Advertising in Tourism and Leisure

Advertising in Tourism and Leisure

Nigel Morgan and Annette Pritchard

OXFORD   AUCKLAND   BOSTON   JOHANNESBURG   MELBOURNE   NEW DELHI

Butterworth-Heinemann
Linacre House, Jordan Hill, Oxford OX2 8DP
225 Wildwood Avenue, Woburn, MA 01801-2041
A division of Reed Educational and Professional Publishing Ltd

℞ A member of the Reed Elsevier plc group

First published 2000

British Library Cataloguing in Publication Data
A catalogue record for this book is available from the British Library

ISBN 0 7506 4531 8

Composition by Genesis Typesetting, Rochester, Kent
Printed and bound in Great Britain by Biddles Ltd, www.biddles.co.uk

Contents

Acknowledgements

There are many people and organizations to whom we are very grateful for their help and support in producing this book. Whilst many of our colleagues in the School of Hospitality, Tourism and Leisure at the University of Wales Institute, Cardiff (UWIC) gave us invaluable support in our research for this book, we would especially like to thank Julia Fallon, Diane Sedgley and Dr Eleri Jones. We would also like to thank all our present and past postgraduate students (particularly Sheena Westwood, Cheryl Cockburn-Wootten, Philip Myers and Mohammed Nassar) for their support and suggestions, and for sharing research experiences, and also the library staff at Colchester Avenue, UWIC – especially Colin and Jenny. We would also like to express our gratitude to our editors at Butterworths for their assistance and guidance throughout the publishing process, particularly Catherine Clarke and Kathryn Grant. The responsibility for any flaws in the final product, of course, as always rests with the authors.

Whilst researching the material for this book we received a tremendous amount of support from the tourism and advertising industries – both agencies and clients – and we would like to record our debts to the following who were particularly helpful, either in providing information or allowing us to reproduce their advertisements: Rowan Chanen (Saatchi & Saatchi, Singapore); Alison Copus (Virgin Atlantic Airways); Shane Crockett (Western Australia Tourism Commission); Craig Davies (Saatchi & Saatchi, Singapore); Ariane Hueneke (DBBO, Hamburg); Neeraj Nayar (International Travel and Tourism Awards); Shin Na (CNBC Asia *Storyboard*); Isabelle Pleissex (Publicis Eureka); Roger Pride (Wales Tourist Board); Tom Rodwell (Court Burkitt); Rob Schwetz (Vickers & Benson Advertising of Toronto); Charlie Thomas (Rainey Kelly Campbell Roalfe/Y&R); Tim Whitehead (Torbay Tourist Board); Leiza Wood (Western Australia Tourism Commission).

Finally, above all, we would again like to express our gratitude to our respective families for all their help and encouragement throughout our lives, and once again this book is dedicated to them.

Figures

Plates

Tables

Abbreviations

AOL	America Online
ASA	Advertising Standards Authority
ATC	Australian Tourism Commission
BA	British Airways
BWA	Brand Western Australia
BBC	British Broadcasting Corporation
BTA	British Tourist Authority
CEO	chief executive officer
CTC	Canadian Tourism Commission
DCMS	Department for Culture, Media and Sport
ESP	emotional selling proposition
EU	European Union
FTSE	Financial Times Stock Exchange index
G7	Group of Seven
GDP	gross domestic product
HRHB	Hard Rock Hotel, Bali
HTML	Hypertext Markup Language
IGTA	International Gay Travel Association
IPA	Institute of Practitioners in Advertising
IT	information technology
PR	public relations
SQW	Segal Quince Wicksteed Limited
SWOT	strengths, weaknesses, opportunities and threats
TAT	thematic apperception test
TTB	Torbay Tourist Board
URL	universal record locator
USP	unique selling proposition
WATC	Western Australian Tourism Commission
WTB	Wales Tourist Board
WTO	World Trade Organization

Part One

Advertising Creation

1

Understanding tourism and leisure advertising

Chapter overview

Advertising bombards us every day – from commercials on television and radio, to advertising on buses and billboards, in magazines and on the Internet – and there is an increasing amount of advertising masquerading as something else – on television travel shows, in the latest blockbuster movie and on children's toys and clothes. We live in a marketing and media-driven world and much of this advertising markets leisure, travel and tourism products and services. In fact, any organization involved in the leisure and tourism business – from local arts centres, museums, sports clubs and small hotels to the largest theme parks, airlines and cruise companies – will be interested in advertising in one form or another. Whilst for the most part in this book, we focus on the strategies of the larger players – the national tourism agencies, the airlines, the global hotel chains and the large tourism operators – many of the ideas and techniques discussed in the following chapters can be adapted by smaller operators seeking competitive advantage and added value from advertising on limited resources. In addition, whilst even the largest organizations often have sizeable budgets for promotional activities, none has a bottomless purse and of course, all advertising activity has to be results driven in today's highly competitive and dynamic marketplace. Lessons can always be learnt from studying good (and bad) advertising practice. This chapter opens the book by reviewing the following:

■ marketing and promotion in tourism and leisure today
■ marketing communications, promotion management and advertising strategy
■ the importance of advertising in tourism and leisure marketing
■ how advertising works in tourism and leisure
■ advertising messages and the audience.

Introduction

Advertising is expensive, its impact is difficult to judge and it usually takes a while before it has any influence on your customers. In fact, Philip Kotler (perhaps today's most quoted marketing expert), goes so far as to say that 'only the very brave or the very ignorant . . . can say exactly what advertising does in the marketplace'.[1] As a result (coupled with the increasing fragmentation of the media and the audience), many companies think that they should cut back expenditure on advertising and redirect it into sales promotions, direct mail, sponsorship, public relations and other forms of marketing communications. Indeed, advertising's share of the communications mix declined in many sectors towards the end of the twentieth century – particularly during the recessions of the early 1980s and 1990s when companies sought to save money on promotional activities.

This view of advertising's role in marketing fails to appreciate that it is not merely a current expense but, rather, is a strategic activity which should be regarded as an investment in the product or brand. Reducing advertising spend may yield short-term savings but may well lead to long-term loss of market share. In the late 1970s Adidas cut advertising spend on its sports shoes and found that the brand was not strong enough to maintain market share in the face of new competitors – and it has struggled to recover its former position. Edwin L. Artzt, chairman and chief executive officer (CEO) of Procter & Gamble (the world's largest advertiser, with an annual ad budget of well over $2 billion) once drew an analogy between advertising and exercise. Both provide long-term benefits and it is easy to postpone both as their results are hard to quantify. But:

> If you want your brand to be fit, it's got to exercise regularly. When you get the opportunity to go to the movies or do something instead of working out, you can do that once in a while – that's [equivalent to] shifting funds into [sales] promotion. But it's not a good thing to do. If you get off the regimen, you will pay for it later.[2]

Yet in the 1980s and 1990s the trend was to allocate more money to sales promotion and between the late 1970s and early 1990s its share of the world's promotional budget grew from less than 60 per cent to well over 70 per cent. This is part of an overall ongoing marketing trend whereby long-term brand equity has often been undermined by short-term interests in which upwardly mobile brand managers have been too tactical, too parochial and too focused on increasing short-term sales volume. Declining brand loyalty is heavily influenced by a lack of advertising, which has much more of a long-term impact on market performance than tools such as price promotions – perhaps a four- as opposed to a one-year impact on sales. Brand equity is the goodwill and reputation that an established brand has built up over its life, and excessive focus on or poorly planned sales promotions can seriously damage that reputation by cheapening a brand's image. Moreover, advertising must be sustained to maintain a brand's market presence since people only buy those products they talk about. Out of sight is out of mind for the consumer – spelling bad news for forgotten products – and on average market leaders spend 20 per cent more of their budgets on advertising than do their nearest competitors.

In its most basic role, therefore, advertising is an economic investment for any leisure, tourism or travel organization, whether it is in the public, private or not-for-profit sector. Effective advertising within a well-planned communications strategy cannot guarantee success, but it certainly increases its chances. With this in mind, this book focuses on the role of advertising within the specific sectors of tourism and leisure, and considers issues such as:

- What is good advertising?
- What makes a well-planned advertising strategy?
- What is the role of advertising research in the creative process?
- What are the implications for tourism and leisure advertisers of the changing global marketing environment?

- How can advertisers use creativity to create ads with attitude?
- How can advertising help build or reposition brands?
- What does the future hold for advertising in an age of virtual reality, Internet marketing, celebrity endorsement and product placement?

Marketing and promotion in tourism and leisure

It is important to remember that advertising is not developed or delivered in a vacuum – it plays an important although limited role within the process of marketing. At the beginning of the twenty-first century, most people have an understanding of the word 'marketing'. To the average person on the street, it is synonymous with advertising and selling, to any student on a business-related course or to any effective manager it means the concept of the marketing mix. There are almost as many definitions of marketing as there are marketing textbooks and that of Gronroos encapsulates many of the ideas of most. He argues that marketing seeks to 'establish, develop and commercialize long-term customer relationships so that the objectives of the parties are met. This is done by a mutual exchange and keeping of promises.'[3]

It has also been said that good marketers see their business from the customer's viewpoint and organize their entire enterprise to develop relationships with the customer based on trust – in this way marketing is part of everyone's job, from front-line staff to the board of directors. Marketing is thus both an organizational function (perhaps expressed as a marketing department in a company) and a business philosophy. It is the ability to develop a mix of marketing strategies to influence customers to buy products and services. This mix consists of a set of four decisions:

- product decisions
- pricing decisions
- distribution decisions
- promotional decisions.

The product component of the marketing mix ensures that the product (which could be anything from a tour package, an airline seat or a destination, to a hotel or a football club) characteristics provide benefits to the customer; the price component ensures the product is priced at a level that reflects consumer value; the distribution component ensures access to the product in the right place at the right time in sufficient quantities to meet customer needs; and the promotional component communicates (through advertising, publicity, personal selling and sales promotions) the product's ability to satisfy the customer's needs. Together these main components work in a synergistic relationship determined by the product's positioning, and all of these have to provide the framework in which advertising is created.

Marketing communications, promotion management and advertising strategy

Together with marketing, marketing communications had dramatically increased in importance in the 1980s and 1990s to the extent that effective, sustained communications with customers is now seen as critical to the success of any organization – whether in the private, public or not-for-profit sector – from global airlines to tourism destinations and museums, theatres and local arts groups. Organizations communicate with a variety of audiences, principally to:

■ inform
■ persuade
■ induce action.

For instance, organizations may want to *inform* prospective customers about their products; *persuade* them to prefer certain brands, products or venues, attend particular entertainment events or perform a variety of behaviours; and *induce* customer action so buying behaviour is directed towards their offering and purchase occurs sooner rather than later. These and other promotional objectives are achieved by a variety of activities, such as:

■ advertising
■ sales promotions
■ salespeople
■ point-of-purchase displays
■ direct mailings
■ product packaging
■ sponsorship and other event marketing
■ public relations.

Although our focus is on tourism and leisure advertising, it is important to note that all these activities and other promotional devices (see Table 1.1) are collectively known as *promotion management*. As such, they are part of the overall marketing mix outlined above and thus promotion is that aspect of marketing that promotion management deals with explicitly. In contrast, *marketing communications* is a much more ambiguous and all-encompassing

Table 1.1   The key tourism and leisure promotional tools

Tool	Comments
Media advertising	Television, press, radio, billboards and the Internet; also tourist board and travel-related guides, books and brochures that sell advertising space
Public relations	All media exposure appearing as editorial, not as paid for advertising space, includes 'ambush' and 'guerrilla' marketing
Personal selling	Meetings, workshops, telephone contact aimed at distributors and trade purchasing to sell on to end users; also aimed at consumers, e.g., at travel agents
Sales promotion	Short-term incentives to induce purchase – aimed at salespeople, distributors and consumers
Price discounting	A common form of sales promotion – aimed at wholesalers, retailers and consumers
Distribution channels	Systems by which consumers access products and services, including computerized networks
Familiarization trips	Educates and raises product awareness through sampling – aimed at wholesalers, retailers and opinion-formers (e.g., journalists)
Exhibitions and shows	Venues for display and distribution aimed at wholesalers, retailers and consumers
Sales literature	Brochures, leaflets and other print used as a selling and booking tool
Merchandising and point-of-sale displays	Atmospherics, store layout, posters, displays and other materials to create image
Direct mail	Part of the wider activity of direct marketing
Sponsorship/special events	Of community-based activities, sports and music events and 'good causes'

term (and activity) that includes communication via any and all of the four marketing mix elements. How a product is packaged, priced and distributed all communicate an image to a customer just as much as how that product is promoted.

The blend of the promotional elements described above (advertising, sales promotions etc.) are known as the *promotional mix* and promotional management is the co-ordination of all the elements, setting objectives and budgets, designing programmes, evaluating performance and taking corrective action. Any organization is likely to use a range of promotional tools in its marketing activities. For instance, Legoland – opened in 1996 and now the UK's third largest theme park – uses television, radio, national and regional press, trade press and educational literature, plus direct marketing through the Internet and door-to-door mail drops in its promotional programme. Advertising is only one element within this promotional mix, and its management at Legoland – as elsewhere – is broadly similar in terms of its remit.

Advertising has been exhaustively defined and is usually taken to mean either mass communication via newspapers, magazines, radio, television, billboards, the Internet and other media or direct-to-consumer communication via direct mail. Whilst word of mouth may be the most credible form of promotion, both of these definitions of advertising are characterized by its two key definers: they are *paid for* and *non-personal*. They are paid for in the sense that the sponsor or advertiser is clearly identifiable (as opposed to public relations activities) yet non-personal in the sense that the sponsor is simultaneously communicating with many receivers (perhaps millions) instead of talking to small groups or individuals as a salesperson would.

Promotion can be a short-term activity (such as a sales offer), but also, when seen at a strategic level, it is a mid- and long-term investment aimed at building up a consistent and credible corporate or destination identity. Promotion, when used effectively, builds and creates an identity for the product or the organization. Brochures, media advertisements, the behaviour of staff, in-store merchandising, sales promotions and so on create the identity of the organization, and all aspects of the promotional effort should project the same image to the customer. There are many components to the promotional mix, but of all these, the tourism and leisure marketer has most control over advertising and sales promotion. Whilst identity creation affects all aspects of the promotional mix, the key vehicles for its projection are in media advertisements and brochures, although, of course, these operate in conjunction with other activities, particularly sales promotions.

The need for integrated communication strategies

Perhaps one of the most important advances in marketing in recent decades has been the rise of integrated marketing communication – the recognition that advertising can no longer be crafted and executed in isolation from the other promotional mix elements. As markets, media and marketing itself have grown more complex and fragmented, advertisers and consumers find themselves in an ever more confusing marketing environment. The answer to this is to convey a consistent, unified message and identity through all an organization's marketing and communications activities – *integrated marketing communications*. This means that the advertiser (and therefore the product and brand) speaks with a single voice in the most consistent, cost-effective way. This sounds logical and simple, yet the biggest problem stems from organizational structures – especially in large, multinational corporations with a varied product portfolio. Advertising agencies have also been caught up in the drive for integration and as it becomes the goal for many advertisers, unless the ad industry works more on providing clients with brand management and strategy development and less on simply securing media slots, it will lose ground.

Why is advertising important in tourism and leisure marketing?

In the tourism and leisure sectors, where the product is a service, promotion is even more vital than in other industries. Despite arguments over the essential differences between the marketing of goods and services, it is well established that where it is a service, the tourism and leisure product is a complex bundle of value – since it is *intangible, inseparable, variable* and *perishable*. Put simply, there is nothing tangible for the customer to examine beforehand or to take away afterwards; the service is inseparable from its production; the experience is variable and often subject to factors beyond the marketers' control; and finally, the product is perishable and cannot be stored for future sale. Clearly, you cannot test-drive a holiday beforehand, and thus promotion becomes critical, having a greater role in establishing the nature of the product than in most other markets. Promotion *is* the product as far as the potential tourist or leisure consumer is concerned. The customer buys a holiday, a theatre ticket or attends a concert purely on the basis of symbolic expectations established promotionally through words, pictures, sounds and so forth. In this way, leisure and tourism experiences are literally constructed in our imagination through advertising and the media. Indeed, it has often been said that tourism marketing is about the selling of dreams and that tourism itself is about illusion, or about the creation of 'atmosphere'.

In addition to these characteristics, the tourism and leisure product is also a discretionary product, which will be competing for both the customer's time and money against essential items of expenditure and other discretionary purchases. These five attributes (*intangibility, inseparability, variability, perishability* and *discretionary purchase*) mean that the skill in tourism and leisure marketing lies in creating the perceived value of the product, in packaging it and in promoting the experience in a way which gives an organization a competitive edge. In this respect, creating an identity becomes paramount – and hence this particular aspect of tourism and leisure marketing is the focus of this book.

Advertising and tourism and leisure promotion

Advertising emerges as a key marketing tool in the tourism and leisure industries where potential consumers must base buying decisions upon mental images of product offerings, rather than being able to physically sample alternatives. As a result, advertising is a critical variable in the tourism and leisure marketing mix, and covers a wide range of activities and agencies. Its role reflects that of promotion in general, which is aimed at influencing the attitudes and behaviour of audiences in three main ways: to confirm and reinforce; to create new patterns of behaviour and attitude; or to change attitudes and behaviour. Thus, tourism and leisure operators use images to portray their products in brochures, posters and media advertising; airlines, hotels, theme parks and resorts do the same, as do destinations, attempting to construct an image of a destination that will force it into the potential tourist's evoked set, or destination short list, leading to a purchase decision. Whatever the tourism or leisure product, its identity is the public face of how it is marketed and the importance of advertising in tourism and leisure marketing should not be underestimated.

Certainly advertising in general is big business – and it is getting bigger. In 1997 total global advertising spend amounted to some $300 billion, with the USA accounting for $110.1 billion, Europe $83.5 billion and Asia Pacific $84 billion. Significantly, much of the expenditure comes from an increasingly small number of megabrands and in 1996 the top 200 brands accounted for over 40 per cent of the USA's media expenditure. In the UK, around 32 500 branded goods and services are advertised each year and over 7000 of these brands spend £150 000-plus annually on their advertising. In terms of total ad spend, tourism and leisure organizations are small players – in fact, if *all* public sector tourism ad spend worldwide was combined it would still be less than a quarter of the ad spend of one company – Sony (Table 1.2). However, individual *private sector* companies in the leisure industries have huge advertising budgets, the largest being Walt Disney Co., which spent $773 million in 1997, 72 per cent of this concentrated on audio-visual advertising.[4]

These advertising figures are also increasing substantially as the tourism and leisure industries continue to expand faster than any other sector – during 1997–9 UK leisure consumer spending grew by almost 6 per cent, whilst all

Table 1.2   Tourism destinations vs other advertisers: global spend, 1995

Advertiser	Global ad spend (US$ millions)
Sony	1277
Coca-Cola	1146
Renault	566
Gillette	400
Tourism	357
Volvo	342
Fuji Film	208

Source: World Tourism Organization and *Advertising Age*.

spending on goods and services grew by only 4.5 per cent. At the same time, marketing gurus such as Bill Gates and John Naisbitt predict that travel – for leisure and business – will be one of the three key industries of the twenty-first century. If advertising is *one* of the world's fastest growing economic sectors, then tourism and leisure is definitely *the* fastest – making for a significant expansion in the specialist area of tourism and leisure advertising over the coming decades. To take one individual country, whilst total leisure and tourism ad spend figures are not available, in the UK *domestic* market alone tourism ad spend totalled £45 million in 1998 (Table 1.3). Moreover, ad spend figures are increasing at a rapid rate – *total* UK hotel ad spend increased from under £20 million in 1996 to almost £30 million in 1998, with Forte spending over £5 million, whilst over the same period, Center Parcs' ad spend increased from £3 million to over £4 million and UK airline advertising leapt from £48 million to £61 million – British Airways, the UK's biggest travel advertiser, alone spent almost £20 million on advertising in 1997.[5]

In the last thirty years, the tourism industry has grown by 1 or 2 per cent more than the global economy each year – regardless of all the major political, economic and technological upheavals which have happened in that time. Today, one in every ten jobs on the planet is linked to travel or tourism; 80 million people are directly and another 150 million are indirectly employed in the industry; and it is worth US$4.5 trillion or 12 per cent of the global gross domestic product.[6] Yet, despite these figures, tourism is still in its infancy and has tremendous growth potential – only 7 per cent of the world's population currently travel internationally – including 14 per cent of Europeans and 8 per cent of Americans. The World Tourism Organization predicts that tourist

Table 1.3   Advertising spend in the UK domestic market, 1994–8 (£ millions)

Sector	1994	1995	1996	1997	1998
Hotels and B & Bs	8.6	9.6	12.8	14.5	19.9
Holiday resorts	9.6	10.0	9.6	10.7	10.1
Tourist offices	6.5	7.4	6.7	7.2	6.9
Tour operator	3.0	5.0	5.2	5.6	5.7
Camping and self-catering	0.1	0.3	0.9	2.0	1.7
Boating	0.1	0.1	0.1	0.1	0.1
Total	28.1	32.6	35.8	40.6	44.8

Source: Mintel, quoted in the *Travel Trade Gazette*, 14 June 1999.

arrivals will more than double from 673 million in 2000 to 1602 million in 2020, whilst tourism receipts are set to triple in the same period from \$621 billion to \$2000 billion.[7] Assuming an Asian economic recovery, over 100 million Chinese are expected to be making international trips each year in 2020. The industry is anticipated to grow significantly even in the medium term and the world's airline fleet and its accommodation base will have to double by 2010 if the travel sector is to cater for the expected growth in tourists. Every tourism region is being marketed and every niche market and interest group is now being targeted by tourism advertisers. 'Troubles tours' are available (and often sold out) in Northern Ireland; in Bolivia the government is promoting Che Guevara adventure tours; and ethnic travel is seen to be a huge growth area, with ethnic Chinese trips to China and African-American visits to Africa being just two of the more obvious examples. Tourism is even expanding beyond the Earth and in December 2001 space tourism will finally become reality when the first sub-orbital flight for tourists is scheduled to launch (tickets priced at \$100 000), whilst Hilton International is already planning its first hotel on the moon.[8]

How does advertising work in leisure and tourism?

Advertising at its simplest is first and foremost a process of communication. Yet it has many different forms and consumers react to advertisements in any number of ways. Today ads are viewed by an increasingly advertising literate consumer base and not surprisingly (given the sheer volume of advertising *clutter*) most advertisements

Clutter results from the ever-increasing number of ads competing for audience attention. 'Noise' and clutter can distort the message and distract the audience so it is vital to think about how the message moves through every step of the communication process.

are of little interest to most people at any one point in time. People engage with advertisements for a relatively few number of reasons: if the product is different; if the ad is unusual; if the ad is relevant to them; and if the ad is seen often enough. Above all, the key challenge for agencies today is to create advertising executions that can penetrate the clutter of everyday life.

The good news for advertisers of tourism and leisure products is that for many people tourism- and leisure-related purchases are items of expenditure which deserve significant consumer attention and effort – unlike other inexpensive consumer goods such as toiletries or convenience foods. Ads are there to persuade and suggest things that the consumer may not previously have considered and the persuasion process is lubricated by ads that are witty, charming and beautifully constructed. This process may have an immediate effect but more likely, it may influence behaviour some time later. Indeed, advertising should have both short- and long-term results, although one thing to bear in mind is that advertising which does not work in the present will hardly work in the future. This is completely different, however, to saying that advertising must produce immediate and measurable effects. The rate and nature of effect will also depend on the objectives underpinning the advertising campaign itself (e.g., sales promotion, brand positioning, brand awareness etc.).

When it is effective, communications (and advertising in particular) moves customers along a continuum from awareness of a product to reinforcing post-purchase satisfaction:

- Stage 1 – *Awareness*. The target market needs to be aware of the product – particularly when it is a new product or a new market.
- Stage 2 – *Comprehension*. Once they are aware of the product, potential customers need to understand its features and benefits. This can be challenging where product parity exists (for instance, between destinations) and substitutability threatens.
- Stage 3 – Acceptance. Potential customers must decide that the product can meet their needs – advertising plays a vital role here.
- Stage 4 – *Preference*. Advertising messages must offer a compelling reason for potential customers to think that the product meets their needs (ideally in a unique way that reduces brand substitutability).
- Stage 5 – *Purchase*. Advertising motivates customers to action or to buy the product (often this objective is linked to sales promotions).
- Stage 6 – *Reinforcement*. One of advertising's key roles is to confirm customers' choices and create a sense of satisfaction about their actions or purchase.

These six stages are known as *the hierarchy of effects model* since it reflects the audience's stages of reaction to advertising, however, our understanding of how advertising works has had to move on from this model, not least because advertising objectives have evolved, as have the nature of brands and the competition. Perhaps a more useful way of understanding how advertising works, is to look at the four key models employed in planning advertising today:

- sales response
- persuasion
- involvement
- saliency.[9]

The first advertising technique – *the sales response model* – is a very simple price-based strategy which encourages the purchase of a product purely on the basis of its price. The second, a widely used and demonstrably successful advertising technique, is *persuasion*. This takes the advertisement as its starting point and, if it is effectively compiled, its impact and message should persuade the audience that the product presented is the most desirable available. Persuasion is not a simple technique, however, for it is capable of sophisticated variation, particularly where the 'brand advantage' is sought through emotional rather than rational appeals. Brand advantage can also be secured through a series of advertisements which each highlight a specific benefit of a product, culminating in an overall impression of a superior brand. This is a topic which will be discussed in much more detail in Part Three of the book.

> Persuasion – the ability of the ad to shift attitudes towards the brand and motivate purchase.

> 'Brand' is defined as a unique combination of product characteristics and added values, both functional and non-functional, which have taken on a relevant meaning which is inextricably linked to that brand, awareness of which might be conscious or intuitive.

The third advertising model is *involvement* – a technique which aims to interest and engage the consumer. Once their interest is aroused, a self-referent relationship is created with the audience – they imagine themselves within the advertisement's framework and feel good about the brand. The next progression is a commitment to the brand, resulting in increased sales. Involvement is a more sophisticated technique, characteristic of style market products such as lager and jeans (Levi's 501 campaigns of the late 1980s and 1990s, discussed in Case study 9.1, are a successful example of

> Involvement – whether consumers relate to and empathize with the advertising.

this advertising technique). At the leading edge of developments in advertising, is the fourth and final technique – *saliency*. This relies on innovative, radical and even controversial brand images. It is more than a simple 'brand' awareness strategy as it attempts to move the target audience emotionally closer to the brand product. Saliency is therefore concerned with the product's presence in the audience's consciousness, generating a feeling of 'that product is for me'.

> Saliency – the ability of an ad to cut through media clutter, arrest the consumer's attention and shift attitudes towards the brand.

The concept of saliency is at the heart of current thinking on advertising impact. In the 1980s advertising was regarded as a tool which contributed significantly to direct sales. However, in the 1990s this assumption became hotly disputed and commentators argued that this 'rush out and buy' impact was usually only applicable to new products or variations in products with an obvious competitive advantage. Today, the widely held view of advertising (particularly in relation to established brands) is that its role is not to directly increase sales and that, even when it does have this effect, the sales generated are generally insufficient to recoup the cost of the campaign. What then is the purpose of advertising, if not to directly increase sales? Amongst today's advertising practitioners, it is argued that its value lies in improving the consumer's attitude towards brands, thus leading to long-term sales. In this way, the real effect of advertising is not at the point of sale but at the point of *consumption*. Consumer brand opinions are only formed after consumers have tried the brand; however, these opinions are clearly influenced by the expectations created by advertising. In this way, advertising – the repetition of arguments, creatively presented – does not influence product perception at the time it is seen, but it does increase the likelihood of a consumer making an exploratory purchase of the brand *and* has a strong influence on how he or she feels the product compares to the competition.[10]

Advertising and the audience

Some advertising campaigns challenge consumer buying decisions, leaving the audience thinking 'I must try that'. Established brands cannot, however, generate this kind of response and instead they face the challenge of maintaining the consumers' interest. This is particularly important as consumers purchase within a limited range of acceptable brands, choosing that which captures their interest and matches their own values at a given moment in time (see Chapter 8). Such engagement is created by the culmination of long-term advertising memories; whilst consumers discard those which are uninteresting, they retain memories of those advertisements which are unusually appealing or provocative. The latter form the basis of successful brand identity building and maintenance. The process is accomplished over a considerable period of time but the rewards are great for the impact is also long-lived.

Advertising need not be complex to be effective – it is simply about creating enough awareness and positive brand associations for it to register as a top-of-the-mind brand when the consumer is faced with a purchase choice. However, with every adult person in the West exposed to between 2000 and 3000 advertising messages every day, the ad appeal has to cut through a lot of marketing clutter – whether by using humour (although the comedy has to be finely balanced to avoid overwhelming the message) or originality. Yet the larger and more diverse the market, the more difficult it is to find arresting messages and symbols that will not offend someone or touch on a controversial area – as in the 1980s when Pepsi ended its endorsement contract with the pop star Madonna following pressure from the American political right over her *Like a Prayer* video which featured her with a black Jesus in a sexual story line. This has driven many agencies to appeal to the lowest common denominator and create middle-of-the-road advertising – which no one hates, but probably no one really loves either. This is particularly true when it comes to issues of sexuality, gender and work/family roles, where there is no longer universal agreement about how they should be presented, and where straightforward appeals to what was once taken for granted no longer work.

The drive to create impactful *and* effective advertising still remains a major advertising challenge, despite the development of sophisticated advertising tracking and evaluation techniques. Whilst there are many examples of successful and effective advertising, calculating the 'ad investment–return' ratio seems at times to have more in common with the search for the Holy Grail than a practical business problem. The famous and much rehearsed quote (variously attributed to several major figures, including Lord Leverhulme) – 'I know that half of my advertising is wasted ... I just don't know which half' – was, in fact, a wildly optimistic assessment and contemporary advertisers operate in an even more unpalatable environment. The fact which advertisers have to face today is, quite simply, not only are consumers still inconsistent, mercurial and unreliable, but they are now also increasingly busy, hard to reach and fickle. With more advertising literate consumers now, at the beginning of the twenty-first century, than ever before, consumers are increasingly bored by ads and blasé about advertising.

Reaching the right consumer

The elusive nature of today's advertising consumer is thrown into sharp relief by the experience of what was the twentieth century's most influential and penetrative media phenomenon – the television – which is now the USA's dominant advertising media, accounting for 40 per cent of media spend.[11] At one and the same time the television has been the most coveted and the most wasteful advertising medium. As a mass medium, it inevitably attracts many people outside an advertiser's target audience and with the plethora of channels created by the expansion in cable, satellite and digital technology the choice for consumers and advertisers has become bewildering. The advent of more specialist channels with their fragmented audiences means it is costing more to reach the same number of people – a major challenge for the $100 billion worldwide television advertising industry. Of course, whilst the age of the mass media is ending, addressable, interactive and database-linked advertising is growing rapidly and more specialist television has also allowed much greater targeting and segmentation of audiences. However, if you add to this fragmentation the downward spiral in audience *interest* in television – particularly amongst younger people – commercial television's dominance as an entertainment and advertising medium is clearly slackening. Table 1.4 shows that the percentage of people paying little or no attention to television increased by 7 per cent in the UK from the early to the mid-1990s.

If fewer people are paying attention to the television – using it instead as mere 'electronic wallpaper' – then they are certainly not going to remember the ads aired between programmes. Not surprisingly, interest in programmes greatly influences advertising recall rates but if an ad fails to be an audience-attention grabber then it does not really matter how interested people are in the surrounding programming – the advertising will have been wasted money. Given this, it is vital that advertisers distinguish between the *total* amount of coverage a campaign is likely to generate and its *sphere of influence* – those

Table 1.4 **Television's loosening grip on audience interest**

Year	1992	1993	1994	1995	1996
(% of UK viewers paying little or no attention to commercial television)	26	29	29	31	33

Source: adapted from Carat Insight Ltd, Television's sphere of influence.

people whom they most want to target. A campaign's sphere of influence depends on the advertising's creativity and involvement factor, together with consumers' attention factor, brand familiarity and advertising attitude. Research in the UK by Carat Insight Ltd. suggests that one particular group of like-minded people have a high probability of falling within a campaign's sphere of influence. These so-called ad *seekers* are people who actively engage with advertising, whether they are looking for information, ideas or entertainment – the other major categories of ad responders being *reactors*, *rejecters* and *ignorers* (Table 1.5).

Table 1.5   Ad-itude groups

	Active	*Passive*
Positive	Seekers	Reactors
Negative	Rejecters	Ignorers

Source: Carat Insights Ltd.

These 'ad-itude' categories are not mutually exclusive and consumers may move between them, depending on the product or service advertised and the quality of the ad. Seekers – as long as the advertising is right – will respond to a campaign (Ad highlight 1.1). Of course, some advertisers are likely to have more seekers than others – and, again, the good news for tourism organizations is that their ads are likely to have more seekers than other products and they are also more effective in generating awareness (Table 1.6). For example, a British Airways promotion offering a limited number of flights

Table 1.6   Targeting the ad seekers

Products being advertised	*% of consumers who are ad seekers and look out for these ads*
Package holidays	24
Food retailers	18
Motor cars	14
Draught lager	10
Chocolate bars	8

Source: adapted from Carat Insight Ltd/BMRB, 1997.

on Concorde for just £10 reportedly stimulated around 30 million telephone calls in one day – despite the fact that the advertising was limited to a one-page advertisement in a selected number of national British newspapers. By contrast, reactors will not actively seek out advertising; however, with sufficient exposure they are likely to respond to it – witness the success of Levi's 501 jeans with this group (see Case study 9.1). Rejecters are aware of advertising but for one reason or another reject it. Finally, ignorers are those people who will always be oblivious to ads for particular products and even high exposure will not normally prompt them to change their minds – although attention-grabbing ads could do so.

| Ad highlight 1.1 | Walt Disney World, Florida ads attract seekers |

One of the package holiday campaigns tested by Carat/BMRB amongst package holiday-takers was for Walt Disney World, Florida. The £1.7 million UK campaign was designed to:

■ tap into the fact that people are planning their holidays
■ persuade viewers to request a video brochure
■ communicate Disney World's magical qualities.

The results of the research were very encouraging:

■ almost 90 per cent were aware of the ad campaign
■ almost 20 per cent said that the advertising made them more likely to consider Walt Disney World
■ significantly, 29 per cent of 'seekers' were positively influenced by the campaign, compared to 16 per cent of non-seekers
■ when awareness and behaviour measures were combined, seekers were 75 per cent more likely to have responded to the campaign than non-seekers.

Source: Carat Insights Ltd.

Table 1.7 Matching creative advertising styles to consumer ad-itudes

Consumer ad-itudes	Seekers	Reactors	Rejecters	Ignorers
Advertising models	Sales response Persuasion	Involvement Saliency	Persuasion Involvement	Saliency

Source: adapted from Carat Insights Ltd.

When you combine these ad-itude groups with the four major advertising effectiveness models then it becomes possible to match advertising styles with potential advertising consumers and appropriate advertising media. Ad seekers often respond to direct sell or persuasion techniques whilst reactors are attracted by involving or saliency measures. Rejecters and ignorers are more difficult to reach with advertising, although persuasion, involvement and saliency techniques have the potential to influence consumer behaviour (Table 1.7).

Chapter summary

Advertising is expensive and its impacts elusive, but it is a crucial long-term investment in any brand and it is most effective when fully integrated with an organization's other marketing activities. In an increasingly competitive, confused marketplace, tourism and leisure organizations must strive to convey a consistent, unified message and identity through all their marketing and communications activities – the essence of integrated marketing communications. In the tourism and leisure industries, where most services and experiences are intangible, and consumers purchase on the basis of promotional messages, understanding the role of advertising is paramount. Whilst tourism and leisure organizations are not large advertising spenders, these economic sectors are expanding rapidly and their share of global advertising spend will increase in the coming decades.

The purpose of advertising is to inform, persuade and induce purchase, although understanding advertising's relationship with consumers is a complex process and there are four advertising models:

- sales response
- persuasion
- involvement
- saliency.

Contemporary consumers are increasingly advertising literate and proving ever harder to reach through these four techniques. As a result, tourism and leisure advertisers and advertising agencies must focus on issues such as the consumer's attention factor, brand familiarity and advertising attitude when planning campaigns.

Notes

1 Philip Kotler (1986). *Principles of Marketing*. Prentice Hall, pp. 347–8.
2 Jennifer Lawrence (1991). P&G's Artzt on ads: crucial investment, *Advertising Age*, 28 October, quoted in Terrance Shimp (1993) *Promotion Management*. Dryden, p. 262.
3 C. Gronroos (1989). Defining marketing: a market-orientated approach. *European Journal of Marketing*, **23** (1), 52–9, 57.
4 John Philip Jones (ed.) (1999). *The Advertising Business: Operations, Creativity, Media Planning, Integrated Communications*. Sage.
5 Belina Archer (1997). Sun, sea, sex, sand and media. *Campaign*, 30 May, 29–30.
6 *Time*, June 1999.
7 World Tourism Organization (1998). *Tourism 2020 Report*. WTO.
8 The Economist (1999). The world in figures: industries. Tourism. In *The World in 2000*. The Economist Publications, p. 104.
9 Alan Mitchell (1994). Rephrasing the question of advertising evaluation. *Marketing*, 10 March, 25–7.
10 Ibid.
11 Jones, *The Advertising Business*.

Further reading

Brassington, F. and Pettitt, S. (2000). *Principles of Marketing*. Financial Times/Prentice Hall.

Horner, S. and Swarbrooke, J. (1996). *Marketing Tourism, Hospitality and Leisure in Europe*. Thomson Business.

Jones, J. P. (ed.) (1999). *The Advertising Business: Operations, Creativity, Media Planning, Integrated Communications*. Sage.

Kotler, P., Bowen, J. and Makens, J. (1999). *Marketing for Hospitality and Tourism*. 2nd edn. Prentice Hall.

Otto, J. E. and Brent-Ritchie, J. R. (1996). The service experience in tourism. *Tourism Management*, **17** (3), 165–74.

Swarbrooke, J. and Horner, S. (1999). *Consumer Behaviour in Tourism*. Butterworth-Heinemann.

Torkildsen, G. (1999). *Leisure and Recreation Management*. 4th edn. E & F Spon.

Wells, W., Burnett, J. and Moriarty, S. (1995). *Advertising Principles and Practice*. 3rd edn. Prentice Hall.

World Tourism Organization (1998). *Tourism 2020 Report*. WTO.

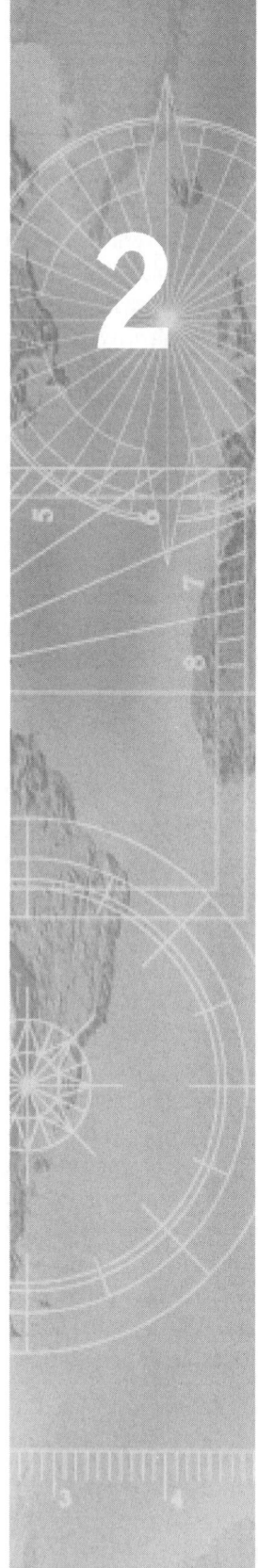

What makes good advertising?

Chapter overview

In examining what makes good advertising, this chapter sets out some of the key themes of the book, examining the role of creativity in advertising, the importance of targeting the right audience, and the 'old' and 'new' rules of good advertising. The second half of the chapter then discusses the centrality of successful client–agency relationships in nurturing a climate in which good advertising can flourish. The case study at the end of the chapter illustrates how the Asian economic crisis towards the end of the 1990s impacted on the creation of effective advertising in Thailand and Japan. The key themes reviewed are:

- generating creative and distinctive ads which get noticed
- building on solid foundations and targeting advertising
- are award-winning ads good ads?
- the old and the new rules of advertising
- working well with ad agencies
- the damage done by politics in advertising

Introduction

Perhaps we should begin by explaining why we are devoting a whole chapter to what makes 'good' advertising: because 90 per cent of advertising is bad and 90 per cent of advertising goes unnoticed and fails. No matter how often an ad is run, if it is uninspired, dull, boring and mediocre the audience will ignore it (even worse, frequent exposure to an irritating ad will actively annoy consumers). Place this against a backcloth of ever-increasing media clutter and audience apathy and it is little wonder that bad ads will not sell in today's communication-saturated society. Ironically, as the effectiveness of advertising is reducing, its use in volume and variety, is increasing. The per capita consumption of advertising in the USA today is over $400 a year.[1] This means that if a company was to allocate $1 million of ad spend next year to the American market, it would be hitting the average consumer with less than half a cent of advertising, spread out over the whole year – a consumer already exposed to $399.99 of other advertising communication. Of course, the USA accounts for over half of all advertising spend and the average American consumer is exposed to twice as much advertising as the average Canadian, four times as much as the average Briton and five times as much as the average French person.[2] In this saturated environment, it will take some pretty slick advertising to attract the attention of the ad-fatigued tourism and leisure consumer, even more so when you think that most advertising is irrelevant to most consumers at any one time – it is only when you are about to book a holiday trip or buy a new tennis racket that you become aware of ads for tour operators and sports goods.

Indeed, a number of surveys suggest that today's advertising is failing the consumer: in Germany consumers feel that advertising is becoming less entertaining and less useful in helping them find out about new products; the Dutch are more and more irritated by advertising; whilst the Swedes are increasingly troubled by ad content and executions. So, most advertising is unwelcome and it is less welcome when it is bad advertising; neither is the situation going to get easier in the future with an increasingly media literate public. So what does make good advertising? A question which is very difficult to answer. In fact, calling this chapter 'What makes good advertising?' might be the biggest mistake of all – advertising is, after all, very subjective and highly personal.

Instinctively people know when they've seen a good ad, and even more so when they've seen a bad ad – although

> 'Good' advertising depends on which side of the fence you are standing. The advertiser's definition is 'cost-effective, stimulating and positive communication of a brand's virtues'; the ad agency's definition is that of 'an unusual (and therefore memorable) twist to a problem, well-executed and supported by sufficient funds'.[3]

liking or disliking ads has little impact on how deeply the repeated messages penetrate your consciousness. If it is a good ad consumers will engage with it, and if it is part of a series of executions they might even anticipate the next instalment. You may know about or remember the phenomenal success of the long-running Nescafé Gold Blend television ads in the UK. Advertisements were even placed in newspapers announcing the timing of the next instalment of the commercials' story and the first screen kiss of the couple featured in the ads made front-page news in the British tabloid press. In many product categories similar brands have similar qualities and consumers see them as interchangeable. In this sense, ads cannot hoodwink people and agencies find it very difficult to say anything special about products such as kitchen cleaners or frozen dinners. Yet advertising in tourism and leisure has the potential to offer so much more – we all care about what we do in our increasingly constrained spare time, where we spend it and who we spend it with – so tourism and leisure brands should have the potential to engender consumer loyalty and emotional attachment.

The role of creativity and planning for success

Advertising is a critical part of marketing – in fact, the future of many brands to a large extent currently depends on the quality of a series of 30-second television ads. So if the advertising is not right, then the brand could be badly damaged. At best, communication in an overcommunicated society is extremely difficult – and sometimes an organization is better off delaying communication – at least until it is ready to position itself for the long term. But, once it is ready to communicate, it will never get a second chance to make a first impression. Andy Warhol once famously said, everyone gets fifteen minutes of fame. When a product gets its chance, its marketers must get it right.

Today creativity has become the entry ticket to the contemporary advertising marketplace, which is shaped by technological innovation and clutter.[4] Indeed new technology has opened a whole new vista for creativity, including: computerized design tools, morphing and digital special effects, digital video-editing, holograms, virtual reality, multimedia presentations, ink-jet personalization, public relations planning software and interactive media. So how do ads get noticed in such saturation? There are a number of steps clients and agencies can take to break through the clutter, including:

- producing a tightly defined, research-based advertising brief
- precisely targeting the audience

- harnessing creative energy – released by revolution, anarchy and the shattering of convention
- being interesting, surprising and relevant
- inventing indelible imagery – such as the Coca-Cola, Sony, Playboy, MGM logos
- perfecting timing
- having a consistent approach – as exemplified by Volkswagen and Fairy Liquid
- appearing effortless – good ads provide the audience with intense experiences, delivered with the maximum of cool.[5]

Advertising as visual metaphor

The majority of advertising is in effect, the resourceful use of visual metaphors. This is not, however, merely the sustained promotion of a logo or a particular brand signature since visual metaphors require emotional connections and associations to work effectively. Those brands that have managed to achieve iconic status (Coca-Cola, BMW, Rolls-Royce etc.) built and retain this position through emphasizing the emotional rather than the functional rewards associated with purchasing the product or service. The visual metaphor of advertising can convey a number of brand values including its superior performance, the psychological rewards associated with it, the people who use it and the social context in which it features. Such metaphors enrich advertising in much the same way as they enrich speech, providing a connection between the images of the user, the brand and the featured social environment. As we will see in Chapter 10, the English Riviera's palm tree is a metaphor for the South of France and an upscale social milieu, whilst Nike's Swoosh has become a byword for 'Just do it' attitude. In a similar vein, the Alaska tourist organization's use of Marilyn Monroe in an advertising campaign after the *Exxon Valdez* oil disaster, could be seen as an attempt to appropriate one of the twentieth-century's most enduring metaphors for beauty and appeal.

To be truly memorable and significant, rather than simply good, advertising must take the brand forward. Some ads are hugely successful because they are a one-off, but most ads will be rerun. Len Weinreich points to a British Airways (BA) television commercial that ran in the UK during the central break of the *News at Ten* every night for a week. Based on the fact that the airline's annual passenger total was equivalent to the population of Manhattan, the ad showed Manhattan being guided into Heathrow instead of a 747. Unfortunately, with such saturation, the unremitting hype began to weaken credibility and after the third or fourth screening consumers began to question the relevance of BA's message. When a single-spot, often repeated ad becomes irritating, as in BA's case, the advertiser is spending money to negative effect.[6] So it is critical to establish whether an ad will bear repetition. Is the concept campaignable – in other words, can it be built up over a period of time and can it be adapted in different executions?

The best creativity is built on solid foundations

To create top-notch advertising there must be a synergy between creativity and strategy – top-class advertising is informed by an effective creative brief that is based on sound market research and accurate goals. Whilst Chapters 3 and 4 discuss these aspects in detail, it is worth mentioning here that it is up to the client to provide explicit briefs – an advertising agency cannot be expected to deliver good work if it is not clear about what the client wants their advertising to achieve. Indeed, fuzzy, inaccurate briefs are often instrumental in agencies delivering inappropriate advertising, unsuited to client requirements. To produce a good brief, organizations require up-to-date market research. They need to think about:

- What is happening in the marketplace and what is likely to happen in the near future?
- Who is the campaign aimed at?
- Does enough information exist to profile the target market or is more required?
- What needs to be done to get this information?

In addition to effective research, a brief needs clearly expressed goals that answer:

- What should the advertising achieve?
- How does an advertiser want to influence consumers?
- Does the advertiser want to raise their awareness?
- Does the advertiser want to change their perceptions?
- Who is the brand competing against?
- How does the brand stack up against them?
- How can it be truly differentiated from the rest?

The answers to such questions must be incorporated into an advertising brief which lays out the current position together with the desired position. It is vital that the creative brief (which defines the advertising's communication) is the best that it possibly can be; clear briefs will help to deliver innovative ideas that will lead to effective advertising, moving the brand forward. More than this, the brief should also enthuse the creative teams, although it is essential that it is honest since the more realistic the expectations, the easier it will be to evaluate the campaign's success. Some creative briefs are developed in client–agency partnerships, others are written solely by the client, but whatever the arrangement, there must be sufficient time to ensure that the brief is properly developed and addressed before any advertising planning. Advance planning is therefore critical, and the ad agency's account planners and managers must ensure that the creatives (so-called because they are responsible for creating and developing the actual ad campaign) keep on track to deliver the most appropriate advertising ideas and concepts for the brief in question (for more on this, see Ad highlight 2.3 and 'Generating creativity' in Chapter 7).

Once the agency is confident that its advertising ideas meet the client's needs, it is in a position to make its presentation to the client. At this stage both the client and the agency need to be flexible enough to make and accept improvements to the advertising concept, whilst they also need to be wary of unwarranted changes which would undermine the advertising's effectiveness. Once agreement has been achieved, then the ideas can be developed into a number of advertising executions and then placed in the most effective media slots – a process framed by an agreed budget and timescale. And that, as they say, is that! If only it was so simple. Unfortunately, at each stage, any number of variables could intervene to upset this model plan. Ambiguous briefs, unreliable market research, personality clashes and uninspiring ideas can, and do, derail the process. That it is so often undermined is evidenced by the fact that most advertising is awful or at best nondescript. But if it was that simple, would not everyone be producing good advertising, and books such as this one would be superfluous.

Targeting the advertising message

Of course, achieving creativity and producing tightly defined briefs is only part of the planning and implementation of good advertising. If the advertising is creative it is a plus, but the campaign's success is by no means assured since, the world's most creative ad will never sell if it is not aimed at the appropriate consumer segments. As we will see in Chapter 3, the fragmentation of today's media means that mass audiences are now much harder to reach, however, very few tourism and leisure products are intended to have mass appeal. Advertisers instead know that one of their major challenges is selecting the right media to reach their intended audience and buying into these media as cost-effectively as possible. Whilst it is likely that for many tourism and leisure products, above-the-line 'traditional' media still remain the most appropriate and effective way to reach increasingly small and specific groups of consumers, accurate targeting of consumer segments is central to advertising success.

It is essential that the tourism and leisure industries become much smarter in defining and targeting the right market segments. Yet, surprisingly, too few advertisers are prepared to resource the research required to target much 'tighter' groups of consumers than current practice allows. Such is the diversity of contemporary brand and product choices that most people will never buy even a minority of them. In spite of this, many advertisers continue to spend large sums of money targeting people who are not

> It is vital to ensure that the media and the message 'fit', for instance, research suggests that loyal viewers of particular television shows are 30 per cent more likely than the casual viewer to buy the products advertised during the show's commercial breaks.

particularly likely to purchase their products. Waste is unavoidable in advertising and in many instances it is still the case that the mass advertising media is a more effective vehicle for reaching consumers than highly targeted, but (in terms of costs per thousand) more expensive direct marketing techniques. Nonetheless, tourism and leisure organizations should try to discover as much about their consumers as is practically possible so that they can eliminate from their media schedule all those customers who will definitely not purchase their products. Whilst prospective customers are far more difficult to identify, the aim should be to identify and personalize the brand's users (to establish their personality and lifestyle traits) in order to facilitate more effective, efficiently targeted advertising. This moves consumer research way beyond its previous reliance on demographic variables which are readily available and frequently used by all organizations in a given product category. Pyschographic profiles of specific brand users (when combined with geodemographic techniques) can make tourism and leisure advertising more relevant, more targeted and more effective – more of which in Chapter 6.

Are award-winning ads good ads?

Before we move on to consider how some of the ideas discussed above have been translated into a number of advertising 'rules', it is worth considering whether there are some objective criteria for 'good' advertising. The 'jury is out' on whether the advertising industry's own awards recognize the best and most effective advertising. In a 1998 CNBC *Media Magazine* survey, when asked whether awards reflect the calibre of an advertising agency, 32 per cent of the industry ranked them as 'very important', 60 per cent as 'somewhat important' and 8 per cent as 'not important'.[7] Of those who said that the awards are somewhat important, not surprisingly, respondents in the agencies' creative departments polled the highest (70 per cent), whilst 17 per cent of those in account services and 13 per cent of management executives felt that awards were not important. Of course, whilst award juries may have loved an ad, consumers in the real world may have deemed it a disaster. Indeed, there is a sense amongst advertisers that some agencies may have lost the plot in their desire to collect awards. This view, however, tends to ignore the fact that many famous, award-winning campaigns have also been extremely successful where it counts – in the marketplace. *Campaign* magazine investigated whether highly creative campaigns were more or less effective than others and found that around a third of Institute of Practitioners in Advertising (IPA) Advertising Effectiveness Award winners had also won some sort of creative award – the converse of this, of course, is that two-thirds had not. Despite this, there does seem to be a correlation between creativity and effectiveness[8] and, whether they win awards or not, world-class ads usually have some common features: they are built around a great idea and they have high production values – the best are beautifully designed, superbly photographed and have great composition and good copy.

Certainly the best advertising involves ideas that are new, original and remarkable – and ultimately good advertising always depends on creative people (Case study 2.1). Creating effective advertising is all about adding value to a product and good advertising captures that product's point of differentiation, the essence of what makes it special, what makes it stand out from the rest. Smart advertisers find out what their product means to consumers, then they exploit it and find a value that they can add to the overall experience. Most tourism products have something that is unique to them and that will appeal to the target market in question – for instance, as we will see in Chapter 10, despite all the intense competition, most destinations tend to have some attribute that has the potential to become a unique selling opportunity. The issue then centres on whether that point of differentiation can be captured in the advertising. Different products require different approaches but, above all, the advertising has to have credibility with the consumer – overenthusing the advertising message will not do anybody any favours. So are there any 'rules' about creating good advertising, and what are they?

The rules of the ad game

Consumers are responding more and more to expressive rather than status-oriented values, seeking out brands which recognize their individuality and reject authority. Whilst there are always exceptions, in one US survey the least persuasive ads were those that used CEOs or celebrities as spokespeople (Table 2.1). One line of thought argues that ads no longer work unless they make people laugh or evoke an emotional bond with a brand and irony is often described as the key to success in today's market where the consumer is both savvy and sceptical. Whatever the twist to make it stand out, a good ad is often built around a strong, simple idea, expressed in a clear fashion. Take the example of a print ad for UTA French Airlines discussed by Jim Aitchison in his book *Cutting Edge Advertising*. This ad breaks all the airline advertising conventions because it has none of the usual features – there are no shots of the cabin, no photos of the plane's exterior or of smiling crew members. Instead the ad focuses exclusively on a French baguette sliced four times. The message – UTA offers more non-stop flights from Singapore to Paris – is conveyed by the sliced bread (which represents the interruptions caused by transit arrangements) whilst the choice of the baguette (a traditional French symbol) evokes the airline's national link. In the small copy type the reader is told that the sliced baguette is a typical flight to Paris with other airlines.[9] A simple idea, cleverly executed and one which is different because it tries to move away from the traditional way to sell an air flight.

Table 2.1 America's winner and loser ads

Winner ads	Loser ads
Ads with humour	Hidden camera testimonials
Ads with children	Company CEOs
Product demonstrations	Ads with celebrities
Real-life situations	Brand comparisons
Ads with pets	Musical commercials

Source: Video storyboard tests of America's favourite ads.

The advertising environment has changed dramatically in recent years and in this climate of constant change it is worth taking some time to ask whether the old 'rules' of good advertising still apply today (Table 2.2).[10] During the 1950s and 1960s, successful advertising was felt to be the result of advertising agencies following certain rules which were grounded in the experience of that time. The applicability of these rules is much more debatable in the contemporary advertising world – although perhaps too often their influence still remains difficult to resist. Take the first rule about having a unique selling proposition. In most product categories today, products and services are so

Table 2.2   The eight old rules of advertising

1	You must have a USP
2	You must offer rational benefit
3	Humour doesn't sell
4	You must have a memorable slogan
5	You must have a logo in the ad
6	You must show the product in the ad
7	Every ad in a campaign must look the same
8	Creative ads don't sell

Source: Jim Aitchison (1999). *Cutting Edge Advertising. How to Create the World's Best Print for Brands in the 21st Century*. Prentice Hall.

similar that unique selling propositions (USPs) are harder and harder to find. Where differences remain, however, is in a consumer's emotional attachment or commitment to a brand. It is this emotional selling proposition[11] (ESP) rather than any USP that differentiates many of today's brands. This emotional connection refers to how consumers connect and interact with a brand's personality and, in the same way that rational benefits previously dominated advertising, emotional appeals and brand personality are the essence of many contemporary advertising success stories. For instance, Stella Artois' proposition that it is 'reassuringly expensive' (something which after all is a highly irrational appeal) – is seen in numerous superbly crafted executions – although it would be wise to remember that such appeals naturally have to have some foundation – even an irrational appeal will fail if the product or service cannot deliver quality features.

A classic example of the pulling power of an emotional appeal is the advertising for Virgin Atlantic. The connection is clearly seen in the ad 'Chase Rainbows' – a 60-second commercial shot in South Africa and produced in February 1999 by Rainey Kelly Campbell Roafe, a small London-based agency. The ad opens with a good-looking biker in a wilderness-style landscape. He sees a rainbow ahead of him, guns his engine and roars off at high speed towards it. The soundtrack 'Crazy Horses' (a heavy rock score by the Osmonds) cuts in. The biker crosses fields and leaps roads in a bid to chase the rainbow down. A blond woman dressed in a peasant-style dress reminiscent of Switzerland or Eastern Europe leans over a gate and watches him with a smile. He roars on, jumps a rise and reaches the rainbow before it vanishes. We see him bathed in all its colours from a number of angles and the endlines appear: 'Some say why?', followed by 'Others say why not?' 'Virgin Atlantic. Chase Rainbows' (together with the Virgin Atlantic logo). There is nothing here about extensive legroom, award-winning in-flight service, attentive cabin crew or punctuality – the usual staples of airline advertising. Instead, we are invited into an image, an attitude, a way to live. Be a chaser of rainbows, be the ultimate dreamer – usually a derogatory term – yet here seen to be a nonconformist, one who attempts and achieves the impossible (one who finds the rainbow's end) – just like Virgin Atlantic and, by implication, those who choose to fly it.

If the first two ad rules about having a USP and a rational appeal are questionable, what about number three – 'humour doesn't sell'? In contrast to the traditional viewpoint, humour is now seen as something which can bridge divides and build relationships, although it needs to be used carefully because at other times it can have precisely the opposite effect. Humour is certainly a great entertainer and the tourism and leisure industries provide much scope for using it in ad campaigns (see Ad highlight 2.1). If humour fits the personality of the brand then it is perfectly acceptable to use it – as seen in the series of television ads produced for Thredbo, an Australian ski resort. A winner at the 1998 International Travel Advertising Awards, these low-budget ads were produced on a handheld camcorder to create an atmosphere of 'guerrilla' advertising. Appealing to advertising aware Generation X skiers, these anarchic ads are the very pastiche of traditional advertising – suggesting in one execution that members of the public have been paid to praise Thredbo over its rival, the Japanese resort of Nagano, and in another that they have been bullied into endorsing it.

Problems can arise when humour is used inappropriately or when it is at odds with a brand's personality, but when it is done well it can cut across cultures (if not language). For instance, a year later, a winner at the 1999 International Travel Advertising Awards was one of a series of television ads for the Kowloon–Canton Railway. Opening with a scene of a man in his flat practising commando-style rolls with a cushion, the commercial's next scene then shows the same man as an office-worker and it soon emerges that the cushion was a substitute for his briefcase. He enters an office in which his boss is seen on the phone through a plate-glass window. Clearly, his boss has arrived before him and he is late. Putting into practice his rehearsed technique, the office-worker rolls under the window with his case – thus avoiding his boss's gaze. The endline appears: 'Why make life difficult? Keep time on your side. Use KCR.' Despite the cultural differences, consumers around the world could identify with the man who tries to avoid his boss when he's late.

Ad highlight 2.1   Thomson's 'We know the feeling' campaign is a hit in Sweden

Tour operator advertising has frequently proved to be a fertile breeding ground for clichéd and even bad ads as operators have often focused on sun, sand and sex clichés or value-for-money concepts. Originality has tended to play a very minor role – although with the Thomson's award-winning and highly amusing 'We know the feeling' 1998 campaign a new standard has been set in tour operator advertising practice.

The brief

Thomson, one of the largest and most successful UK tour operators, wanted to establish themselves in the Swedish package holiday market and the creation of memorable advertising was seen to be critical to the success of this initiative. The advertising proposition centred on Thomson's dominance of the UK package holiday market for more than thirty years – a market that has been described as the most demanding in the world. At the heart of the ad concept is the influence and impact of the British weather on the British people, something which everyone can sympathize with and which the Swedes themselves witness on their television screens in their own weather bulletins. The weather of course, is something the British package holidaymaker seeks to escape – more often than not, via one of Thomson's holidays.

The ads

Made in English, with English actors communicating in a very English style, the ads made good use of national stereotypes to communicate their central message. In a variety of executions, each ad opens in black and white and focuses on a character who describes the 'joys' of the British weather in an ironic and humorous way. In one ad a young Englishwoman describes her fondness for grey, whilst her less than contented boyfriend looks on in the background. In another, a bowler-hatted, pinstripe suit-wearing businessman tells us quite seriously that the sun shone over the whole of the British Isles for 43 seconds once. Yet another ad shows a downtrodden divorcee in the pouring rain bravely telling the camera how happy she is compared to her ex-husband who has just emigrated to Hawaii with his new wife. Each execution ends with the line 'We know the feeling' as the Thomson's logo appears and the ad switches into colour and cuts to a scene of tropical beach.

Rules four, five and six concern the appearance of slogans, logos and the product itself in the ads. None of these really have to feature in ads and yet many companies are still reluctant to leave out these standard elements, largely because most ads have them. There is a very real concern amongst clients that if an execution does not have these features, then somehow it is missing something vital. Yet this overlooks some extremely successful campaigns which have just featured a logo, or maybe an element of the product, or even a stylistic association – one only has to think of the success of the Silk Cut and Benson & Hedges cigarette campaigns in the UK. Not all advertising needs an endline or slogan – they can sometimes be too unsophisticated or too 'uncool' for the brand image – such as in the case of the Levi's brand – whilst media fragmentation and advertising costs also make universally acclaimed endlines increasingly expensive (see Table 2.3). Of course, when they are done well, endlines can be a very useful resource in advertising. Everyone remembers some of the classic endlines that have become cultural icons in themselves, used in everyday speech. However, many commentators feel that the advertising industry has lost its way because famous endlines just are not being written any longer. Not only that, but companies are jettisoning highly successful endlines in favour of much weaker executions – thus Heineken ditched the famous 'Heineken refreshes the parts other beers cannot reach' in favour of 'only Heineken can do this', and more recently adopted 'How refreshing, how Heineken'.

In dropping successful endlines, companies are turning their backs on what are vitally important assets – not only in terms of consistent advertising but also significant components of their brand's image. If one is used, an endline

Table 2.3 Endline legends and lame ducks

Legends	Modern classics	Lame ducks	Corporate gobbledegook
Happiness is a cigar called Hamlet	You know when you've been Tangoed	It talks your language	An essential British company piping gas for you
Heineken refreshes the parts other beers cannot reach	Just do it	Because I'm worth it	A company from over here that's also doing rather well over there
Beanz Meanz Heinz	Australians wouldn't give a XXXX for any other lager	Welcome to the world	Together we make some alliance
It's a lot less bovver than a Hover	Who would you most like to have a One 2 One with?	The airline for Europe	For all our tomorrows
Schhh . . . you know who		More than just a bank	

Source: Harriet Green (1998). The end of the endline. Campaign, 12 June, 28.

should be designed to communicate what is unique or special about that product or brand – it has to mean something to the consumer. Successful endlines also seem to be written in the vernacular with a rhythm or quirkiness to the speech that is easy on the ear. Most importantly, they are central to mid- to long-term campaigns, featuring in each ad instalment. Successful endlines can sum up the essence of a campaign, whilst the worst ones can become corporate positioning statements which are rarely entertaining and frequently targeted at the wrong audience, appearing to be aimed more at enthusing employees than the consumers themselves.

The basic guideline in producing good advertising must be to utilize whichever combination of slogans, logos or endlines works best in terms of the creative execution and the brand strategy. Advertising for hotels is a case in point. Much of this advertising is not creative – frequently featuring the hotel itself, the reception desk or some of its other facilities. And yet what impact can this have on a potential consumer? Hotels are buildings, some have grand entrances, others have less than imposing receptions and lobbies, but is this what brings hotel advertising to life? Is this the kind of advertising that creates a point of differentiation for a hotel or a hotel chain? The answer has to be 'no', yet it is still difficult to find hotel advertising which attempts to break new ground – difficult but not impossible, as the advertising for Camino Real in Ad highlight 2.2 shows.

Ad highlight 2.2	Camino Real leads the way in hotel advertising

Camino Real, a major Mexican hotel chain, launched a series of highly successful, award-winning television ads in the late 1990s. The ad premise was not that the Camino Real has the best hotel façade, reception or guestrooms but that the Camino Real goes that step further for its visitors. This relatively simple idea was communicated in humorous and entertaining executions that featured animals as the central characters. Animals selling hotels – sounds strange, after all what do they have to do with Camino Real – or any other hotel for that matter? Yet it worked superbly. In 'Mosquito', a mosquito buzzes angrily in a guest room. It lands next to the hotel guest's pillow but instead of biting him serenades him with a lullaby that sends him to sleep. The message? We go further for our guests' comfort. In 'Lobster', another in the series, the commercial opens with a lobster that is making its way along a kitchen table. It climbs a ladder and stands poised on the edge of a huge cooking pot. With a flourish and a wave to the camera, it jumps into the pot – sacrificing itself for the guest's dinner. Again, the message is: 'We go further for our guests.'

These two clever executions, part of a bigger campaign, manage to make a memorable statement about how far Camino Real hotels will go for their guests – and not a hotel lobby shot in sight. The Camino Real ads are useful because they also illustrate how a campaign can have consistent tone and style whilst retaining elements of surprise and spontaneity which engage people's interest and attention – undermining rules seven and eight. Whilst consistency is critical in brand-building campaigns, today's incessant drive towards the 'identikit' ad where every aspect is planned for sameness is negating surprise – particularly in global advertising campaigns. Throughout this discussion of the rules of advertising, what is abundantly clear is that the rules are changing and becoming more fluid. This can be unnerving and somewhat scary – after all, rules make life safe and comfortable for all of us, even creative people. New rules have emerged to challenge the old ones and whilst no doubt these in turn will also reach their sell-by date, they are more relevant in today's environment (Table 2.4). In many ways, of course, these new rules are largely adaptations of the old ones discussed by Aitchison – reflecting not only the shifts in advertising production capabilities and a higher level of service in most industries, but also changing consumer preferences, attitudes and behaviours.

Table 2.4 The eight new rules of the ad game

1 Emotional selling propositions are paramount
2 Irrational appeals are legitimate and predominate
3 Humour can and does work for many brand personalities
4 Slogans are good but only if they are memorable
5 You don't always need to feature your logo
6 You don't always need to feature your product
7 Ads in a campaign should be linked but don't need to be identical
8 Creative ads do sell

Source: adapted from Jim Aitchison (1999). *Cutting Edge Advertising. How to Create the World's Best Print for Brands in the 21st Century.* Prentice Hall.

Whilst the rules might change, one fundamental premise remains the same – each ad must be built around ideas. Without the idea, the ad is merely a parody or a pastiche. It is the idea which should energize people to engage with the brand in the ad and whilst an ad's execution and production values should build on and enhance the idea, in themselves they cannot replace the idea. It is important to remember also that ads do not have to be complex and ground-breaking to be successful and effective. Sometimes simple ideas with basic appeal work best, as in the case of Marriott UK's leisure breaks campaign which won the 1998 Hotel Marketing Association's Best Leisure Marketing Campaign. Run in the national press and on the London

Underground, the ads showed thirty-something couples enjoying themselves with the strapline 'Take a leisure break', followed by 'When you're comfortable you can do anything' – a simple campaign which increased sales across all the group's hotels by 20 per cent.

The role of client–agency relationships

The creation of successful advertising is not merely about using and applying ad rules and devices. It is also about building successful relationships between clients and agencies, which can then facilitate the germination and nurturing of effective, creative advertising. Increasingly, our world is dominated by corporate giants that are intent on becoming bigger and better than ever, which has had an effect on the expectations placed on advertising agencies. In this world, the agency that proposes to sustain a company's market share in the face of growing competition is likely to be eclipsed by those offering campaigns designed to greatly increase a brand's market share at the expense of its rivals. This, despite the view of many advertising agencies that advertising effects are incremental most of the time – particularly as we live in a world where competitor products and services rarely differ significantly over an extended time period.

Types of agencies

Advertising agencies are often described as being either full-service or limited-service agencies. A full-service agency offers the client the total range of services required to develop, create and execute an advertising campaign. In the 1990s many of these larger agencies moved to offer a variety of activities including sales promotion and public relations to complement the ad campaign. By contrast, limited-service agencies offer a pick-and-mix style whereby clients can mix a range of services from a number of agencies. One such specialist service is the creative boutique, an agency that may not offer research or media buying but deals strictly in developing innovative concepts and messages. The big idea of the 1980s and early 1990s – the one-stop-shop concept which held that mega-agencies like WPP Group (London), Omnicom Group (New York), Interpublic Group (New York) and Saatchi & Saatchi Co. (London) should offer a multiple network to avoid client conflict and be able to offer brand owners services ranging from recruitment to printing – is now seriously challenged.

Today, agencies are increasingly being seen as purely suppliers of creative input. Apart from the issue of client conflict, there is little to distinguish one giant advertising conglomerate from another and, arguably, the client's primary need is for a creative agency – an ideas company or a boutique – that can rejuvenate a brand. One of the problems with big agencies is that their administrative costs can eat up a significant portion of an advertiser's budget – which could be much better spent in media buying (Ad challenge 2.1). Other commentators see a future of consolidation, with the bigger players getting even bigger – arguing that scale generates resources that can deliver a competitive edge and that, in order to take advantage of global media opportunities, advertisers must be organized on an international basis with an international network of offices.

> The growing fragmentation and diversity of the marketplace may mean that in the future agencies will become increasingly specialized – maybe by function (commercials, print, direct marketing, brochure specialists) or by market (e.g., to reach Hispanic, African-American or Asian-Americans in the USA).

Ad challenge 2.1   British advertising industry faces a crisis

British advertising is envied for its consumer insights and creativity but according to a recent report, the top fifty advertising agencies are by and large poorly managed, overstaffed and with costs and salaries running out of control, whilst productivity per head fell by 1 per cent in 1998. The report condemns their profit margins (which at 6.5 per cent is well below the 15–20 per cent experts agree well-run service firms should be making), saying they undercharge for their core strategic and creative inputs and then try to recoup revenue by overcharging clients for extra services. The picture is not universally gloomy but it is the big foreign-owned agencies that perform the worst. This is because multinational agencies often duplicate roles and have an expensive tier of managers in large, local offices. Ultimately, if agencies are not managing themselves well, their clients will end up paying for it and, in a drive for further efficiency, many large advertisers are beginning to turn their attention to their advertising agencies.

Source: Alex Benady (1999). Wanted: substance to match style of adland. *Observer*, 26 September.

What clients look for in an agency

More than ever, with tighter ad budgets and increased competition, advertising managers are in the firing line, so how can a client select an agency which will produce advertising that is more relevant, persuasive and effective? First, a client should consider its relationship with the agency. Should the agency merely supply a product or should it be a longer-term partner who will advise strategically as well as tactically? The answer to this question will dictate the type of agency that will suit the client's needs. Agencies are extremely varied organizations and the vast majority are small companies consisting of a handful of specialists and employing freelancers as and when required. This means they can pull in people from a large pool of talent without sustaining high overheads and their clients only pay for the services needed. By contrast, there are a small number of giant international agencies with offices worldwide and annual billings of billions of dollars. These giants may own several advertising agencies and they offer a full range of advertising services virtually anywhere in the world. In general, agencies should be able to fulfil the following functions for a client:

■ perform a strengths, weaknesses, opportunities and threats (SWOT) analysis of the advertised product, including its current and potential market
■ examine all appropriate methods of distribution, sales and media
■ prepare an advertising plan, create and produce the ad campaign, buy media space and time, and liaise with the client to co-ordinate the campaign with other marketing activities.

Advertising agencies should never be mere providers of advertising. Instead, they should be in the business of providing advertising solutions to clients' briefs. *Marketing Week*'s tenth annual survey into agency reputation in 1998 – a survey which asks clients to judge the agencies they work with – indicates what clients want from their agencies. Clients were asked to judge agencies on nine categories ranging from creativity to value for money. This survey reveals that clients now want agencies who will act in their longer-term best interests (based on understanding their business and markets), together with the always regularly acclaimed top two criteria of creativity and value for money. Amongst the remaining factors which clients are identifying as increasingly important in their agencies' portfolio are those of media planning and marketing strategy (Ad highlight 2.3). If an advertiser wants to hire an agency or change agencies, whatever the size of their budget, there are a number of common factors which they should consider:

■ *Reputation* – what image does the agency have and what do other clients, agencies and the media say about the agency? Has it produced quality work – are its ads creative and effective?
■ *Expertise* – how well does the agency understand the product, market and industry and has it got a proven track record of working well on similar briefs?
■ *Cost* – can the agency work within the budget and deliver an advertising campaign of suitable quality and effectiveness?

Table 2.5 What clients want from agencies

1998 rank	Criteria	1998 rating (%)
1	Creativity	62
2	Value for money	61
3	Ability to act in clients' longer-term best interests	58
= 4	Media planning, buying and placement	44
= 4	Quality of account managers	44
5	Marketing strategy and analysis	37
6	Attentiveness and adaptability	32
7	Financial stability and strong agency management	19
8	Coverage of markets outside UK	7

Source: Marketing Week, 26 November 1998.

Whilst clients have to consider a range of issues when choosing an agency, it is as well to remember that there are bad clients as well as bad agencies – notably those who do not listen to their agencies' advice and yet are too closely involved with the brand to be objective. Honesty is critical in successful brand management and good clients are brave and encourage their agencies to be bold and original.[12] Weinreich highlights four attributes that make a good client, suggesting that they are:

- communicative – willing to share plans and research
- stimulating and encouraging – desiring good advertising
- receptive – knowing when they are on to something positive
- courageous – refusing to bow to ultra cautious critics.[13]

Ad highlight 2.3   The role of the account executive

The account executive (also sometimes known as a management supervisor, account manager, account supervisor or account director) manages all the ad agency's services on the client's behalf and is responsible for delivering the creative ideas on time, to budget and according to the agreed strategy. He or she should be able to select the advertising team most appropriate for a particular brief and should be well appraised of the client's needs. This appraisal should be based on a thorough understanding of the client's business, in particular:

- the product or service to be advertised
- the client's marketing strategy
- the client brand's advertising and promotional history (including successes and failures)
- competitor positionings

- distribution mechanisms and strategies
- the target market and the consumer profile
- the required time frames and the advertising budget.

Source: Jay Quinn (1999). Agency management. In *The Advertising Business: Operations, Creativity, Media Planning, Integrated Communications* (J. P. Jones, ed.) pp. 17–28, Sage.

Building client–agency trust

This brings us to one of the essential ingredients in the client–agency relationships – trust. When the client–agency chemistry clicks it can produce exciting and effective advertising which can become legendary – for instance, Lever Brothers have been with the J. Walter Thompson agency for almost 100 years. Although this is exceptional, trust is essential in the partnership and without it, it may be difficult for the client to have faith in the executions presented to them. If a client–agency relationship is not based on trust and mutual respect, it will fail and any advertising produced will be sterile. Client–agency relationships can last a relatively long period of time and whilst seven years is the average, successful partnerships can last much longer. This could lead to a problem for many publicly funded agencies in the tourism and leisure industries as they often have to renew contracts which on the whole tend to be issued for around three years. Of course, regular reviews of advertising relationships are not necessarily a bad thing – they can be constructive and can prevent agencies from becoming complacent and keep the relationship fresh. The downside of this regular tendering is that publicly funded organizations are often pressed to accept the least cost rather than the best value option. This destroys successful partnerships with more regularity than in the private sector and damages both the client, the product (which may be a country, region or resort) and the agency. Equally, frequent changes of agencies can waste time since the 'getting to know you' process takes quite some time – clients have to educate new agencies and agencies take time to get to know the client, its aims and marketplace.

> Clients should never trust an agency that presents more than one campaign at a time – creative agencies will put their faith in a single campaign, and presenting a range of options is a sign of indecision.

Other aspects of building trust are frankness, enthusiasm and flexibility, and it requires both sides to be receptive to new ideas or to new ways of looking at things. There is also an onus on clients to be upfront about their gut reactions to a piece of work – if they do not like it and are worried about it, then they should come out and say so. In such cases clients and agencies should discuss and explore the reasons behind the reaction. One client that felt uneasy about an execution but still went ahead with it was the Wales Tourist Board (WTB). Some years ago the WTB and a London-based agency were developing a campaign aimed at England (Wales's biggest tourist market). The campaign had quite beautiful, faultlessly executed, unusual almost surreal photography depicting the Welsh landscape. To complement these, the agency was looking for something 'vaguely Welsh' as a strapline. It came up with 'Now there's Wales for you'. The rhythm and cadence was supposed to represent Welsh speech without being 'too' Welsh – in other words, to be distinctive without actually using the Welsh language. Almost immediately the client was nervous about how this execution would be received in Wales, and its instincts were right since it quickly became seen as parodying Welsh speech.

This should remind us that advertising has many audiences, not just the consumer – and in destination advertising marketers ignore the other audiences and stakeholders at their peril. In this case, after much discussion, the client went with the agency idea but it did not take long to realize that this had been a mistake. Media coverage within Wales mushroomed, reactions were overwhelmingly negative and within a year the campaign was dropped. Having said this, clients should, above all, retain an open mind during the advertising process. It is undoubtedly true that whilst everybody loves good finished advertising, rather fewer react positively to storyboards and unfinished ideas whose virtues and impacts are not always readily apparent. One way in which agencies can better empathize with their clients' needs is to understand their business and, whilst agencies are not specialists in their clients' business (their task is being expert at persuading people to want their clients' products), they can include an industry-specific management consultant on the team, together with a client representative.

Politics in advertising

The advertising process is fraught with politics which some observers see positively, injecting some much needed scepticism into the more 'off-the-wall' executions, whilst others take a more negative view, seeing such politics as inhibiting the development of creative advertising. Certainly, the advertising process is by no means a seamless and safe transition through all its stages of research, development, implementation and evaluation. Designing an advertising campaign involves a range of people and organizations at various times throughout the process – most obviously the client, the agency and the market researchers. When clients and agencies collaborate over a campaign, two different cultures are coming together, and whilst both are discussing the same objectives, they have differing agenda. The client wants a campaign which sells the product, whilst the agency wants to develop a campaign it can put on its showreel – and sometimes the two desires are not compatible. Moreover, within agencies different coalitions and divisions exist, particularly between the so-called 'suits' (account managers) and the creatives – a gulf between, what has been termed, one person trying to run a business and another who is trying to run an art gallery.[14]

There can be no doubt that politics genuinely affects the outcomes of advertising and particularly the research process which should inform the brief. Politics can intervene to the extent that the wrong marketing decisions are taken or it can encourage compromise and trade-offs that produce poor ads. It similarly devalues the advertising research, which can become a mere prop for particular arguments rather than a source of illumination. It is easy to understand why politics intervenes in advertising. After all, advertising is the public face of the brand; it is also a very costly element of the overall marketing mix and its performance and effectiveness are difficult to evaluate. At the same time, the advertising process is characterized by continuous negotiation – both between and within the agency and the client. Moreover, many of a client's real decision-makers – the CEO, managing directors, even marketing directors – are unlikely to be intimately involved in the advertising process, and without clear communications this can lead to a lack of synergy between the overall marketing strategy and the advertising campaign. Negotiation is also endemic because agencies, clients and research companies are all made up of individuals, and if five people are involved immediately there are eight relationships to negotiate in the advertising process (Table 2.6).

Table 2.6 Relationships that can 'kill' creativity

The client killer	*The researcher*	*The creative*
Career based on killing other people's ideas	Power at last!	The idea owners
There's always a reason not to run an ad	Comes late to the ad development	Not involved elsewhere
Advertising research often provides the excuse not to run an ad	Value for money dominates	Suspicious of advertising research

Source: adapted from L. Green (1993). Unpublished paper on politics in advertising, Market research conference, Nottingham.

Whilst such politics and relationships will never disappear, it is important that all the parties involved attempt to understand and overcome them – otherwise the advertising will inevitably be compromised.

Chapter summary

It is very difficult to distil what is special about good advertising. There are many more advertising failures than successes and much of what is produced today is so much 'wallpaper'. If advertising was easy, every piece of advertising produced would be wonderful – and this is patently not the case. Good advertising is based on solid research and planning, as well as creativity and skilful media buying. Effective ads are founded on:

- producing a tightly defined, research-based advertising brief
- precisely targeting the audience
- harnessing creative energy
- being interesting, surprising and relevant
- inventing indelible imagery
- perfecting timing
- having a consistent approach
- appearing effortless.

These guidelines indicate that good advertising incorporates a number of features and is often centred on effectively creating an emotional appeal that inextricably links the brand and the consumer. It is generally agreed that award-winning advertisements are of a particularly high standard and the best ads have high production values, in particular they have:

- skilful design
- beautiful photography
- good composition
- great writing
- superb layouts which are not too 'busy'.

With the right combination of these factors, impressive advertising can be produced and the very best tourism and leisure advertising seeks to transcend the commodity nature of the product and offers the consumer the promise of a unique benefit. Whilst there is no point in producing advertising which is different merely for its own sake, advertising which is both original and relevant is highly desirable. Within tourism and leisure there is much scope to produce advertising which is stylish, eloquent and witty, and it should also be remembered that tourism and leisure advertising, after all, is not the same as advertising for washing powder – since it is about selling dreams and aspirations (Table 2.7).

Table 2.7   What makes good and bad advertising

Good ads	Bad ads
Are relevant	Use unrelated gimmicks
Advance the brand	Are a clone of someone else's ad
Are based on a simple idea	Are badly timed
Are uncomplicated	Use bad jokes
Tell a story	Are invented by committees
Talk to the target audience	Are produced for an international audience
Challenge and provoke comment	Let technique and technology hijack the idea
Are long term and cumulative	Have unrealistic aims and budgets

Case study 2.1

Asia produces creative advertising

In Asia, Thai advertising is number one, beating both Australia and Japan to top CNBC's *Media Magazine* survey for the most creative and original advertising. The 1997 economic slump hit Thailand hard – Thai advertising spending plunged by 30 per cent year on year in the crisis and, while it was not as depressed as Indonesia, it was badly damaged, resulting in salary cuts, downsizing and more emphasis on effective management. Yet this did not limit the industry's imagination – in fact, agencies have had to use their ingenuity to come up with powerful ideas for fewer dollars. For some that has meant getting back to what advertising is all about and the ad idea itself has become much more important because there is not a lot of money to spend on elaborate production. A creative idea was central to the ad promoting tourism in Thailand that won a top award for creativity and production in 1998. The ad opens with a man with his back towards the camera. He faces a huge Thai parade, headed by a bedecked elephant, as brightly coloured floating market canoes with parasols glide by, seemingly travelling in the air, as city-clad workers look on in amazement. This commercial was to the point and uses a simple and strong idea – and whilst good ideas do not depend on big budgets they do have to be distinctive enough to sell products to Thais living on limited budgets of their own.

The state of the Thai ad industry is in direct contrast to the Japanese industry which once represented the cutting edge of Asian advertising – pulling in international awards for funny, quirky and moving ads. Recently Japanese ads lost their international appeal and in this case there does seem to be a correlation between advertising budgets and awards – paralleling the rise and fall of the Japanese economy. As the Japanese economic machine faltered and stopped in the late 1990s, companies became desperate to move their products off the shelf, resulting in campaigns which were short term in strategy and in impact – with a shift to 15 second commercials, leaving less room for creativity. As a result, ad breaks became a cacophony of short, competing claims. With six different brands competing in the same space as three once occupied, brands really have to stand out. Yet, with everyone attempting similar strategies, the ad environment becomes much more cluttered, tempting the agencies to take short cuts which Japanese viewers recognize but which draw a blank internationally. It may well be that as the economy continues to recover, companies will move back to the 30-second ad slot format which allows them more opportunity to build brand images – but that remains to be seen.

Notes

1 John Philip Jones (1999). Introduction: the advertising business. In *The Advertising Business: Operations, Creativity, Media Planning, Integrated Communications* (J. P. Jones, ed.) pp. 1–17, quote p. 4, Sage.
2 Al Ries and Jack Trout (1986). *Positioning. The Battle for Your Mind.* Warner Books, p. 15.
3 Len Weinreich (1999). *11 Steps to Brand Heaven: The Ultimate Guide to Buying an Advertising Campaign.* Kogan Page, p. 67.
4 Simon Anholt (1999). Travel and tourism companies: global brands. *Journal of Vacation Marketing*, **5** (3), 290–5.
5 Adapted from Weinreich, *11 Steps to Brand Heaven*, pp. 69–74.
6 Ibid., pp. 14–15.

7 Reported on CNBC Asia *Storyboard* in 1998.
8 Winston Fletcher (1994). *How to Capture the Advertising High Ground.* Century Business Books, p. 95.
9 See Jim Aitchison (1999). *Cutting Edge Advertising: How to Create the World's Best Print for Brands in the 21st Century.* Prentice Hall.
10 Ibid.
11 Ibid., p. 42.
12 Weinreich, *11 Steps to Brand Heaven*, p. 110.
13 Ibid., p. 99.
14 Ibid., p. 128.

Further reading

Aitchison, J. (1999). *Cutting Edge Advertising: How to Create the World's Best Print for Brands in the 21st Century.* Prentice Hall.
Anholt, S. (1999). Travel and tourism companies: global brands. *Journal of Vacation Marketing,* **5** (3), 290–5.
Anholt, S. (2000). *Another One Bites the Grass: Making Sense of International Advertising.* John Wiley.
Bond, J. and Kirshenbaum, R. (1998). *Under the Radar: Talking to Today's Cynical Consumer.* John Wiley.
Cialdini, R. B. (1993). *The Psychology of Influence.* William Morrow.
Dru, J.-M. (1996). *Disruption: Overturning Conventions and Shaking Up the Marketplace.* John Wiley.
Fletcher, W. (1994). *How to Capture the Advertising High Ground.* Century Business Books.
Green, H. (1998). The end of the endline. *Campaign,* 12 June, 28–9.
Jones, J. P. (ed.) (1999). *The Advertising Business: Operations, Creativity, Media Planning, Integrated Communications.* Sage.
Quinn, J. (1999). The account executive in an advertising agency. In *The Advertising Business: Operations, Creativity, Media Planning, Integrated Communications* (J. P. Jones, ed.) pp. 29–34, Sage.
Weinreich, L. (1999). *11 Steps to Brand Heaven: The Ultimate Guide to Buying an Advertising Campaign.* Kogan Page.

3

Planning the complete campaign

Chapter overview

This chapter will discuss the advertising process as a complete strategy, from campaign brief to evaluation and should be read in conjunction with Case study 3.1 which details how Publicis Eureka constructed a campaign for the Hard Rock Hotel which opened in Bali in 1998. A clear, well planned strategy should provide the starting point and blueprint for a campaign, and the centre point of that strategy must be a clear proposition which serves to frame and develop the advertising. Of course, intuition (from both agency and client), as well as logical process is critical to the production of strong creative work (as we will see in Chapter 7), but this must be produced within the framework of a sound research-based strategy (see Chapter 4).

One aspect of campaign planning that is frequently overlooked is media planning. Making media choices used to be a comfortable business – companies would launch brands on national television and reinforce this launch with print ads in newspapers and a handful of key magazines, and in doing so they could rely on reaching much of their target audience. No longer. Broadcast, cable, satellite and digital channels abound; the magazine market has fractured into thousands of specialist publications; on-line, multimedia interactive advertising has arrived in earnest; automated kiosks carry ads and act as sales points; and markets are global. This makes the choice of media a highly complex, specialist and critical area of advertising strategy and this chapter evaluates the range of options open to advertisers. The key themes of the chapter are:

- strategy development
- creative development
- communication assessment
- campaign evaluation
- media strategy and media choices
- the advantages and disadvantages of different media for tourism and leisure advertising.

Introduction

In Chapter 2 we looked at what makes good (and bad) advertising and focused on the role of creativity in breaking through the media clutter and arresting audience apathy. However, creativity is only part of what makes good, effective advertising. To produce good advertising, both advertisers and agencies must work in partnership to combine the appropriate message (creatively conceived and flawlessly executed) with the right media to effectively influence a clearly defined audience. In essence, the final advertising campaign will only be as good as the planning which underpins it and at all stages in the advertising process it is important to have clear objectives. At the same time, of course, the advertising strategy is likely to be only one component of a wider promotional strategy set within an overarching corporate plan which steers the organization's development. In this way, advertising planning does not exist in isolation and needs to be guided by clear business and marketing objectives which, in turn, will establish the context for any advertising research requirements (see Chapter 4). The organizational strategy and the advertising plan within it need to be developed holistically – if they are not, the organization, the marketers, the product developers, the advertisers and the researchers will be pulling in different directions – with all the negative impacts such confusion brings.

Plate 1 Music sells the Hard Rock Hotel, Bali (Courtesy of Publicis Eureka)

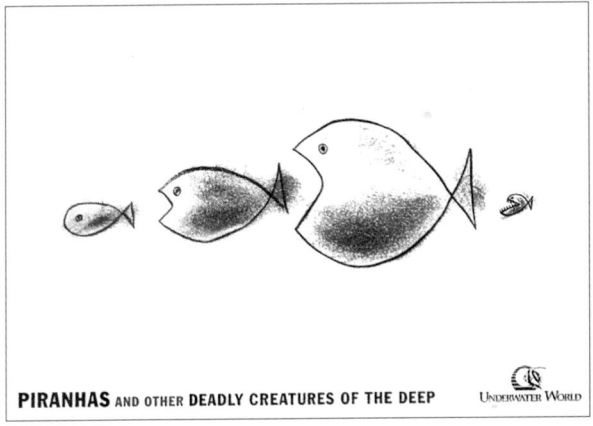

Plate 2 'Deadly creatures of the deep' at the Underwater World Aquarium, Singapore (Courtesy of Saatchi & Saatchi, Singapore)

Piranhas and other deadly creatures at Underwater World
Singapore

1,000 gods.

And not one to protect

against tourists.

SPEND SOME TIME IN THE COUNTRY

Fares from London Waterloo to:	Adult Day Return fare
Royal Botanical Gardens (Kew Bridge)	£3.00
Sherborne	£20.00 (Apex)
Exeter	£20.00 (Apex)
Dorchester South	£21.00 (Apex)
New Forest (Brockenhurst)	£21.70
Isle of Wight - Ryde Esplanade (via Portsmouth Harbour)	£26.50*

CALL 0345 48 49 50   A better day out **SOUTH WEST** TRAINS

Plate 4 South West Trains: 'A better day out'
(Courtesy of Court Burkitt)

Plate 3 *(opposite)* 'Eternal Egypt' at the Singapore Museum
(Courtesy of Saatchi & Saatchi, Singapore)

Plate 5 Royal Peacock Hotel: 'A brothel before, a hotel now'
(Courtesy of Saatchi & Saatchi, Singapore)

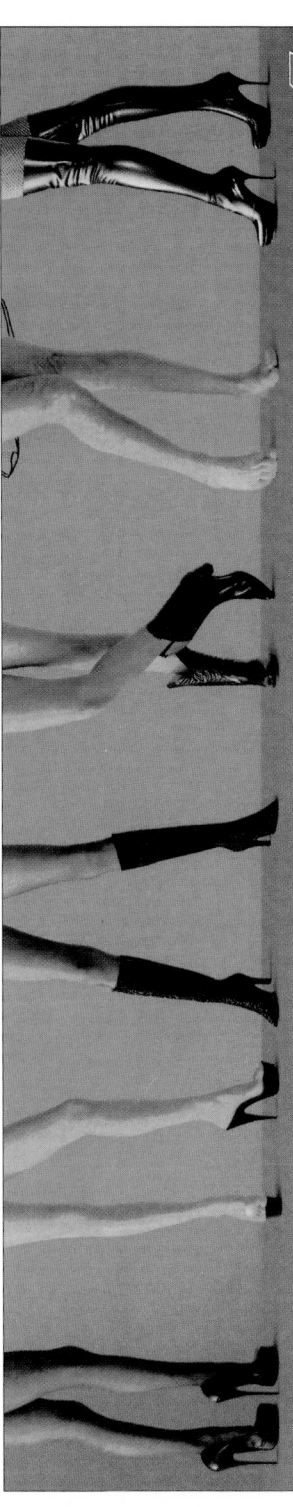

Upper Class Outrageous legroom.

virgin atlantic

BA don't give a Shiatsu.

Upper Class   Free onboard massage.

virgin atlantic

Plate 6 Examples of Virgin Atlantic's award-winning poster campaign: 'Outrageous legroom', 'BA doesn't give a shiatsu' and 'bald man' (*overleaf*)
(Courtesy of Rainey Kelly Campbell Roalfe/Y&R)

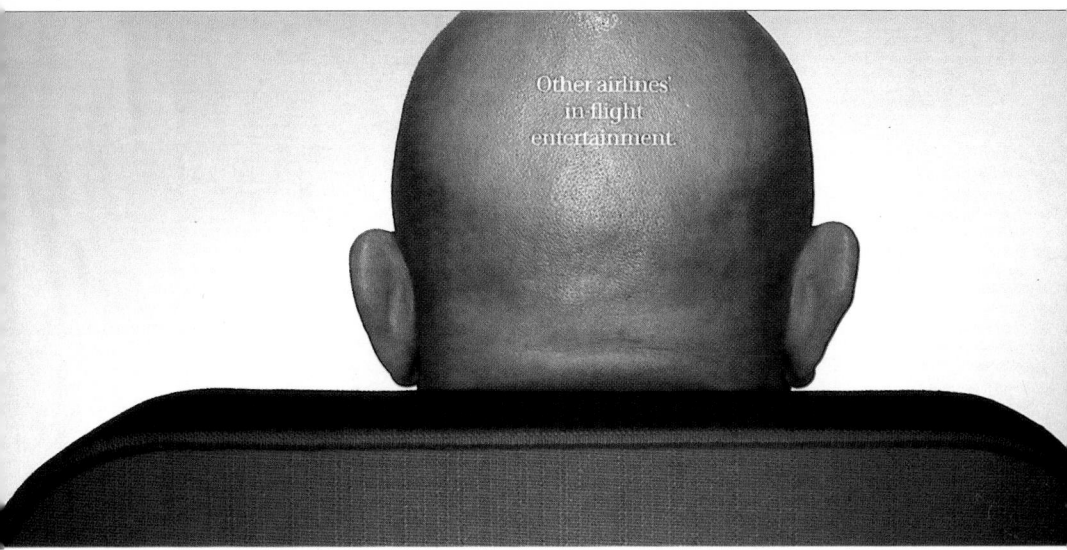

Other airlines'
in-flight
entertainment.

Fly Virgin. And get a seat back TV in Economy.

virgin atlantic

Plate 6 (continued)

THE ENGLISH RIVIERA
TORQUAY · PAIGNTON · BRIXHAM

Plate 7 Modern style and service in the Torbay 1985 brochure illustration (Courtesy of Torbay Tourist Board)

The advertising strategy should outline the existing advertising situation and the current advertising objectives, along with a more detailed discussion of executions, media plans, the advertising budget and the required timescales. The ad strategy is the culmination of a process which itself is highly complex and challenging. Not surprisingly, the development of an advertising strategy is guided by some very familiar, tried and tested business planning cycle principles and consists of the following eight steps:

1 *Analysing the current situation* – where are we now, how did we get here?
2 *Defining the audience* – who do we want to communicate with?
3 *Developing marketing goals* – where do we want to go?
4 *Developing advertising goals and a plan* – how are we going to get there?
5 *Agreeing an advertising budget* – how much money can we spend?
6 *Developing and executing a creative strategy* – how shall we communicate?
7 *Developing and implementing a media strategy* – where are we going to place the ads?
8 *Evaluating advertising effectiveness* – how successful were we?

This advertising process has to be framed within the overall marketing strategy and each campaign has to be co-ordinated with other promotional tools such as sales promotion, public relations and sponsorship to create effective and seamlessly integrated communications. The advertising plan is a blueprint for answering where an organization is now and where it wants to be in the future, for learning about the target audience, determining how it will achieve its objectives and for evaluating the campaign outcomes.

> A campaign is defined as an advertising programme designed to achieve specific goals during a specified period of time.

Advertising strategy

The advertising cycle, which builds on and adapts general business planning principles, should enable advertisers and agencies to give a brand direction and will ensure that resources are used wisely and effectively. A continuous process, it is more often than not repeated annually, although in certain instances it might be used more or less frequently. The agency's role in the process will be dictated by the nature of their relationship with the client – those who have built up a close relationship over the long term may well

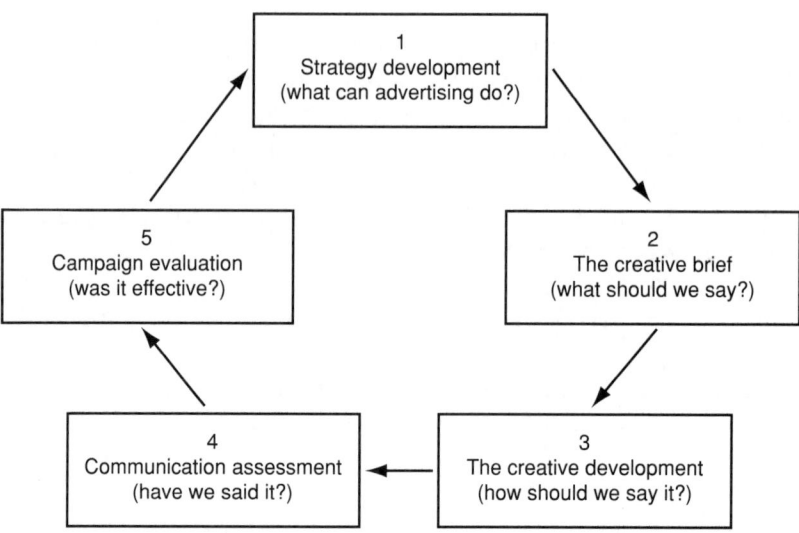

Figure 3.1 The advertising cycle

collaborate at each stage of the cycle, whilst others will only become involved once the brief has been determined. There are five key phases in the advertising process: strategic development, creative brief development, creative development, communication assessment and campaign evaluation (Figure 3.1), each of which we will discuss in turn.

Phase one: strategy development

Successful advertising is founded on clear objectives that direct the creative advertising effort. Time should be realistically allocated to the setting of these objectives as it is a challenging process. Advertising objectives are usually, in effect, communication objectives whilst, by contrast, sales objectives are much more likely to be marketing objectives since they are driven not merely by advertising goals but also by decisions arising from the other components of the promotional mix (sales promotion, public relations, sponsorship, etc.) and from the overall marketing mix (pricing, distribution, product develop-ment strategies, etc.). The advertising strategy needs to clearly identify the problem, the desired outcome, the current and desired operating context, current consumer perceptions of the brand and the ability of advertising to contribute towards the desired outcome. It cannot be emphasized enough how important it is to get the ad strategy right. Without an accurate analysis of the context or problem, then the advertising effort will be flawed from the start – there will be no clear objectives, the brand's current position will not be understood and there will be no way of measuring the advertising's impact. There are a number of key questions that the advertising planning team need to consider to get the strategy right:

- What is the problem?
- Can advertising solve it?
- What do we want the advertising to do?
- Who do we need to be talking to?
- What is the market situation (current and future)?
- How does the consumer feel about our brand and those of our competitors?
- What motivates the consumer and what do they find relevant?
- What do we need to say in our advertising?

Too often, this phase in the planning cycle can be neglected since people are always busy and, in the rush to develop the best ad execution in the time available, clients can treat this phase somewhat complacently – after all, in any organization, surely everybody knows what it is trying to achieve with the advertising, everyone knows who needs to be targeted and is not everyone familiar with the consumer base? These assumptions should not be made – and even if they prove to be correct, good general knowledge is no substitute for well-researched, detailed plans which will produce much more highly targeted and specific advertising. Effective planning at stage one should make it much easier to move to phases two and three of the advertising cycle.

Phases two and three: the creative brief and its development

Phase two, the creative development phase, establishes the advertising's creative brief whilst phase three develops and examines the advertising idea itself, finalizes the executional details and arranges the media schedule. The creative phases are often the most enjoyable and fascinating stages of the advertising process. Creativity is all about producing original ideas, finding new ways of looking at existing ideas or even about juxtaposing previously unrelated concepts (see Chapter 7). The most obviously creative element in advertising is the final product – the artwork and the copy – yet this is only the last stage in a complex creative process which attempts to connect a brand with the preferred market. The bulk of creative thinking is geared towards producing the creative concept or the 'big idea' around which an advertising campaign is built. It probably comes

> A campaign brief sets out the nature and scope of the advertising objectives and defines the target audience – in practice they can vary from just a few lines to highly detailed documents!

as no surprise that the most creative ads frequently develop from a thorough understanding of a brand's relationship with its customers and competitors (for more on this see Chapter 4).

The creative concepts generated should be relevant (to the ad objectives and the consumer), original (to generate interest or surprise) and rich (to allow them to be 'mined' for further ad executions). The creative concepts, and ultimately the finished ad, need to appeal and to make a connection between the brand and the audience. Appeals can be rational (logical and cognitive) or emotional (based on feeling) or could be a combination of the two. They can be based on any number of variables (including price, quality, celebrity endorsement, etc.) and can make sensory, emotional, ego or novelty appeals. Above all, the executions should, wherever possible, be fresh, original, witty, personal, relevant, simple and attractive. In order to make creative development as effective as possible, there are a number of questions which the client and the agency need to address:

> Appeal – the extent to which consumers react positively towards an ad and actively like the advertising.

- Who are we trying to persuade?
- What do we want people to think and feel about the brand?
- Does the idea communicate the strategy?
- What kind of consumer responses does it evoke?
- Are these the right kind of responses?
- How is the idea working?
- Is some of it working for us and some against?
- Can we develop it further or have we taken it as far as it will go?
- Have we got the executional details right?

Phase four: communication assessment

This phase of the planning cycle – unlike the previous phases, which were concerned to develop and implement the creative concept – is concerned with evaluating the creative executions before the campaign is run. It is important to understand that this phase cannot guarantee the success of the campaign, but it certainly increases the advertising's chances of meeting its goals. Of central importance is the extent to which the advertising executions have communicated the strategic goals established in phase one. The exact method of analysis will differ depending on what the advertising was designed to achieve in the first place, although the communication assessment should consider:

- To what extent is the strategy communicated?
- What are the execution's strengths and weaknesses?
- What kinds of impact could the execution achieve?
- Is the execution well branded?
- Can we improve it?

Phase five: the campaign evaluation

This is often the most difficult stage in the advertising cycle, largely because, whilst it is relatively easy to establish certain advertising measures (such as consumers' awareness of a brand before and after the campaign), it is much harder to establish shifts in consumer attitudes or brand perceptions – more of this in Chapter 4. Despite this, the evaluation phase is significant, not only because it establishes what a campaign has achieved, but also because it will provide guidance in terms of how further campaigns could be improved and developed. Clients and agencies should consider the extent to which:

- the message reached the right people
- the ads actually said what was intended
- the ads achieved what was expected
- consumer perceptions were changed
- product sales increased
- the media mix was effective
- lessons could be learned from the campaign
- campaigns could be improved in the future.

Making media choices

Whilst creative development and evaluation are essential components of the advertising campaign planning cycle, even the best execution will never work if it is in the wrong media. The range of advertising media available to today's advertiser is increasingly bewildering and it is becoming ever more fragmented, and whilst this offers the prospect of greater targeting it also makes the job of the media planner ever more difficult and specialist. Certainly the plethora of media choices brings with it a real sense of clutter and confusion in the marketplace, and magnifies the possibility that the wrong choices will be made. In this environment, which medium is the most persuasive? The answer is that this depends on the brand in question, the target audience and the message – as well as being influenced by a range of other factors. Table 3.1 provides a quick reference guide to the range of the main advertising media and points out their major advantages

Table 3.1   The advantages and disadvantages of the major advertising media

Print media	Advantages	Disadvantages
Local press	High market coverage Short lead time Easily laid out Frequency/immediacy Relatively inexpensive Allows for repetition of ads Creates local image	Audience reads selectively Short life span Low attention Media clutter Poor reproduction quality
National press	Large circulation Many creative options for layout Appeals to all income levels Relatively cheap for national coverage Frequency allows repetition Allows audience/geographical selectivity	Audience read selectively Short life span Poor reproduction Low attention Clutter
Consumer magazines	Large circulation High pass on readership High-quality reproduction and colour Relatively long life and read in leisurely fashion Well-segmented audience High information content Allows sales promotion inserts	Expensive Distant copy dates Clutter
Specialist trade journals	Well-segmented audience Short lead times Potential for high information content ads	Clutter Competitors' ads may be featured
Circulars	Low production and distribution costs Blanket coverage in target areas	Poor image Distribution abuse Short attention span
Inserts in free press and magazines	Relatively cheap Good for direct response ads	Short life span May be seen as having a poor image
Posters	Cheap Target specific areas/groups Longevity (especially on public transport – buses, etc.)	Short exposure time Poor image Clutter Audience segmentation difficult

Print media	Advantages	Disadvantages
Billboards	High impact Low cost and large readership Longevity	Brief exposure Limited message – unsuitable for complex ads Needs large-scale distribution Creativity needed for impact

Electronic media	Advantages	Disadvantages
Television	Opportunity for high creativity and impact (sound, visual, etc.) Good for image Appeals to all income levels Relatively cheap for national coverage Frequency allows repetition Allows audience/geographical selectivity High attention gaining	Relatively high production and airtime costs Short life span Clutter Fleeting attention
Commercial radio	Large localized audience Gains local recognition Flexible deadlines Well-segmented audience Allows repeat messages	Production can be expensive Allows audio message only Clutter Short life span Fleeting message Low attention/audience distraction high
Cinema	Possibility to segment audience or mass market Allows frequent exposure Potential high creative impact of colour and visual – large screen and sound	Relatively high production and airtime costs Competitors' ads may be featured Fleeting message Difficult to establish audience profile
Internet	Global impact Immediacy Many creative options for design Possibility of direct response and audience profiling	Short life span Creativity and Web design costs Attention low Targeting can be difficult

Table 3.1 continued

Other media	Advantages	Disadvantages
Direct mail	Allows tracking Prepared mailing lists Allows audience/geographical selectivity High information content	Relatively high production costs of creating and maintaining databases Potential poor image
Exhibitions/trade fairs and shows	Large target audience Reach large numbers of customers simultaneously Good for attracting new, maintaining existing customers	Costs of set-up and staffing can be expensive Clutter
Sponsorship and events	Possibility to reach attractive segments or mass market Allows company to build credibility and benefit from reflected success Potential for unusual, attention-grabbing, impactful activity Builds company recognition	Relatively costly Transience of celebrity and lack of control over others' actions Time-consuming to build relationships and links with partners Difficult to evaluate impact
Point-of-sale displays, in-store merchandising	Relatively inexpensive Reinforces ad message Incentive for trade to stock your product	Reaches customers already likely to purchase
Ambient media	Good coverage Good segmentation potential Many creative options	Creativity a constant challenge Targeting can be difficult

and disadvantages – note that the Internet, which is probably the most significant recent addition to the list of media vehicles, is touched on here but is more fully discussed in Chapter 11.

There are many components to the media mix, and how an organization blends them depends on a number of factors, particularly the nature of the product or service and the target audience. For example, tour operators rely heavily on television advertising, but niche players such as special interest operators tend to focus on printed media advertising in specialist publications. Whilst tourism and leisure advertising makes use of all the main media, the key vehicles are print and electronic media advertisements and brochures. In selecting the correct media mix, the media planners and media buyers need to consider the following:

- the target audience's media habits – what do they watch and read and where are they?
- striking a balance between the media image and the product – the media must be able to convey the correct appeal
- the complexity of the ad – the more complex the message, the more frequent exposure it needs to be remembered
- media costs
- audience attention – media should be chosen where noise and clutter will be minimized.

If an advertising agency has £1 million of advertising budget and a blank sheet of paper, how do they decide where the client's money should be spent? Should it go on 'saturation advertising'? This is an all-or-nothing strategy where an event, television programme or media route is monopolized by a short burst of advertising for a particular brand – tried recently by, amongst others, Pepsi, Tango and Castlemaine XXXX. Pepsi spent £330 million in 1996 on its packaging relaunch, including painting Concorde blue, advertising inside the Mir space station and having *The Mirror* (a tabloid UK newspaper) printed on blue paper. Yet this is a high-stakes strategy that runs two important risks: either missing the target audience completely or boring an already sceptical consumer. Pepsi claimed that 70 per cent of the UK population were aware of the colour change within 48 hours, but whilst it scored well on awareness, the campaign failed to increase sales. Similarly, in the same year Carlsberg-Tetley spent £1 million on one night – running nine versions of the same commercial around one film on ITV to relaunch its Castlemaine XXXX. Again, just like Pepsi, sales remained static and the brand has not repeated this strategy.

> Alastair Macdonald, in a study of advertising effectiveness concludes: 'The key to effective media planning remains the issue of coverage and frequency, and to expose the advertising as often as is required to as many of the target audience as possible.'[1]

The alternative to such blanket approaches is to spread out the media spend over several months, buying into a small number of spots each week, although a choice here may be whether to use all the available television channels or to limit exposure to, say, one terrestrial channel and satellite television. Part of the answer to this and similar questions depends on the advertising objectives and yet the advertising agency's media planner and buyer (who operationalizes the planner's ideas – evaluating, planning, recommending and buying media space and time) will probably have little control over setting those objectives. In this case, much of the media planner's contribution is to determine how often the advertisement needs to be seen. Only then can he or she determine essential questions such as:

■ How many weeks should the campaign be on air/in print?
■ What should the weight of advertising be each week?
■ How should airtime slots be spread over each day?
■ What would be the optimum allocation of airtime to each television channel?
■ What would be the optimum time-length strategy (given the budget)?
■ What would be the impact of a change in the ad budget?[2]

Despite the severe penalties for getting the answers to such questions wrong, media planners often have to rely on their past experience of campaigns and their 'gut feeling' (see Table 3.2 for the four steps to effective media planning). As we shall see in the next chapter, trying to establish a link between levels of advertising exposure and levels of sales or market share is a highly complex task, since the advertising impact cannot be isolated from the influence of other company communications, competitors' actions, changes in distribution or even seasonality. Moreover, the quality of exposure is not the same across all media, within different dayparts or across all television programmes, but there is still no way to quantify such effects with

Table 3.2   Four steps to effective media planning

1 Where?	Know your brand not just in terms of facts and figures but its brand essence. How does it speak to consumers? Is it a loud or soft brand – this will influence media choices.
2 When?	Know your brand's consumers and their lifestyles. When is the best time to reach consumers with your brand message – this could be relatively straightforward in an era when vast amounts of consumer data are stored by advertisers.
3 How?	In what ways can you speak to your consumers? Know when to use the different media.
4 What?	Treat the media environment imaginatively but remember that accountability in media planning and spending is vital.

Source: adapted from Carla V. Lloyd (1999). Advertising media. In *The Advertising Business: Operations, Creativity, Media Planning, Integrated Communications* (J. P. Jones, ed.) pp. 89–100, Sage.

consistent accuracy. Such issues should underpin a campaign's media schedule which will, more often than not, combine a range of media vehicles – and could include traditional media such as newspapers, magazines, television, cinema, radio, billboards and brochures, as well as emergent media such as ambient advertising.

The remainder of this chapter will discuss each of the main media vehicles in turn, starting with the more traditional and, for many tourism and leisure advertisers, still the most frequently used media – newspapers and magazines.

Traditional media

Newspapers and magazines

Newspapers and magazines form the backbone of tourism and leisure advertising – in the UK they account for almost 60 per cent of travel ad spend, compared to television's 30 per cent, radio's 6 per cent, cinema's 4 per cent, with 1 per cent being spent on outdoor ads.[3] The attraction of newspapers and magazines is that they offer advertisers the flexibility of targeting consumers in an area as small as a group of postcodes (or zip codes) or as large as an entire country and, as a result, their advertiser client bases range from small bed and breakfast operators to airlines, tourist boards and tour operators. Many of these advertisers tend to focus either on targeting the affluent leisure traveller or the business traveller – the latter being a prime money-spinner for the tourism industry (Ad highlights 3.1 and 3.2). Since so many specialist publications are now available (there are over 11 000 different magazines in the USA alone), advertisers can reach any group – if they understand their reading habits. Countries, states, cities and tourism organizations often buy full-page advertisements in widely read business magazines such as *Time*, *Fortune*, *Forbes* and *The Economist*, and newspapers offer an easy way to communicate messages about a place, including news about festivals or events. Moreover, newspapers are flexible enough to run late holiday deals and responsive enough to accommodate brochure request hotlines. The attraction of magazines is that they can frequently offer advertisers an upmarket audience without wastage. In the UK the upscale glossy *Conde Nast Traveller* was launched in September 1997 and now has a circulation in excess of 60 000. According to its publisher it caters for '30-plus professionals with high disposable income who are passionate about travel', although it does not exclude aspirational readers.[4] Its advertisers include Elegant Resorts, Abercrombie, Mauritius Tourism, Abu Dhabi Airport and a number of luxury hotel chains.

| Ad highlight 3.1 | Targeting the business traveller |

Business travellers generate significant revenues for travel and tourism companies, particularly hotels and airlines – the 15 per cent of British Airways' passengers who travel on business account for more than a third of the airline's total revenue. During prime business hours, the business traveller spends 82 minutes in an airport and there are a wide range of media targeting every leg of this consumer's journey – the ride to the airport, the check-in area, the departure lounge, the duty-free zone and the flight itself are all covered by some medium or other. Whilst television does not really reach this busy, discriminating consumer, there are a plethora of magazines catering for executive travellers. One such publication is *Business Traveller*, launched in the UK in 1976 and distributed around airports. Its readership embraces frequent airline and hotel users and its advertisers (which provide 70 per cent of the magazine's revenue) include major hotel chains and airlines, with a sizeable number of Asian companies keen to reach UK business travellers. Other media owners targeting the business traveller include Sky Sites, the official airport advertising body that owns the poster contract at the seven major UK airports, as well as the Eurostar train terminals at Waterloo and Ashford in Kent.

In-flight media are also a growth area for advertisers in this market, offering the opportunity for a one-to-one dialogue with a captive audience – around $350 million was spent globally on in-flight media in 1996, compared to $270 million the year before. Charles Vine, account director of Spafax Inflight Media, an in-flight entertainment and media company which works with forty airlines, says: 'Everyone wants the business traveller who is an ABC1 decision-maker [yet who is] a light television viewer, and thus elusive to reach on the ground'. With 300 000 people flying around the world at any one time (whether for work or play), on-board advertising is a significant market. In-flight interactive services also provide attractive niche targeting and advertisers can identify passengers precisely, by route structure, class and even journey purpose. The services can be tailored for a business audience, or can work throughout the aircraft – offering travel-related advertisers the chance to book into movies, video games, shopping, gambling, destination information programming and services such as car hire.

Source: Belina Archer (1997). Sun, sea, sex, sand and media. *Campaign*, 30 May, p. 29.

One of the major drawbacks with print ads, however, is that there is also a tremendous amount of clutter in this medium and a question mark must hang over its effectiveness given the amount of information overload experienced by the average consumer. For example, the Sunday edition of a large metropolitan newspaper like the *New York Times* weighs about 4.5 pounds and contains 500 000 words. To read it all would take about 28 hours – taking all of Sunday and most of the rest of the week! It is important to remember, however, that quality Sunday newspaper and magazine readership is spread over a period of time after the issue date. For all magazines there is some time-lag between when the issue is bought and when it is read, although it varies significantly between types of magazines. For instance, half of the readership of the larger quality monthlies such as *Vogue* happens at least nine weeks after the issue date, and 20 per cent five months afterwards. This means that brands placing ads in such magazines should not look for an immediate response and – unlike television ads – magazine ads will be noticed significantly less and less over time, probably after three or four exposures. The good news, however, is that print ads do achieve high initial branded visibility and – in relation to the ad spend – can be two or three times more efficient initially than television advertising (see Case study 3.2).[5]

Television, cinema and radio advertising

As we mentioned above, whereas television is now the dominant advertising medium, it is the second most important medium for leisure- and travel-related advertisers, with about a third of the travel ad spend, followed by cinema and radio which account for much smaller proportions of spend. Since the first commercial television station was launched in the USA in 1941, television has become the most powerful and successful ad medium for the simple reason that it can reach a bigger audience more quickly than any other. More than 99 per cent of all US households own a television and the number of commercials has almost doubled since 1975.[6] Commercials have also become shorter and, whilst more than 90 per cent of all commercials were 30 seconds long in 1975, by the mid-1990s just about a half were lasting 30 seconds and 40 per cent 15 seconds.[7] Although television's dominance of the entertainment world is under threat (see Case study 3.2), it is still a highly effective, attention-gaining media vehicle. As an audiovisual medium, it offers advertisers opportunities for high levels of creativity, it enables a commercial to be run as frequently as is required (and as far as the budget will stretch) and offers national and international coverage across all income levels (Ad highlight 3.2). It is, however, frequently an expensive medium – £1 million spent on airtime at Christmas in the UK will buy less than 6 minutes to persuade the consumer[8] – and its effectiveness is threatened by viewer habits such as channel surfing and the 'zapping' of ads on videos.

| Ad highlight 3.2 | CNN International: a global advertising platform |

CNN, the 24-hour global news channel launched in the USA in 1980, and its sister network CNNI, launched in Europe in 1985, are together distributed to more than a billion people in 185 million households across 212 countries and territories via twenty-three satellites. With more than 80 per cent of its programming generated specifically for the international audience, CNNI offers advertisers a platform to reach all the key worldwide markets. CNN is available in 3.6 million hotel rooms around the world (70 per cent of branded hotels with cable or satellite channels offer CNN), as well as in cruise ships, health clubs, on aircraft and in airport departure lounges. Through the CNN Airport Network, the channel can be seen in more than 1420 gate areas in thirty-three major US airports, plus Frankfurt and Amsterdam – representing more than 350 million enplanements annually. With such coverage, the channel is 'a cross-cultural "familiar face" able to put travellers at ease whether they come from the Americas, Asia Pacific, Europe, the Middle East or Africa'.[9]

Leisure- and travel-related advertisers can buy advertising across all of CNNI, providing a consistent worldwide branding message, or individually by region, and time slots can be planned within specific programmes, at certain times of the year or to coincide with the channel's country- or region-specific theme weeks. For hotels, the campaign can direct viewers to an information page on CNN text for more details on seasonal offers or special promotions – a text service broadcast to over 50 million homes in Europe, the Middle East and Africa and used by at least 1.5 million high-income Europeans every week. As part of the Time Warner group, CNNI also offers partner hotels discounts on other media within the group – and *Time* magazine and *Fortune* (increasingly found in airline business and first-class lounges, on aircraft and in quality hotels) are particularly appropriate for advertisers attracting a business and upscale clientele.

The channel also has its own magazine. Launched in 1998, *CNN Traveller* is a high-quality, glossy quarterly in which destination articles are complemented by lifestyle articles, interviews with leading personalities and pieces on art, fashion, business and the environment. Hotel groups can distribute a customized version of *CNN Traveller* featuring a four-page bound insert promoting new properties, loyalty programme benefits, upgrade programmes and weekend break offers. In addition, CNN has designed a website specifically for hotels. Positioned as 'the website for the discerning international traveller', cnn.traveller.com consists of travel and travel industry news, travel features drawn from *CNN Traveller* magazine, and an on-line reservations facility. Here, advertisers can benefit from discounts on banner advertising and sponsorship and the editorial and cross-promotional power of the CNN News Group since the website is promoted in CNN's television, Internet, text and publishing activities.

One company, Best Western, extended their marketing campaign via direct sponsorship on CNN Interactive. They sponsored a City Guides section on CNN.com/travel guide that was customized to indicate the locations of Best Western hotels, as well as creating the facility for CNN.com users to link directly to Best Western reservation and booking facilities. The campaign enabled Best Western to enhance its branding elements via millions of page impressions, increased traffic to Best Western websites by 300 per cent and boosted sales, achieving a 35 per cent reservation response by Best Western site users.

Source: Time Warner European Profile, 1998, Time Warner Europe, Brussels, 1998 and CNN & Travel, CNN, London, 1999.

Cinema and radio, whilst only accounting for about 12 per cent of advertising are useful media vehicles for tourism and leisure advertisers seeking to target specific niches. Today radio is a vibrant medium used by local, regional and national advertisers, and there are approximately 5000 AM and 4000 FM radio stations operating in the USA alone. Cinema advertising has also become very popular, particularly with leisure advertisers, as it offers marketers a captive audience – television viewers can switch channels or head for the kitchen during a break; junk mail can be put unopened in the bin, but at the movies the audience is tied – once they have a ticket they are not likely to leave. Not only is the audience captive, but it is also very attractive – filmgoers are young (generally under twenty-five) and they have disposable income (after all, the cinema is no longer an inexpensive night out).

Brochures and other print literature

The most popular medium used by travel and tourism advertisers is undoubtedly the travel brochure. It has been said that 'The travel world is awash with brochures'[10] and for many organizations the design, production and distribution of their annual tourism brochure is the single most important and most expensive item in the marketing budget. The advantages of brochures are their relatively low cost, flexibility and portability. Indeed, the brochure is arguably the key image-creating tool in tourism and Holloway and Plant have described it as 'probably the most important single item in the planning of tourism marketing'.[11] Brochures are produced for both promotional and information purposes and tend to involve the use of colour photographs and prose laden with adjectives to sell attractive images of destinations, resorts and hotels to potential customers. Whilst hotels and attractions use brochures extensively, it is tour operators and destinations who rely most heavily on the brochure, which is often a thick, glossy, full-colour catalogue, designed to persuade people to purchase the product. It is a vital tool in tourism marketing, not least because of the product substitute role of printed material and the extent to which it establishes expectations of quality, value for money, product image and status.

The brochure is seen to be significant in the holiday destination selection process and it is argued that potential consumers compare brochures and, on the basis of that comparison, subsequently make a decision on their preferred holiday destination. Yet, despite this contention, little definite evidence exists to explain the process in any detail. Now, research examining the decision-making processes of people taking domestic holidays in the UK reveals that (although different decision-making processes may apply when consumers are

65

considering overseas holiday destinations) the process is more haphazard than might be expected.[12] Few clear patterns emerge to explain people's actual holiday choices and, in fact, people find it extremely difficult to explain their decisions and the brochure seems to be used to confirm, rather than to identify holiday choices. On top of this, the position of the brochure as a major travel medium is threatened by new technology, such as CD-ROMs, videos (Ad highlight 3.3) and the Internet. As a result, the medium-term future of the brochure seems unclear – as we will see in Chapter 11.

Ad highlight 3.3   Disney's video success

Disney began to use videos rather than brochures to market Walt Disney World, Florida, to the UK in 1995 as their distribution was seen as a good marketing strategy because the UK lacked access to Disney's direct sell US operation. The videos, together with high-profile television campaigns, provided a new and unusual way of pushing the Disney brand and the 30-minute video also encouraged potential visitors to consider staying longer at Disney World by highlighting the other attractions in the 43 square mile site (Epcot, Disney MGM, six golf courses, three water parks, etc.). Demand for the videos soon became enormous and the 1996 campaign generated 670 000 calls – 20 per cent more than the 1995 campaign. Disney was now also in possession of a database numbering over a million households, which could be very profitably mined for future target marketing. Research showed that:

- 50 per cent of the videos were passed on to family or friends
- 80 per cent of requesters intended to visit Disney World sometime (before they watched the video)
- 90 per cent of requests for the video came through television ads.

Almost 1.5 million videos were sent out and Disney analysed specific ad breaks to see which family members were requesting the video and in which part of the UK they lived. As a result of this analysis, Disney decided to place more emphasis on daytime television because of its effectiveness in advertising the product. At the same time, Disney also ensured that its telemarketing systems were as effective as possible because dealing with customers on the telephone was felt to be one of the most important aspects of the marketing effort. Disney's telemarketing system can deal with well over 2500 calls at any one time, sufficient for 99 per cent of all response periods.

Whilst videos are just one of the newer media threatening the brochure, it is changing in response to such challenges. For instance, some destinations are presenting their brochures as magazines, and including guest articles and short stories. The brochure produced by the Wales Tourist Board is an excellent illustration of the way in which the traditional travel brochure is changing.

Presented as the *Wales Tourist Board Holiday Magazine*, it contains personal, individual views of Wales and its attractions written by well-known Welsh celebrities and people with connections with Wales. The managing editor, Roger Thomas's editorial comments that: 'The magazine is intended as a good read. I hope you'll be entertained – and surprised – by its contents.' The contributors have included Oscar-winning actor Sir Anthony Hopkins, UK prime-time news presenter John Humphrys, internationally renowned botanist and broadcaster David Bellamy, world record-breaking athlete Colin Jackson, historian Sir Roy Strong, and Carlo Rizzi, Musical Director of the Welsh National Opera. There is also evidence to suggest that such brochures are likely to be retained for longer, almost as 'coffee-table magazines' and some brochures for the new generation of 'fashion hotels' are objects of beauty in themselves – where once they would be illustrated by the inevitable shot of a couple in soft focus on the balcony, now they contain images which would not look out of place in *Elle Deco* and the *World of Interiors*.

Many travel brochures and other types of printed promotional literature – including flyers and direct mail shots – are distributed through direct marketing, facilitated by detailed customer profile databases. For example, many of the city and state tourism agencies in the USA – including those at Scottsdale (Arizona), Greenville (South Carolina), Fort Worth (Texas), New York and Virginia – are successfully using direct marketing techniques to target vacationers. Scottsdale is benefiting from a strong co-operative advertising campaign. This centres around an award-winning video of the area produced by the convention bureau which has a 2-minute slot of blank space in the middle which hotels can purchase and insert their own ad (a similar campaign has also been adopted for radio advertising). Meanwhile, to inform South Carolina's advertising strategy, geodemographic analyses were conducted to highlight potential visitors. These were then targeted by placing inserts in newspapers that served these markets and response rates to each insert averaged 40 000 returns. This campaign has proved highly successful and South Carolina estimates that every $1 spent on advertising (of a total ad budget of $2.8 million) has generated $45 in visitor spend.

There are pitfalls with direct marketing, however, and the tone and style of direct mail literature needs to be appropriate. This problem was highlighted in James Rosenfield's analysis of the 1992 Club Med campaign which was felt to have misjudged the mood of the 1990s consumer.[13] In the early 1990s, Club Med embarked on a highly personalized UK direct mail campaign using authentic-seeming, personalized handwriting fonts to create intimate post-cards from two fictitious characters – Richard and Kim. The campaign was condemned for a number of reasons, including its phoniness, insincerity and invasiveness. The personally addressed postcards contained a range of messages, including one that read:

> When we went ashore for an afternoon at St Barths, I wanted to see the nude beach, but Kim wouldn't go for it. So instead we found a four-star restaurant and had a few sunset cocktails with duck liver appetizers in cherry sauce. May sound strange, but they were great! Then back to the ship. A real beauty isn't she? Will write again and tell you more about it. Best to All . . . Richard.

In subsequent instalments, Kim wrote to say how Richard was talking about marriage. The postcards were then followed up by directly mailed Club Med brochures. Whilst the campaign was involving and well executed, such strategies were not really suitable for the consumers of the 1990s and are even less so for those of the 2000s. Marketing tricks which might have appeared to be cute or creative in the 1980s had already become inappropriate for the early 1990s as consumers became more sophisticated and advertising aware.

Outdoor media and billboards

Whilst representing a small proportion of leisure and tourism ad spend, this is still a popular medium and in the UK alone advertisers spend close to £500 million on outdoor advertising a year. The billboard is a spatially fixed medium and it can advertise nearby attractions to road travellers; airlines use them to advertise at airports and destinations, and tour operators use them extensively in their ad campaigns. Yet, whilst billboards are a popular advertising medium, it is often one where creativity seems to desert agencies – with some exceptions. For instance, the 1997 poster for the Disney Channel which showed a hand holding a remote control and a series of overlapping, colourful shapes which, the viewer eventually realizes, are Mickey Mouse silhouettes, was a clever execution,[14] as are those of Virgin Atlantic which has established a reputation for innovative poster ads (see Chapter 8). Despite the fact that billboards are perhaps not as creative as they could be, industry commentators suggest that this outdoor medium has huge potential in an era of media fragmentation precisely because it is the one medium guaranteed to reach a mass audience. David Berstein, for instance, has developed a set of rules designed to generate effective poster advertising:

- Keep it simple.
- Use a single dominant image.
- Be bold.

- Do not overload on text – use few words, with clean, legible and large type.
- Make use of eye-catching and contrasting colours.
- And most of all, ensure that the poster design belongs to and develops the brand.[15]

Emerging media

So far, this review of advertising media has focused on the traditional sector, discussing newspapers, magazines, television, cinema, radio, brochures and print literature, and outdoor advertising, which dominate most of today's media schedules. But this might not always be the case – particularly as newspaper advertising revenue is increasingly threatened by the Internet.[16] That is why we need to examine some of the newer trends in the media to explore their potential for the tourism and leisure industries. These so-called emergent or non-traditional media include ambient media, sponsorship and event marketing, and ambush advertising. Perhaps one of the most noticeable recent trends in leisure advertising, however, has been the development of public relations (PR) related advertising.

Advertising and public relations

Projecting a supermodel in her underwear on to the side of Battersea Power Station in London and smuggling a 40-foot flag of French footballer Eric Cantona into Manchester United's games are just two of the publicity stunts that companies have pulled off to increase awareness of their brands. Playtex Wonderbra and Nike, the beneficiaries of these two ideas, have been the most conspicuous so far, but PR stunts are playing such an increasingly important role in the communications strategies for a range of companies that in the mid-1990s Tango's advertising agency, HHCL & Partners, set up a division called Environment Marketing to create PR 'happenings'. As well as communicating directly with existing consumers, PR stunts increase brand awareness in highly competitive markets.[17] Mike Perry, managing director of Nike's advertising agency, Simons Palmer Denton Clemmow & Johnson, sees such communications as a significant addition to an organization's promotional activities: 'Because the media is increasingly fragmented it is less and less easy to hit people via traditional television or press advertising. You have to stand out.' Perry and his team were responsible for creating from an Eric Cantona Nike poster a flag that was unfurled during an important match between Manchester United and Barcelona. An estimated television audience of 80 million watched as the flag was passed around the ground. The biggest advantage of such PR stunts is that they save money – the Nike flag cost £5000 to make but was seen by a worldwide audience for much less than the cost of the equivalent advertising airtime.[18]

Alasdair Ritchie, chief executive of TBWA, the advertising agency behind Playtex Wonderbra's Battersea Power Station laser project, agrees that it is a cheap way of raising brand awareness. It cost £20 000 to mount the laser scheme – whereas a 30-second commercial costs around £60 000 – with media transmission costs on top. The amount of media coverage generated was priceless since the media is much more prepared to run stories about such advertising and PR activities.[19] However, the nature of this media phenomenon means that agencies have to keep developing bigger and better ideas to excite jaded tabloid journalists and an increasingly media literate public. You cannot just laser project an advertisement on to a building and expect to create headlines, because TBWA has already done it – although the men's style magazine *FHM* did take the idea a step further in 1999 by projecting an image of a naked female television presenter on to Big Ben to promote one edition of the magazine.

Ambient media

Such activities overlap to some extent with one of the newest additions to an organization's list of media choices – ambient media. This is the fastest growing sector of the media worldwide and in the UK it has outstripped commercial radio's growth rates during 1995–9 – increasing from a spend of £10 million in 1995 to almost £60 million in 1998. It includes place-based advertising and is all about finding new, unexpected ways of getting advertising messages across (Ad highlight 3.4). Examples of ambient advertising include skywriting, ads on the back of tickets, on straps in underground carriages, on washroom walls, on the lids of takeaway food cartons, on supermarket floors, supermarket trolleys and parking meters, or on computers and video screens. Business travellers are being targeted with welcome mats in limousines, commercial messages on tickets and ticket wallets, and boarding card promotions. Even food can carry ads – as when advertisers employed The Fruit Label Co. to place 12 million tiny stickers of Jim Carrey on apples in the USA to promote the video release of the Universal Pictures film *Liar, Liar*. Fruit label advertising, by comparison with television commercials (which can cost $500 000 for 30 seconds), costs less than 1 penny per piece of fruit and the consumer has to notice them, at least for the few seconds it takes to peel them off. The one danger with this approach is that consumers can become numb to the message and the medium – just as they have to others.

Another of these 'new' advertising environments is telephone kiosks, which carried mainstream advertising for the first time in the UK in 1998 when big companies turned their attention to targeting young people in their teens and early twenties. In a trial in May 1998, 3000 kiosks outside record shops, fast-food restaurants and nightclubs carried Tango ads in south-east England. Outdoor advertiser Taxi Media, which originated the idea of putting ads on taxis, launched a new company, Phonsites, aimed at young people. The company estimates that 76 per cent of young people aged sixteen to twenty-four use payphones every month and average about nine calls, with most made from entertainment, shopping or leisure locations. In the 6.3 minutes it takes to make the average payphone call, the ad has ample time to capture the caller's attention and there is more scope to be creative in the future – with the possibility of using changing images or holograms.

Ad highlight 3.4   Washroom advertising hits the target in the UK

Washroom advertising is part of the vibrant ambient media scene – having evolved from glorified fly posters to proper, vandal-proof, graffiti-proof mini poster sites. In the UK it has grown from just twenty panels in 1994 to over 27 000 in 1999, with revenue up from £35 000 in 1995 to almost £5 million. The first advertisers to use this medium were films, men's magazines, cable television and computer games – attracted by its ability to reach the elusive eighteen to thirty-five year old male in pub washrooms – and whilst five years ago it would have been inconceivable that brands such as Mars, Gillette and Nestlé would be advertising in such environments, their ads are now commonly seen. In cost per thousand terms it is an expensive medium but it is a good way of reaching a hard to target market and cost savings can be made by using existing creative work for press and posters and simply scaling them down. For some campaigns – such as anti-drink and drive messages, the washroom wall – with an average impact on the consumer of 30 seconds – can be the ideal advertising environment. By expanding the concept to shopping centres advertisers can also reach parents with small children (through the baby changing facilities), and in motorway service stations, businesspeople, motorists, leisure travellers and sports fans can be reached. Sports stadia, leisure centres and health clubs also provide significant opportunities as venues for such advertising.

Source: Ruth Nicholas (1999). Toilet trading. *Marketing Week*, 13 June, pp. 51–2.

One innovative use of ambient media came in 1999 when Virgin Atlantic painted the traditional green and white Hong Kong harbour's Star Ferry bright red with its own logo – for the first time in the ferry company's 100-year history the livery changed, at a cost of $20 000–25 000 a year. A further advance in ambient advertising is the use of artfields, which in essence are advertisements cut into fields. Attempting to capture the interest of the highly desirable, although elusive international business traveller, the artfield concept is seen as having the potential to create impact amongst jaded consumers who are already overloaded by traditional advertising. In a recent example, passengers arriving on flights to Munich airport saw a giant ad for Swissair growing in the fields below. A 250-metre long aircraft (grown in green barley) against a background of brown straw, depicted the red and white Swissair logo – created using ecofriendly pigments. The artfield was chosen because it also communicated positive things about the Swissair brand – in this case that Swissair is an environmentally friendly airline that cares about nature. In a similar vein, a Beck's beer bottle has been cultivated in wheat, accompanied by the slogan 'Only natural ingredients' alongside the main railway line into London's Euston station. Some ad pundits feel that these examples are only the beginning and that the future of ambient media will be to develop advertising akin to that which dominates the movie *Bladerunner* – where advertising is projected on to the sides of buildings and dominates the skyline – although other commentators are rather less convinced about the role of technology in driving the development of ambient media, arguing that ideas are much more significant.

At the moment, however, most of the better known examples of ambient advertising have tended to rely on novelty or their ability to shock, and technology has been vital in providing such opportunities. Developments in technology have also enabled advances in poster advertising, allowing for the printing of giant posters (130 metres by 17 metres) which would not have been commercially viable previously. Technology has also driven the development of wraparound ads on trains, buses, aeroplanes and even rockets. For instance, the Heathrow Express (which provides a 15-minute link between Paddington and Heathrow) has carriages filled with large, flat-screen television monitors, and programming includes advertising. As an advertising medium it has real potential precisely because it will provide a tailor-made environment to reach the highly desirable business traveller market (60 per cent of passengers) who do not tend to pay much attention to traditional media. The technology does not always have to be particularly new or complicated, however – when ScotRail wanted to project ads on to the side of Scottish monuments, it initially thought it would have to use an advanced computer imaging system but a 35 mm projector was all that was required. Whilst technology can provide an advertiser with plenty of publicity – as the Adidas ad projected with laser beams on to the white cliffs of Dover proved – ultimately advertisers using ambient media should be more concerned with finding additional ways to build brand presence in their target markets.

Advertising, sponsorship and event marketing

One way in which many tourism and leisure organizations have sought to create brand presence is through sponsorship and event marketing – particularly in relation to sports events. Sponsorship is growing at a phenomenal rate as more clients attempt to reach more elusive target audiences. Although quite distinguishable from advertising, sponsorship is becoming increasingly synergized with the advertising component of the promotional mix and many organizations in the leisure industry are seeking to capitalize on sponsorship deals. For instance, in order to offset declining visitor figures and greater competition, museums and art galleries are increasingly seeking sponsorship. Advertising spend has increased massively in other leisure sectors – such as cinemas, family entertainment centres, play centres, tenpin bowling arcades and leisure parks – all of which present appealing alternatives to museums. There are almost 2000 UK museums attracting an average of 46 000 visitors a year – still the most popular type of visitor attraction – yet the sector's overall market share and visitor numbers have fallen in the face of competition from other leisure alternatives and rising ticket fees which make them offer less value for money. Yet with tight budgets that preclude high ad spend, they have turned to other marketing options in the more competitive environment and many museums are now involved in sponsorship deals for exhibitions.

When a firm sponsors an exhibition the company raises its profile and the museum gains income. Sponsors are drawn by the museum's attractive target market – a third of adults visit a museum or art gallery every year, the majority are likely to be male, aged fifteen to fifty-four and from the more affluent ABC1 group. Other peaks occur amongst people with children aged ten to fifteen, amongst working managers, better-off families and empty-nesters. However, since the sponsor has a direct interest in the subject matter and expects to influence the content there can be tensions in the relationship. For example, Nuclear Electric PLC's sponsorship of some of the exhibitions at the Science Museum in London caused tension. When an exhibition on Alzheimer's disease was planned, Nuclear Electric's PR office expressed concern over the suitability of the topic – because it was about elderly people and therefore seen to be 'depressing and unappealing' to a younger audience.

Whilst the not-for-profit sector such as museums has benefited from sponsorship deals, the most popular link-ups occur around sports events. In the new global leisure market sport seems to operate increasingly as a world language that helps to dissolve the traditional, commercial, financial, geographical and political barriers to multinationals selling world products in a global market. Sponsors of major sports events use them to showcase their brand as having an international presence. As Umbro's director commented in relation to the firm's involvement in the 1996 European Football Championships: 'We aspire to be more of an international brand. The international scope of the tournament was very attractive to us.' In a similar vein, the sports sponsorship co-ordinator of Canon Europe described the company's involvement in Euro '96 in the following terms: 'in providing these essential services we are able to demonstrate how Canon can support a global event of such magnitude, which can only reassure our customers'.[20]

Examples of successful sports sponsorship deals include the now terminated sponsorship by Cornhill Insurance of the English Cricket Board, which raised public awareness of the firm from a lowly 2 per cent to 21 per cent. Similarly, Marlboro chose to invest in Formula One motor racing to more effectively increase awareness in its major target market – which matched Formula One's audience demographic profile, whilst Puma's sponsorship of Boris Becker paid dividends when he won Wimbledon in 1984 and their racket sales increased from 15 000 before he won to 150 000 after his victory.

| Ad challenge 3.1 | **The risks of sports sponsorship** |

In January 1999 the Nationwide Building Society became the main sponsor for the English Football Association, the England team, the Football League and the Scotland team in a deal worth £8 million over four seasons. The firm's aim was to use the sponsorship to change its rather staid and boring public image and the Football League (as opposed to the Premiership) provided the company with an opportunity to connect with the public at a grass-roots level and capitalize on the widespread popularity of football. Yet Nationwide is by no means a passive sponsor of football and as a company it has suggested that it is the sort of sponsor who would ask players to 'toe the line' precisely because its image is of vital importance to it.

Nationwide did not balk from letting the Football Association know its concerns when Glenn Hoddle, the then English national coach, made various comments regarding disability and reincarnation – suggesting that disabled people were reaping what they had sown in a former life. The company pointed out that they had many disabled members and that Nationwide was contractually protected should the Football Association bring it into disrepute. Glenn Hoddle subsequently left the England job although Nationwide denied any direct involvement in his departure. This case reveals the potential benefits and dangers associated with sponsorship, and although evaluation studies have shown some sponsors suffer little or no negative effect as a result of damaging actions, brands still run the risk of being contaminated by such controversy or scandal.

More recently, the 1999 Rugby World Cup staged in Europe and hosted by Wales was estimated to have generated an additional £30 million in direct tourism spend and an extra 55 000 visitors to Wales in 1999 but, more importantly for its sponsors, it was estimated to have been watched by a worldwide audience of 3 billion – making it the world's third largest sports event. The globe's most watched sports event is the soccer World Cup and the last one was France '98 where the audience per game was 500 million, making a cumulative total of 37 billion or over six times the world population. For the duration of the '98 World Cup it was 'Eat football, drink football, sleep football' – at least that's what Coca-Cola and a host of other sponsors paid for. France '98 spawned a whole merchandising industry (T-shirts, key chains and even condoms carried the official logo) as sponsors were willing to do virtually anything to get their name associated with the event.

Of all sports, football's image changed the most in the 1990s and clubs such as Manchester United and Chelsea in the UK are expanding into hotels, restaurants, megastores, health clubs and museums. A new breed of soccer fan has emerged – the so-called soccerati – high-brow, middle-class fans who once disdained the game. Today a quarter of Wimbledon and a fifth of Chelsea fans earn more than £30 000 a year. Football now accounts for well over 50 per cent of UK consumer spending at live sports events and it is the dominant sport on television. In Britain there are over 4300 hours devoted to football on terrestrial, digital, cable and satellite television channels. Boosted by all-seater stadia and a greater proportion of female spectators, gate receipts still constitute 45 per cent of the average club's income – although it is becoming less important as clubs rely more and more on pay-per-view fees, merchandising and sponsorship – the BSkyB and BBC deal with the Premiership in 1997 for four years until 2001 was worth £670 million.

The soccer World Cup, more than any other sports event, enables sponsors to establish themselves as the premium global brand within their category – everyone loves the World Cup and it has a very positive association for advertisers. Any global brand wants to be either directly involved or associated with the World Cup, since they are looking for the largest television audience to reach their target market and it is the world's biggest sports event – it touches every continent and World Cup fever is one of the reasons soccer is known as the beautiful game. This creates a win-win situation for the event and the sponsors – the additional sponsorship means more money for the sport's development and further television coverage means that football can reach more people in more countries than ever before, whilst the sponsors gain from the size of the event. However, sponsorship of sports events can become a huge waste of marketing budgets – you cannot own an event if yours is one of eight to twelve brands trying to do the same thing and in 1998 the World Cup had twelve official sponsors. A World Cup sponsorship survey in *Marketing Week* in July 1998 showed that the official sponsors – including Coca-Cola, McDonald's, Adidas and Snickers – failed to achieve public awareness, whilst Nike, not an official sponsor, became the most talked about brand because of its hijacking or ambushing of the event.[21]

Ambush advertising

Ambush advertising, as the term implies, refers to unofficial advertising at major events. This unofficial advertising is designed to get the maximum exposure for a product or service for the minimum outlay – advertising costs are hugely reduced precisely because the product or service is not a major or official sponsor of an event. The 1998 football World Cup in France provided a number of examples of ambush marketing at work – from snack food manufacturers to sportswear giants. Pepperami, a spicy salami sausage snack food produced by Vanden Bergh foods, gained free advertising worth thousands of dollars for little more than the cost of a sausage suit. Despite the heavy security surrounding the England football team's final training session, a man dressed as a large salami sausage, with a bobble hat and Union Jack shorts invaded the pitch. The next day, photographs of this marketing stunt were splashed all over the UK newspapers.

Nike is the company that has long cultivated maverick approaches to both its brand management and its advertising. Nike does not merely found its advertising on linking the brand to sports stars with attitude (John McEnroe, Michael Jordan, Ian Wright and Eric Cantona, to name but a few), it is also a major practitioner of ambush marketing. In essence, Nike likes to pretend that it is an official sponsor of events – as in Euro '96 when it bought all the billboard space outside Wembley stadium. It adopted the same hijack tactic at the 1996 Atlanta Olympic Games. For the period of the games, Atlanta was bombarded with Nike ads on hoardings – the company even built a fake Olympic village in an out-of-town car park – and it saturated television with ads paid for out of the money saved by not paying for official sponsorship. Although it was not an official sponsor, three-quarters of Americans believed it was, whilst Reebok (which had paid to kit out a third of competing athletes and teams) did not even register as an official sponsor. Table 3.3 shows the percentage of Americans who replied 'yes' when asked if a company was an official Olympic sponsor – making happy reading for ambushers.

Whether such advertising tactics are legitimate or ethical is open to question and some advertisers have likened ambush marketing to theft. It is

Table 3.3 Advertising recognition at Atlanta '98

Official sponsors	%	Ambush marketers	%
McDonalds	85	Nike	73
Visa	70	AT&T	63
Coca-Cola	68	Pepsi	55
IBM	65	Mastercard	49
Kodak	63	Sony	43

Source: *Marketing Week*, 9 July 1998.

unlikely that the general public is either aware of or particularly concerned by this tactic but steps have been taken by events to inhibit the success of ambush marketing. The 1998 football World Cup learnt from Atlanta and organizers managed to persuade official sponsors to buy up all the advertising hoardings to prevent an ambush by 'marketing terrorists'. Despite this, such events remain vulnerable to hijacks and Nike was again able to buy bus shelter advertising sites on all the main routes into Cardiff (the host city of the event) during Rugby World Cup '99 – as well as draping a massive banner ad proclaiming 'I love rugby' over the side of a large multistorey car park outside the main entrance to the city's Millennium Stadium – directly opposite the official merchandising outlet! Nike's television ads, featuring well-known rugby players from both the northern and southern hemispheres, also ran during the commercial breaks in the televised matches – no doubt confirming the impression that Nike was a major sponsor of the tournament. Perhaps cleverest of all was Nike's ploy during the semi-final match between Australia and South Africa. Here, fans were seen waving free placards emblazoned with 'Joost do it' above a Nike Swoosh (capitalizing on the fans' enthusiasm for Joost Van Der Westhuizen, the South African captain).

Chapter summary

A precise, well-planned, research-based strategy is the starting point for any ad campaign. The development of an advertising strategy consists of eight steps:

1 *Analysing the current situation* – where are we now, how did we get here?
2 *Defining the audience* – who do we want to communicate with?

3 *Developing marketing goals* – where do we want to go?

4 *Developing advertising goals and a plan* – how are we going to get there?

5 *Agreeing an advertising budget* – how much money can we spend?

6 *Developing and executing a creative strategy* – how shall we communicate?

7 *Developing and implementing a media strategy* – where are we going to place the ads?

8 *Evaluating advertising effectiveness* – how successful were we?

These eight steps can be summarized into five key phases in the advertising process: strategic development, creative brief development, creative development, communication assessment and campaign evaluation:

1　Strategic development is concerned to identify the problem, the desired outcome, the current and desired operating context (including competitor relationships), the current images and perceptions held of the brand, and the ability of advertising to contribute towards the desired outcome.

2/3 Creative development establishes the campaign brief, develops and examines the ad idea, finalizes the executional details and arranges the media schedule.

4　Communication assessment is concerned with evaluating the creative executions.

5　Campaign evaluation establishes what a campaign has achieved and provides guidance on how further campaigns could be improved and developed.

Advertising planning is only one element of producing a campaign; making the right media choices is equally important. Today media planning is a highly complex, specialist and critical area of advertising planning and the final media mix and the time-length strategy hinges on:

■ the target audience's media habits
■ the match between the media image and the product
■ the complexity of the ad
■ media costs
■ audience attention.

A campaign's media schedule will usually combine a range of media vehicles – and could include traditional media such as newspapers, magazines, television, cinema, radio, billboards and brochures, as well as emergent media such as ambient advertising. The traditional media still dominate tourism and leisure advertising – with newspapers and magazines having the highest ad spend, followed by television, radio, cinema and billboards. Whilst it is rarely the case that one medium completely replaces another (rather the old medium adapts around the new where there are areas of overlap), the emerging forms of media are expanding rapidly and will be more significant in the future. Today ambient advertising is the world's fastest growing media sector.

Case study 3.1

The Hard Rock Hotel, Bali: from brief to campaign

The Hard Rock Hotel, Bali (HRHB) opened in May 1998. As a brand extension of the Hard Rock Café, it was the first 'theme' hotel in Asia and was recognized as 'New Player of the Year' by Travel Asia.

The brief
Publicis Eureka (Singapore) and Optimedia were appointed to develop the advertising campaign for the Hard Rock Hotel, Bali. The advertising aimed to:

- generate interest by capitalizing on the established brand of Hard Rock Café chains
- create awareness among frequent travellers (looking for new style vacations) and families (a growing market)
- demonstrate the hotel's uniqueness (from other hotels and from the Hard Rock Café concept)
- build a sense of privilege and membership.

The point of differentiation
The hotel's major competitors were other resort hotels in the region, particularly those which were themed – as some exotic Balinese hotels or

those adopting a sports theme, such as Club Med. However, there were several unique features that set the Hard Rock Hotel, Bali apart from the competition, namely:

■ the concept (music, rock 'n' roll, trendy)
■ the mood (trendy, rocky, refreshing, surprising)
■ the service (the guest is a star)
■ the facilities (music facilities as well as traditional resort features).

The campaign faced several difficulties, however, including the need to identify Hard Rock Hotel, Bali with the Hard Rock Café concept and the problems generated by the external operating context, namely the Asian economic crisis.

The target consumer

Target consumers were very specific in terms of demographic and psychographic characteristics (Table 3.4). Potential Hard Rock Hotel visitors were seen to be people looking for something new – new hotels and new entertainment themes – and who were able to pay a premium price for the product.

Table 3.4 Consumer characteristics for the Hard Rock Hotel, Bali

Demographics	Psychographics
18–30-year-old yuppies/newly weds	'I love travelling but I'm looking for something different where I can wear my clothes and meet funny, fancy people'
35–60-year-old families	'I want to see and be seen' 'I want to have fun with new faces and do new things but at the same time I want to enjoy my vacation and rest with my friends and family'
Business (meetings, conventions, incentives)	'I want my family to have fun with me. I don't want to feel obliged to be always with them' 'I do what I want and not what I'm supposed to' 'I am living a branded life and look for branded things'

The campaign aim

The aim of the campaign was to shift the consumer choice process away from choosing the destination and then the hotel to one where the consumer chooses the hotel (in this case the Hard Rock Hotel, Bali) and the destination merely comes with it. Within this, the campaign would have to generate a distinct shift in consumer attitudes (Table 3.5). The positioning was about a hotel which embodies a revolution in hotel and resorts management, offering new, all-star excitement in a tropical paradise, and travel trade partners (agencies) were seen to be key to attracting the consumer.

Table 3.5 Illustrative shifts in consumer attitudes to Hard Rock Hotel, Bali

Before	After
'I'm fed up with the classical image of holidays with sport or exoticism.'	I have stayed at Hard Rock Hotel, Bali, not you.'
'Another Hard Rock in Bali? So what, I have that in my own city.'	'Hard Rock Hotel, Bali is happening and refreshing, this is the place to go for a change.'
'I don't go to Bali to listen to music.'	'Everybody enjoys it: my children, my grandparents, my friends, my wife and myself.'
'What, a Hard Rock Hotel for my children? Never!'	'Where is the other Hard Rock Hotel?'

Key insights and triggers

Various insights and triggers were felt to be central to the campaign, including:

- a fun, different, happening, rock 'n' roll attitude (food, drink, sleep, rock = Hard Rock Hotel, Bali)
- song taglines (1960s, 1970s and contemporary success – the Rolling Stones, Madonna, Spice Girls)
- central theme – 'feel like a star', 'experience it – stick to it'.

The ads

The ads developed to bring the campaign to life all combine famous lines from well-known songs with a suitable supporting picture – as a concept, these ads could run and run (Plate 1). The executions include:

- 'Just another day in paradise.'
- 'You don't have to be a star, baby, to be in our show.'
- 'Hungry like the wolf.'

The campaign adopted a single medium – print – approach which worked well and ran in Asia Pacific travel titles such as *Travel News Asia, Travel Trade Gazette Asia* and *Travel Weekly*; and consumer lifestyle titles, including *IS* magazine (Singapore), *Who Weekly* (Australia) and *HK Magazine* (Hong Kong). Interestingly, because of the Asian economic crisis and the knock-on reduction in advertising costs and increased incentives, Hard Rock Hotel, Bali's advertising was able to run more frequently and prominently – there was approximately a 70:30 ratio – trade to consumer media – ad spend. The success of the campaign in Asia prompted Hard Rock Hotel, Bali to invite the agency to propose a similar European strategy with the emphasis on targeting the tourism industry directly – particularly travel agencies. Various trade titles were considered and those selected included some of the best selling publications in Europe, particularly in Germany and the UK.

Source: Publicis Eureka.

Case study 3.2

Comparing television and newspaper effectiveness

Television is regarded by many as the premier advertising medium since it is generally much more effective than print media such as newspapers for building advertising awareness. Millward Brown International's 1993 study found that magazine ads are better than television ads at drawing attention to the fact that a brand has been advertised, but that the detail of the ad content – illustrations, headlines and copy – are less well remembered than that of television ads and over time become less noticed. This pattern is explained by the consumer's differing relationships with television and print ads. In the case of television, the consumer's relationship is both passionate and limited. The aim of a television ad is to use audiovisual images to prompt people's memories of those images when they are confronted with the brand at the point of consumption. To work effectively, those images must have been associated with the brand in the first place and they must create an emotional relationship.

By contrast, the consumer's relationship with print ads is very different as it offers greater potential for the mind to be actively engaged and for readers to dictate the length of time they spend looking at an ad. Provided the ad pulls the reader in (either through involvement and interest in the product or through its attention-grabbing creativity), the reader will work through the content of the ad in a way that the passive television viewer would not do. This active processing of the content leads to better brand linkage and more rational processing of ad messages than for television. It also means, however, that once it has been assimilated, the visual imagery is soon forgotten and there is less reason for the consumer to take notice of the ad the next time he or she sees it. This explains why a more recent UK research study by Carat suggested that, in most cases, television created more than double the awareness of newspapers.

Table 3.6   Television and newspaper advertising awareness: percentage who are certain they have seen advertising

| | Brand | | | | | |
	K	L	B	E	D	F
Newspaper	18	19	17	20	16	14
Television	35	35	45	45	51	59

Source: adapted from Carat/BMRB Television's *Sphere of Influence*.

However, awareness is only one measure of advertising effectiveness and the same study also showed that the newspaper campaign for brand K (which was actually Thomson Holidays) generated a more positive consumer response than the television campaign. In overall terms, 16 per cent of respondents were more likely to consider taking a package holiday with Thomson's as a result of the print campaign, compared with 10 per cent for the television campaign. The value-for-money ratio is actually much greater than this, given that newspaper-based campaigns tend to cost much less – around a quarter of the price of television campaigns. This study is also noteworthy because it showed that more people were turned off the idea of buying a Thomson's package holiday by the television campaign. On this basis, media choices need to be driven by the campaign objectives. Similarly, the nature of the target market is important. Tables 3.7 and 3.8 show how the various groups of advertising consumers, discussed in Chapter 1, react to package holiday and lager campaigns which feature across a range of media. Interestingly, in both product categories and across all types of consumers of advertising, radio scores quite poorly.

From Table 3.8 we can see that lager drinkers largely react to advertising stimuli – particularly television advertising. As a result, beer manufacturers can generate substantial interest in their brand if their

Table 3.7 Advertising consumer reactions to package holiday ads (percentage)

Package holiday	Seekers	Reactors	Rejecters	Ignorers
	'I look for television ads for ideas and info'	'I don't look out for these ads but find some interesting'	'I notice these ads but take little interest'	'I can't remember seeing ads for any of these'
Television	24	29	41	5
Newspapers	24	20	34	20
Magazines	21	23	32	22
Radio	14	14	14	53

Table 3.8 Advertising consumer reactions to draught lager ads (percentage)

Draught lager	Seekers	Reactors	Rejecters	Ignorers
	'I look for television ads and talk about them in the pub'	'I don't look out for these ads but find some interesting'	'I notice these ads but take little interest'	'I can't remember seeing ads for any of these'
Television	10	58	29	2
Newspapers	4	30	41	25
Magazines	4	15	36	45
Cinema	3	22	24	46
Radio	3	11	18	67

advertising is stimulating and interesting rather than factual or informative. Over two-thirds of respondents were in fact willing to be persuaded if the advertising was good enough (seekers and reactors) and in Chapter 4 we see how one beer manufacturer – Murphy's Stout – built its advertising around this premise (Ad highlight 4.1). Just over half of package holiday-takers were prepared to be persuaded by television campaigns but it is also interesting that the percentages of those open to newspaper or magazine ad persuasion were not far behind – both recording rates of 44 per cent. Such results may also reflect the quality of advertising in both these industries. Currently, lager advertisers are certainly well ahead of tourism operator advertisers in terms of creating interesting, stimulating, entertaining and involving advertising.

Source: adapted from Colin Aubury (1993). Print vs TV – balancing the learning. *Researchplus,* November, p. 12; Carat/BMRB Television's *Sphere of Influence.*

Notes

1 Alastair Macdonald (1994). Quantifying the effect of advertising: the implications for advertising strategies. *Journal of Targeting, Measurement and Analysis for Marketing,* **3** (1), 48–59.
2 Ibid.
3 Belina Archer (1997). Sun, sea, sex, sand and media. *Campaign,* 30 May, 29–30.
4 Andy Fry (1998). Fantastic journeys. *Marketing,* 26 November, 35–7.
5 Colin Aubery (1993). Print vs TV – balancing the learning. *Researchplus,* November, 12.
6 Courtland L. Bovee, John V. Thill, George P. Dovel and Marian Burk Wood (1995). *Advertising Excellence.* McGraw-Hill, p. 20.
7 Ibid.
8 Len Weinreich (1999). *11 Steps to Brand Heaven. The Ultimate Guide to Buying an Advertising Campaign.* Kogan Page, p. 69.
9 CNN & Travel, CNN, London, 1999.
10 Victor T. C. Middleton (1989). *Marketing in Travel and Tourism.* Butterworth-Heinemann.
11 Chris Holloway and Rob V. Plant (1992). *Marketing for Tourism.* 2nd edn. Pitman, p. 148.
12 Wales Tourist Board (1994). *Marketing Areas Study.* WTB.
13 James R. Rosenfield (1992). Club Med. *Direct Marketing,* **54** (10), February, pp. 15–16.

14 David Bernstein, quoted in Nick Higham (1997). Today's outdoor market needs a dose of creative simplicity. *Marketing Week*, 30 October, p. 19.

15 Ibid.

16 Emily Bell and Jamie Doward (1999). Fighting for survival.com. *Observer*, 26 September.

17 Sheila Wright (1997). *The Financial Times Marketing Casebook*. Pitman, p. 180.

18 Ibid.

19 Ibid.

20 S. Easton and P. Mackie (1998). When football came home: a case history of the sponsorship activity at Euro 96. *International Journal of Advertising*, **17** (1), 100.

21 *Marketing Week*, 9 July 1998.

Further reading

Bernstein, D. (1997). *Advertising Outdoors: Watch this Space!* Phaidon Books.

Delpy, L., Grabijas, M. and Stefanovich, A. (1998). Sport tourism and corporate sponsorship: a winning combination. *Journal of Vacation Marketing*, **4** (1), 91–101.

Easton, S. and Mackie, P. (1998). When football came home: a case history of the sponsorship activity at Euro 96. *International Journal of Advertising*, **17** (1), 100.

Howard-Brown, J. (1999). Consumer evaluation of direct mail in the travel and leisure sectors. *Journal of Vacation Marketing*, **6** (1), 55–61.

Jones, J. P. (ed.) (1998). *How Advertising Works: The Role of Research*. Sage.

Jones, J. P. (ed.) (1999). *The Advertising Business: Operations, Creativity, Media Planning, Integrated Communications*. Sage.

Lloyd, C. V. (1999). Advertising media. In *The Advertising Business: Operations, Creativity, Media Planning, Integrated Communications* (J. P. Jones, ed.) pp. 89–100, Sage.

Macdonald, A. (1994). Quantifying the effect of advertising: the implications for advertising strategies. *Journal of Targeting, Measurement and Analysis for Marketing*, **3** (1), 48–59.

Mounser, I. (1999). Identifying, keeping and valuing profitable customers. *Journal of Vacation Marketing*, **6** (1), 62–8.

Nicholas, R. (1999). Toilet trading. *Marketing Week*, 13 June, pp. 51–2.

Tapp, A. and Clowes, J. (1999). The role of direct marketing in football clubs: a case study of Coventry City FC. *Journal of Database Marketing*, **6** (4), 339–55.

4

Advertising research

Chapter overview

This chapter builds on Chapter 3 by examining a key aspect of the advertising planning process – advertising research. The first part of the chapter discusses how research should underpin the planning cycle and provides a practical discussion of how research can be used to fine-tune and evaluate the final advertising execution. The second part of the chapter then provides a toolbox of research techniques that may be used by practitioners, researchers and students to investigate the effectiveness of the messages communicated by tourism and leisure advertising. This discussion of research techniques is complemented by the first of our end of chapter case studies which reviews how qualitative approaches can be used to inform destination advertising by analysing consumer perceptions of Las Vegas. The key themes of the chapter are:

■ whether research is killing creative advertising
■ the role of research in advertising
■ research and the advertising cycle

- when to research
- whom to research
- pretesting ads
- campaign evaluation
- research techniques.

Introduction

Given the recent trend towards results-driven advertising, it is not surprising that many tourism and leisure companies and organizations have increasingly turned to research in an effort to cut down on wasted expenditure and to reduce the risk of running potentially brand-damaging campaigns. Certainly good, well-timed research can vastly improve the content and effectiveness of advertising. It can also demonstrate accountability and cost-effectiveness – two criteria that are increasingly significant given that advertising is usually an expensive element of the promotional budget. This kind of marketing research is a highly specialized area precisely because it attempts to evaluate the effectiveness of advertising as a method of marketing communications and persuasion. It is also, however, a highly controversial area because many advertising practitioners and commentators, themselves, often disagree over whether the creation of a successful campaign is pure inspiration or calculated science. As one has said:

> Just when it looked as though a stake had been driven through its heart, research mania is threatening to rise Dracula-like from its coffin to haunt . . . advertising again . . . summoned back to life by ultracautious clients who are driven to seek safety in number crunching by the sheer expense of advertising and tighter margins that leave little room for error.[1]

The role of advertising is largely competitive – to gain or defend market share at someone else's expense. Not surprisingly, a significant proportion of ad campaigns fail.

Clients and agencies are both concerned with the twin challenges of how to create an appealing campaign and how to measure its success. Dedicated, made-to-measure research is often the only option when attempting to solve these problems and it is certainly the most desirable approach. Unfortunately, limited resources can lead to multipurpose surveys that fail to gauge advertising impact, often because of their nature, approach or audience. For instance, existing tourism research projects, such as national visitor surveys (even where they can be disaggregated down to a local level, which is infrequently) will not tell an attraction's manager the extent to which his or her visitors were influenced by the latest advertising campaign or whether their perceptions of the brand or facility have changed. Even if ongoing national surveys could provide such information, the time involved in the collection and analysis of national tourism statistics usually means that they are only available long after the next year's advertising budget has been agreed.

Is research killing creative ads?

Before beginning a detailed discussion of the role of research in advertising planning, it would be useful to look at some of the wider debates which have been taking place – with varying intensity – in the advertising industry over the last decade or so. The area of advertising research, whilst extremely important, is highly sensitive and politically charged, and some of the more controversial questions asked in agencies today concern whether research is killing rather than creating cutting-edge advertising. Some practitioners in the ad world believe that instead of debating which techniques should be used to inform and evaluate their latest campaign, they should instead be asking whether advertising campaigns should be researched at all. They contend that advertisers should be basing their decisions more on their own experience because research simply cannot really capture life in the real world. As Silvester has argued, researchers often talk to the wrong people, at the wrong time and ask the wrong questions. He points out that 'there is no substitute for sound creative judgement', saying: 'If you seriously want a campaign which will make your brand fly, you cannot delegate the task of selecting it to a group of housewives in Pinner.'[2]

> Research does not need to kill creativity. If it is used properly it should enhance and stimulate it.

Unfortunately, reality for most – if not all – clients and agencies today is a business environment dominated by the demands of performance indicators, output measurement and impact evaluation.

The drive to measure and evaluate every aspect of business is so strong that many organizations – in the public, private and not-for-profit sectors – recruit the services of marketing research companies with ever greater frequency and alacrity. Advertising – as a cost-intensive activity for many organizations – has not escaped this evaluation ethos and to meet this demand, the number of marketing research companies has mushroomed in recent years. Similarly, just as the number of companies has grown so, too, has the number and range of techniques to satisfy these objectives. Given this scenario, we could be forgiven for believing that the case for more, rather than less, research seems to be universally accepted by both clients and agencies. Indeed, the need for more research has been given further impetus by the proliferation and diversification processes that have affected markets, brands and media since 1970. Mass markets have been transformed into niche markets, the range of leisure and tourism services and products has exploded; and, at the same time, the media available to market these services, products and brands have grown beyond all recognition and technological advances stimulated by the Internet continue to push the frontiers of media beyond all previously established boundaries.

Ad challenge 4.1	Information overload for clients

We are living in an information-saturated world – where 1000 books are published daily and traffic over the telephone lines is increasing at over 10 per cent each year. We have access to everything but control over nothing. We are unable to receive, sift and filter the avalanche of information potentially available to today's marketers. In fact, it is not information at all, but a hailstorm of data. There is a widening gap between what we understand and what we think we should understand. There is too much information and not enough communication. This presents genuine problems for advertisers in leisure and tourism, as in other sectors. Research is commissioned, yielding a wealth of potentially useful data, but clients only have time to read executive summaries – they can only handle snapshot, sound-bite research.

Given the proliferation of services, products, brands, media and data, it is vital that clients and agencies clarify what role, if any, research should play in the advertising process. On the side of those who dislike research, the basis for their concern lies with whether 'the public' is an effective, reliable and suitable sounding board against which campaigns should be developed and evaluated. Initially we might be forgiven for wondering whether this concern is in fact spurious. After all, who is better placed to judge the effectiveness of advertising than those who consume it? Who better to say whether an idea or campaign should stay or go? Such an approach is dangerous, however, precisely because it would be easy for the public to end up replacing the creative judgements and skills of the practitioner – even though there is little evidence to suggest that consumers can be relied upon to endorse effective campaigns or reject ill-founded executions. In effect, research could, and in some cases has, become a dangerous substitute for judgement (Ad challenge 4.2). In the rush to consult and to rely upon consumer opinion, there is a real danger that creative and potentially powerful campaigns may be rejected on the basis of interpreted and assumed 'research fact'.

| Ad challenge 4.2 | **To be truly innovative do not ask the consumer** |

Many marketers spend most of their mature working lives acting on information and beliefs which are outdated, and most of the senior managers running tourism and leisure companies today were last on the front line with customers at least ten years ago. In this ever-changing marketplace, being so out of touch makes products irrelevant, organizations redundant and managers obsolete. In the same way, marketing research is based on the historical beliefs of customers and their perceptions of the products and services they buy. By its very nature market research investigates existing markets, and refines existing propositions, it rarely attempts to talk to customers about their views on new concepts. Similarly, benchmarking helps managers to compare companies, but cannot help them to leapfrog the competition. In fact what most companies are doing is watching their rivals not watching the customer.

Since 1970 the marketplace has seen three waves of marketing philosophy. In the 1970s, business was supply driven; the 1980s were research driven when companies spent a great deal of time asking the customers what they wanted. The third and prevailing wave is concept driven. 'We need to establish what the customer might want if it were available or what the customers might want but were too ill-informed to ask for,' says Glen Peters. Companies that do not evaluate how customer values are changing and merely seek to keep pace are likely to be ones that are too oriented to the present – they are probably trading on the historical loyalties of their customers and the company's established position in the marketplace.

Source: adapted from Glen Peters (1996). *The Next Wave. Imagining the Next Generation of Customers*. Part 1. Pitman.

The crux of the problem is that consumers are being asked to give their opinion about often complex or controversial messages in a very short space of time and usually in artificial environments. In this situation people are forced to suspend the fact that they are normally far too busy to pay much attention to advertising since the research forces the ads to the centre stage and makes consumers react to them differently. In such a scenario it is quite likely that the overall impact and 'feel' of the ads may well get lost in the 'hothouse' discussion which follows. The need for consensus in such research also brings problems. What if in a focus group half the respondents love a campaign and half hate it? Ninety-nine per cent of researchers will recommend that the advertisement be changed. It is not surprising that this approach may end up providing a pseudo-scientific way of dismissing the quirky or distinctive ideas that are often the essence of good advertising. What remains are ads which appeal to the lowest common denominator – bland, uncontroversial and unlikely to get noticed. The short-term focus of much advertising research is also problematic as much of the power and value of advertising is grounded in a long-term campaign. The time spans involved in building a successful brand, and therefore the limited weight which can be assigned to specific ads or campaigns, pose interesting questions regarding the role that research can properly play – after all, an individual ad or even campaign will not be particularly effective in a brand-building strategy.

Advertising research, in essence, is designed to generate phenomenal amounts of information at any given point in the advertising process. It is all too possible, however, for advertisers to end up with schizophrenic brands or multipersonality advertising campaigns, at least in part because of an overreliance on research data. Take research that is designed to elicit potential brand values. Almost without exception this will generate a range of associations, but is it possible for such research to generate a core value or unique communication proposition? More likely, it will generate several primary and secondary communication possibilities – as our Las Vegas example (Case study 4.1) illustrates. It is the job of the agency to use this research to identify the essential communication message, as the temptation to recommend that the advertising material should reflect all of these values in some way may be overwhelming, particularly for the client. After all, who can resist telling the whole world when consumers say good things about their product or service? Identifying a singular association may also be difficult (as consumers are usually willing to discuss a product's or service's diverse qualities in great detail), yet a failure to do so may have a serious impact on the long-term well-being of the brand. Remember that most highly successful long-term campaigns are very simple. They tend to communicate only one thing about the brand, which is clearly linked to the communication proposition. Moreover, powerful communication propositions rely on singular concepts – British Airways' use of 'The world's favourite airline' is an obvious case in point, as is Torquay's use of the strapline 'The English Riviera' – an association which began some ninety years ago and still continues today (see Chapter 9).

The role of research in advertising

Despite some of the pitfalls of advertising research, it is a fact of life that only the very brave or the very foolhardy organization would be prepared to completely exclude it from the advertising process. Perhaps the real debate surrounding the relationship between advertising and research should focus not on whether research is 'killing' advertising, but rather on what advertising research is and how it can be effectively incorporated into the overall advertising process. Less a matter of if and rather a matter of when to use research (Table 4.1). We need to establish how research can help to produce the kind of advertising which inspires positive brand associations and induces product purchase. In doing so, we also need to recognize that a lot of research fails because it is used for the wrong reasons – frequently as a substitute for decisions and instead of sound creative judgement (remember that research is least useful when it's testing the unfamiliar). Above all, research may often be hampered by hidden agendas which interfere with what should be technical advertising decisions – some clients use research to undermine internal opposition, to deflect external criticism or to appease partner organizations.

> Good advertising is likely to be founded on a thorough understanding of the brand, its relationship with the consumer and its place in the market.

Table 4.1   The ten research rules

1 Think not if to research but, rather, at what stage to research and for what purposes?

2 Consider what the general public is good at measuring – the communication proposition of advertisements and what specific advertisements are saying. Being able to interpret an advertisement is not the same as being able to establish the impact or power of particular advertisements or campaigns.

3 Remember that consumer research is not particularly helpful in the selection of a long-term campaign idea.

4 Use research to improve the communication presentation, packaging and, ultimately, the reception of the message, not to replace judgement. Unfortunately, executional research is often strategic research that should have been done before the advertising was actually written. Do not fall into the trap of undertaking research to confirm rather than to question advertising material.

5 Good strategic research is essential, as is good stimulus material (mood boards, statement boards and video clips). Such strategic research should 'test' hypotheses developed prior to undertaking the research.

6 Take time. Advertising research requires good analysis and this is dependent on time – a factor which is usually in short supply. Researchers need time to consider: the core findings; conflicting responses; the impact of the researcher; the research process; and the impact of recruitment.

7 Talk to the target audience. It is essential that research should be conducted only with the target audience. Time and money spent on non-core target research is at best wasted and, at worst, potentially highly damaging.

8 Talk only to consumers. Organizations should also be careful to ensure that research is only conducted amongst real consumers, not 'paid up' market research professionals (rent-a-participants).

9 Do not be afraid to exercise judgement. The consumer is not always right and clients and agencies should reserve the right to say no, and be prepared to exercise it.

10 Talk plain English. Many researchers dress up their reports with jargon to make them sound more authoritative and valuable. For instance, 'the work elicited a polarized reaction', means half the respondents liked it, half hated it.

Whilst academic advertising research has taken a number of directions, industry-orientated research has tended to focus on advertising for particular brands and perhaps should be better termed 'brand research'. Within the context of brand research, the researcher tries to explain what the consumer understands from stimuli such as advertisements or, if the research is at a more formative level, advertising concepts and ideas. At this stage it is important to note that the consumer has an interactive relationship with both the brand and the brand advertising. Although it would be fair to say that it is neither possible nor desirable to establish predictive or causal relationships from research data (i.e., $a + b = c$), accurate interpretation should enable judgements to be made on the sustainability and efficiency of particular executions. We have already seen that promotion can be an extremely expensive business and that corporate and destination marketers are operating in a very crowded and competitive tourism and leisure marketplace. Brand research at one and the same time offers them the prospect of reducing the risks whilst producing more effective research. No wonder its popularity is increasing.

Research in the advertising cycle

The challenge facing advertisers is to know when, where and how to use brand research. As we saw in Chapter 3, planning cycle principles are well known and frequently utilized in the tourism and leisure industries, following such steps as determining status profile, performance to date, desired status and performance required. The core task facing those responsible for designing and implementing brand campaigns is the development of a strategic plan, within which the roles and extent of advertising and research are clearly identified. This plan should then dictate the work of the advertising researcher and indicate at which stages brand research can be usefully undertaken (see the advertising cycle in Figure 3.1). The success of the advertising depends upon the effective development of such a strategy and the success of the research depends upon an equally considered and carefully targeted approach, identifying when and where research should be used to inform advertising decisions during the exploratory, strategic, creative and evaluative stages.

Who should you research?

Whilst there is widespread agreement on the need to establish the objectives for brand research, of equal importance is the need to target research effectively (see Case study 4.2). This may be a seemingly obvious point but it is surprising how many times this core priority just disappears in brand-orientated research. It is also important to choose the right location for audience research. Unfortunately, this may be more cavalier than clients would expect – a survey into group research locations in the UK in the mid-1990s showed that 25 per cent of focus groups were done in Buckhurst Hill (a suburb of London), 'far enough out of London to look representative to clients, but easy enough to get home from in time for *News at Ten*'.[3]

In most sectors, including in tourism and leisure, product appeal is limited since very few products appeal to everybody and the trends towards the increasing diversification and fragmentation of products and markets is predicted to accelerate further in the next century. Yet, despite the fact that segmentation is the buzzword recognized by clients, advertising agencies and research agencies alike, as a principle, it often 'disappears' in the research undertaken to underpin a particular campaign. The research process itself appears to take on its own dynamic, which requires mass research regardless of market targets, a trend that requires positive action to halt its progress. Ad challenge 4.3 is an anonymous illustration of this problem and discusses a situation with which many practitioners can sympathize. Given this scenario, clients and agencies need to ensure that they tightly target the research to replicate the campaign brief's criteria. Failure to do so almost guarantees a dilution – and possibly the failure – of the campaign before it even gets off the ground, wasting valuable time and resources.

Ad challenge 4.3   Dangers of listening to peripheral groups

A destination was about to undertake an ad campaign that was directly aimed at the more upmarket, higher income couples market in a defined geographical area. Research amongst this market segment was a priority, qualitative research methods were preferred and subsequently focus groups were arranged. Historically, however, the main markets for this destination have traditionally been the middle- to lower-income family market segments. Therefore, there was a strong feeling that research needed to be undertaken with representatives from these markets to ensure that they were not alienated – despite the fact that this was to be a highly targeted campaign. Although initially it might have seemed perfectly reasonable to extend the research audience, the end result was a research profile where only 40 per cent of the respondents were actually from the target market (Table 4.2).

The question which should have been asked here was 'what happens if (and quite likely when) those outside the core target market reject all or some of the campaign?' By involving them in the research process these peripheral markets assumed great significance (and few researchers and clients would find it easy to ignore or discard their opinions) – despite the fact that these are not the consumers the campaign was intended to reach. The end result could well be a campaign sufficiently diluted to appeal to all the groups yet lacking any appeal to really inspire one group.

Table 4.2   Research profile

Socioeconomic group	Gender mix	Age	Life stage status
AB	Male/female	30–39	Pre-family couples
AB	Male/female	40–49	Pre/post-family couples
C1	Male/female	25–40	Full-nest family
C2	Male/female	25–40	Full-nest family
D	Male/female	25–40	Full-nest family

When to research?

Having established the audience parameters, client and agency can consider undertaking research during the key exploratory, strategic, creative and evaluative phases of an advertising campaign's life cycle. Exploratory research can be used to establish initial concepts and ideas about the brand in question; strategic research is more concerned to establish the context for the image campaign; creative development research provides advice about the direction of communication strategies and positioning executions. The final phase in the research process is to measure the success or failure of a campaign (Table 4.3). Exploratory research, as the name suggests, is designed to understand both the existing and potential market, to understand how consumers within these markets interact with advertising and to develop a comprehensive analysis of the brand (including consumer awareness levels,

Table 4.3   Research and the campaign life cycle

1 Exploratory	2 Strategic	3 Creative	4 Evaluative
Conceptual	Contextual	Directional	Measurement
Establish market	Consumer motivations	Effective communication	Campaign objectives
Brand audit	Brand distinctiveness	Consumer responses	Market context
Brand potential	Brand credibility	Advertising refinement	Advertising performance
	Advertising directions		

growth potential and impact measures). Only when a sound knowledge of the brand (sometimes termed a brand audit or competitive review) has been established can clients and agencies begin to make key decisions on the brand's target markets and the communication approaches to be developed for them.

The second stage is strategic developmental research, which can sometimes blur into or be confused with creative developmental research. It should, however, precede the development of the creative brief. The overriding objective here is to establish what factors motivate consumers, what they believe to be distinctive about the brand and what they are prepared to accept as credible about the brand. Following on from this, it will be possible to explore what direction the advertising should take, what it should say and how it should say it, providing a good base from which to launch the creative research phase. Strategic developmental research is all about establishing how campaign objectives and advertising propositions might work within intended target markets; ultimately it should be used to inform and enlighten the communication strategy, but never to replace sound judgement.

Creative development research is one of the most sensitive areas of advertising research as a result of a variety of factors. There is, for instance, the political context of the client/advertising agency relationship and the fact that creative development research will provide the first opportunity for the client to really evaluate the advertising material which its agency has produced. There is also the fact that the campaign itself will have developed its own momentum amongst the agency creative staff and, finally, there is the issue of timing, which will probably become increasingly critical. Ideally at this stage the research should be used to nurture creative ideas and to refine communications to make them more memorable and distinctive to the consumer – at worst it should be serving as a damage limitation exercise.

Although success can never be guaranteed, sound research depends on a number of factors, including a proper understanding of the brand and what it means to consumers and how the advertising communication 'relates' to this 'reality'. It also requires agreement on the preferred consumer response to the advertising. Is the advertising trying to reinforce or change existing beliefs about a brand or is it simply trying to increase its saliency? Appropriate methodologies are of course, also essential. More problematic, yet of vital importance, is the need to recreate, in so far as is possible, the consumer context for the research (see Ad highlight 4.1). Artificial situations undermine the effectiveness of research and every effort needs to be made to replicate the conditions in which consumers usually consume advertising. For instance, depth interviews are more appropriate for discussing press advertising and mini-groups for examining television advertising. Recruitment to these groups is also critical, although 'sadly the recruitment of creative development respondents is still too lax'.[4] Despite all these precautions it should always be remembered that there are times when creative development research will have no role to play – particularly where the concept is very novel and consumers are resistant to change and new ideas.

Pretesting advertising executions

The pretesting of advertising is a specific phase within the creative development process that is also integral to the overall evaluation of the material. It is usually undertaken after the qualitative creative development research has been completed, but prior to the campaign launch. Despite the fact that media budgets are coming under ever increasing pressure, advertisers have never been more interested in testing the effectiveness of advertising – whether to make sure it is 'right' or to anticipate how it will perform. A variety of research methods can be used to assess if and how advertisements work before the critical step is taken to launch. Unfortunately, with the best of intentions, advertising researchers have made pretesting a foggy, and overtechnical subject for the non-expert. In the USA, advertising has tended to be valued in so far as it encourages people to buy products, whilst in the UK the emphasis has been on whether advertising adds value to products. This difference in approach (although an oversimplification and possibly increasingly less relevant in an era of globalization) has quite naturally influenced the methodological approaches to pretesting. However, with an increasing emphasis on value for money and performance measurement, quantified testing procedures are proliferating and are usually preferred by advertisers (Table 4.4).

> Each research agency will often have its own preferred pretesting measures – which usually evaluate market or brand effects or aspects of the advertisement itself.

Table 4.4　Key pretesting evaluation measures

Market effects	*Ad measures*
Pre/post preference	Copy point recall
Persuasion	Impact/standout
	Interest/attention
Brand effects	Employment/likeability
Brand attributes and image dimensions,	
e.g., relevance, empathy, brand recall	

Pretesting systems do offer a number of advantages and disadvantages. The advantages include its potential to reduce risks and its apparent objectivity (where all ads are subject to the same key measures and analysed by an 'independent' third party). The disadvantages centre on whether the whole procedure itself is flawed – is pretesting just a substitute for good management? Will it reduce advertising to the lowest common denominator – in other words is research the great leveller?[5] A further issue of concern is the timing of pretests. Too frequently, advertising is tested much too late in the day to enable any meaningful changes to take place as the brochures and posters will have already been printed, the advertisements filmed and the media slots booked. In this scenario, minor improvements are usually the only changes possible and the research money spent is money wasted. Whatever its perceived advantages or disadvantages, pretesting is here to stay and is now regarded as an essential part of the advertising development process. Tests are, when compared with the overall marketing budget, relatively inexpensive and, when used properly, they can enhance the prospects for success and reduce the risks involved with the campaign.

Evaluating advertising performance

The final phase in the campaign life cycle is critical in today's results-driven marketing world, where brand recognition and purchase intention charts are expected to go forever upwards. Moreover, failure frequently attracts awkward questions and possibly slimmer advertising budgets, either from the corporate headquarters or, in the case of national tourism organizations, from the sponsoring government department. Yet the difficulty is that advertising has the potential to work on a variety of levels, only some of which are open to measurement and evaluation. Popular measures can, as Table 4.5 shows, simply assess ad spending impact *vis-à-vis* revenues generated through consumer spend, although common sense alone tells us that this single measurement focus cannot lead to an adequate evaluation of advertising impacts. Given the increasing demands for evaluation and proof of a campaign's success, it is vital to recognize that the only honest and appropriate evaluation of such a campaign occurs when it is measured against a brand's stated strategy in conjunction with the prevailing market context. It is vital that the research agency, the ad agency and the client work together to ensure that such a detailed briefing takes place beforehand. Without knowing how and why a campaign is expected to work the outcome is more likely to be destructive rather than

> Campaign evaluation in tourism requires a much broader time frame than that allowed by the paymasters of many public sector organizations who demand year-on-year increases (and may be constrained by political event horizons).

Table 4.5   Promotional performance of selected destinations, 1997

Country	1997 budget (US$ millions)	Promotional spending per tourist arrival (US$)	Additional tourism revenues generated for every US$1 spent on tourism promotion
Singapore	99	15.20	80
UK	82	3.15	250
Spain	72	1.66	369
Thailand	67	9.30	129
Australia	65	15.47	143
France	61	0.91	464
Austria	58	3.48	213
Puerto Rico	45	13.50	44
Netherlands	43	6.44	153
Mexico	40	2.06	189

Source: World Tourism Organization, 1998.

constructive. Yet, despite the fact that it is essential that criteria for evaluation are agreed prior to undertaking evaluation, 'Unbelievable as it may seem, quantitative advertising evaluation research is often conducted without a true understanding of what individual campaigns are trying to do for a brand, or the way in which a creative execution is attempting to work'.[6]

A framework for advertising evaluation

Advertising campaigns perform three basic functions, to persuade, to change or reinforce brand values and to raise the brand's profile.[7] As a result, the nature of the advertising evaluation should reflect the differences of each type of campaign (Table 4.6). Persuasive advertising seeks to present new 'news' or make old news freshly motivating, and evaluation research here should seek to establish whether the message has been absorbed, the extent to which the message is believed, the message's relevance to the consumer and whether the brand is now considered in consumer choices. However, as consumers and markets have become increasingly sophisticated, advertising itself has tended to move from persuasion through product benefits to persuasion through establishing close consumer relationships. This second approach aims to position a particular brand as a brand 'for me' – one with which consumers will identify. Such strong brand relationships are particularly critical in product or service areas where 'the demonstration of any tangible motivation benefits over competitors is too complex or difficult', as in financial services or tourism and leisure.[8] Advertising that seeks to change or reinforce brand values is an extremely subtle form of advertising which addresses the relationship between the consumer and the brand on a personally motivating level. In other words, positioning or repositioning a brand as the brand to be seen with. Advertising that attempts to do this needs to be measured and assessed in terms of its ability to reposition the brand with the consent and acceptance of its target market. Where the advertising objective is to reinforce rather than reposition particular brand values, the research should establish the extent to which the ad was involving and enjoyable, and a high degree of advertising recall might be expected in the target market.

Finally, advertising which aims to raise a brand's recognition rating (largely because consumers prefer well-known brands) should focus on making the ads themselves salient to the consumer. Saliency refers to an advertisement's ability to 'cut through media clutter and arrest the viewer's attention'[9] – standing out from the crowd because it is so distinctively different. Salient advertising: 'is especially relevant for small brands which want to achieve consideration levels closer to their more well-known competitors ... They become better known through having famous advertising – it has nothing to do with rational persuasion or even likeability.'[10]

However, reliance on a single measure such as saliency may not be particularly appropriate because, although a campaign may be well recalled, recall itself provides little indication of the campaign's ability to influence brand perceptions. Fortunately, however, where saliency fails, some would

Table 4.6 Potential advertising evaluation measures

Message	The extent of the ad's ability to communicate service or product benefits (rational and non-rational)
Saliency	The extent of the ad's ability to cut through media clutter and attract attention
Appeal	The extent of the ad's appeal and ability to provoke positive reactions
Branding	The extent of the ad's linkage and reinforcement with the brand
Persuasion	The extent of the ad's ability to shift consumer attitudes towards the brand and stimulate purchase

Source: adapted from Research International. *The Research International Approach to Advertising Evaluation Research*, p. 4.

argue that involvement measures succeed. Involvement is defined as 'whether consumers can relate to and empathise with the advertising',[11] and involvement measures try to establish the relevance of executions to consumers.

Advertising research techniques

As we have seen so far in this chapter, research can influence the advertising at various stages in the campaign's development. At each stage, however, it is vital that those involved in the research select the most appropriate techniques. The sheer range and diversity of techniques now available can make this a challenging and confusing task, and clients (either alone or in conjunction with their agency) may appoint specialist research companies to conduct the research. Even if this is a viable option for a client, some understanding of the nature of advertising research techniques is always useful for a manager and the remainder of this chapter reviews the most popular and well-used advertising research techniques.

Research that seeks to explore, probe and investigate the perceptions and attitudes of consumers towards particular brands is best suited to qualitative research techniques. Qualitative research, as the name suggests, seeks to provide quality information, usually in the form of deep and rich insights into a particular issue. It may be used to establish a brand's values or to investigate whether the target audience will respond to the brand values and messages communicated in a specific ad or campaign. In essence, qualitative research provides a conceptual link between consumers and advertising decision-makers in the development of advertising, helping to 'define the most consumer-relevant strategy, and subsequently to guide the creative process towards the most consumer-relevant but also executionally exciting expression of that strategy'.[12]

It was only during the 1990s that qualitative research became recognized as a stand-alone research method used in its own right, rather than one used as a precursor to quantitative techniques – which deals with the quantification of a particular measure. Quantitative techniques may be used in advertising research to evaluate factors such as copy point recall and levels of pre- and post-campaign product awareness. Historically, the choice between using qualitative or quantitative techniques was based on whether sensitivity or statistical reliability was the key research goal. Qualitative research offers depth and flexibility, whilst quantitative data provides the reassurance of the large numbers from which many organizations take comfort. The divide between the two forms of research is increasingly blurring, however, at least with some of the 'quali-quant' techniques being developed within the market research industry – techniques which allow quantitative advertising research greater depth, flexibility and freedom of expression. Two of the most frequently used research methods in advertising are both qualitative techniques – depth interviews and focus groups. With these, qualitative research is conducted with small numbers of people in non-random samples, in other words, the sample is selected by the interviewer from within the target audience and selection criteria may include age, gender, socioeconomic grouping and geographic location.

Depth interviews and focus groups

Depth interviews are normally informal one-to-one conversations lasting for up to an hour in which the respondents are encouraged to talk extensively about particular issues and, whilst the interviewer usually has a list of concerns to be addressed, the conversation is very much directed by the respondent. By contrast, focus groups consist of between eight and ten people (mini-groups of five to six people are also becoming increasingly popular) and the discussions usually last anything up to 2 hours. The running of focus groups is a demanding form of research that places a heavy responsibility on the interviewer to moderate the discussion. In so far as it is possible, moderators need to ensure equal participation from all respondents, which means dealing with domineering respondents at an early stage and encouraging shy group members to participate. Moderators also need to be able to control the 'hothouse' dynamic that sometimes threatens to overtake a discussion when potentially sensitive or emotive issues are being discussed. In fact, moderator quality is essential to ensure good focus group research and impartiality is vital – however, since it does vary there can be problems of moderator impact.

Both depth interviews and focus groups can provide invaluable insights into consumers' attitudes towards and experiences of particular brands. They are designed to probe beyond the more easily accessible thoughts to mine people's deeper feelings and deep-seated associations. As a result, some of the most relevant information may be obtained from non-verbal responses and focus groups are usually video-taped. This not only enables the interviewers and moderators to devote complete attention to the actual discussion, but also facilitates greater data depth and insight at the analysis stage. In this way, focus groups are more about consumers' emotional rather than rational reactions to ads and, given this, focus groups are in no way scientific – they are unpredictable, interactive and illuminating precisely because they are designed to explore and uncover consumer attitudes. Ad highlight 4.1 explores how focus group research played a significant role in revitalizing a particular Irish stout in the UK beer market.

Ad highlight 4.1   Revitalizing Murphy's Stout

In the UK, various stouts compete for beer drinkers' attention – including Murphy's, Guinness and Beamish. One of the best beer advertising campaigns of the 1990s was developed for Murphy's Stout. Directed by Alan Parker, the ads were built around witty, laid-back observations of small-town Irish life by a young male Murphy's drinker. They provided the brand with a distinctiveness it had previously lacked (by comparison with Guinness). Various bittersweet scenarios were developed in a series of ads centring around the life of the young drinker each of which finished with him wryly commenting 'Like the Murphy's . . . I'm not bitter'.

The market

Although this mid-1990s campaign was extremely successful, by 1998 it was felt to have outlived its usefulness, primarily because Murphy's now had to compete not only with other stouts but also with an expanding beer and lager market. Murphy's – although extremely pleasant and enjoyable – was failing to impress young drinkers as a cool, night-out drink. Research had shown that whilst Murphy's was accepted as a restful weekend or lunchtime drink, it was definitely not considered appropriate for clubbing on a Friday night – as Jo Franks, Murphy's marketing manager, commented: 'Murphy's had become a Sunday lunchtime drink with your dad'. In addition, stout drinking had old-fashioned overtones for young drinkers and in a market saturated by cool, trendy drinks (including alcopops) this was a potentially serious problem. As a result, a new ad campaign was developed to revitalize Murphy's Stout, in which focus group research played a hugely significant role.

Campaign development research

Using a variety of techniques to mine a range of data sources, the first phase in the development of the campaign (based on in-house brainstorming at the client and the agency) sought to establish and explore:

- the overall beer market
- the roles of stouts within this market
- the roles of Murphy's brand within the stout market.

The second phase sought to provide an analysis of how beer advertising works and how the Murphy's campaign fitted into that market. Guidance was sought from consumers on how advertising could be used to reposition the brand and research was conducted amongst eighteen to thirty-five-year-old male beer drinkers in London and Manchester in standard focus groups and usually in 'friendship groups' – that is, people who normally drink together. The campaign's developers rationalized that as beer drinking was a social activity, more effective and meaningful data would be produced by replicating the situation in which the product was consumed. Thus, the research locations included participants' homes, and pubs and bars. This phase of the research generated extremely rich data, both in terms of attitudes towards Murphy's, the significance of beer advertising and future directions for Murphy's ad campaigns. The rough, consumer-generated ideas were then assessed by the agency and client. New creative treatments were developed, and then tested and refined with many of the consumers who had been involved in the previous stage.

The research findings and the new campaign

Whilst there was a lot of affection for the brand and the 'I'm not bitter' campaign, the first research phase revealed that Murphy's needed much more energy if it was to successfully compete in the cutthroat beer market and attract new markets. Interestingly, within these markets the choice of beer was seen by consumers not only as a matter of preferred taste, but also as significant for consumers' self-images and as an indicator of masculinity. As a result, the new Murphy's ad campaign sought to appeal to eighteen to thirty-five year old male beer drinkers by positioning it as a trendy, energetic, sexy brand by completely revamping the tone and style of the advertising. No longer positioned as an Irish, slightly bemused beer, the new campaign centred around three 'ordinary Irish girls' who transform into 'The Sisters of Murphy's' whenever any danger threatens any laddish young Murphy's drinker and his pint (whether it be falling cars or more surreal threats from Valkyrie-like singing women). These sexy, black-leather-clad superwomen with their modern (*Loaded* magazine) and classic cult associations (*Charlie's Angels* and *The Avengers*) were felt to be more in tune with the late 1990s and early 2000s than the earlier campaign. They also shifted the campaign and the product beyond associations of rural, gentle Irishness and transformed it into a young, modern, urban brand with sex appeal. Research to date suggests that the target market responses to the campaign have been very encouraging.

Source: adapted from Michele Witthaus. *Marketing Week*, 28 January, 1999.

Projective techniques

Projective research techniques have a chequered history. Introduced in the 1950s under the guise of motivation research, they were once extremely popular in advertising and consumer research, although their general usage has declined, largely as a result of the practical difficulties associated with their application. Despite this, projective techniques continue to be important in research that attempts to investigate and establish images, perceptions and attitudes towards brands, and also reactions to advertising material. More recently, they have been incorporated into quantitative analysis through brand profiling techniques. Projective techniques require skilled interpretation and some advertising agencies employ psychologists, anthropologists and other social scientists to undertake and interpret them.

In a world where consumer choices are difficult to explain and describe, researchers use a wide range of non-directive and projective techniques to probe underlying emotions and attitudes towards brands and buying situations. Particular techniques in use today include mapping, word association, inkblot or cartoon interpretation tests, projective drawings and thematic apperception tests (TATs). In addition, it is not unusual for agencies to ask consumers to describe their favourite brands as animals, people or cars, whilst a further technique involves consumers drawing figures or making clay models of typical brands or brand users. One well-known example of the use of such techniques was when the credit card firm American Express asked people to draw likely users of its gold card and its green card. Respondents sketched gold-card holders as 'active, broad-shouldered men' and green-card holders as '"couch potatoes" lounging in front of television sets'. On the basis of this analysis American Express positioned its gold card as 'a symbol of responsibility for people capable of controlling their own lives'.[13]

Mapping brands spatially locates how relevant particular brands are to individual consumers. Maps may have bipolarities such as very/not important, very/not desirable, for me/not for me, although this is not essential. These maps can be used to indicate the relative desirability of particular destinations and tourism or leisure products. Word association or sentence completion are similar techniques which require respondents to say what immediately comes to mind when faced with words or partial sentences. Such techniques can reveal images, feelings and associations which respondents hold of particular brands (Case study 4.1). Cartoons with blank speech balloons where respondents are asked to write what they think is the appropriate response for that particular setting can also be used. Researchers using projective drawings ask respondents to draw the pictures they visualize, given particular criteria such as, how did you feel before a holiday, during a holiday or after a holiday? Consumers may also be asked to write imaginary postcards from a destination and draw the picture they most associate with that place. Thematic apperception tests depict a series of cartoons showing a person in particular contexts, such as choosing a particular service or product, for example, a health club membership or sports equipment, and respondents are then asked to describe that person in detail (Table 4.7).

At times such projective techniques can seem at best slightly unusual, or for the more sceptical client, quite bizarre, and these techniques do have an image problem in some quarters. Despite this, marketers, advertising agencies and researchers are finding these 'touchy-feely' techniques increasingly useful, first, in understanding how the consumer thinks and feels and, second, in developing more effective marketing strategies, campaigns and executions. As with all techniques, if incorrectly used or interpreted, projective research can be misleading or downright wrong. Used within agreed parameters, however,

Table 4.7 Projective techniques and research applications

Projective technique	Research use
Maps	Relevance/closeness/desirability
Word association, sentence completion	Images/feelings/associations
Cartoons, TATs	Responses to scenarios
Drawings, modelling, presentation	Feelings/images/associations/beliefs
Brand fingerprinting	Experience/relationship

it can provide a very flexible and effective way to 'get into consumers' heads' to establish the deep-seated beliefs and motivations which determine consumer choices and attitudes to tourism and leisure brands.

Ad highlight 4.2   Advertising research stimuli

All the qualitative techniques discussed may well make use of stimulus material – items which either represent the ad idea or which might stimulate consumer responses. Material can be direct or indirect stimulus. The former is used to convey a particular advertising idea to consumers, the latter is used more to illuminate consumer responses or reactions, but the material may appear to bear no obvious resemblance to the finished idea. A combination of direct and indirect material can prove to be invaluable in assessing the advertising and how it relates to the overall creative strategy. Naturally, the material will be filtered through the respondents' own perceptions, experiences, sociocultural conditioning and circumstances and therefore has no intrinsic meaning.

Direct stimulus material:

- Concept boards
- Animatics
- Storyboards
- Narrative tapes
- Photomatics.

Indirect stimulus material:

- Words, drawings and pictures
- Projective technique material
- Collage boards
- Film clips and music
- Videos/tapes
- Mock interviews.

Chapter summary

The need for effective rather than simply well-crafted advertising is becoming increasingly vital in tourism and leisure marketing. In this context, advertising research seems set to become even more important given the increasingly competitive environment and the fragmentation and diversification of products in this marketplace. Research can help a brand manager to understand the competition, it can reveal consumer perceptions and attitudes towards products and brands, and it can monitor market trends. Yet whilst research can make a client and agency more sensitive to the market, it cannot generate a campaign or guarantee its success by itself. In addition, its use is very limited when the product is a new one, unfamiliar to the consumer. Research is most effective when it provides a thorough understanding of a brand's market (whether existing or potential), allowing clients and agencies to produce effective, intuitive advertising. Research can also be very useful in illuminating the creative possibilities of advertising executions but it must not be used as a substitute for decision-making. However, the drive to seek consumer prelaunch endorsement of campaigns is unrelenting in an era dominated by performance evaluation, and some clients use research more to avoid failure than to ensure success.

Whilst the need for greater accountability and for better performance evaluation have stimulated a growth in research agencies and research techniques, researchers have not been able to develop truly predictive and diagnostic methodologies. Advertising works on a variety of levels and no single methodology can satisfactorily meet all these levels. Instead, organizations need to mix and match techniques to arrive at the best possible package, which requires effective selection of research respondents who fit a campaign's target market. Finally, remember that research should seek to make campaigns more powerful and more salient, and ad campaigns should be judged and evaluated on these criteria.

Case study 4.1

Researching Las Vegas's brand personality

Various research techniques have been developed in order to establish the images, attitudes and perceptions which people hold of particular brands or products. However, given their very nature, the measurement of such factors is frequently problematic since images, attitudes and perceptions are subjective and, in many cases, even subconscious. As a result they are not easily quantifiable. However, accurate measurement is essential as strategies for marketing and promoting destinations are frequently based on such research findings. One study to explore Las Vegas's brand personality amongst UK consumers used a variety of projective techniques to construct a comprehensive analysis of the overall image strengths and weaknesses of the destination. Taken as a whole, these measurements enable a powerful picture of respondents' impressions of Vegas and its competitors to be developed. The key measures used to establish these brand impressions were:

- destination saliency
- user and product imagery
- brand fingerprinting
- brand personality.

Destination saliency

Destination saliency provides a measure of how emotionally close an individual feels to a destination. A measure of saliency is vital in order to determine:

- how relevant Las Vegas is to potential UK vacationers
- how potential holiday-makers feel about Las Vegas. Do they feel good about it, do they feel it is for them?
- how Las Vegas is regarded as a destination. Is it viewed as being a potential current or future vacation destination?

Destination saliency was measured by the respondents mapping their emotional proximity to a number of vacation destinations. The map provided an analysis of destinations respondents felt either emotionally close to or distant from. It was then used as a prompt to further analyse interpretations of how close they felt to particular destinations. Destination saliency was also measured by exploring the respondents' top-of-the-mind associations of Las Vegas. These centred very much on the 'traditional', adult Las Vegas product, and gambling, sex, Mafia-connections and entertainment were the key descriptors. Personalities associated with Vegas included Howard Hughes, Busy Seagal, the 1950s 'bratpack' and Tom Jones. There were also glamorous overtones of limousines, champagne and glittering nightlife; family associations, including family entertainment, were notably absent from this initial discussion.

User and product imagery

Investigations of user imagery help to establish how well respondents identify with the destination by establishing respondents' perceptions of the typical vacation visitor to Las Vegas. Product imagery reflects what respondents would expect to find there in terms of accommodation, attractions, entertainment and environment. Here user and product imagery was explored by using two techniques – visual collage boards and sentence completion. Using visual collage boards, respondents were asked about the types of people who went to Las Vegas and the type of product it offered, including its hotels and entertainment. From this, similar brand themes emerged. The people who would go are relatively affluent, empty-nesters, largely American, 'brash', 'loud' and 'self-confident'. International visitors were thought to be first-time visitors. They are overwhelmingly described as in search of 'fun', a 'good time' and entertainment.

Word association or sentence completion are similar techniques which require respondents to say what immediately comes to mind when faced with words or partial sentences. Such techniques can reveal images, feelings and associations that respondents hold of particular destinations and tourism products (and their competitors). In the case of Las Vegas, these tended to confirm this view of a traditional, adult product. One respondent completed the sentence, people who go to Las Vegas are 'pseudo-riche unhappy Americans, glamorous but bored and looking for happiness'. When asked what Las Vegas offers there was unanimity in that it offers 'everything and anything you want', '24-hour entertainment of your choice' and above all 'escape'. This last was a common theme and one respondent who had been there commented that: 'Las Vegas offers dreams, glitz, glamour and a chance to forget reality'. It was 'not pretentious – it doesn't pretend to be something it's not – but what it is, fun and spectacle. It's for all sorts of people out for fun and entertainment.'

Hotels in Las Vegas are 'like theme parks with rooms', they are big, 'bright', 'brash' and 'entertainment centred'. For those who had been there was a sense that parts of the hotels were also 'oases of calm, away from the noise and clamour of the casinos'. For those unfamiliar with the product many thought the hotels would be expensive, whilst those who had been to Vegas considered them value for money. Both groups of respondents considered the hotels to be modern and offering quality. Entertainment in Las Vegas was seen as varied, comprehensive and offering a wide range of choice, with something for everyone. For those who had been it was 'over the top, with show-girls everywhere', it's 'in your face, you can see a volcano explode, watch a sea-battle, then go and see showgirls all in the space of a five minute walk'. One respondent who had experience of the product commented that entertainment is 'non-stop . . . and often free'. It was a similar story for those with only naïve images of the destination – they saw it as 'like Butlins, only bigger, a lot bigger'. Above all it was 'fun, fun, fun'.

Brand fingerprinting

Brand fingerprinting investigates the respondents' experience of, and their relationship with, a brand. It was one of a series of key measures used here to establish the brand imagery of Las Vegas and its competitors as vacation destinations. Brand fingerprinting examines the thoughts and feelings held about Las Vegas and its competitors through the senses (sights, sounds, smells, tastes, touch and feelings). Respondents were asked to describe in detail their images and impressions of the destinations under consideration (Table 4.8).

Brand personality

When the respondents were asked to describe Las Vegas as if it was to come to life as a person, the results were interesting. Although some saw it as a large, middle-aged man and others as 'a sexy, young showgirl, all feathers and lipstick', the overwhelming personification was of Las Vegas as a middle-aged, American lady 'acting and trying to look younger'. She seems glamorous but in a faded way, with 'gaudy, expensive clothes, driving a big car and wearing lots of jewellery, make-up and perfume'. She would also be 'chattering away in a loud voice about anything and everything but on a superficial level'. Underneath this exterior, however, there is a sense of insecurity – she is 'gregarious, outgoing and extrovert but maybe underneath desperate and lonely', even being seen as 'the original whore with a heart of gold' and 'big, brash, crude but refined in some ways'.

Table 4.8 Las Vegas's brand fingerprint amongst UK tourists

Sights	*Sounds*
Bright neon lights and dark skies	Loud, up-beat music and 'buzz'
Limousines	Traffic
Showy clothes and make-up	Gaming machines and roulette wheels
Sparkling diamonds	Last bet calls
Amusement parks	People and many languages
Smog	Clinking glasses and champagne corks
Wide, straight streets and large buildings	
Lots of people hanging around	
Smells	*Taste*
Perfume	US fast-food, steak, ribs and meat
Sweat	Cosmopolitan food
Alcohol, smoke and food	Alcohol and cigarettes
Cars	Bitter taste
Pollution, rotten bins and dirty	Coca-Cola
Touch	*Feelings*
Money	Overwhelmed and frantic
Metal	Surprised, amused and happy
Heat	Exhilarated, adrenaline
	Guilt, fear, loneliness
	Excitement, expectation and anticipation
	Distaste and turned off

These are all echoes of 'traditional' Las Vegas, however, there was one suggestion of the newer Vegas. One respondent who was familiar with the product saw Las Vegas 'as a child. Each new toy has to be bigger, better and more expensive than the last – old toys are discarded as new toys appear. Like a child's birthday party, it's indulgent and over-the-top but it's harmless, fun and amusing. It wants to entertain and to be entertained.'

Taken as a total package of research techniques, these and other similar projective methodologies can provide a powerful and comprehensive profile of people's perceptions of destinations and the strengths and weaknesses of their images. In this case, the destination was Las Vegas, but the same techniques can and have been successfully applied to other destinations, with the results serving to inform revised advertising and marketing strategies.

Case study 4.2

MTV's research puts it ahead in the youth market

The youth market is notoriously difficult to target, they are often described as the future of brands but how do advertisers keep pace with a generation constantly ahead of itself – do they target attitude or age? As many marketers fight to maintain appeal in the youth market, one major brand – MTV – is finding new ways to defend and enhance its position as youth market leader. It is not the only market it targets but it is the most popular music channel among this core audience. In 1997 the channel completely revamped itself and rather than operating on a Europe-wide basis, it opted to regionalize all television coverage for each specific market, with dedicated feeds in Germany, the UK and Italy, and with a research manager for each region. In July 1999 MTV Networks Europe – encompassing MTV, VH1 and M2 – further expanded to launch three new digital channels – Extra, Base and VH1 Classics.

MTV is synonymous with the youth market and enjoys a position from which it can exploit the brand to its utmost. Whilst many brands have tried to target this media-literate audience, few have succeeded – Nike, Levi and Coca-Cola being some of the few exceptions. The value of the MTV brand transcends all international barriers and because of this consumers will be attracted to brands advertised on the channel – offering an attractive environment to sponsors and advertisers. It is the strength of the channel's research department, however, which gives the station an added edge. With a sixteen-strong team across Europe and an annual budget of £2 million, the variety of its research activity is huge. It conducts a fortnightly call-out tracker in the UK, Sweden, the Netherlands and Germany whereby clips of music are played down the phone to a random sample who are then asked about its relevance and 'fit' to the MTV brand. Its large-scale quantitative studies also include the lifestyle study *Turned on Europe* which takes place with 200 sixteen to twenty-four-year-olds in six European countries, whilst Continental Research undertakes *The Monitor* – a yearly study on perceptions and attitudes to MTV. Also included in the research mix is qualitative research – encompassing what MTV terms 'non-traditional' research such as vox pops, event research, and in-school and on-site interviewing – the latter taking place among participants of a programme at a studio.

Future MTV research projects include looking at ways of utilizing its website to test video clips and conduct questionnaires and focus groups on-line. The channel is also seeking research collaborations with other marketing companies and media owners on a pan-European level and when commissioning a piece of research, whether it is marketing, youth or music oriented, the station collaborates with its international channels so that the project becomes global rather than regional – for instance, Viacom, MTV's US parent company, also owns the American children's channel Nickelodeon.

Source: Sylma Etienne (1999). I Want My MTV. *Research*, June, 36–7.

Notes

1 Anonymous, quoted in Sue Moss (1994). *The Planning and Role of Research*. Advertising research. Market Research Society.
2 S. Silvester (1994). Why pretesting sucks. Speech to the Association of Qualitative Research Practitioners.
3 Ibid.
4 Andrea Berlowitz (1994). *Stimulus Material*. Advertising research. Market Research Society, p. 3.
5 S. Silvester (1994). *Is Research Killing Advertising?* Background papers. Market Research Society.
6 Research International. *The Research International Approach to Advertising Evaluation Research*. Research International, p. 2.
7 Terry Prue (1994). *Tracking and Effectiveness*. Advertising research. Market Research Society.
8 Research International, *Approach to Advertising Evaluation Research*, p. 6.
9 Ibid., p. 4.
10 Prue, *Tracking and Effectiveness*.
11 Research International, *Approach to Advertising Evaluation Research*, p. 8.
12 Berlowitz, *Stimulus Material*, p. 2.
13 P. Kotler and G. Armstrong (1994). *Principles of Marketing*. Prentice Hall, pp. 284–5.

Further reading

Birn, R., Hague, P. and Vangelder, P. (eds) (1990). *A Handbook of Market Research Techniques*. Kogan Page.
Chisnell, P. M. (1991). *The Essence of Marketing Research*. Prentice Hall.
Department for Culture, Media and Sport (1998). *Measuring the Local Impact of Tourism*. DCMS.

Gilmore, A. and Carson, D. (1996). Integrative qualitative methods in a services context. *Marketing Intelligence and Planning Special Issue: Qualitative Market Research,* **14** (6), 21–7.

Greenbaum, T. L. (1998). *The Handbook for Focus Group Research.* Sage.

Hallberg, G. (1995). *All Consumers Are Not Created Equal: The Differential Marketing Strategy for Brand Loyalty and Profits.* John Wiley.

Hornig Priest, S. (1996). *Doing Media Research: An Introduction.* Sage.

Jones, P. J. (ed.) (1998). *How Advertising Works: The Role of Research.* Sage.

Morgan, D. (ed.) (1993). *Successful Focus Groups: Advancing the State of the Art.* Sage.

Peters, G. (1996). *The Next Wave: Imagining the Next Generation of Customers.* Pt 1. Pitman.

Ryan, C. (1993). *Researching Tourist Satisfaction.* Routledge.

Schutt, R. K. (1996). *Investigating the Social World: The Process and Practice of Research.* Sage.

Segal Quince Wicksteed Limited (1998). *Tourism Marketing: A Practical Guide to Evaluation.* SQW.

Shimp, T. A. (1993). *Promotion Management and Marketing Communications.* 3rd edn, pt 2, Behavioral foundations of marketing communications, pp. 55–148. Dryden Press.

Swarbrooke, J. and Horner, S. (1999). *Consumer Behaviour in Tourism.* Butterworth-Heinemann.

Trembath, R. (1999). Best kept secrets: an evaluation of South Australia's direct marketing campaign. *Journal of Vacation Marketing,* **6** (1), 76–85.

Wertheim, M. E. (1994). Market research for heritage attractions. *Journal of Vacation Marketing,* **1** (1), 70–4.

Part Two

Advertising Challenges

5

The dynamic advertising environment

Chapter overview

Advertising is influenced by a range of external or environmental forces that are beyond the marketers' control. These include sociodemographic, economic, political and technological developments as well as changes in legislation and regulation. This chapter focuses on a range of global sociodemographic and economic developments and explores their implications for tourism and leisure advertising. They include the rise of women, changing age dynamics, the emergence of multicultural societies and the impact of technological change (although this last issue is covered in more detail in Chapter 11). The chapter concludes with a discussion of the influence of ethical consumers (including ethical issues in advertising) and the regulation of advertising, and the end case study focuses on the gay and lesbian consumer. The key themes reviewed are:

- today's changing leisure consumer
- the transformation of work and leisure

- the rise of women
- global age dynamics
- global income dynamics
- the global competitive economy
- emergent markets of Asia, Latin America and Eastern Europe
- ethical issues in advertising.

Introduction

Our world is constantly changing, economic power centres are shifting, old markets are giving way to new, and there are emergent countries offering both new business opportunities and new sources of competition – all changes which have important consequences for tourism and leisure advertising. The world is rapidly shrinking as businesses become internationalized and technology goes global and, hand-in-hand with globalization as a key shaper of today's advertising, are massive sociodemographic changes. Far from the start of this millennium heralding an age of leisure, as many commentators once suggested, today's consumers now lead more harried, fragmented and less predictable lives than ever before. With the growth in dual-income households in many post-industrial countries, both women and men have less discretionary time and the result has been a massive increase in time control and a demand for flexible services. In addition, Western markets are becoming more middle aged, middle class and discriminating, and many societies are increasingly diverse and multicultural, creating new challenges for tourism and leisure marketers. Many countries have seen a liberalization of sexual mores (Case study 5.1) and the opportunities for women are rising both in the ageing West and in the youthful East, where many of the most significant changes are occurring. In addition, the world is witnessing the emergence of marketing opportunities in the transitional economies of central and Eastern Europe, southern America and Asia, as seen in Table 5.1.

The key economic developments that are impacting on the leisure industries are the growth of the global tourism industry, particularly in Eastern Europe, Asia and South America and the increasing professionalization and liberal-ization of the sector. The main political developments include more democracy which means more tourism and, within a European context, the expansion and integration of the European Union. Social developments include the rising pressure on and importance of leisure time, increasingly flexible working time and a loss of long-term security, a move to an urbanized world, especially in Asia and South America, a boom in long-haul travel for

Table 5.1 Where advertising will grow, 1997–2000 (top ten countries)

Country	% growth
China	87
Portugal	50
Czech Republic	45
South Africa	26
Philippines	21
Belgium	20
Ireland	19
Chile	19
India	19
Greece	17

Source: Zenith Media, quoted in The Economist (1999).
The World in 1999. The Economist Publications, p. 97.

the affluent and greater polarization between rich and poor worldwide. We will also see more mobility with flying commonplace, although environmental concerns are likely to spur the search for more forms of non-polluting transport. Indeed, green issues are likely increasingly to impact on politics and organizations in every sector, whilst in technology the new media will be very important, providing ever more access to information and new forms of distribution that will bring greater opportunities for tourism, sport and all types of leisure products and services.

Not surprisingly, these socioeconomic trends are also impacting on consumer behaviour. With more emphasis on the price:quality ratio, for instance, low-quality destinations are now only attracting mass tourism, whilst at the same time, spurred on by a rising sense of individualism, made-to-measure holidays are on the increase – offering more activities, variety and opportunities for self-development. As a result, there is more demand for new products and for 'unique' holiday experiences – moving from an emphasis on relaxation towards sensationalism. One marketing expert, Luis Moutinho, predicts that this new 'socioquake' will enhance cocooning (increasingly privatized lifestyles) and promote 'customer vigilantism', fantasy adventure experiences (through virtual reality), moves towards conservation, decon-sumption, and emphasize small indulgences in privatized leisure where the home will become 'hot'. He also sees the future as an age of the downwardly mobile with more people retiring earlier and downshifting to less stressful jobs, a society in which non-linear career paths, redundancy, self-employment, rising divorce rates and fewer marriages will combine to fracture 'traditional' lifestyle patterns.[1]

This chapter will examine the increasingly fragmented reality of consumers' lifestyles, especially in the post-industrial tourist-generating societies. In particular, it focuses on demographic and economic trends and explores their impact on tourism and leisure marketing. In recent decades consumers and markets have changed radically, resulting in a 'demassification' of markets – a process which has not been so much one of market segmentation but rather of market fragmentation. Clearly, marketers can no longer describe and target consumers in simple terms, but have to develop sophisticated marketing strategies and, in doing so, they are experiencing varying degrees of success. A discussion of the importance of targeting consumers with the right type of advertising appeals forms the basis of Chapter 6. First, however, this chapter identifies and discusses some of the ways in which the world is changing at the start of a new millennium.

The changing leisure consumer

As consumers' lives become ever more stressful and hectic, the value of time increases and is becoming as much a concern for many consumers as achieving value for money. As a result, consumers are placing more faith in brands and are demanding tailored leisure experiences. More people are looking for a greater variety of activities and unique holiday experiences, responding to a sense that holidays are no longer merely about relaxation but also about recharging and rediscovery (Table 5.2). In this new environment, travel commentators are predicting big increases in cruising, cultural tourism,

Table 5.2   Our changing holiday needs

Yesterday	Today
I want to escape	I want to discover people, places and experiences
I want to go far away	Let's go anywhere to learn
I need to have a holiday space	Holiday is life, life is holiday
I need to relax	I need new experiences
I need fun	I need excitement and mental stimulation

Source: adapted from R. Passarielo. Paper presented at the 1997 International Travel and Tourism Awards.

longer-stay holidays, themed holidays and 'retirement' products (such as health, thalassotherapy and educational activities), most of which involve increased interaction between people and greater creativity. Similarly, against this backdrop of personal development and exploration, advertising appeals that focus on elements of discovery (of the world, oneself and others) are likely to be more successful.

The overworked consumer

Whilst some commentators once predicted that the start of the third millennium would herald the end of traditional work patterns, it seems that the reality for many consumers is that they are working longer and harder than ever before. One exception is Japan where working hours are being reduced to bring them into line with their European and American counterparts and, as a consequence, a new leisure class is emerging in which the younger generation is central. Yet in the USA, many organizations are increasingly demanding that workers be at their desks earlier in the mornings and later at night, in addition to expecting many white-collar workers to sacrifice weekend time. Since 1969, the average American man's working time has increased by 100 hours a year, whilst for women the increase has been much greater, rising by over 300 hours a year. Ironically, these increases in working hours are not providing greater opportunities for those who are unemployed or underemployed. As a result, these people continue to be denied leisure opportunities because of a lack of disposable income, whilst those who do work (and have a reasonable income) are overworked and too time-poor to enjoy extended leisure activities.

> My workload has increased, I have taken on more responsibility, my job is not as secure as it was – these are all common sentiments heard in surveys at the start of the new millennium.

It comes as no surprise in this case that vacation travel in the USA is significantly affected by such work patterns. In a recent poll almost 25 per cent of all those planning a vacation said that 'getting time off from work' was a big problem. This also explains why a 1998 survey by the American Management Association International (www.amanet.org) revealed that rather than attempt to negotiate some sort of leave, almost 2000 managers and executives decided to stay at home for their summer vacation.[2] Interestingly, summer vacations now only accounts for 32 per cent of all annual vacation travel as people take shorter breaks and travel shorter distances – the typical journey is between 200 and 299 miles.[3] These rising work pressures are encouraging more and more people to opt for alternative lifestyles – accepting and exchanging a reduction in their income to gain more leisure time and more control over their lives. Often highly educated and motivated, most of these US 'downshifters' are positive about their decision, questioning the 'all-consuming' American dream's costs in terms of time, emotional energy and quality of life.

Europeans, unlike their American counterparts, have tended to enjoy much more free time, having experienced the sharpest postwar decline in working hours and a huge increase in leave entitlement. Now, however, these gains are being significantly eroded by employer practices and employment trends. Fuelled by higher levels of self-employment, greater female employment and more dual-income households, a greater number of European consumers are following their American counterparts and working harder than ever. A recent UK survey found that 66 per cent of fathers work in the evenings and 60 per cent work at weekends, whilst a new word has found its way into organizational vocabularies – 'presenteeism' – coined to describe the way in which many employees, worried about job insecurity, have to be seen to be indispensable to their companies, always the first into work and the last out. As a result, these trends have had a number of impacts on leisure patterns, including:

- the time-rich/poor–money-rich/poor paradox is a real issue – those who have money have no time and those who have leisure time have no money
- the money-rich account for 40 per cent of the total leisure market
- time is now a premium commodity and consumers are switching from time-intensive to experience- and capital-intensive leisure (increasing shorter holidays, expensive home entertainment systems and multi-attraction venues)
- the affluent retired are the main group bucking the time–money paradox.

The transformation of work and leisure

Just as globalization (facilitated and accelerated by technological change) is a key force in shaping the world, a major shift is occurring in work practices. Indeed, particularly in the post-industrial world, work is being transformed and 'the job' as we understood it in twentieth-century terms may well disappear as outsourcing and consultancy increase part-time and short-term arrangements between employee and employer – certainly the dominance of the 'nine to five' work pattern has all but vanished. Technology is the prime agent of this transformation, as telecommuting and self-employment increase. The Internet and its associated technologies represents the most significant opportunity for companies and individuals to shape the future, and whilst the growth in the number of Internet hosts is slowing, it still grew at a rate of 70 per cent in the late 1990s. The implications of these changes will be far-reaching, creating greater job insecurity, heightening the importance of self-marketing and speeding up the drift to a low-wage future for many people in many countries. By necessity, as work itself is transformed – its nature and very definition being reshaped – so the construction and role of leisure and tourism in people's lives will also change.

As the computer becomes part of everyday life and as it becomes more flexible – with the proliferation of smart mobile phones, laptops and palmtops (often with miniature high-speed fax/modems) – the traditional boundaries between where we live, where we work and where we play are becoming blurred. Working from home is not a new phenomenon as freelancers and the self-employed can testify, but what makes this a revolution is not its novelty but the *scale* on which it is occurring. The growth of information technology and the restructuring of large corporate and governmental bodies around the world is making work flexible on an unprecedented scale. Up to 2 million people in the UK currently work at home full-time and, while half of these are self-employed, a third are 'telecommuters', the numbers of which are growing rapidly. In the late 1990s over 60 per cent of UK companies reported some form of telecommuting and in the USA almost 12 million people are already telecommuting – working digitally from the home or on the move. The latest figures suggest that this could soon be an option for as many as one in three workers in some countries.

Whilst technological change offers new opportunities for some workers, for others it poses more of a threat, creating a heavier workload for some and taking work away from others. The digital revolution has not eased the workload of many busy executives, it just means they can take their work with them wherever they go. Technological advance has also reduced the requirement for many skills, resulting in downsizing and an increase in early retirement in many developed economies. The shift from a manufacturing to a service-based economy in the post-industrial world has also been key in encouraging the trend towards flexible employment. Over the last two decades the contribution of manufacturing to gross domestic product (GDP) has declined in the developed world, whilst that of services has increased. In some countries, such as Japan and Germany, the manufacturing sector remains important, responsible for about 40 per cent of GDP, but in others, such as the USA, the UK and France it is down to less than 33 per cent.

Manufacturing jobs in the developed economies have also been hit by automation and high labour costs – for example, in Germany factory labour costs are about $25 an hour, whereas in China the figure is between 50 cents and $1. If the countries of the developed world are to maintain employment they must look to providing value-added activities and concentrate on what they do best. Japan and Taiwan have a niche in electronics, Germany in designing and building reliable machines, the USA in communications, whilst London is the world's top financial centre. There is a trend towards shifting the traditional labour-intensive manufacturing jobs into the lower-wage economies of the developing world whilst the developed world seeks to compete in the higher value-added service industries – marketing, distribution, media, communications and leisure are the established areas where the developed world will continue to grow jobs. Even with information-related services, cross-border competition is increasing and cheap networking and communications will make it possible to run most information-oriented services from almost anywhere in the world.

Against this backdrop of highly dynamic social, economic and competitive forces, advertising takes on an even more critical role in contemporary marketing. The key trends in marketing today are saturation (with growth rates of below 5 per cent in most markets), globalization (with global giants in every industry/sector being larger and fewer than previously), fragmentation of markets and diversification of providers (for instance, in the UK, supermarket grocery retailers have moved into financial services), and downsizing (as a result of flatter structures and automation). As a result, we are seeing the rise of new customer-centric organizations that are process based, cross-functional, information technology (IT) driven and based on clusters of teams with different backgrounds. In the future of global marketing operations companies will have to be hybrid and hyperflexible, and managers will have to think laterally and strategically, envisioning and influencing the future rather than merely reacting to it.

In marketing terms, today's world is also one of increasing product parity in which products and brands are increasingly the same everywhere, yet (somewhat ironically) people are looking for more difference and more tailored services with a sensitivity to detail, seeing an emphasis on quality and brand information as a major product differential. Moutinho describes this as the growth of 'prosumerism' – allowing consumers themselves to be involved in the design and tailoring of products through new technology. In particular, children, teenagers and young adults all want to customize and personalize their image and like to take products and redefine them. As tomorrow's consumers (as well as today's) these groups have a 'do it my own way' culture which advertisers must recognize.[4] Certainly consumers want the solution benefits of products and marketers will have to emphasize quality and service to maintain customer loyalty – they need to shift from a 'make and sell' mentality to a focus on 'listening and serving'. The emergence of these new structures will have significant implications for the tourism and leisure industries and, therefore, for those involved in promoting its images and creating its dreams.

The global rise of women

Perhaps one of the greatest phenomena of the second half of the twentieth century was the global rise of women. Flexibility and self-sufficiency will be the keys to survival in the next millennium and since women already adopt a flexible approach to life through juggling careers and families, they are set to prosper and face a rosier employment future than men in the years ahead. In fact, men are likely to be those worst equipped to deal with the future, especially those baby boomers born between 1946 and 1961 – the group most likely to feel alienated and ill-prepared for the new lifestyles set to emerge. Significantly, where educational opportunities are available to them, women around the world are increasingly gaining higher standards of education than their male counterparts and where they have political representation they are more likely than men to vote for welfare and environmental protection.

In the West, the position of women has changed dramatically in recent decades and their importance as consumers, and as influences on buying behaviour and political change is greater than ever before. As Beeghley comments, whereas women used to be asked what their husbands did for a living, now men are frequently asked what do their wives do?[5] Women's consumer needs have long been neglected by marketers, but their rise in power and influence should be ignored at marketers' peril in the future. Today white females account for almost 40 per cent of the US workforce, having risen by 11 per cent since 1960. Carol Nelson comments that this is in stark contrast to 'Thirty-five years ago ... [when] the typical American woman graduated from high school, married, had children, and stayed at home with her family ... "Career" woman as a peer of the career man was practically unheard of.'[6]

Yet, although the gap has narrowed, women in the USA continue to earn less than their male counterparts – 72 per cent of male earnings in the mid-1990s, compared to 61 per cent in 1960 – and, given the slow narrowing, will not achieve parity for some time. It is also perhaps a misnomer to talk about 'the rise of women', precisely because 'women are an ever-more fragmented market'.[7] Throughout the West women are divided in terms of their responsibilities, their level of financial security and their amount of free time, as well as on a range of socioeconomic factors. There is also a significant difference between the experience of women in industrialized and developing countries and of those in parts of the less developed world.

In parts of Asia, we are witnessing what Naisbitt has described as a 'quiet, yet powerful revolution'. For example, Japan and Sweden now share the oldest average age for first-time marriage – twenty-seven for women and thirty for men. Within Asia, we can discern the beginning of two Asias – whilst most women continue to live traditional lives, there is also the emergence of millions of affluent Asian women as a force the world must reckon with. In China, women are participating in all aspects of Asian life in unprecedented ways, as workers and consumers, constituting 25 per cent of all entrepreneurs. Asian women are increasingly achieving educational parity with their male counterparts and their participation in the workforce compares favourably with US and European figures. In this sense, in this part of the world, where women's lives have been 'role bound' for centuries, new opportunities are emerging. These options are the culmination of many processes, including labour shortages, full employment, education and 'gender-blind' technology. As one Singapore newspaper has commented: 'in only one generation some Asian countries have created a corps of career women who are upwardly mobile, globally minded, affluent and ambitious. That is no mean feat.'[8]

Despite this success story, women in Asia are also paid less than men and are subject to the same glass ceiling as those in the West, whilst their emerging economic success has yet to be echoed in social and political change. Women in Asia are, however, being politicized and there are a number of examples of women organizing to demand change. The achievements of women in Asia should not be denied and, indeed, it should be recognized that change has occurred against a social and cultural tradition in which women have been home-makers and in which 'males are strong and aggressive (yang), women passive and nurturing (yin)'.[9] Women are clearly challenging the old male power bases and, as Naisbitt concludes in his analysis: 'Asia in the twenty-first century will find leadership in its own women and they, in turn, will find partnership with women in the West, moving towards global critical mass.'[10]

Shifting household patterns

The lessening of women's dependency on men is accelerating as a result of a number of forces, including industrialization, urbanization, widening marital choices, premarital sex, contraception, abortion, divorce and women's employment. These are trends that are by no means confined to the West as Asia is beginning to experience the same changes in response to the incorporation of women into the workforce. As a result, 'traditional' family life has been affected and perhaps one of the most fundamental challenges facing the West (although less so elsewhere) is the rise of the household and the parallel decline of the family. Certainly the family is changing out of all recognition in the Western industrialized world. The term 'family' refers to two or more persons related by blood, marriage or adoption, who reside together – a pattern which is declining in the West as the number of 'households' rises. A household may include unmarried couples, family friends, roommates or

> Today less than 4 per cent of American families consist of what was once considered the 'traditional' arrangement of a bread-winning husband and a home-making wife.

boarders. At the same time, there has been a sharp decline in the nuclear family, an increase in 'blended' families and in single-parent families. In the USA 30 per cent of all households are non-family households, outnumbering the once traditional family (married couples with children) and 33 per cent of children are now born outside marriage. In addition, divorce is rising throughout the Western world and changing working patterns have also changed the concepts of what constitutes a traditional family.

Social and demographic change is also enhancing the importance of the singles markets and single males are expected to become an especially important target market in the future. The number of UK single-person households is predicted by Mintel to rise by 11 per cent during 1998–2002. In the UK the number of people marrying each year has been declining for over twenty years, from seventeen per 1000 in 1975 to eleven per 1000 in 1995. Even in 1990 in the USA 23 million or 22 per cent of home-makers were adult males and that number is rising as household size shrinks and the number of one-person households increases. Male home-makers are typically found in non-family type situations as single persons – over 80 per cent have no children, compared to 58 per cent of women. They are also concentrated in the under thirty-five and over sixty-five age groups. Thus, with many people postponing marriage and children, there has been a decline in the nuclear family and a concomitant growth in leisure and tourism products aimed at childless couples – in the UK 66 per cent of current holiday trips do not involve children.

Ad highlight 5.1   Britain's diverse leisure consumer: today's pub drinker

Constantly evolving fashions and trends, along with persuasive advertising, has meant that pub-goers in the UK have more sophisticated tastes and higher expectations of their social environment than ever before. Today's consumer could be anything from seventeen to thirty-five years old, black, white, gay, straight, female or male. He or she has become accustomed to outlets that offer service, atmosphere and value for money. Although the traditional British pub for all still exists, the habits and consumption patterns of British drinkers are increasingly more complex. There are four main types of venue that dominate the sector: the working-man's bar, the local for regulars and families, the night-out pub such as the Rat and Carrot chain, and the trendy preclubbing bar. Moreover, despite the plethora of theme bars, there seems increasing demand for them. Research by Mintel shows that 50 per cent of consumers want to see more theming, 42 per cent were interested in sports-related theme bars, twenty to twenty-four-year-olds were particularly interested in film themes, whilst music-related bars were also very popular.

Pubs are no longer male preserves, and operators are designing female-friendly bars to attract women who have more money to spend than ever before and who are putting off having children until later in life. As well as a pleasant atmosphere, food also keeps consumers on the premises for longer and brings extra revenue into a market already worth £4.8 billion a year. The gay consumer is also a highly lucrative market for Britain's pubs – the gay scene is full of potential customers who enjoy a drink and night out, who have disposable incomes and are not constrained by the time or financial commitments of a nuclear family. Pub and bar designers are creating unusual and fun surroundings – such as at the Freedom Bar in Soho with its Jelly Baby adorned walls – in a bid to attract these profitable consumers.

If the twenty-first century might be the era of the household, in an age of increasing sexual liberalization, it might also see the wider recognition of 'alternative' lifestyles. In particular, homosexuality has been openly recognized and, although it has not necessarily been accompanied by general acceptance, many marketers have begun to see the economic power of the so-called 'pink pound'. A number of commentators have recognized that the gay and lesbian tourism market includes a potentially large market of upscale, well-educated professionals. In the USA almost 40 per cent of unmarried partners of homosexuals hold a college degree, compared to 18 per cent of unmarried heterosexual partners and 13 per cent of married spouses. While 86 per cent of the partners of gay men and 81 per cent of the partners of gay women have an above high school education, only 74 per cent of heterosexual unmarried partners have a high school diploma. Readers of US gay magazines also have an upscale profile – 7 per cent have doctoral degrees, compared to less than 1 per cent of the general US population and their median household income in the 1990s was $51 300 compared to a national average of $30 050. It is widely reported that gay male couples have higher average incomes and more free time than heterosexuals, since fewer than 5 per cent of gay male couples have children, although it is important to remember that such surveys may create a simplistic view of the homosexual market – as in other market segments, there are upscale and downscale gays (see Case study 5.1).

The ageing 'West' and youthful 'East'

Of all the demographic changes shaping the world, perhaps the greatest single demographic event is the age split between the developed world, which will continue to age, and the developing world which is younger than ever. An ageing population is not an exclusively developed-country phenomenon, since in China, with its one child per couple policy, over a fifth of the population will be over sixty by 2030, and Thailand, Taiwan and South Korea face a similar situation. Nevertheless, it is the case that more than half the world's population today is under twenty years of age and 90 per cent of them live in the poorer developing world. In contrast, an 'age wave' is sweeping the developed world's population, a process that has been well documented elsewhere. Increased life expectancy as a result of improving medical care and rising standards of living is shifting the age profile ever upwards. In the developed world people live, on average, twenty-five years longer than they did at the beginning of the twentieth century, and at the start of the twenty-first century about one in seven people in North America and Japan are aged over sixty-four. In the USA the number of elderly consumers is growing twice as fast as the overall population – over 30 million Americans, or 12 per cent of the population, are over sixty-five and that number will double in the next fifty years. At the same time, falling birth rates mean that in most Western European countries the birth rate is too low to sustain even the current population and by 2020 half of Europe's adult population will be over fifty years old.

This 'greying' trend is well established in the tourism marketing literature but, as we shall see in Chapter 6, advertisers do not always know how to craft messages which appeal to this segment. In particular, many of the images are very stereotypical and often alienating. The main target of the marketers are the baby boomers rather than the over-fifties generation, who, together with younger consumers – generation X – are frequently overlooked. Recently the definition of the X generation was convincingly shifted by Karen Ritchie to the birth years 1961–81, in other words, those aged between twenty and thirty-nine in 2000. Interestingly, thus defined, they have actually out-numbered boomers in the USA since 1980, accounting for 78.4 million, or 30 per cent, of the population by the mid-1990s, whilst boomers accounted for a smaller, if noisier, 26 per cent.

These demographic statistics should be of interest to all tourism and leisure marketers, particularly with the arrival of 'new' tourism generating regions with younger age profiles, notably in Asia. A new, younger leisure and travel consumer group may emerge, defined by globalization, itself accelerated by technological innovation and the emergence of a global youth culture. These Xers, 'marketing savvy, cost-conscious and skeptical of "hype" '[11] are the first generation to have grown up in a media, information-saturated environment – an environment of sophisticated advertising, video games and personal computers, in which television has been a mature medium throughout. They have been described as having a healthy scepticism of advertising and marketing, and it will be interesting to watch how advertisers frame their appeals to these consumers in the future.

The global, competitive economy

Perhaps the most critical of all the forces which are shaping advertising is the accelerating trend towards global competition and the opportunities and threats this creates. For many large tourism and leisure organizations, today's advertising objectives, budgets and messages are formulated with world (or at least regional) markets in mind, media are transnational and ad agencies have offices across continents. In addition to globalization, widespread government deregulation has also led to an increased emphasis on advertising and promotion in general. Deregulation in the US airline industry, for instance, has created many mergers and fewer competitors. This has resulted in increased advertising expenditures and a multitude of promotions such as frequent-flyer schemes.

Faster communications, increasing travel opportunities, falling trade barriers, multicultural societies and a convergence of tastes and preferences are all contributing to the creation of a 'smaller' world, although there are also counter-forces to globalization, particularly the rise in nationalism and anti-immigration policies. This move towards globalization is an influential contemporary trend, one that will create both threats and opportunities for tourism and leisure marketers. The new world economy is increasingly dominated by intercompany trade and person-to-person communications, and multinational companies and not states are the dominant power players. Indeed, there are a number of significant threats to the power of nation states, both from within and without, including pressures for internal devolution and decentral-ization as communities, countries and regions seek more self-determination.

The internationalization of business

Of all the challenges facing today's managers, 75 per cent identify globalization as their greatest concern. Indeed, such is the acceleration of internationalization that some commentators have written about the end of nations and the rise of markets. Many companies now have subregional marketing programmes, with, for instance, a South-East Asian, a European and a North American policy, whilst many international non-commercial organizations (such as Greenpeace) are also gaining unprecedented prominence. Investment flows between countries have risen dramatically since the mid-1990s as trade barriers have come down and more and more businesses have developed global portfolios to reduce vulnerability to regional downturns; for instance, whilst Europe suffered a major recession for most of the 1990s, many of the Asian economies experienced a boom before the financial meltdown towards the end of the decade.

Globally focused Western companies (particularly those providing consumer goods and services) have enjoyed greater profitability than those who concentrated on domestic markets. Although many Western companies have been *multinational* since the 1960s, few have been truly *global* companies. This involves companies taking advantage of global markets and their economies of scale, *and* being culturally representative of the markets in which the companies operate. At the end of the 1990s British Airways responded to this rise of a global economy, and the much heralded world traveller, by seeking to become the first truly global airline – although this policy seems to be under threat as a result of bad publicity at home and falling profits (see Case study 8.1). However, just as there appears to be a recognition of the need for companies to be culturally representative, and thus more diverse, this itself is being challenged by the emergence of a parallel trend which suggests that what we are witnessing is a convergence of global tastes.

The convergence of tastes

For years marketers have sought to create homogeneous global brands so companies can achieve economies of scale in management and marketing and promotional costs. Now, despite the continuance of local, national and regional differences, there is growing evidence of the rise of cross-cultural tastes and the entertainment and software industries are already truly global industries. The USA has been the most successful society in packaging its culture and its brands for global consumption. It has been largely responsible for promoting a 'world snacking-culture' and Coca-Cola, McDonald's, Disney, Levi and Hollywood all promote individualism, free-market philosophies and a youth culture.

Entertainment and sport are the leading agents of this global culture, as satellite television channels and corporate sponsorship promote soccer to the USA and Asia, American football and baseball to Europe and golf to the world. As we have already noted, CNN is seen in almost 100 countries worldwide and MTV in over forty – providing global platforms for advertisers. As tastes converge, arguably we can see the emergence of cross-national consumers as in the case of the first Euro-consumers – the well educated, the young and the frequent business travellers. These consumers can be reached via advertising in English, the language which has the highest comprehension level in Europe, especially in northern Europe, averaging over 55 per cent comprehension in Scandinavia. This will be accelerated by the growing availability of pan-European media, such as the increasing penetration of cable and satellite channels across Europe, projected to reach almost 60 per cent of European households by 2003. As Glen Peters (amongst others) has suggested, what we are witnessing is a globalization of tastes and cultures, but one which, in the medium term, will still cater for more local preferences with a micro overlay of attention to local tastes and preferences.

The trend towards globalization and a convergence of global culture is not yet irreversible, however, and indeed the iconic representations of this phenomenon (largely drawn from American culture) have been attacked in countries as diverse as India and France. In India demonstrators have smashed Pepsi bottles and set fire to Kentucky Fried Chicken restaurants whilst in France some politicians believe that the French culture is under threat from Americanized, English-speaking cultural and ideological saturation. Steps have been taken to combat this with legislation requiring French radio stations to broadcast at least one-quarter of their daily output in the French language. At the beginning of the twenty-first century we are clearly witnessing a collision of tastes, but at this point it is difficult to predict whether it will result in the emergence of some composite and shared identity or whether we will see the powerful Americanized culture succeed at the expense of other, weaker ones. Despite the convergence of cultures, there remains a strong desire to retain difference in the face of homogeneity so that, even in the most multicultural, multiethnic societies, cultures and customs appear as a mosaic, with each contributing group retaining their individuality whilst contributing to a new, richer whole.

The rise of multicultural societies

Just as we are seeing trends running towards and against globalization, we are also seeing significant changes within nation states. Multiculturalism has arrived, particularly as previously powerless ethnic minorities grow in economic, cultural and political influence. To illustrate the implications for tourism and leisure advertising it is useful to focus on the world's most significant multicultural nation – the USA. The USA is one of the world's key tourism-generating countries and although most Americans do not travel beyond the borders of the USA, many take vacations within the States and their domestic tourism market is huge. A country of over 250 million, it is an extremely ethnically diverse market. The major racial subcultures in the USA are Caucasian (itself divided along ethnic and cultural lines), African-American, Hispanic-American, Asian-American and American-Indian. The USA is in the midst of one of its largest immigration waves in decades.

> Less than 10 per cent of US citizens have passports as they are not required for travel to Canada, Mexico or many Caribbean destinations.

At the beginning of the 1990s 8 per cent of the population, or 20 million people, were foreign born, about 25 per cent of them having arrived since 1985. Of these foreign-born persons, over 4 million were Mexican, by far the largest group, with Filipinos accounting for over 900 000. The foreign-born immigrants are making the greatest impact in California, where over 20 per cent of them live.

Differences in lifestyles, economic wealth, political influence and consumer spending patterns exist between all these groups, yet it was only during the 1990s that tourism marketers began to look beyond the needs of white tourists and, to date, the overwhelming majority of consumer research has focused on Caucasians. By far the largest and most politically powerful racial minority in the USA are African-Americans, currently accounting for 30 million people, or 12 per cent of the population, and spending an estimated $250 to $270 billion annually. Recognizing the power of this market, over $750 million is spent annually on advertising to African-Americans. The decision facing marketers is how best to reach this segment: whether to advertise in the general mass media on the assumption that African-Americans have the same consumption habits as Caucasians, or whether to advertise in media directed exclusively at African-Americans. While it remains true that a significant portion of the African-American population is not as well off economically as the white majority, there is an important and growing African-American middle class and it is these consumers who are beginning to attract the interest of the tourism marketers.

The fastest growing minority in the USA are the Asian-Americans yet despite their importance, there is little evidence of any tourism- or leisure-related market research focusing on this group, which at the beginning of the 1990s accounted for 7 million people or 3 per cent of the population. Of these approximately 23 per cent were Chinese, 19 per cent Filipino and 12 per cent Japanese. In fact, about 40 per cent of all new immigrants to the USA are currently from Asia and they are concentrated in a small number of large cities

– about 58 per cent of them living in Los Angeles, San Francisco and on Hawaii. By the early 1990s about 10 per cent of California's population was Asian and today approximately 5 million Asians live in the state. Asian-Americans are largely family oriented, highly industrious and strongly driven to achieve a middle-class lifestyle. They are also high academic achievers, more computer-literate than the average and many of them own businesses or are in managerial or professional occupations. In particular, the ethnic Chinese are extremely influential, both in the USA – where 1 million ethnic Chinese live in California alone (the largest Chinese community outside Asia) – and globally. The ethnic Chinese, from Taiwan to Los Angeles and London, are the most successful entrepreneurs in the world and Chinese around the globe hold between $2 trillion and $3 trillion in assets. These attributes make them an attractive market for an increasing number of marketers.

Although Asians are the fastest growing minority group, it is the Hispanic-Americans who will outnumber African-Americans as the largest minority group in the USA within twenty years. Representing about 9 per cent of the US population, or 22 million people, they are younger than other segments, have larger families and experienced approximately a 25 per cent growth rate in the decade 1990–2000. They are already the dominant minority in New York, Los Angeles, San Diego, Phoenix, San Francisco and Denver, and are the majority in San Antonio, Texas. The largest three Hispanic subcultural groups are Mexican-Americans (60 per cent of Hispanic-Americans), Puerto Ricans (12 per cent) and Cubans (5 per cent). They are heavily concentrated in certain geographical locations, with over 70 per cent living in California, Texas, New York and Florida.

Whilst the USA is the most influential multicultural and multiracial society, similar societies also exist in Canada, New Zealand, Australia and Europe. In the UK there are almost 300 000 black households in London alone, forming a significant market for products and services. In fact, the UK has a large ethnic minority population, numbering 3 million, or almost 6 per cent of the population. As in the USA, different ethnic communities vary in economic power and it is extremely misleading to speak of such minorities as a single, homogeneous category. One of the most striking facts is the growing success of the Indian community, which outperforms all other ethnic minorities (except the Chinese) on most counts and often the white ethnic majority as well. A profile is emerging of the UK's Indian community, which is increasingly self-employed, home-owning, privately educated and white-collar professional. For instance, 61 per cent of Indians between the ages of twenty-one and twenty-three have two A levels or their equivalent, compared with 43 per cent of whites and 40 per cent of blacks. The Afro-Caribbean UK communities have been rather less successful and only 40 per cent of black families are owner-occupiers compared with 83 per cent of Indian households. Multiculturalism holds many implications for tourism and leisure marketing and, as we can see from the USA, there are elements within ethnic minorities who have secured substantial economic power and will provide attractive opportunities for marketers.

Global income dynamics

Certainly the 1990s witnessed a widening gap between the rich and poor countries and between the 'haves' and 'have nots' within those countries, accelerated, in many ways, by technological advance and the transformation of work. In this age of information and knowledge, the speed with which countries, companies and individuals rise to the challenge of technology will depend on the time and money they are able and willing to invest in the training and infrastructure needed to compete in a reshaped marketplace. Those who do make effective use of the new channels of information will be able to access global markets, but those who do not are likely to become increasingly peripheralized. These new media channels are likely to be shaped in certain ways – thus the prevalence of the English language in media and communications as the language of business is likely to give English-speakers a competitive advantage. Sixty per cent of radio broadcasts, 70 per cent of addressed mail, 85 per cent of international telephone calls and 80 per cent of *all* data transfers are currently in English.

If three main segments of world markets are identified – industrialized countries, developing countries and less developed countries – the second segment accounts for 19 per cent of the world's population and 32 per cent of the world's income. Since these countries are outpacing the industrialized countries, they offer very attractive business prospects, both in terms of generating tourists and offering a higher-quality destination product. Yet, despite this, there is no doubt that the rich are becoming richer and the poor relatively poorer. For example, the gap between Africa's rich and relatively stable countries and its poor and sometimes collapsing countries is growing every year. Certainly, technological change has the potential to empower the world's disadvantaged countries and the new global infrastructure – the information superhighway – could erase the differences between centre and peripheries. People living in hitherto isolated rural communities will be able to compete with urban workers via the information superhighway. To date, however, its liberating potential has yet to be widely felt and the information society is a reality for a very small portion of the globe – North America accounts for over 70 per cent of the world's Internet connections (and traffic along America's electronic superhighways triples each year), Europe for just under 25 per cent, and Australia and Japan for 4 per cent – the rest of the world accounts for only 1 per cent of connections.

The world is not simply being divided into rich and poor countries: within rich nations the gulf between the 'haves' and the 'have-nots' is widening. In the 1990s many of the world's developed countries saw recession, falling property and real estate values, and high unemployment rates with associated insecurity about jobs and the future. Clearly the free-spending leisure future predicted in the early 1980s has not materialized and many countries have seen the gap between their rich and poor widen. Of all the Group of Seven (G7) economies, only Germany has seen this gap narrow (as a result of more prosperity in the former East Germany), whilst in the USA and the UK the gap has widened considerably. The distribution of income has become increasingly unequal in recent years in the UK – the bottom 40 per cent of households accounted for only 12 per cent of expenditure in 1995, half that of 1979. Moreover, basic essentials account for over a half of their spending, whilst the richest households devote almost 60 per cent of their spending to luxuries, especially travel and leisure activities. In the USA almost 25 per cent of children under the age of six live below the poverty line and the figures for ethnic minority groups are startling. Fifty per cent of all African-American children and 40 per cent of all Latino children under six live in poverty.

As *between* countries, one of the main divisions *within* such societies in the future may well be related to access to technology. Some adults are technophobic but those with access to the information society are still more likely to be drawn from the higher socioeconomic groups in the developed world. Relatively more people in the Third World are likely to be excluded from the Internet (at present over 80 per cent of the world's population has no access to a telephone, let alone a computer) – a medium which has huge potential for tourism and leisure advertising. Yet, despite such inequality, emergent markets will become very powerful in the next decades. Today's international tourists from Asia and the Pacific account for only 11 per cent of the potential markets in those countries, whilst in Africa the figure is 5 per cent, but by 2020 the World Tourism Organization predicts that China will be the world's fourth biggest tourism-generating country (as well as the world's top destination) – see Table 5.3.

Emerging tourism and leisure markets

Despite the recent financial turmoil in South-East Asia, one of the regions which is likely to emerge as a major market in the twenty-first century is Asia.

Table 5.3   Countries predicted to be the top tourism generators in 2020

Country	Tourist arrivals generated world-wide (to nearest million)	Market share %
1 Germany	164	10.2
2 Japan	142	8.8
3 United States	123	7.7
4 China	100	6.2
5 UK	96	6.0
6 France	38	2.3
7 Netherlands	35	2.2
8 Canada	31	2.0
9 Russian Federation	31	1.9
10 Italy	30	1.9

Source: figures from the World Tourism Organization, 1998.

The Asian continent from India to Japan, from the old USSR to Indonesia, now accounts for 3 billion people, half of the world's population, half of whom are under twenty-five. By the middle of the first decade of the twenty-first century, more than half a billion of these Asian households will be 'middle class' – a market the size of the USA and Europe combined. Asia is dominated by countries that are not only demographically, but also politically, young since for most of these states the Cold War was a period of post-colonization with independence only being achieved in the 1940s and 1950s. The last bastions of colonialism have been breached with Hong Kong's 1997 return to China, and with Macau returning to China in 2000, every inch of territory in Asia will be controlled by Asians for the first time in 400 years.

Whilst the region as a whole holds such potential, the patterns across Asia are changing. The old Asia was divided by culture, language, politics, religion and geography, but the new Asia (created by economic integration, technology, travel and mobility of people) will look like one coherent region. Many Asians, especially the Chinese, are characterized by hard work, thrift and education orientation, and the new economies of Asia have created millions of entrepreneurs. Clearly, Asia is reaching high levels of sophistication – as Naisbitt comments about perceptions of the East: 'Many in the West who have never been to Asia, or who have not been there for a long time, have the mindset that Asia is a fairly primitive place, when, for example, Asia's best hotels and best airlines are better than those in the West.'[12] In recent years advertising has penetrated more than ever before into China, home to over a billion consumers. Foreign brands are increasingly available in many of China's cities, they are advertised on Chinese television and Chinese consumers are eager to purchase well-known brands, fuelling a business boom.

The news is not all good, however, as the 'financial tsunami' that struck Asia in July 1997 was the most powerful economic blow since the Great Depression of the 1930s.[13] In its wake hundreds of billions of dollars were sucked out of emerging markets, from Thailand and Russia to Brazil. The economic meltdown caused major problems in the Asian advertising industry with downsizing and revenue problems and whilst before the crisis there were waiting lists for companies wanting to book television advertising space, now the television channels are short of advertisers and have had to rely on public service advertising for revenue. In Indonesia television ad revenue dropped by as much as 60 per cent year on year in the crisis, and during 1998 Japan's economy deteriorated and growth rates in China slowed from 9 to 7 per cent. The impact of the Asian crisis was felt across the globe: in 1998 Las Vegas casinos' baccarat takings were down between 10 and 30 per cent because of the fewer numbers of Asian high-rollers; Coca-Cola's falling Asian sales reduced the company's profits by almost a tenth; McDonald's closed fourteen restaurants in Indonesia because of sluggish local sales; and EastmanKodak saw sales in the Asia-Pacific region decline by between 20 and 25 per cent.[14]

In terms of its impact on tourism, the crisis had serious repercussions and Japan – for so long a driver of growth because of its official policy to encourage travel abroad – suffered dramatically. Hong Kong, Thailand, the Philippines and Malaysia also suffered and the USA, UK and Australia, recipients of large numbers of Asian tourists, also experienced fallout from the downturn. Towards the end of 1999 political instability in Jakarta and Indonesia's activities in East Timor saw foreign tourist arrivals on Bali collapse – with hotel occupancy levels at between 20 and 40 per cent in August 1999 – a stark contrast to the same month in 1997 when they were at 100 per cent. At the same time, however, stock markets and growth rates around the world have begun to recover, although the world economy remains fragile and the recovery has been patchy – South Korea, Singapore, Taiwan, the Philippines and Thailand did particularly well in 1999 – not so Hong Kong and Indonesia.[15] Other emerging markets have also recovered faster than anticipated – Brazil's economy contracted by only 1 per cent in 1999, whilst Russia's output fell by 2 per cent, rather than the predicted 7 per cent. Yet at the start of the next century the global economy is certainly weaker than before the 1997 crisis, much of Latin America remains in recession, whilst a growing list of countries (including Ecuador, Russia and Pakistan) are close to defaulting on tens of billions of dollars owed to private lenders.[16]

| Ad highlight 5.2 | **Eastern European advertising expands** |

One of the fastest emerging markets for advertisers is Eastern Europe, particularly in Poland where in 1998 the advertising 'cake' grew by a massive 65 per cent to 5.3 billion zlotys, or US$1.3 billion (Table 5.4), as a result of Polish economic growth, a rise in consumer purchasing power, the introduction of a whole range of new products and brands, and a large media expansion, especially in television. Closely following is the Czech Republic where ad spend increased by 11 per cent in 1998, tripling the total ad spend figure over the period 1995–8 – again heavily driven by a huge expansion in television advertising which grew by almost 60 per cent in that time.

Table 5.4   Advertising spend in selected Eastern European countries, 1998

Country	Poland	Czech Republic	Slovenia	Slovak Republic
Total ad spend (US$ millions)	1.300	390	135	159
Television	59%	40%	42%	49%
Print	27%	42%	44%	36%
Radio	7%	8%	9%	8%
Other	7%	10%	5%	8%

Source: *Golden Drum*. Official magazine of the New European Advertising Festival, Slovenia, September 1999 (13), 4.

Other important emerging markets are the countries of South America and South Africa. Whilst millions of South Africans remain in desperate poverty (10 million live in shacks and black unemployment levels are at 42 per cent, compared with those for whites at 4 per cent), modernization is progressing at a rapid pace – 35 per cent of homes now have a telephone, up by a quarter since 1994. Yet the economy is only growing slowly: in 1998 the rand lost 16 per cent of its value as a result of the world economic crisis and the country remains heavily dependent on foreign investment. Despite such problems, South Africa has huge potential – both as a tourism destination and as a leisure market, with most of the population under twenty years of age, it is a young and growing consumer market. Moreover, many tourism experts have dubbed the country 'the new California' as a result of its climate, wine industry and tourism potential – reflected in a massive expansion in its luxury hotels and tourism infrastructure – such as the five-star Blue Train which rivals the

Orient Express in luxury and reputation. South America at the start of the twenty-first century is also experiencing little economic growth, currency pressures and little foreign investment. Its short-term future could in fact be even bleaker if the world economy continues to slow and exports (mainly oil, minerals and grains) command even lower prices. Also significant will be the performance of the Brazilian economy, which accounts for 45 per cent of the region's GDP.[17]

Consumer power, ethics and responsibilities

In view of trends such as the polarization of global wealth, researchers are increasingly finding that consumers want businesses to act responsibly and respectfully towards them – if they feel that is not the case they are voting with their dollars and choosing to spend their money elsewhere. Yet consumers face increasingly hard choices – the average UK supermarket stocks 60 000 brands so the 'ethical' consumer is confronted by an array of products – information overload is acute and consumers are increasingly confused by the plethora of choices and are 'turned off' when they see cynical marketing practices. Whilst time is precious to many people, so too is quality and service, and consumer power is increasingly evident. Recently, consumer fears over genetically modified foods in Europe have forced giant companies to reconsider their strategies, and pressure over cheap child labour has created negative publicity for firms ranging from Nike to Gilbert (manufacturers of the rugby balls used in the 1999 Rugby World Cup). Other examples of such consumer pressure include anti-smoking campaigners attacking British American Tobacco over the company's sponsorship of the Indian cricket team, claiming that the company's aim was to promote the brand amongst children.

Ad highlight 5.3   What happens when the agency gets it wrong?

The advertising industry is in a state of alarm after a US judge decided to allow a $10 million lawsuit to proceed against the New York office of Saatchi & Saatchi, the UK's most famous agency, for making a bad television ad which the client later claimed was forced on them. If the case succeeds and establishes a precedent, multinational agencies could find themselves in court in the USA every time a client dislikes the campaign. Whilst complaints about ads are common, this time the agency really got it wrong. After one showing during the Superbowl when 175 million households watched the ad, the client, Just for Feet (an American chain of sports shoe stores), saw its share price drop from $19 to $6 and lost the cost of the

$7 million campaign in a massive sales fall. Described by *Advertising Age* as 'neo-colonialist . . . culturally imperialist, and probably racist' the ad was designed to illustrate how far the stores will go to supply sports shoes. It opens with a barefoot, black runner being followed by white men in a military-style vehicle. When they catch him, they force a pair of Nikes on his feet and he scrambles away trying to shake the shoes off. Whatever the ethics or taste of this particular campaign, the case has worried agencies as it may result in only safe, bland campaigns which will not land agencies in lawsuits.

Source: Paul McCann (1999). US client sues Saatchi over 'disastrous' ad. *Independent*, 16 June.

Most countries have a regulatory framework for advertising and in a global marketplace this creates considerable challenges for advertisers who may be trying to create multinational campaigns – in Sweden, for example, advertising to children is highly controlled and tough laws prevent advertising from targeting children. Ads during children's programmes are banned altogether, and in the evening ads must not be designed to appeal to children under twelve – those who contravene the rules can face fines of £250 000. In the UK all television commercials have to be checked at key stages of their development by the Broadcast Advertising Clearance Centre – a body employed by the broadcasting companies to ensure viewers are not offended or misled by the advertising.

The legal barriers to cross-border campaigns are considerable and anyone looking at a checklist of what is possible within the European Union will see a range of possibilities – from almost all ticks in the UK column to nearly all crosses in the German column, with every combination in between. One company very committed to the idea of using its local offices as sources of specialist knowledge in such matters is British Airways – it has a strong global brand identity which it combines with local input to reflect different conditions. Not all pitfalls are legal ones, of course – often they are cultural. Even for a package tour company promoting holiday travel, for instance, images of women in bikinis cannot be shown in Israel and whilst in many countries birds are seen as symbols of freedom and often used by airline advertising, in southern Europe their use is not recommended as they are seen as threatening and represent the darker side of life.[18]

Whilst there are many legal and regulatory constraints to consider, there is a significant move towards liberalization in some sectors. In Chapter 9 we will see how the UK bingo industry benefited from a recent change in the laws governing advertising and, similarly, in the USA in 1999 the Supreme Court's decision to overturn a ban on broadcast advertising depicting casino gambling saw agencies and casinos rethink their media plans. Whilst all the major casinos had been advertising before the ruling, they could not show or mention the actual gaming in radio or television spots (casinos owned by Native Americans were exempt from the ban), so it is likely to impact more on ad content than volume. However, those cities where there is a very competitive casino scene – such as in New Orleans – will see a massive increase in casino advertising.[19]

Ad highlight 5.4	Potato chips leave bad taste

In 1999 the agency Leo Burnett had to pull a controversial campaign in Thailand which featured Adolf Hitler munching on a certain brand of potato chips and being transformed into 'a good person'. He was seen stripping off his Nazi uniform whilst dancing and prancing around. Meanwhile the Nazi swastika morphs into the logo of the Thai potato chip brand. The agency initially argued that the ad was intended to be funny and that it had received a warm response in early testing. However, following a growing number of complaints, including the Israeli embassy's condemnation of the ad as disgusting, the agency pulled the ad from television and Bangkok's tuk-tuks, saying it regretted any offence.

Source: CNBC Asia (1999). *Storyboard.*

Chapter summary

This chapter has provided a selective overview of the global trends which tourism and leisure organizations, marketers and advertising agencies will have to address in the early twenty-first century. We have tried to identify key trends, although recognizing that there are equally significant trends which space has not allowed us to consider – notably the rise of movements dedicated to promoting environmental concerns. Those we have identified include:

- the changing nature of work and leisure in a world shaped by globalization and technological innovation
- the increasing opportunities for women as leisure consumers and entrepreneurs
- the global age dynamics of the ageing West and the youthful East and South
- the global income dynamics of rich and poor consumers and countries

- the impact of emergent markets in Asia, Latin America and Eastern Europe offering both new business opportunities and new sources of competition
- the increasing demands of more 'ethical' consumers.

Massive global changes are occurring and a key theme in this discussion has been the increasing fragmentation of lifestyles, which means that advertisers will have to become more niche-orientated and targeted in their media selections, yet simultaneously more 'inclusive' in their ad appeals. Far from the start of this millennium heralding an age of leisure, contemporary consumers now lead more harried, fragmented and less predictable lives than ever before. With the growth in dual-income households in many post-industrial countries, both women and men have less discretionary time and the result has been a significant increase in time control and a demand for flexible services. In addition, Western markets are becoming more middle aged, middle class and discriminating, and many societies are increasingly diverse and multicultural, creating new challenges for tourism and leisure marketers. Those tourism and leisure organizations that recognize and cater for these new markets may well outperform their less innovative rivals and, in one scenario, perhaps the future will hold more acceptance for currently often marginalized groups like gay and lesbian travellers and better provision for previously neglected groups like consumers with special needs.

Case study 5.1

The gay and lesbian leisure consumer

The true size and value of the gay and lesbian market is impossible to ascertain, since few reliable statistics exist on sexual orientation. There are also practical problems in obtaining data about marginalized activities, and research on gay and lesbian consumers often relies on 'anecdotal' evidence, informal 'interviews' and participation observation. It does seem, however, that the market is expanding as a result of greater social permissiveness, growing out of the gay pride movement. The market is also increasing as more and more homosexuals (especially lesbian women) openly develop families, conceive or adopt children and build 'quasi-traditional' families. It also appears that gays and lesbians are more likely than average to buy discretionary items, such as consumer goods, health club membership and, especially, travel products. As a result, in the late 1990s, this high income, free-spending gay and lesbian community became the latest target of mainstream marketers as a viable consumer group.

In the USA, with 10 per cent or 18.5 million of the population estimated to be homosexual, companies have been targeting the gay community for some time. Absolut Vodka has been targeting gay consumers since 1979 and sponsors of the IV Gay Games in New York included AT&T, Continental Airlines and Miller Beer. Although gay tourists who attend events like the Gay Games are a minority of consumers, they tend to be 'hyperconsumers' who not only consume more, but also influence the purchases of their gay and straight friends and colleagues, thus providing vital word of mouth endorsements for products, brands and companies. Gays are also extremely brand loyal to gay-friendly companies and once gay and lesbian consumers see that a company is reaching out to them they are much more loyal to those efforts than straight consumers – sponsorship of gay events makes them much more likely to buy the sponsor's products or services. Absolut Vodka, for instance, has built so strong a franchise among gays and lesbians that the brand is automatically acknowledged as a sponsor or presence at major events, even when it is not there. Such marketing can have a lasting impact, providing the effort made is sustained.

In terms of travel options, there are, of course, many homophobic destinations – including Brazil, Colombia, Mexico, Nicaragua, Peru, Iran, Afghanistan and Bavaria – places which do not welcome openly gay tourists. Even destinations which may on the surface seem liberal, such as popular Caribbean resorts, may not welcome gay tourists. Despite such problems it seems that gay couples travel more frequently than their straight counterparts and gays have been described as the closest thing to a recession-proof market. The New York Gay and Lesbian Visitor Center, for instance, estimates that gay couples average 4.5 trips a year compared to a 'straight' average of one trip. Similarly, whilst in the early 1990s most cruise companies experienced a downturn, RSVP, a US gay travel company, reported consecutive annual increases in cruise business. It is important to point out that any figures on the size of the gay tourism market cannot take into account travel purchases made by gays through mainstream operators or booked directly, yet despite this, its recent growth is nevertheless unmistakable. The Tourism Industry Intelligence suggests that an estimated 5 million to 25 million gay men and lesbians spend more than US$10 billion on travel products each year. The International Gay Travel Association (IGTA) is a global umbrella organization of over 1500 gay and gay-friendly organizations, 900 of them based in the USA. The IGTA estimates that its members book over a billion dollars in airline tickets alone, with almost US$450 million expenditure in other travel purchases.

Gay destinations are not confined to the USA, and London, Blackpool and Brighton in the UK and Ibiza, Mykonos and Gran Canaria in the Mediterranean are all popular with gay travellers. In the UK the fastest emerging destination is Manchester. The city has a significant gay and lesbian population that has created a more gay-friendly atmosphere and provided the infrastructure for the Phoenix Mall Project, whose businesses include many types of gay-friendly stores and services, as well as bars and restaurants. This, Europe's first gay shopping mall, opened in early December 1996 in an old textile mill in the city's Gay Village. The largest and most significant gay event for Manchester, however, is its annual Mardi Gras, previously known as the 'Carnival of Fun', 'Tickled Pink' and the 'Absolutely Fabulous Event of the Year'. The event began as a small-scale one-day street market in 1991 and has grown into a four-day festival attracting 60 000 to 80 000 person visits. The festival currently includes carnival parades, fireworks displays, a funfair, street markets, discos and a candle vigil commemorating those who have died of Aids. The event organizers are the Village Charity, a group which sees it not only as a fun festival but also as a vehicle to break down barriers, to raise HIV and Aids awareness and, most importantly, to raise funds for its Aids projects and charities in north-west England.

Source: Annette Pritchard, Nigel J. Morgan, Diane Sedgley and Andrew Jenkins (1998). Reaching out to the gay tourist. *Tourism Management*, **19** (3), June, 273–82.

Notes

1 Luis Moutinho (1998). Paper presented at the third international tourism conference in Benidorm.
2 Robert P. Libbon (1999). How far do people travel on summer vacation? *American Demographics*, August.
3 Ibid.
4 Lisa Goff (1999). Don't miss the bus! *American Demographics*, August, 49–54.

5 L. Beeghley (1996). *What Does Your Wife Do? Gender and the Transformation of Family Life.* Westview Press.

6 Carol Nelson (1994). *How to Market to Women.* Visible Ink, p. 33.

7 John Naisbitt (1997). *Megatrends Asia: The Eight Asian Megatrends that Are Changing the World.* Nicholas Brealey, p. 281.

8 Quoted by Naisbitt, *Megatrends Asia*, p. 219.

9 Naisbitt, *Megatrends Asia*, p. 227.

10 Ibid.

11 Karen Ritchie (1995). *Marketing to Generation X.* Lexington Books, p. 165.

12 Naisbitt, *Megatrends Asia*, p. 3.

13 Adam Zagorin (1999). Shoring up the house. *Time*, 4 October, 60–4.

14 *Time*, 14 September 1998.

15 Zagorin, Shoring up the house.

16 Ibid.

17 The Economist (1999). *The World in 2000.* The Economist Publications, p. 83.

18 David Reed (1998). Across the divide. *Marketing Week*, 10 September, 45–51.

19 Rachel X. Weissman (1999). Money to Burn. *American Demographics*, August.

Further reading

Beeghley, L. (1996). *What Does Your Wife Do? Gender and the Transformation of Family Life.* Westview Press.

Bradshaw, Y. W. and Wallace, M. (1996). *Global Inequalities.* Pine Forge Press.

Carey, S. and Gountas, Y. (1999). Changing attitudes to 'mass tourism' products: the UK outbound market perspective. *Journal of Vacation Marketing*, **6** (1), 69–75.

Economist (The) (1999). *The World in 2000.* The Economist Publications.

Goff, L. (1999). Don't miss the bus! *American Demographics*, August, 49–54.

Horner, S. and Swarbrooke, J. (1996). *Marketing Tourism, Hospitality and Leisure in Europe.* International Thomson Business.

Lazer, W. (1997). *Handbook of Demographics for Marketing and Advertising: New Trends in the US Marketplace.* Lexington Books.

Mintel International Group Limited (1995). Targeting the rich and poor. *Executive Summary*, 17 July.

de Mooij, M. (1998). *Global Marketing and Advertising: Understanding Cultural Paradoxes*. Sage.

Morgan, N. J. and Pritchard, A. (1998). *Tourism Promotion and Power: Creating Images, Creating Identities*. John Wiley, ch. 5.

Mulryan, D. (1995). Reaching the Gay Market. *American Demographics*, **17**, May, 46–8.

Naisbitt, J. (1997). *Megatrends Asia: The Eight Asian Megatrends that are Changing the World*. Nicholas Brealey.

Nelson, C. (1994). *How to Market to Women*. Visible Ink.

Peters, G. (1996). *Beyond the Next Wave: Imagining the Next Generation of Customers*. Pitman.

Quelch, J. A. and Bartlett, C. A. (1999). *Global Marketing Management*. 4th edn. Addison Wesley Longman.

Ritchie, K. (1995). *Marketing to Generation X*. Lexington Books.

Swarbrooke, J. and Horner, S. (1999). *Consumer Behaviour in Tourism*. Butterworth-Heinemann.

Usunier, J.-C. (1996). *Marketing across Cultures*. 2nd edn. Prentice Hall.

6

Matching markets and advertising appeals

Chapter overview

Chapter 5 outlined the dynamic marketing environment, focusing on the ways in which today's tourism and leisure market is becoming ever more fragmented and its consumers more difficult to reach. Segmentation (as part of a strategy of target marketing) holds the key to cost-effective and efficient ad spend. However, at the beginning of the twenty-first century variables such as sociodemographics cannot be used in isolation to predict consumer behaviour, and advertisers have to seek to combine these more traditional forms of segmentation with techniques such as psychographics and lifestyle attributes. This chapter examines the importance of matching ad appeals to the target audience. It focuses on the difficulty of crafting appeals based on demographic characteristics and discusses the challenges of targeting groups such as older and younger consumers, women and gay and lesbian consumers. The chapter ends with a discussion of the importance of recognizing difference in today's global, multicultural marketplace. Key themes reviewed are:

- the role of segmentation in tourism and leisure advertising
- demographic appeals – appealing to families, older and younger consumers
- advertising to women
- does sex still sell?
- recognizing difference in the marketplace
- meeting the challenge of global and multicultural advertising.

Introduction

Before the widespread adoption of modern marketing concepts, the main way of reaching consumers was by mass or undifferentiated marketing, that is, offering the same product and marketing mix to all consumers. If all consumers were the same, with similar needs, wants, desires and profiles, then mass marketing would be the logical strategy. It would also cost less because there would be one strategy, one standardized product and one promotional message. Some companies still employ an undifferentiated strategy very effectively, but for most tourism and leisure products there are major drawbacks in this approach. When trying to sell the same product with a single strategy, the marketer must portray the product as providing a common benefit which, whilst not alienating anyone, may have the affect of appealing to no one in particular.

Segmentation is very useful to marketers as, if used effectively, it can aid planning and lead to increased sales, lower costs and higher profitability. In particular, it helps marketers identify 'prospects', get closer to their customers and allows them to call smaller groups of consumers their own. Marketers have discovered that the higher costs of segmentation (such as consumer research and differentiated promotional campaigns) are more than recouped by reduced wastage and increased sales, and in most cases consumers accept the higher costs for products since segmentation provides a greater choice of products that are more closely matched to their needs. In general terms, segmentation can be said to have two main purposes: to identify gaps in the market and to position a brand in relation to its competitors. Advertising and media messages both play

> Segmentation can also be used to identify the most appropriate media in which to advertise, since almost all media (from satellite television channels to magazines and newspapers) use segmentation research to determine their audience profiles.

major roles in positioning tourism and leisure products, and advertising can even expand markets by tailoring messages to new consumer segments, as in the case of Torbay (see Chapter 9).

The appeal of segmentation

Such has been the fragmentation of tourism and leisure products and markets in recent decades that it is becoming increasingly important for marketing professionals to be able to select the most strategically important segments and design brands, products, packages, communications and marketing strategies which are specifically tailored for them. However, segmentation operates within a dynamic environment in which social, economic, political and technological changes are constantly affecting consumers and their buying behaviour – their needs, wants and abilities to pay. As we have seen, the 1990s was the decade of micro-segmentation, it saw a polarization between the haves and have nots and witnessed the emergence of new markets in Asia, Eastern Europe and the Americas, and the rise of new consumer groups in the West – particularly women and gay and lesbian consumers. Direct marketing technology became important, as did interactive approaches and now, at the beginning of the 2000s, there is a shift in marketing emphasis from seeking 'market share' to 'customer share' in which the importance of matching advertising appeals to a tightly defined target audience is paramount.

The term 'market segmentation' first appeared in the late 1950s and since then, has received considerable attention in the marketing literature with Theodore Levitt once famously proclaiming that 'If you ain't segmenting, you ain't marketing'.[1] Segmentation has been variously defined, although most of the definitions are very similar. Perhaps one of the most succinct is that of Chisnall who defines it as a tool which:

> assists marketing management by dividing total market demand into relatively homogeneous sectors that are identified by certain character-istics. Market strategy can then be devised which will be related to the needs of these market segments. There may be changes in styling . . . or in advertising appeals.[2]

Market segmentation is widely considered to be at the very heart of marketing. It recognizes that consumers differ in their tastes, needs, lifestyles and motivations, and maximizes market demand by directing marketing efforts at what are regarded as economically significant groups of consumers.

Segmentation enables marketers to avoid direct competition in an increasingly crowded marketplace because it provides opportunities to differentially distinguish their particular product, perhaps on the basis of price, more often through styling and promotional appeal. It is important to remember that market segmentation is not itself a marketing strategy, but merely the first phase in a three-step strategy. After segmenting the market into relatively homogeneous sectors, the marketer then has to identify one or more segments to target with a particular product or promotional appeal. The final phase is to position the product so that the target market regards it as satisfying its needs better than other offerings. Positioning and repositioning can be accomplished through any aspect of the marketing mix, but particularly through branding – the focus of Part Three of this book. Although market segmentation is a key element in marketing theory, many practitioners are dissatisfied with segmentation as a concept and it is often difficult to apply to certain markets. It is important to recognize that segmentation is a creative tool that should not be regarded as a one-off exercise but rather should be seen as a process that needs constant monitoring and re-evaluation. Segmentation will be different for every situation; there is no single right way of segmenting a market and most markets can be segmented in many different ways. Nevertheless segmentation is a very widespread tool and there are high stakes: marketers receive plaudits for getting it right, but they can severely damage a brand when they get it wrong.

Developments in segmentation

Some twenty years ago, segmentation meant demographic and geodemographic analysis, then the addition of psychographics into the geodemographic equation enabled segmentation techniques to reflect consumer attitudes and motivations (Case study 6.1 discusses a more unusual approach to segmentation, based on astrology!). In the 1990s the buzzword was 'micro-marketing', a strategy whereby advertisers try to focus only on those consumers who are interested in their product. The drive towards micro-marketing has been fuelled by technological innovation, particularly the increased availability of point-of-purchase information which allows greater customer profiling. Indeed, advertisers are ever more able to locate and communicate with customers and potential customers, and to tailor both the ad message and medium so that people outside the target market are excluded – saving expenditure and increasing effectiveness. However, despite such progress in database management, it is important to remember that marketers should not allow themselves to be overly seduced by the attractions of one-to-one marketing – after all, people tend to be as much alike as they are different and the costs of one-to-one marketing are frequently prohibitive for many tourism and leisure organizations.

Currently segmentation theories are realigning to take account of retention marketing, greater computer power and more recognition of the demands placed on that increasingly rare commodity – brand managers' time. Retention marketing focuses on working out who are the most profitable and important customers for the company – exploring their purchases and analysing how they differ amongst themselves. This data is then used to target like-minded customers who fall outside the existing customer base. Advances in computer database management have also enabled marketers to start with the essential building blocks of markets – the individual consumer – and then search for similarities and contrasts amongst them. Some commentators would argue that even this is a simplistic approach to consumer analysis, and that advertisers should target 'consumption events' rather than people. As the same person's behaviour differs depending on their circumstances at any given time, the purchase under consideration and the rationale behind this choice (relaxation, indulgence, stress relief or whatever), it follows that different ad appeals will engage them at different times.

Demographic advertising appeals

The decisions as to which segments are deemed viable are also influenced by the perceptions and priorities of the marketers themselves. This emerges clearly when age is used as a criterion for segmentation. Since the 1950s it has been the baby boom generation that has dominated marketing in the post-industrial world, both because of their numbers and because most senior marketers are themselves drawn from their ranks. Marketers have learned 'that the sheer weight of this birth cohort we call Baby Boomers was often the difference between success and failure for a marketing concept'.[3] The boomer generation has been the dominant postwar target audience: as 'kids' in the 1950s; as 'teens' in the 1960s; as 'hippies' in the 1970s; as 'yuppies' in the 1980s; and as 'woopies' in the 1990s. As boomers have aged, so too have marketing targets crept towards older age groups. In the early 1980s, the main audience were eighteen to thirty-four-year-olds, in the mid-1990s it became the twenty-five to fifty-four age group – now it is slowly moving towards the third age consumer, although, as we will see, the older age groups have often been misunderstood by advertisers.

Ad highlight 6.1	Center Parcs' ads find the target

One company which has carefully segmented the market and targeted the ABC1 consumer with children, extended families and young peer group consumers is Center Parcs. Wholly owned by Scottish and Newcastle since 1991, Center Parcs is a Dutch concept which set a new trend for the holiday centre market – beginning with the first Dutch site in 1967. The centres are designed to complement the ecology of the local environment and offer a range of leisure facilities and activities that place emphasis on a healthy lifestyle. Since introducing the first forest holiday village at Sherwood Forest in the UK in 1987, Center Parcs now has three centres in the country with a 12 per cent share of the holiday centre market. It has a 90 per cent year-round occupancy rate and over 60 per cent of its business comes from repeat customers.[4] Whilst it has segmented the market, the company's advertising is also increasingly emotionally based and its 1998/9 campaign appealed to people who are feeling jaded or stressed. The range of ads included a print ad which pictures a traffic jam, with the strapline 'your nearest Center Parc is as far away from here as you can get', followed by the line 'To escape, call now for a free brochure'. A second execution features a picture of a tranquil forest, with sunlight filtering through the trees and a single rabbit on the road, with the words 'rush hour', underneath which is the line 'Experience a different way of life at Center Parcs'.

Appealing to older leisure consumers

As we outlined in Chapter 5, one of the biggest marketing challenges in the 2000s will be the record numbers of senior citizens in most of the developed countries of the world, which are the main tourism-generating countries. Older people and their needs will become increasingly important to post-industrial societies in ways they have never been before, in any place or time. This mature and informed segment is already impacting on tourism and leisure, demanding high standards and value for money. Healthier than ever before, keen to travel and willing to experiment – with new foods and cultures – these are consumers with huge potential. They are today's discerning leisure travellers equipped with the necessary time and financial resources, and whilst the propensity to travel amongst the older age groups has traditionally been relatively low, today's seniors are changing that. Older consumers are cash-, time- and experience-rich but cynical about marketing – surveys show that they are rather less positive about advertising than younger people.

Although the population is ageing, recent research suggests that older consumers are enjoying increasingly active lifestyles. First, the Henley Centre (which provides UK leisure research information) argues that older people are taking part in more and more active leisure pursuits, such as swimming and aerobics. Second, the Henley Centre suggests that they are also increasingly participating in more upmarket activities such as concert and theatre visits and short breaks, and leading the shift towards eating out at restaurants. Finally, although one might expect this market segment to be among the more conservative in terms of participation in traditional activities, they are turning to more varied leisure activities, becoming less homogeneous and less easy for marketers to reach. This evidence complements other recent research that indicates that in many areas the behaviour and attitudes of older and younger people are becoming similar as older people are becoming younger in outlook. Leisure activity patterns, including going to the cinema, participating in do-it-yourself activities, eating out and watching videos, are blurring across age groups. Described as a process of 'attitudinal convergence', it seems reasonable to suggest that this will also be translated into a convergence in tourism consumer behaviour patterns. This will be accentuated as today's cohort of third age consumers, aged forty-five to fifty-nine, move into the older age groups, giving a further boost to the leisure profiles of tomorrow's older consumers. Clearly, marketers are going to have to become adept at providing a range of active and varied leisure services and appeals to people in their fifties, sixties and seventies, previously marketed only to those under fifty years of age, particularly as this market will enjoy twenty to thirty years of post-working life (Table 6.1).[5]

> Half of US individuals sixty-five-plus take vacations and their vacation expenditure is above average, whilst the European Travel Intelligence Centre predicts that at the beginning of the 2000s total travel by Europe's seniors will be 80 per cent above the 1990 level.[6]

Such lifestyles are the result of the relatively high disposable incomes enjoyed by many older people who are benefiting both from earned income and inheritance. For instance, the forty-five to fifty-nine-year-old age group have amongst the highest levels of earned income of any UK group and, despite the

Table 6.1 What's in and what's out in the US fifty-plus market

Arrivals	*Departures*
Red wine	Soda
Adventure travel	Bus tours
E-mail	'Why don't the kids ever write?'
E-commerce	Malls
Four-door sedans	Sports-utility vehicles
Personal fitness trainers	Exercise videos
Working as long as you want	The silver ceiling
Ageing	Immaturity

Source: Trend central. *American Demographics*, August 1999, p. 27.

exaggerated importance of inherited income and decreasing mortgage costs, the real value of inheritance rose by 50 per cent during the 1990s – over half of this going to the forty-five to fifty-nine age group. However, it is not simply the sheer numbers and the disposable income of consumers in the older age groups which attracts the interest of tourism and leisure advertisers – it is also the lifestyles of many of them. It has been said that the 'third age' in particular is as much 'an aspirational category as a new demographic classification, as much a personal affair as a collective circumstance'.[7] The relevance of this senior segment to tourism and leisure marketers is therefore of crucial significance. Even if its full potential is only partially realized, it implies the existence of a large cohort of older consumers with very different lifestyles and consumption habits from older people in the past.

Targeting this market should be of critical importance to tourism and leisure professionals since, for the first time, it has the ability to make choices about consumption habits and, unconstrained by the responsibilities of employment and childcare, this group are increasingly able to enjoy leisure and travel – today almost half of the people taking winter holidays in the UK are aged between forty-five and sixty-five. Targeting older consumers may be a profitable activity, but it is not easy, since they are by no means a homogeneous group. In fact, it has been suggested that older consumers are more diverse in interests, opinions and actions than any other segment of the adult population. Moreover, age is not necessarily a major determinant of how older consumers respond to marketing activities and, recognizing that they are not a uniform group, marketers have tried to segment these consumers. Whilst one basis is simply age, splitting them into the young-old (sixty-five to seventy-four), the old (seventy-five to eighty-four) and the old-old (eighty-five and over), a more useful method is on the basis of motivations and quality of life orientation, splitting them between the 'new-age old' and the 'traditional older consumer'.

The travel industry is increasingly aware of the lucrative nature of this emerging segment and the British industry has a long history of targeting seniors, particularly through Saga – the best known operator in this sector. The growth in the seniors' vacation market has stimulated all the major UK operators (First Choice, Cosmos, Sunworld, etc.) to develop packages specifically designed to attract them. Nevertheless, despite the appearance of some of these newer packages, there remains considerable doubt whether most of these marketers really understand older consumers and recent research suggests that many marketers and market researchers still ignore older people.[8] It seems that many marketers regard them as only responsive to price inducements or as too old to be persuaded to try new products and/or switch brands. It has also been argued that many marketers take the view that it is young consumers who are the future for their products. Perhaps not surprisingly, at the same time, many older people are rejecting much of the advertising for the products they are likely to buy as the implicit assumption in the style and tone of the messages underlines the fact that they are not the primary market. 'Lifestyle' advertising is seen as patronizing in tone and content, and stereotypical seniors in casting and styling are particularly disliked – unfortunately, this is how they often appear in tourism brochures.

Certainly there is overwhelming evidence that older people do not think of themselves as old and should not be treated as such. Moreover, research consistently suggests that people's perceptions of their ages are more important in determining behaviour than their chronological ages, since people may have a number of cognitive or perceived ages. Older consumers perceive themselves to be younger than their chronological age on four perceived age dimensions: feel age (how old they feel), look age (how old they look), do age (how involved they are in activities favoured by a specific age group) and interest age (how similar their interests are to a specific age group). Whilst many older consumers have relatively younger cognitive or ideal ages than their chronological ages, recent research supports the argument that marketers regard these consumers as uniformly 'old'. In particular, many seniors do not feel that the tourism industry caters for them, tending to reject the brochures aimed at them in favour of making their own arrangements. Interestingly many (including a high number of people over seventy) do not feel that they are old enough to go on the typical seniors' package holidays.[9]

In contrast, those tourism and leisure advertisers who have thought about this market have done very well. For instance, Nike has run specific campaigns targeting older consumers who account for a considerable proportion of its sales. Its advertising avoids the subject of age, focusing instead on attitude, and a number of older people were chosen as role models for the brand because they symbolized its attitude and personality. Ads have featured a fifty-year-old marathon-winning female jogger and an eighty-year-old who runs 6 miles a day. The ads attracted a lot of publicity because of this seemingly 'shocking' juxtaposition of young, aggressive, fashion-conscious product images and older people. In the same way, Levi's has also run advertising featuring older models in 'the original jeans, the original wearers' campaign – ads aimed at a younger audience but symbolizing the brand values. The executions included one featuring a rodeo cowboy, which had copy reading: 'Alonzo, eighty-six, is the oldest surviving black cowboy in Colorado and still rides in the rodeo. He wears Levi's Type 11 Jacket.'

Appealing to the younger leisure consumer

If they have a long way to go to successfully appeal to older people, the tourism and leisure industries also need to become a lot smarter in targeting younger people (Case study 6.2). For the foreseeable future, the number of sixteen to twenty-four-year-olds in the UK is likely to remain stable, although the under sixteens will decline. But across Europe, of the European Union's (EU's) 360 million people, nearly a quarter are between fifteen and twenty-nine years old.[10] Yet, these younger consumers have little sense of shared identity and, despite marketers' repeated efforts at labelling, today's youth is a highly fragmented market in which simple demographic segmentation by age seems a clumsy tool. Generation X, a term coined by American novelist, Douglas Coupland in 1991, 'has evolved into little more than a convenient term for twentysomething'.[11] The experience of young people across Europe is one of individuality, splintered by the fractured early twenty-first-century politics of gender, race, religion and sexual preference.

At the same time, the tourism industry has forecast an increased demand for specialist, youth-oriented leisure holidays which are more likely to be taken with friends than with families. Young people are likely increasingly to demand customized holidays that are flexible, specialized and tailored. This demand could suffer, however, if the travel industry fails to get to grips with young consumers' changing lifestyles, their holiday preferences, their decisions and their attitudes towards travel advertising. Whilst the rewards for those who can secure brand loyalty through effective marketing communications stand to be great, brand loyalty demands effective understanding and market segmentation is an obvious tool to achieve this, although it must take a more sophisticated approach than one based purely on age. A good example of a more effective approach is that of Carat Insight, one of the UK's largest advertising companies, who have classified

Table 6.2   British holiday-makers (aged fifteen to twenty-one) attitude groups

Activity seekers	Like activity-driven British holidays and make their own travel arrangements;
British seasiders	Go back time and again to familiar British beach resorts;
Backpackers	Like holidays off the beaten track and go for longer periods; prefer to take non-package holidays;
Sun, sea and sangria seekers	Want to eat, drink and lie in the sun, and always use a travel agent to book their package holiday.

fifteen to twenty-four-year-olds into four relatively homogeneous travel groups: activity seekers, British seasiders, backpackers, and sun, sea and sangria seekers (Table 6.2).[12]

Once these consumer groupings have been established, then their media habits can be analysed so that advertising can more easily target them. It seems as though, in this case, backpackers watch little television and are more likely to read quality newspapers like the *Financial Times*, the *Guardian* and the *Observer*. They are also heavy users of the London Underground and are the most likely group of all to have access to the Internet at home. Sun, sea and sangria seekers are much more likely to watch television and be commercial radio listeners. Young women's magazine readership (*19*, *Looks*, *Minx*, etc.) is high, and both men and women in this group are regular cinema-goers. They also love, watch and read everything to do with travel and their top four television programmes are; *Wish You Were Here*, *The Real Holiday Show*, *Holiday* and *Airline*. The behaviour, interests and media habits of just these two groups are diverse enough to warrant equally diverse communication strategies, yet to date the UK travel industry has tended to rely on a single communications strategy when appealing to such fifteen to twenty-four-year-olds. It seems as though, if it is to survive and prosper, it needs to quickly come to terms with consumers' increasingly diverse lifestyles and attitudes, and to recognize that old demographic and geodemographic segmentation analyses are no longer enough.[13]

Appealing to today's echo boomers

Whilst older consumers are extremely significant for the future of many tourism and leisure products, as the demographic surge known as the 'echo boom' (people now aged five to twenty-two) works its way through the populations of Europe and America, advertisers are also targeting children as never before. Currently there are 31 million children in the USA between the ages of twelve and nineteen – projected to grow to 34 million by 2010, this is the largest teen population in US history. They are prized as a much coveted consumer group, both for their own spending power and for their influence on parental purchases – growing to the extent that US teens now direct a fifth of weekly household expenditure. Not only are children consumers today, but they also have a lifetime of spending ahead of them. In the early 1990s US children aged four to twelve were spending over $10 billion a year, teenagers about $100 billion and all children were indirectly influencing another $150 billion in family spending; figures which have since soared – in 1998 $168 billion was spent by or on youths aged four to nineteen in the USA.[14]

Realizing this potential, some firms deploy the ultimate marketing tool to influence adult purchases – the nagging child. Hyatt Hotels Corporation collects names and addresses of children who stay at its resorts and mails them promotion brochures, indirectly influencing their parents.[15] The London Transport Museum is just one of a host of British tourism and leisure organizations which are increasingly targeting children for their own spending power. Its latest poster, commissioned in conjunction with the toy store, Hamleys, the London Aquarium and listings magazine *Time Out? Kids Out*, is a modified underground map designed to appeal to children with fun facts about well-known landmarks such as Nelson's Column and Buckingham Palace. Other UK organizations to target children include Shrewsbury Tourism, which designed a separate brochure for young visitors in 2000 as a marketing tool to break into the family market. Similarly, the children's theme park – Legoland Windsor – has teamed up with snack manufacturer, Golden Vale, to target six to twelve-year-olds via promotions, supported by television ads, in children's press and marketing activity at the theme park.[16]

According to Wendy Liebmann of WSL Strategic Retail in New York, advertisers must adjust their pitches to the very different lifestyles, attitudes and spending patterns of today's kids and teens. Studies suggest that, in contrast to previous generations, echo boomers are engaged and enthusiastic. 'Bred' on the Web, these kids are informed and marketing-shrewd but not sceptical. When they buy, they do not just wander into the nearest store – they research product and brand names on the Internet, exchange e-mails in on-line chat groups, plot the best, 'hottest' buys and perhaps even buy on-line. They also have family responsibilities (many have two working parents), value family, relationships and work success – more than half of fourteen to twenty-four-year-olds in the USA have some kind of a job – and they have high aspirations for the future. So generation Y scores high on optimism, maturity and independence. If advertisers talk down to them and do not treat these experienced, informed consumers with respect, they will lose them – as Myra Stark, Saatchi & Saatchi's director of knowledge management, says: 'Advertise up'.[17]

Ad highlight 6.2 | Reebok's ad speaks to today's echo boomers

Reebok's film short 'Doppelganger', starring the Manchester United and Wales soccer star Ryan Giggs and his clone, is an example of a very creative and successful ad concept primarily aimed at the advertising-aware younger consumer, although the beautifully drawn cartoon characters (in the style of Tim Burton's *A Nightmare Before Christmas*) appeal to both young and old. The ad is concerned to tell a story about a hero and his legendary weapon – in this case Ryan Giggs and his Reebok football boots – rather than to obviously sell the product itself. In the ad, the 'United' player (Giggs) has been cloned by the fictional villain, 'City' chairman Reginald Backhander. The real Giggs is locked in a laboratory, the clone signs for City and makes his debut against United. In true heroic fashion, the real Giggs escapes just in time and manages to save the day for United – but only because Peter Schmeichel (the then United goalkeeper) recognizes him by his Reebok boots. The ad is a very convincing way of saying that Giggs is dedicated to his Reeboks – after all, he must be to allow himself to be caricatured by a puppet and this is something of which the younger consumer is aware. This ad recognizes the level of consumer sophistication in this market and, because it does not obviously sell the product, it works on a number of different levels in a highly effective and entertaining way.

Advertising to women

As we saw in Chapter 5, the last two decades have seen a sea change in the position of women in many countries, so that today their significance as consumers and managers is huge – in the USA five out of six households are managed by a woman and 60 per cent of women work, so they are massively impacting on consumer and business purchasing.[18] In the USA, women are starting businesses at twice the rate of men, whilst in the former East Germany, one of the unforeseen results of the collapse of communism was the numbers of women starting new companies. Between the fall of the Berlin Wall and the mid-1990s over 150 000 businesses were set up by women, employing a million people and contributing $15 billion to Germany's GDP. In the UK there are 3.5 million women in managerial and professional positions and, as we have seen, women are highly significant as entrepreneurs in Asia. In the USA, almost 40 per cent of the 35 million-plus business travellers are women – a multibillion dollar market segment in which women spend well over $10 billion on business travel each year.

> Today's woman is more time-constrained than ever. Women's leisure hours lag behind men's, with women in two-income households being squeezed the most. In 1975 45 per cent of women said they had enough leisure time, by 1990 the figure had fallen to 35 per cent and it is still falling – today it is women who are more likely to say that they need a holiday to get away from it all.[19]

Yet, despite the economic power of women and their potential as tourism and leisure consumers, even in the mid-1990s, a survey by Grey Advertising found that the majority of women felt that advertising failed to 'respect them in terms of the people they really are'.[20] Advertising does not necessarily need to adopt a separate set of standards when targeting women, but advertisers must recognize them as a viable target group and, far from offending them, must become more sensitive in the way they craft their advertising appeals. Even thinking of aiming marketing communications at *women* (51 per cent of the world's population) is facile, since it fails to recognize the diversity and the fragmentation of women's lifestyles. There is no such thing as a typical woman (just as there is no typical man), so advertisers must appear to be talking to an individual woman and seek to build rapport, rather than appear condescending (Ad highlight 6.3).

Ad highlight 6.3   Sexist airline advertising and the female business traveller

It seems that despite the importance of women as business and leisure passengers, airlines are, in fact, failing to appeal to women. A British Airways survey in 1990 revealed that sex discrimination was an issue among almost half of all the women interviewed. Many respondents thought that men were served first and were 'pampered' by stewardesses, whilst they were often treated as partners of men – even those simply seated next to them! A decade later, it seems as if the airlines are still failing to address these issues – in fact, if anything, women's discontent has grown. 'Attitude, attitude, attitude. Stewardesses virtually ignore or are rude to business-women travellers.'[21] In addition to the in-flight service, the airline's advertising has also attracted substantial criticism.

Airlines spend more on advertising than any other sector of the travel industry. Between June 1995 and June 1996 airlines spent £62.4 million on advertising compared with the £18.8 million spent by hotels and £43.2 million by travel agents. However, a recent study suggests that half of their customers – women – continue to feel that airline advertising is consistently out of touch with today's woman. Old stereotypes, particularly those of submissive and smiling Asian female cabin crew, were criticized by women who thought that the promise of being 'pampered by Oriental handmaidens' was not only demeaning to women but also very distasteful. One campaign that generated much controversy was the 1996 BA campaign. These executions included a series of print and poster ads where the heads of male business travellers were superimposed on to the bodies of young children and infants, sometimes in 'Oedipal' situations. The advertisements were designed to appeal to the business traveller by conveying the message that the new business-class seats on BA flights were 'as embracing as a mother's arms' but some women were uncomfortable with these ads which they thought appealed to the 'little boy' in men.

Another ad campaign that was strongly disliked was one for Air France. Here an ad focused on a beautiful woman, with the endline: 'The chances of her being seated next to you are so slim that you won't regret the extra space between our seats'. This provoked universal condemnation amongst the women in the study, with participants commenting that it conveys 'all the wrong sentiments', that it was in 'bad taste' and that it appealed to 'some men harbouring [ideas] about travelling in the mile high club and all that sort of thing'. Perhaps the strongest view expressed by those women who travelled frequently on business with airlines was that there was a real need for women to be recognized as legitimate business travellers in airline advertising: 'I want to feel recognized as an equal in the workforce and as a customer . . . advertisements don't need to have pictures of women, but they should somehow recognize women have just as serious travel requirements as men . . . certainly less of this underlying sexist rubbish.'

Source: Sheena Westwood, Nigel Morgan and Annette Pritchard (2000). Gender-blind marketing: business women and airlines. *Tourism Management*, **21** (1), August 353–62.

Does sex still sell today?

Sex appeal has long been used by advertisers to grab attention – with so many 'wallpaper' ads, sex can shock, create humour and arrest attention. It is still one of the strongest tools advertising has to draw consumers into the ad, although ads which use sex today, particularly in the UK, are more witty and tend to be more thoughtful than those of the 1980s and early 1990s. The simplistic sex approach of a generation ago is now a tired and potentially damaging approach for advertisers – a pretty woman in a bikini holding an automobile tyre has nothing to do with the product and consumers know that, so except for specifically sexually orientated items, marketers must use sexual appeals with care. A recent example of a UK car ad that used sex humorously was for Goodman's stereo equipment; it featured a couple making out in the backseat with the slogan 'Britain's second most popular in-car entertainment'. Similarly, an ad for Triumph bras – featuring a woman in red underwear with the slogan 'When I'm feeling naughty, I go bright red' – was a tongue-in-cheek concept which moved away from the sexist ads of the past since women enjoyed the joke as well. Sex is still used in very seductive ways, however, as typified by the Häagen Dazs ads (with slogans such as 'Lose control' and 'Intense fresh') which were based on research in which consumers linked sexuality with ice cream – ads which were later parodied by a Fosters lager ad in which a guy opens a fridge containing a tub of Häagen Dazs and cans of the lager, but he opts for a beer and leaves his girlfriend frustrated.

> Advertisers are realizing that women are now more confident and this is beginning to be reflected in ads – as in a recent one for a New York kick-boxing club which depicted a woman and carried the slogan, 'So much for that weaker sex thing'.

The vast majority of sexually aimed ads have historically featured conventionally attractive women, but advertising steadily increased its use of the male body as a sex object throughout the 1980s and 1990s – perhaps the most well-known in Britain being the Diet Coke 'Coffee-break' ad in which a male window-cleaner is seen stripping off outside an office full of female executives. Yet, to be effective, such ads also run the risk of being seen as tired if the same premise is overused. A 1997 ad for Lee Cooper jeans fell into this trap. The European jeans market is dominated by Levi's (as a result of their highly successful advertising campaigns of the 1980s and 1990s) and consequently their competitors have to take drastic action to get noticed. Some campaigns have been very imaginative – such as Wrangler's rodeo rider, rivets on the outside ad – many, however, have been poor imitations of Levi's own campaigns – like the Lee Cooper ad in which a male model goes through customs and is scanned by a female customs officer with a handheld metal detector. He is asked to strip, but stops short of taking off his jeans, hence the endline, 'Hard to be parted from'. The ad fails to engage the audience, it has become quite old-fashioned and the premise that these are just two ordinary people in an everyday situation is completely undermined by the fact that the central characters are obviously both models.

As we have seen above, by failing to recognize the specific needs of women in either their product attributes or their advertising, many tourism and leisure advertisers are ignoring consumer demands that women are a distinctive segment, requiring different marketing approaches and that, far from appealing to women, their advertising is sexist since it is designed primarily to appeal to a male audience. Whilst this is a real danger in crafting appeals based on sexy story lines, it is widely seen across tourism advertising and some of the most successful applications of such sexual imagery can be found in campaigns aimed at the younger market, especially young singles and couples (Ad highlight 6.4). The celebration of youth, beauty and sexual encounters lies at the core of much tourism marketing, and ads produced by the US all-inclusive couples-only resorts of Sandals, Couples and Hedonism II and by the UK tour operators Twenties, Priority and Club 18–30 are merely some of the most prominent examples of this.

| Ad highlight 6.4 | If you use sex, target your message |

In 1995 Club 18–30, the UK holiday company which targets the young package holidaymaker, having briefly experimented with marketing campaigns which focused on good clean fun, returned to its tried and tested and, above all, successful core campaign of 'sun, fun and sex'. Posters were launched carrying slogans such as 'Discover your erogenous zone', 'Summer of 69' and 'Girls, can we interest you in a package holiday?' with a picture of a man, described by *The Times* as wearing 'a well-padded pair of boxer shorts'. In addition to this high profile poster campaign (which was later extended to cinemas), the company continued the sexual theme in the pages of their brochures. Indeed, sexually-orientated marketing messages dominate the Club 18–30 brochures. The brochures are highly visual and photographs of attractive, fun-loving young tourists fill the brochure pages – nightclubbing, lounging by swimming pools, playing in the sea and, above all, enjoying the company of the opposite sex. The sheer dominance of these images – many of them taking up a whole page – creates the brochures' atmosphere of sexuality.

Club 18–30 ran an ad campaign known as 'Beaver España', developed by Saatchi & Saatchi. The campaign, which was based around sexual innuendo, provoked a huge reaction in the UK press and caused quite significant offence amongst groups outside the target market. The press coverage provided the campaigns with far more attention and publicity than the company expended on advertising. Indeed, Club 18–30 commented that: 'If we'd bought the same amount of space in the national press, or on the radio and TV, it would easily have cost twice as much.' Club 18–30 knew that the campaign would be controversial but decided to go with it, believing that the only people who would be offended by the ads would be from outside the target market – following the campaign, sales rose by over 30 per cent!

Source: Annette Pritchard and Nigel Morgan (1996). Sex still sells to generation X: promotional practice in the youth package tourism market. *Journal of Vacation Marketing* **(3)**, 1 December, 69–80.

Recognizing difference

Understanding difference is crucially important in today's environment of greater cultural diversity, individualism and fractured lifestyles. In this context, marketers have begun to target gays and lesbians with advertising which has gay or lesbian characters, appeals and subcultural themes. Some advertisers (such as Sony, Toyota, Microsoft, Levi's, American Express, Miller and Absolut) commonly use gay media, whilst others (such as IKEA, Calvin Klein, Kronenbourg and Benetton) have gone further and used homosexual imagery in advertising aimed at general audiences. This latter strategy of using homosexual images and themes, remains highly controversial even at the start of the twenty-first century. Studies in the mid-1990s suggested that just under 60 per cent of the American public believed that homosexuals are not good role models and in 1998 the UK fashion chain, Sisley, came into conflict with the Advertising Standards Authority (ASA) over a poster campaign showing two women in a clinch on the point of kissing. TDI, the company which sells advertising on buses and the London Underground, banned the entire campaign after taking advice from the ASA which decided that it would uphold any complaints received if the campaign went ahead.[22]

Given the diversity of attitudes towards homosexuality and the relatively small size of the gay and lesbian markets, companies have to weigh up the risks of extending ads aimed at the homosexual community to a wider audience.[23] Research suggests that heterosexuals' reaction to the portrayals of homosexuals in ads depends on their emotional and attitudinal response to homosexuality and, of course, consumers do not react to ads in the same way, but relate to ads on the basis of their ethnicity, gender, life themes or experiences. Developing an ad campaign that appeals simultaneously to multiple target markets remains a huge challenge for advertisers. Those who want to run an inclusive ad campaign should avoid stereotypical images and emphasize common needs and concerns, and certainly those who want to be seen as morally or socially responsible and inclusive may want to be perceived to be at the 'cutting edge' of social issues – a desire which may outweigh any negative aspects of such a campaign offending prejudiced consumers.

Some tourism and leisure marketers are recognizing the gay and lesbian market as a viable market segment – as highlighted in Chapter 5. This recognition demonstrates the economic power of gay and lesbian consumers and, as their profile is raised, gay and lesbian clubs, events and festivals are also becoming increasingly popular with straight consumers. Awareness of the gay and lesbian market is clearly already well established in the wider leisure sector, attracting the attentions not only of the media industries, but also the fashion, food and drinks industries, and now the gay and lesbian travel consumer is becoming a rapidly growing, if relatively recently recognized, segment of the tourism industry.[24] To cater for this lucrative segment there are a number of gay travel guides, including *Spartacus*, *Best*, *Gai Pied* and *Ferrari for Men* and an increasing number of specialist gay and lesbian travel companies. These include RSVP in the USA; Man Around, In Touch Holidays and Pride Travel in the UK, and Beach Boy Holidays, the Netherlands' largest gay-only travel company which advertises regularly in the *Gay Krant*, one of Europe's most popular gay newspapers.[25]

In addition to these specialist gay and lesbian companies, there are an increasing number of large-scale gay and lesbian-friendly companies, such as American Airlines, Qantas and Virgin Atlantic Airways, which are recognizing homosexual consumers by sponsoring events or advertising in gay media. Interestingly, Sandals Resorts which had ten clubs accepting only heterosexual couples, has now launched a Beaches brand that welcomes singles, families and any couples. The first opened in January 1997 in Negril, Jamaica, the second in April in the Turks and Caicos Islands, and the third in Barbados in 1998. 'We are a couple of years behind' in reaching out for a wider market said the company chairman, Gordon Stewart, who had been criticized for years for excluding gay travellers, singles and children.[26] The tourism industry does seem to be slowly recognizing and accepting gay and lesbian tourists, and whilst many hotels are still reluctant to accommodate promoters of lesbian events, as the wealth of the market becomes apparent that is changing and now annual events such as 'The Dinah Shore Weekend' – a huge lesbian party which runs alongside a US women's professional golf event – attract sponsors including American Airlines and Absolut Vodka.

Creating multicultural advertising

'Difference' is not confined to sexual orientation, and advertisers must be much more sensitive to the racial and ethnic diversity of markets, tailoring how they frame their advertising appeals and messages. Close to 33 per cent of the US population is non-white and by 2025 that percentage will have grown to 48 per cent. Moreover, today's fifteen to twenty-four-year-old Americans are the most racially mixed group the USA has ever seen and are 60 per cent more likely to be non-white than their grandparents. Some 14 per cent of US residents aged five and older speak a language other than English at home and several major cities and about 200 US counties have a 'minority majority', where their combined non-white and Hispanic populations exceed their non-Hispanic white population.[27] This means that diversity matters to the American consumer and it must therefore matter to advertisers. Furthermore, the influence of diversity goes much further than the sheer numbers of different groups since it is leading to increasing cultural crossovers. A typical example is in music. Whereas a few years ago, if an American teen was Hispanic he or she found a Spanish brand, now the attitude is, 'I like this music and I happen to be Hispanic'; similarly, white teens are increasingly identifying with other ethnic groups' music and culture – as the contemporary worldwide success of Hispanic and rap music demonstrates. In addition, ethnic diversity amongst young people at home (whether the USA or elsewhere) is reinforced by more and more active communication with youth around the world – once they start e-mailing someone in Kosovo or Queensland, young people begin thinking of themselves not in the context of their home town or country, but of the world. As a result, the message to advertisers is 'be inclusive'.[28]

The challenge facing the advertising industry in this context is that it is a predominantly white sector, yet how can these marketers readily understand ethnic minority self-image and satisfy non-white consumers as ethnicity is a variable which affects self-imaging and consumer behaviour, as with all other demographic variables. Unfortunately in the UK (for instance) largely white senior executives in client companies and at advertising agencies have failed to adopt a more ethnically diverse approach to marketing. There are far fewer black product, brand or marketing managers in Britain than there are black doctors, and at marketing director level their numbers are much sparser. If marketers have little insight into the attitudes, beliefs and lifestyles of ethnic groups outside their experience, then it should come as no surprise when their marketing fails to communicate effectively in an ethnically diverse society.

In the USA, however, there has been a growth in tourism products marketed specifically to a black audience, reflecting the emergence of African-Americans as the fastest growing segment of the US travel market, a trend which itself reveals the growing economic power of that particular community. In the late 1970s the African-American travel market was estimated to be worth just over $7 billion, but by the beginning of the 1990s this figure had grown to $25 billion. Ten million black Americans attend a historical or cultural event each year and the minority business meetings market is now worth an estimated $40 billion annually.[29] Moreover, research indicates that African-American convention delegates spend around one and a half times more per delegate per visit than their white counterparts and are much more likely to extend their business visit into a family short vacation. To cater for this lucrative segment marketers from Ontario to Philadelphia, Alabama and Louisiana are beginning to promote products specifically aimed at black tourists.[30] This recognition of the requirements of black travellers is still relatively new, however – as Tamara Real says, the Windsor Convention Bureau 'luckily discovered its gold mine just as interest in African-American travel opportunities was emerging'.[31] Considerations for those attempting to attract African-American travellers include attractions of specific interest to African-Americans and service provisions for black travellers (such as comfort and welcome afforded to black travellers and a sensitivity to their needs), as well as promotional material which reflects cultural diversity.[32]

Ad highlight 6.5   **'Musical chairs' a hit for BA's multicultural advertising**

BA's recent strategic image and sub-brand ad campaign (First Class, Club World and Concorde) is proving very successful. In a 1999 television ad campaign run in Asia (and globally) the airline successfully returned to its brand heart and tackled some of the Asian public's negative perceptions of BA. In fact, 'Musical chairs', one of the executions in Saatchi & Saatchi's BA Worldwide cabin service campaign, was voted *Adweek Asia*'s Ad of the Month. Set in a schoolroom, the ad opens with children from a range of races and ethnic groups playing a game of musical chairs. The camera focuses on a young boy who has missed out. He shrugs and the word 'philosopher' appears on screen. Next a boy wearing a reversed baseball cap pushes someone out of the way to get the last seat and he is labelled 'sportsman'. A young girl is the next to be featured – having missed out she stamps her feet and appears as 'actress'. A serious young boy in glasses looks on disapprovingly – a 'critic'. The remaining children circle the seats – one girl counts each one – she is destined to be a 'banker' – and a bespectacled young boy throws up his hands in a temper having lost his seat – a 'managing director'. Then a young girl looks up, smiles and gives him her seat. The words 'cabin crew' appear under her face. The voice-over tells the audience:

'Some people will naturally put themselves out for others. Which is why one day we hope Angie's favourite job will be with the world's favourite airline.'

The final shot is of Angie seated on a bench facing the camera whilst the game of musical chairs continues behind her. The line 'Angie's favourite airline' transforms into the endline 'The world's favourite airline – BA'. This ad is a soft sell proposition for an airline at a time when many are pushing their range of destinations and their cheap fares. As a brand promise it is entirely convincing since, whilst every airline can compete on destinations, it is not necessarily the only communication and if there is parity it is difficult to isolate as the key consumer benefit. By contrast, this ad is really promising the audiences that the airline is totally committed to their needs: it is the BA attitude which is convincing here, persuading the consumer that the airline is a good one to choose.

The challenge of global horizons

In parallel with the increasing diversity of the marketplace, today's advertising environment could be said to be characterized by two seemingly contradictory (but complementary) trends – the move towards globalization and the rise in highly tailored marketing, where advertisers reach out to smaller and smaller targets. Certainly advertising has changed dramatically over the last thirty years, becoming more truly international – particularly in travel, tourism and leisure. However, most international companies are not doing as well abroad as domestically, by any indicator – sales, customer retention or loyalty, brand tracking and profit margin – and this is true in 90 per cent of cases.[33] These figures suggest that most advertisers are not as successful as they could be in creating good, effective advertising outside their own domestic markets.

Some ads are aimed to be truly global (such as Nike's 1998 soccer World Cup and 1999 Rugby World Cup ads), others adapt a global brand to a region of the world (as in the Australian Tourism Commission's advertising, discussed in Chapter 9), whilst still others are purely local (as in the case of a BA 1999 UK ad, aimed solely at a domestic consumer, which based its appeal on the virtues of Britishness as discussed by an American business-man). The challenge for advertisers and agencies is deciding which strategy to choose and the critical factor must be to balance the consistency of the brand identity with the particular cultural similarities in different markets – often the choice depends on the product and the message in question. The nature and receptiveness of the target audience is also critical – whether they are ready to accept the message from Singapore to Malaysia or from Finland to Spain. Variations are inevitable in different countries – but there are also similarities. For instance, an advertiser may be able to appeal to a yuppie audience in Kuala Lumpur with a global message (because the aspirational similarities across groups with similar lifestyles outweigh the national or ethnic differences), but to reach a rural market in Malaysia the organization may have to adopt a much more local execution.

For advertisers whose markets are global, the advertising challenge is not to focus narrowly but to develop a consistent and cost-effective approach to reach audiences across the world. There are very few truly global brands – Coca-Cola being perhaps the most successful. Its advertising is much the same in over 170 countries – and whilst it does change the media and the delivery (by using local actors), the ads are very similar in content, cost-effectively reinforcing the company's international identity. Such international or global advertising requires total consistency, except in translation, as during the 1998 soccer World Cup when Nike ran a worldwide ad which showed Brazilian star Ronaldo (who was paid $1 million to wear Nike boots) playing a friendly game of football on the beach with Italy's Christian Vieri, Argentina's Hernan Crespo and Spain's Luis Enrique.[34] The same format was also used for ads featuring Ireland's Keith Wood and England's Lawrence Dallaglio run during the 1999 Rugby World Cup. Such universal campaigns are inflexible and restrictive, however, and for most companies, it is unlikely that they will ever come to dominate their advertising. In addition, one of the potential pitfalls with international advertising is its tendency to produce superficial ads which, by omitting any culturally and locally specific content, are offensive to no one but which few people really love or find engaging.

Underpinning the ability of international companies to succeed globally is one key issue: their capacity to negotiate language and culture. The main concern with international advertising today stems from the power of language because there have been some major advertising blunders in copy content and translation as a result of a lack of local knowledge. For instance, Japan's second largest tourist agency was mystified when it entered English-speaking markets and began receiving requests for unusual sex tours. The company – Kinki Nippon Tourist Company – soon changed its name. Similarly, Pepsi translated its slogan 'Come alive with Pepsi' into 'Bring your ancestors back from the dead' in Taiwan and there are many, many more equally disastrous examples. However, as Simon Anholt suggests in his *Another One Bites the Grass. Making Sense Out of International Advertising*, arguably the real problem with creating good international advertising lies not in the dangers of translation errors, but in the ability of advertisers and agencies to understand the role of cultural differences.[35]

The real key to good international advertising is to balance sensitivity to the culture of the brand with sensitivity to the local culture of the consumer, but the problem is that most companies are obsessed with consistency and marketing structures discourage recognition of difference. So, for instance, although a company may appoint a marketing director to oversee advertising in Europe, the Middle East and Africa, for most companies there is no way that the same advertising message will appeal to consumers in all those regions at the same time. Not surprisingly, many of these campaigns fail because advertisers assume a homogeneity that does not exist, a failure likely to be incredibly expensive in terms of both resources and brand value. Many international advertisers have certain rules that must be abided by in any campaign, regardless of country or culture, and for agencies' creative staff, adapting global campaigns for the local market are rarely exhilarating experiences since, more often than not, it involves merely translating advertising copy. (Case study 6.3 examines the success of an international agency that has adopted a much more local approach.) However, this tendency of international advertisers to develop global campaigns based on the experience of their own home markets – usually the USA or Japan – rarely results in memorable advertising in other markets.

The difficulty for many companies that demand advertising consistency to build global brands (and to save money) is that most good advertising is sharp and culturally distinct. With international advertising there are a limited number of international cultural symbols on which to draw – such as Wall Street yuppies, muscled men nursing babies, etc. – and most of these have become overused in ads. Moreover, since international advertising is highly hierarchical and all the key decisions are made at head office (in New York, London or Tokyo), there is little room for any local offices to tailor executions to reflect cultural individuality. For instance, whilst UK advertising is generally recognized as the creative market leader, Americans tend to regard British advertising as a bit too clever and Ad highlight 6.6 illustrates the hurdles negotiated by the UK office of an American corporation to adapt a global campaign.

| Ad highlight 6.6 | American Express 'Blue Monday': adapting a global campaign |

American Express traditionally has very consistent global campaigns and with the launch of the Blue American Express card, its advertising was intended to follow the same pattern – a global campaign developed and executed in New York. However, American Express in the UK saw an opportunity to put together a television campaign that specifically suited that market based around an alternative soundtrack. After a number of battles with the US head office, American Express UK gained approval for what became a highly effective campaign. Centred around a hugely successful anthemic pop song, New Order's 'Blue Monday', which had enjoyed UK chart success in three decades – the 1970s, 1980s and 1990s – the Blue American Express campaign was designed to appeal to precisely that market which had grown up with Blue Monday (successful, upwardly mobile, twenty- or thirty-somethings).

As an alternative to global advertising, many advertisers choose to maintain a brand's personality, but adapt the tone, style and delivery of the message in individual countries through multinational campaigns. Multinational advertising involves running different ads in various countries – currently it is difficult to estimate how much advertising is multinational, despite leading advertising commentators' views that all advertising will be multinational in the not too distant future. For instance, in contrast to Nike, in the 1998 soccer World Cup, Adidas, founded in the European environment of tribal football, was careful to focus its marketing and advertising locally. In France the slogan was 'La victoire est en nous' – 'Victory is within us'. In Germany, however, the television ads featured German players earnestly discussing the value of teamwork and tactics. Such campaigns are taking an increasing share of the multinational advertising market, grounded as they are in a 'think global, act local' philosophy.

> Globalization offers market opportunities as well as challenges and Sandals (85 per cent of whose business comes from North America) launched a year-long advertising and marketing campaign in 1999 to realize its potential in Europe.

Purely local campaigns, in contrast, take as their starting point the premise that people are all different. Those who favour such an approach argue that if advertising is to work, it needs to be grounded in a nation's culture, in its shared stock of knowledge and values, wit and idiosyncrasies – factors which consistent and universal campaigns are unable and unwilling to recognize. Such a philosophy requires different advertising in different countries – a factor that substantially increases a campaign's advertising production costs and that has certainly contributed to its decline in popularity. Champions of diverse advertising argue that the increasing standardization of multinational campaigns is destroying local effectiveness and is unnecessary because as long as a brand's positioning strategy remains consistent it is irrelevant if the advertisements themselves vary.

Whichever strategy an organization adopts – global, multinational or local – firsthand knowledge or feel for the chosen market is important. For instance, it is very difficult to make broad judgements about what works in the diverse Asian markets (see Case study 6.2). Some people in the region may look at an animal and see something sacred, others may see food. Thus, the idea of creating warmth in an ad through using an image of an animal may well be universal but the animal chosen will have to be culturally and socially specific. Similarly, the idea of advertising being able to tap into some universal language is probably misleading (even though sport and film both have many global dimensions) since, whilst many countries and cultures may share similar sensibilities in how they perceive advertising, there is never truly an ad which can reach everyone everywhere at once – whether within or across countries. Advertising is a complex phenomenon and some multinational campaigns are extremely successful, as are some local campaigns – there is no single right or easy answer. Simplicity, imagination and clarity are central features of cutting-edge advertising and many in the industry have struggled with whether an unconventional campaign can communicate with consumers who differ culturally, politically, economically and socially. However, all the focus on difference can lead to us losing sight of those things which bind us together and it is these shared aspects of the human condition that can form the centrepiece of leading global advertising – as John Hegarty has said:

> It strikes me as odd that if Hollywood manages to do it, and Picasso managed to do it, yet advertising can't. And yet advertising is the one industry which is supposed to bring people together. Physical borders are put up by people. The skill of great advertising is to come up with an idea that does cross borders . . . You should look for things that unite us, not divide us. Then you can create advertising that crosses borders.[36]

Chapter summary

One of the key tasks for advertisers is the importance of matching their advertising appeals and media choices to the chosen target audience. In this, effective market segmentation (as part of a strategy of target marketing) holds the key to cost-effective and efficient ad spend. However, in our highly fragmented world, variables such as sociodemographics will not work alone in predicting consumer behaviour and advertisers have to seek to combine these more traditional forms of segmentation with techniques such as psychographics and lifestyle attributes.

Whilst sociodemographics remains one of the most used methods of segmenting and targeting consumers, advertising appeals have to establish rapport and empathy with the consumer, whether they are older, younger, male, female, white, black, Asian, gay or straight. Two of the challenges facing advertisers are the need to be inclusive without alienating key groups and the drive to recognize diversity within and across countries without compromising core brand values and messages by a confusion of approaches.

Case study 6.1

Astrology as a segmentation criterion

It has been suggested that marketers may soon be enlisting stargazers as a legitimate weapon in their battle to conquer the consumer's heart and mind, and this may not be as far-fetched as it first sounds! Astrological experts are regularly consulted to help forecast the future of the Financial Times Stock Exchange index (FTSE) – apparently with similar success rates as orthodox analysts. Could astrology help in psychographic consumer profiling? Given that 50 per cent of British consumers read their horoscopes on a weekly basis, astrology could potentially provide considerable insight into consumer psychology and lifestyle. Dr Vince Mitchell from the Manchester School of Management has analysed the UK government's British General Household Survey and shown that astrology has 'a significant, and sometimes

Table 6.3 Shelley Von Strunckel's astrological guide to consumer behaviour

Aries	Impulsive and demanding, intolerant of shoddiness
Taurus	Thorough, dislikes change, hyperconscious of quality
Gemini	Fascinated by innovations and gadgets, not loyal consumers
Cancer	A creature of habit, threatened by change and likes products that give a feeling of safety or protection
Leo	Conscious of style over practicality, likes being catered to
Virgo	Practical, thrifty, but knows and appreciates quality, likes organized information
Libra	Refined taste, looks as important as function, likes to be won over
Scorpio	Investigates all products thoroughly but, once sold, a creature of habit
Sagittarius	Loves all things new and gimmicky, an impulse buyer with broad tastes, but considers brands unimportant
Capricorn	Will save for quality, knows and values brand names
Aquarius	The trendiest of all the signs, intrigued by innovation
Pisces	Idealistic, needs to be seduced by an appealing image

Copyright: Shelley Von Strunckel 1997
Source: Robert Dwek (1997). Starstruck marketing. *Business*, July/August.

predictable, effect on behaviour in the leisure, tobacco and drinks market'. For example:

- hyperactive Virgoans appear to have no time for gardening, television or listening to music
- inventive, intelligent and eccentric Aquarians shun mainstream activities in favour of more solitary pursuits like do-it-yourself
- Sagittarians (solitary, tactless and impulsive) prefer outdoor activities and like diversity.

Regardless of whether these are the results of 'genuine' astral influences or of 'self-attribution', this analysis can be of use to marketers (Table 6.3). By providing insight into a target audience it can help create more effective advertising as personality endorsements can be tailored to star signs – successful sportsmen and women to appeal to Arians; powerful and big-spending but socially minded high achievers for Leos; honest and fair-minded diplomats for Librans; rugged, independent outdoor 'Marlboro-man types' for Sagittarians, and so on. Whilst much of the marketing industry remains sceptical about the potential of astrology, there remains a recognition that because so many people believe in astrology, it could be used to package messages in the right way, thus providing an effective advertising hook.

Case study 6.2

Appealing to the Asian youth market

Young people are big business and if an organization does not go after them their brand could lose out, yet trying to crack this consumer group is far from easy. In Asia marketers are in hot pursuit of the youth market – a huge segment of the market – and advertisers and agencies alike are asking themselves whether there is a sure-fire way to target these elusive, cynical, highly diverse but cash-rich consumers. Certainly what has worked before is not working now and it is no longer acceptable to use the familiar old marketing tricks, waving corporate banners and signing celebrities to endorse labels. Those tactics are not going to get kids spending on a brand since they are much more sophisticated, more media-shrewd and more sceptical. Yet advertisers cannot afford to give up on the youth market who are not only the consumers of today but also of tomorrow – marketers of any sort of leisure product, have to crack the youth market if they are to be successful in Asia. It is particularly important because the majority of the population falls into the sixteen to thirty-four age group – young people make up two-thirds of Asia's population and they are still spending like they used to despite the recent economic downturn. They are big spenders, particularly on enter-tainment, travel and the latest electronic gadgets and computers. They are also Internet-friendly, which means that they are attractive to high-tech companies that have not gone after this market in the past. Yet the challenge remains – how do you market to this huge, ethnically diverse segment? Marketers have to be sensitive to which values tie them together and which draw them apart.

Take two appeals that are frequently used in youth marketing – sex and music – and some of the problems become clearer. Sex has long been used to sell to the youth market but in Asia problems are posed by the cultural diversity. In India, for instance, men consider a heaving bosom to be sexy, yet in China the desirable feminine form is lighter. Similarly, in music there is tremendous diversity: Bangla might work in Bangalore but it is Hinto-hop in Canton, and in Taiwan dance music means Western-style such as the Spice Girls. In this case, the answer might be to go local and tailor the message to particular youth markets, like MTV Asia which uses local production teams playing local music. Essentially any marketer here has to be in touch with the audience and has to interact with it. That strategy has proved extremely effective for brand marketers and gives them a different twist to the way they market their brand. If all else fails, the only other option is to break the mould – since breaking out might be just the way to get in with the young crowd.

Case study 6.3

DDB Needham: a successful global agency

Active in ninety-six countries worldwide with forty-two multinational clients (and growing), DDB Needham has grown into the world's second largest advertising agency, having been ranked sixth in the early 1990s. Its global billings have risen from $4 billion in 1988 to over $12 billion today. In 1997 it was voted Global Agency Network of the Year by *Advertising Age* and in 1998 it won twenty-seven Lion awards at the Cannes Advertising Festival – more than any other agency. Its global billings were:

- 1988 $4 billions
- 1991 $5.4 billions
- 1994 $6.7 billions
- 1995 $8.1 billions
- 1996 $10.5 billions
- 1997 $11.7 billions

Bernard Brochand, its CEO, puts DDB's success down to its local approach (Table 6.4) in an age of globalization – saying that agencies should think and act local in the first instance and then become global, rather than imposing global solutions on local problems. Whilst most ad services can be unbundled, the client will always need an orchestration and there will always be a need for an ad agency which can act as a client's brand consultant. Whilst the dilemma over whether to unbundle or integrate services is the issue facing many agencies today, Brochand feels that DDB's success lies beyond such questions – arguing that structures do not generate good ideas, solve ad problems or bring results. Instead it is the best advertising and the best ideas that yield results and agencies should be paid according to performance since advertising must be about successful selling.

Table 6.4 DDB's success is spread locally: offices voted agency of the year

Amsterdam	1989, 1990, 1991, 1994
Argentina	1995
Australia	1997
Brazil	1996
Canada	1995, 1997
Chicago	1997
Chile	1997
Dallas	1997
France	1993, 1994, 1995, 1997
India	1992, 1994, 1996, 1997
Italy	1994, 1995, 1996
Poland	1992, 1993, 1996
Russia	1996
Slovenia	1995, 1996
Sweden	1995
UK	1992, 1994, 1997
USA	1995

Source: CNBC, *Storyboard*, 1998.

Notes

1 Theodore Levitt, quoted by S. Silvester (1994). Why pretesting sucks. Speech to the Association of Qualitative Research Practitioners. Background Papers, Market Research Society, Advertising Research Seminar.
2 Peter M. Chisnall (1994). *Consumer Behaviour.* 3rd edn. McGraw-Hill, p. 323.
3 Karen Ritchie (1995). *Marketing to Generation X.* Lexington Books, p. 3.
4 http://www.mintel.co.uk/on-line/lt/o/British_on-Holiday-At_Home.
5 Nigel Morgan and Annette Pritchard (1998). European seniors' tourism: a marketing challenge for the new millennium. In *Leisure, Culture and Tourism in Europe* (W. Nahrstedt and T. P. Kombol, eds) pp. 153–64, Bielefeld.
6 Henley Centre (1994). Today's older consumers: an emerging third age of personal fulfilment or a wasted era of frustrated possibilities? *Leisure Futures*, **1**, 100.
7 Ibid., p. 7.
8 Beth Salmon (1994). Third agers and brand loyalty. Unpublished paper by The Research Business.
9 Annette Pritchard and Nigel Morgan (1997). Marketing practice and opportunities in the tour operators' seniors travel market. *Journal of Vacation Marketing*, **3** (2), March, 153–63.
10 Elizabeth Gleick (1998–9). The new youth. *Time Special Issue, Visions of Europe*, Winter, 174–5.
11 Ibid.
12 Alison Drummond (1999). The travel industry needs to be smarter in targeting the young people of tomorrow. *Travel Trade Gazette*, 4 October.
13 Ibid.
14 Lisa Goff (1999). Don't miss the bus! *American Demographics*, August, 49–54.
15 Michael F. Jacobson and Laurie Ann Mazur (1995). *Marketing Madness.* Westview Press.
16 'London Transport Museum targets children' and 'Legoland runs cheesy promo', *Leisuremarketing*, 14–27 September 1999.
17 Goff, Don't miss the bus!
18 Carol Nelson (1994). *How to Market to Women.* Visible Ink Press, p. 112.
19 Ibid., p. 16.
20 Ibid., p. xii.
21 Chambers Travel (1995). *The Business Woman Traveller Survey.* Chambers Travel, quoted in Sheena Westwood, Nigel Morgan and Annette

Pritchard (2000). Gender-blind marketing: business women and airlines. *Tourism Management*, **21** (1), August, 353–62.

22 Female embrace falls foul of advertising watchdogs as TDI pulls new Sisley poster. *Campaign*, 27 March 1998.

23 S. Bhat, T. W. Leigh and D. L. Wardlow (1998). The effect of consumer prejudices on ad processing: heterosexual consumers' responses to homosexual imagery in ads. *Journal of Advertising*, **17** (4), Winter, 10, 9–25.

24 Annette Pritchard and Nigel Morgan (1997). The gay consumer: a meaningful market segment? *Journal of Targeting, Measurement and Analysis for Marketing*, **6** (1), 9–20.

25 Annette Pritchard, Nigel Morgan, Diane Sedgley and Andrew Jenkins (1998). Reaching out to the gay tourist: opportunities and threats in an emerging market segment. *Tourism Management*, **19** (3), June, 273–82.

26 Resorts are embracing the all-inclusive trend. *USA Today*, 11 November 1996, p. 8A.

27 Goff, Don't miss the bus!

28 Ibid.

29 Tamara Real (1996). Looking good; how cultural tourism has changed the face of North American travel destinations. In *Tourism and Culture: Image, Identity and Marketing* (Mike Robinson et al., eds) pp. 171–84, Centre for Travel and Tourism Sunderland, p. 178.

30 Ibid.

31 Ibid.

32 Ibid.

33 Simon Anholt (1998). Paper presented to the Second International Advertising Festival, Valencia.

34 Wendell Steavenson (1998). Battle of the big brands. *Time*, 27 July, p. 53.

35 Simon Anholt (2000). *Another One Bites the Grass: Making Sense Out of International Advertising*. John Wiley.

36 John Hegarty, quoted in Jim Aitchison (1999). *Cutting Edge Advertising. How to Create the World's Best Print for Brands in the 21st Century*, Prentice Hall, pp. 300–1.

Further reading

Anholt, S. (2000). *Another One Bites the Grass: Making Sense Out of International Advertising*. John Wiley.

Chisnall, P. M. (1994). *Consumer Behaviour*. 3rd edn. McGraw-Hill.

Dibb, S. and Stern, P. (1999). Internet-stimulated thoughts on market segmentation. *Journal of Targeting, Measurement and Analysis for Marketing*, **17** (3), 277–87.

Drummond, A. (1999). The travel industry needs to be smarter in targeting the young people of tomorrow. *Travel Trade Gazette*, 4 October.

Goff, L. (1999). Don't miss the bus! *American Demographics*, August, 49–54.

de Mooij, M. (1998). *Global Marketing and Advertising: Understanding Cultural Paradoxes*. Sage.

Morgan, N. J. and Pritchard, A. (1998). *Tourism Promotion and Power: Creating Images, Creating Identities*. John Wiley, chs 5 and 6.

Nelson, C. (1994). *How to Market to Women*. Visible Ink Press.

Pritchard, A. and Morgan, N. J. (1996). Sex still sells to generation X: promotional practice in the youth package tourism market. *Journal of Vacation Marketing* (3), 1 December, 69–80.

Pritchard, A. and Morgan, N. J. (1997). The gay consumer: a meaningful market segment? *Journal of Targeting, Measurement and Analysis for Marketing*, **6** (1), 9–20.

Pritchard, A. and Morgan, N. J. (1997). Marketing practice and opportunities in the tour operators' seniors travel market. *Journal of Vacation Marketing*, **3** (2), March, 153–63.

Pritchard, A., Morgan, N. J., Sedgley, D. and Jenkins, A. (1998). Reaching out to the gay tourist: opportunities and threats in an emerging market segment. *Tourism Management*, **19** (3), June, 273–82.

Quelch, J. A. and Bartlett, C. A. (1999). *Global Marketing Management*. 4th edn. Addison Wesley Longman.

Ritchie, K. (1995). *Marketing to Generation X*. Lexington Books.

Stone, G. J. and Nichol, S. (1999). Older, single female holiday makers in the United Kingdom – who needs them? *Journal of Vacation Marketing*, **5** (1), 7–17.

Stone, M. (1999). Managing good and bad customers: part 1. *Journal of Database Marketing*, **6** (3), 253–66.

Stone, M. (1999). Managing good and bad customers: part 2. *Journal of Database Marketing*, **6** (4), 299–313.

Swarbrooke, J. and Horner, S. (1999). *Consumer Behaviour in Tourism*. Butterworth-Heinemann, especially part 6: Topical Issues in Consumer Behaviour, pp. 195–248.

Usunier, J.-C. (1996). *Marketing across Cultures*. 2nd edn. Prentice Hall.

Westwood, S., Pritchard, A. and Morgan, N. J. (1999). Businesswomen and airlines: a case of marketers missing the target? *Journal of Targeting, Measurement and Analysis for Marketing*, **8** (2), 179–98.

7

Creativity and advertising opportunities

Chapter overview

In this chapter we explore what has been termed the creative 'toybox'[1] – in other words, the resources which advertisers can mine to produce cutting-edge advertising. We discuss the creative opportunities open to advertisers, including how creatives can use popular culture as an inspiration for their executions, and examine the increasingly important link between tourism and leisure advertising and the media industries – particularly film and television, including the rise of product placement. In addition, we also look at the potential of celebrity endorsements and the importance of getting the right face to fit a product. Key themes reviewed are:

- generating creativity
- the ad opportunities of popular entertainment
- harnessing film and television shows
- the pull of the travel programme
- using music in ads and sonic brand triggers
- the rise and rise of product placement
- using celebrity endorsement – does the face fit the brand?

Introduction

People choose brands and services with which they have empathy, which hold emotional attachment for them and have resonance. So, whilst we have discussed how advertising should try to build a relationship between consumers and brands, it is vital to remember that it is an interactive process. Consumers are not passive recipients of advertising – instead they interact with, respond to and interpret advertising, and they can choose to embrace or reject its message. As a result, advertising needs to break through not just the media and information clutter which surrounds today's consumer, but it also needs to break through the barriers and filters people erect to protect themselves from information overload. If the advertising is not relevant then it will never penetrate and any possibilities for interaction will be lost. But, to be effective, it has to be more than simply relevant, it has to be built around a strong idea. Some advertising can be ground-breaking; Nike, Benetton and Absolut are all examples of brands whose advertising has made them not just household names but also style icons. In general, however, advertising for most products and services secures gradual and incremental change in moving a brand forward. The key issue which each brand manager and agency executive faces in attempting this is how to most effectively harness the opportunities which exist to create appealing and breakthrough ads that will engage consumers.

Generating creativity

For every advertising campaign that is created there is a marketing problem to be resolved – whether it is to persuade and induce purchase, maintain or increase brand saliency or reposition a brand. In a sense, then, an advertising campaign is in fact problem-solving within a certain time frame and budget. It is the advertising brief that provides the creatives with the 'stimulus for invention', ensuring relevance and encouraging original thinking[2] and, as we saw in Chapters 2 and 3, it should include an indication of what has to be communicated, how that is to be done and when it has to be done by. Once clients and agencies have established the parameters of the creative brief, it is time for the hard part – the development and production of the ad itself – and whilst planning, research and media strategy can all be semi-scientific activities, creativity is totally different.

> 'the greatness of an idea can be measured with the speed with which it enters our consciousness. The faster it does so, the longer it is likely to stay there . . . Remember the space you are buying is not on a poster site, TV commercial or in print. It is inside someone's head. That's the only space worth buying.'[3]

Part inspiration, part sweat and tears, the quest for creativity is both an intuitive and deductive process where ideas are generated and then rationally examined to assess their import and significance. It is often an intimidating affair. Being creative is about being different: 'When everyone is zigging, you need to zag'.[4] As Len Weinreich says: 'Talented, intelligent, courageous, individual and different: it is difficult to be all five. Which perhaps accounts for the rarity of hot agencies – and memorable advertising'.[5] The creative process usually begins with brainstorming sessions in which ideas are generated and then pulled apart to assess their functional value. Creativity should not be about indulgence, it is about making the message believable and persuasive, and above all it is about remaining relevant to the consumer and the brand personality. If an idea can stand up to this process then its value is confirmed, although of course it may not necessarily always be the best idea.

Just how do creatives make a message engaging? Often by reducing the advertising problem to its bare essentials and aiming for simplicity, first by isolating the brand proposition to discover which emotion they want to evoke and then by considering how to approach it psychologically. When the relevant stimulus is identified, they can then think of ways to dramatize the message. John Hegarty (the man behind the Levi's revival of the mid-1980s) has said of creativity:

> if we are suffering from information overload, surely the answer isn't to overload our advertising. Surely the answer is to simplify. To make less say more. Not only does this view breathe added life into our work, challenging us to be more single-minded, daring and distinctive, but it also goes to the heart of creativity in advertising. It is said that the foundation of wit is brevity. So it is with advertising. The power of our ability to reduce, to simplify a seemingly complex brief down to a memorable, engaging idea.[6]

Whilst clever techniques can gain attention, simple ideas are what make advertising memorable – ideas which reverse conventional ways of seeing the world, use parallels, similarities or paradoxes and translate them into a metaphor that stands for the brand message. A great idea lies at the heart of every good ad and technique should not overwhelm the idea – if an ad is driven by a desire to be ever more technologically innovative, then that will become its sole goal, instead of selling the brand. Creative stimulation can come from any number of sources – visiting art galleries, reading books, listening to music, watching television and, above all, observing life – which could all trigger those much sought after original thoughts. Essentially, ideas for a campaign could come from the intrinsic value of the brand itself, the people who use (or do not use) it, topical events, popular culture or the general environment.

Capitalizing on inherent value

Tourism and leisure products and services, like any others, have inherent value in, amongst other things, their name, product, logo, location or history and any of these attributes could provide the foundation for an advertising campaign. A certain Australian beer – Castlemaine XXXX – has made its brand name and the culture of its country of origin central to its advertising – the tone and content of its ads vigorously and humorously confirm the centrality of this beer in the lives of Australians. A recent UK ad centres on an illicit liaison. After their assignation, the woman asks the man if he would like a Castlemaine. He replies, genuinely shocked, that he could not possibly drink his best mate's beer (although he has just slept with his wife), thus confirming once again the long-running slogan that 'Australians couldn't give a XXXX for anything else'. Location has also served a British beer brand equally well – 'The cream of Manchester' has been the centrepiece of Boddington's advertising for a number of years, whether used directly or indirectly. Poster and television executions have built on this concept, variously representing Boddington's in a range of humorous 'creamy' situations – as ice cream, shaving cream and even vanishing cream. The concept is also confirmed at the point of sale by the distribution to pubs and clubs where the beer is sold of drinks coasters depicting a cutout silhouette of an ice-cream cone above the brand name and website address.

The advertising seen in Plate 2 also cleverly focuses on aspects of the product – again with a twist of humour – in this case the 1999 exhibition of sea creatures at the Underwater World Aquarium in Singapore. Produced by Saatchi & Saatchi, Singapore, using the strapline 'Deadly creatures of the deep', each poster execution highlights in an amusing, charming and anarchic way the impacts such creatures make on their environment. 'Piranhas' features a cat that came off badly in an encounter with the fish and whose leg bears a remarkable resemblance to Long John Silver. The childlike drawing, the blue ringed octopus and the electric eel all convey similar messages using the same tone and style. This poster campaign was run in conjunction with a television ad that opens with visitors to the aquarium photographing the exhibits. Things are not always as they seem, however, and slowly a lollipop is lowered into view which a child spots and leaps at. As she is pulled up on a line, the viewer realizes that it is the people who are the exhibits here. A simple yet striking approach, this advertising appeals to the anarchic sense of humour of generations X and Y using very well choreographed and executed photography.

A similar approach – featuring the product in a striking way together with a dash of humour – was also used by the same agency in the 'Eternal Egypt' campaign to publicize the travelling exhibition of Egyptian artefacts (belonging to the British Museum) on display at the Singapore Museum in 1999. Aimed at the general public, the agency's strategy was to put the ancient world in a modern context. Taking a number of things about ancient Egypt that most fascinate people – such as mummification, hieroglyphics and religion – the agency created a series of ads and posters intended to be as striking as possible (Plate 3). One execution made the ironic appeal '1000 gods . . . and not one to protect against tourists'. Appearing in newspapers and magazines and at poster sites around Singapore, the ads drew huge lines of people – 150 000 in all – to the exhibition and were successfully sold at the museum shop as exhibition souvenirs. In a city with a population of only 3 million, many of whom are only just discovering the arts, this particular campaign was highly successful and the ads themselves became popular art objects.

Whilst the product itself can provide an extremely prolific source of ideas for creative campaigns, it is not always the best approach to adopt. There are dangers in focusing excessively on the product – especially when it is problematic or consistently fails to meet consumer expectations. Rail advertising in the UK is particularly difficult precisely because consumer surveys consistently report increasing perceptions of poor service, unreliability and a lack of punctuality. Three train companies that have experienced particularly high levels of complaints are Great Western Railways, South West Trains and Virgin Trains – all of which invested in advertising campaigns in 1999. The challenge for these companies and their ad agencies was how do they craft successful ads when there is such a strong possibility of negative consumer reaction? Interestingly, whilst they all offer the same product, each adopted a different approach. Great Western opted for quite traditional advertising that highlights the appeal and role of the train in people's lives. Happy, contented passengers beam out at the audience whilst the train meets their every need. Unfortunately, given Great Western's performance, such ads may lack consumer credibility.

By contrast, in a much more creative approach, South West Trains avoided this problem by focusing on the role of the train in opening up great days out for the consumer – at the seaside, funfair, races or on a shopping trip. These television commercials are very simple but cleverly done. The ads use basic line graphics that utilize the colour of the South West Trains' livery to great effect. A speeding red and yellow line appears to the left of the screen and forms a variety of outlines in each execution – a tree (countryside), a sand castle (seaside), Big Ben (London shopping), a Ferris wheel (fairground) – set to a simple soundtrack representing each location – singing birds (countryside), waves (seaside), marching bands (London) and crowds (fairground), followed by a train whistle. This is then followed by the endlines for each ad, such as 'London's closer than you think. Southwest Trains – a better day out'. The message – the benefits of travelling by this company's trains – is complemented and reinforced by the repetition of the concept in poster ads (Plate 4).[7] This advertising shows what can be achieved even when budgets are extremely tight. Its simplicity and consistent message are memorable, whilst the ads avoid provoking adverse reactions by deliberately eschewing any claims about the product that may not have credibility. VirginRail ads have also avoided making any such claims. Instead, in keeping with the overall tone and style of the Virgin brand and its advertising, the ads make a conspiratorial appeal to the consumer. Rik Mayall (a popular UK actor known for his anarchic sense of humour) plays a businessman facing a variety of situations when flying from London to Manchester. Whatever could go wrong does – and the very simple message that underpins this campaign is that it would have been so much easier by train.

Seeking inspiration from the past

The product's history (whether real or invented) can frequently provide a rich vein of inspiration for creative advertising in tourism and leisure and there are many examples where history dominates executions, particularly in the case of destinations. Egypt's destination advertising (not unexpectedly) focuses almost exclusively on its historical landmarks and personalities – the pyramids and sphinx at Giza, Moses, Cleopatra, Alexander – the list is almost endless. Other destinations use historical associations to construct the brand strapline or essence. Virginia has positioned itself as 'The birthplace of Presidents', Greece as 'The birthplace of democracy' and Florence as 'The centre of the Renaissance'. Windsor, Ontario, has packaged its historic sites (which are central to the African-American nineteenth-century struggle for emancipation) into 'The road that led to freedom'. In a similar vein, Philadelphia, in its guide to the city's African-American historical and cultural attractions, positions itself as the 'City of brotherly love'.

The use of historical associations is, of course, by no means the exclusive preserve of destinations. P&O's branding of the *Oriana*, its flagship liner, is inextricably linked to consumer associations of its predecessor, the *Canberra*. In the UK market the *Canberra* possessed both a strong history and a powerful personality, not least because of its role in the Falklands-Malvinas conflict of the early 1980s. *Oriana* has carried on the tradition of empire in its branding, celebrating its 'British' style and all-British officer crew in its marketing and advertising.[8] Similarly, on the other side of the world, the Royal Peacock Hotel in Singapore provides an extremely effective and appealing example of how to combine aspects of a product's past in its advertising and brand building. The hotel is one of a new breed of boutique hotels that have become very popular in Asia in recent years. Aimed at the budget business traveller, the campaign used the rich and colourful history of the hotel and its surrounding location – as a brothel in Singapore's red light district – as the perfect vehicle to differentiate the Royal Peacock from all its skyscraper competitors in this most modern of cities. After all, it is rare to have the opportunity of legitimately sleeping in a brothel – former or otherwise!

In order to enhance the concept, the agency (Saatchi & Saatchi, Singapore) decided that the poster ads should be designed to look old as well, so each stylish and elegant execution uses Chinese-style posters of the 1920s and 1930s in sepia-toned, 'hand-painted' illustrations (Plate 5). Each execution is different and shares particular aspects of the hotel – both historical and contemporary – with the reader. Headlines include 'At the Royal Peacock, we'll still leave a light on for you. Understandably, it will no longer be red'; 'The staff of the Royal Peacock Hotel. Trained in the highest professional standards, but no longer in the oldest profession'; and 'You'll rest comfortably all night at the Royal Peacock Hotel. My, how times have changed'. Each poster shares the same endline: 'A brothel before, a hotel now. Good service always'. The ads caused quite a stir, winning several local and international awards, and featuring in a range of tourist-orientated magazines, as well as in publications likely to reach secretaries responsible for booking company accommodation. The client reported excellent business at the Royal Peacock – with some guests rather too keenly enquiring about the hotel's former residents!

Another example of a late-1990s ad campaign that used the past as an inspiration, although in a rather different way, was that for Sarawak Tourism. Here a series of ads were produced inviting the consumer to explore 'the hidden paradise of Borneo'. Based on 1950s USA adventure paperback dust jackets, executions included 'Rainbow end in Sarawak', 'The leopard sang in Sarawak' and 'Golden days in Sarawak'. Central to each poster layout was a colourful jungle scene with native people seen in full dress, together with several animals, including orang-utans and monkeys. Whilst this example demonstrates how the agency found inspiration in the past, it is also interesting in that it used illustrations rather than photographs (just like the Royal Peacock Hotel ads).[9] This can be a somewhat dangerous strategy as people like to see what they are going to buy – particularly in tourism where consumers are quite literally buying into the promise of the ad without having experience of the product. At times, however, illustrations can become central to an ad campaign, and in this instance the poster illustrations were chosen for three reasons. First, they made the Borneo rainforest less intimidating and off-putting whilst still retaining a sense of myth and adventure. Second, the budget could not stretch to the costs of high-quality photography. Third, the illustrations were seen to be critical in building a unique, distinctive brand for the destination.[10]

Ad highlight 7.1   The role of the art director

In today's ever more advertising-saturated, visually led world, with consumers watching more and reading less, 'the artistic ability to conceive and produce powerful and persuasive communications and images will inevitably become an even more necessary and valuable commodity'. As a result, the job of the art director in creating effective advertising is becoming more and more challenging and important. A good art director must be 'an artist with type and images' and he or she is responsible for:

- planning and executing all the visual elements of an ad campaign
- liaising with copywriters to ensure that the ads' visual and verbal concepts complement each other
- producing storyboards and comprehensive drawings to communicate the desired finished ad
- hiring and/or supervising photographers, illustrators and directors once the executions are approved.

Source: adapted from John L. Sellers (1999). The art director. In *The Advertising Business: Operations, Creativity, Media Planning, Integrated Communications* (J. P. Jones, ed.) pp. 61–76, Sage.

The advertising opportunities of popular entertainment

In Chapter 3 we suggested that sport has become almost a world language, dissolving sociocultural, economic and political boundaries. In the same way, popular entertainment is increasingly global and offers rich pickings for advertisers trying to construct attractive messages. Celebrities, music, literature, art, films and television programmes have all been extensively used in tourism ads – the supermodel Claudia Schiffer has promoted Montenegro in the former Yugoslavia, whilst Elle Macpherson advertises Western Australia, and innumerable films and songs provide emotive symbols for tourist destinations (as Elton John's 'O Georgia', does for Georgia, USA). Perhaps one of the oldest sources of inspiration for advertising appeals is literature. Borde Failte (the Irish Tourist Board) features not only the country's built heritage and natural environment in its marketing, but also its literary giants, including, amongst others, Oscar Wilde, George Bernard Shaw, Samuel Beckett, W. B. Yeats and James Joyce.

In fact, literary figures are now prominent in the marketing of a number of destinations, appearing in brochures and even on road signs. In the UK Dorset is 'Hardy country' after Thomas Hardy, Yorkshire is 'Brontë country' after the Brontë sisters, Stratford is associated with William Shakespeare and Swansea in South Wales with the poet Dylan Thomas. In the USA New Orleans actively associates itself with the *Vampire Chronicles* novels of Anne Rice and Salem with Arthur Miller's play *The Crucible* (Ad highlight 7.2). Interestingly, the same piece of literature can be used to promote very different places. Bram Stoker's novel *Dracula* and its many movie versions provide Transylvania in Romania with a powerful tourism message, whilst Whitby, on the north-east coast of England (also featured heavily in the book), hosts an annual Dracula festival and has a Dracula experience attraction.

| Ad highlight 7.2 | Salem, Massachusetts is the witch city of *The Crucible* |

In the search for differentiation, some destinations turn to rather unusual associations to create a distinctiveness – as in the case of Salem, Massachusetts, which has branded itself 'The witch city'. When Arthur Miller visited Salem in 1952 to research his *The Crucible* he described the town as 'morose and secret', bypassed by industry, 'dripping . . . in the cold black drizzle like some abandoned dog'. Centuries after the trials, the town was still embarrassed about what had happened. Yet after the triumph of Miller's play, a Witch Trail was set up and today signs show where various citizens were arrested, interrogated, or hanged whilst even the local police carry the Salem branding, featuring 'Salem, the witch city, Massachusetts, 1626' on their patrol cars and uniforms.

Together with literature, perhaps art is the oldest source of tourism imagery and today provides a creative opportunity for tourism advertisers and marketers. One of the many destinations that makes active use of its association with the arts is Italy. The Italian State Tourist Office's brochure, 'Italia: travels in wonderland', is laden with images of paintings, sculpture and architecture, and with references to literature and music from classical antiquity to the Renaissance and the Romantic movement. The brochure's cover sets the pattern, depicting Bernini's sculpture, *Apollo and Daphne*, whilst its first page of text reminds the potential traveller that 'the history of art as we understand it today could never have been written without Italy and its masterpieces'. In addition, 'Goethe, Stendhal, Dickens, Montesquieu, Taine, Byron, Shelley and Dumas' all journeyed through Italy on 'the Grand Tour', 'as did all the cultivated youth of Europe, for whom a journey to Italy was a sort of conclusion to their education, a great University in the open air'. The message and implication in this marketing is clear – that for the modern traveller to complete his or her education, a visit to Italy is essential.

Whilst literature and art continue to offer creative inspiration for tourism and leisure advertising, the defining media of the second half of the twentieth century were undoubtedly television and film. Television is a sensory medium and, more than any other form of media communication, it is intimate, multimodal and multisensory, transmitting voice, music, sound effects, graphics and imagery. Television is the most effective medium for promoting the look and the sound of a place, whether in the form of a 15-second network commercial or a half-hour narrowcast cable or satellite 'infomercial' on a travel channel. As an advertising vehicle for the broadcast of leisure- and tourism-related commercials it is undoubtedly significant but, equally, the popular entertainment featured on television also offers advertisers creative opportunities.

The value of television shows

Who can estimate the impact of showcasing Hawaii on the television detective series *Hawaii Five O* and *Magnum P.I.* or of setting the UK detective show *Bergerac* on Jersey? More recently, in the UK the BBC1 series *Sunburn* helped Cyprus achieve a 10 per cent increase in UK bookings for summer 1999 despite the overall market being down by 2 to 3 per cent on 1998. *Sunburn* generated many enquiries and helped to keep the momentum for bookings going following the Cyprus Tourism Office's £550 000 ad campaign. The decision to set a television series in a destination can also have unexpected spin-offs, of course. In the early 1980s when *Miami Vice* first appeared on American television screens, the city authorities were wary of a negative impact as the show was heavily associated with crime and drugs. Yet the programme became a platform for the revitalization of Miami as a chic destination (associating it with designer fashion, designer stubble, vibrant music and beautiful people), actually becoming the catalyst for environmental and economic regeneration.

191

The show's producers needed brightly coloured visuals and energetic Latin music to crystallize a certain image of Miami, so, for shooting purposes, many of Miami Beach's faded Art Deco buildings were repainted in pinks and oranges. However, amongst the millions of television viewers who saw the show were Miami's residents and marketers, who so embraced it that they began to take renewed pride in the city's buildings and internationally renowned Art Deco architecture, repainting and renovating their own buildings as seen in the show. Now, of course, many of these Miami icons (fashion, style and architecture) feature prominently in Miami's tourism advertising. Unfortunately, however, for tourism marketers, celluloid exposure is uncontrollable and it is as well to remember that it can have negative results. In this way in the late 1980s the film *Mississippi Burning* attracted negative publicity for Philadelphia, Mississippi, a small town which had gained notoriety in the 1960s when three civil rights workers were murdered there by the Ku Klux Klan. The film was shot on location in Philadelphia but in the resultant publicity, the town gave the impression that it had changed little in twenty years.

The magic of the movies

Despite some of the pitfalls, there is evidence which indicates that television shows and films can create both good publicity and increased tourism spend, although their impact is still underresearched. Moreover, tying an advertising campaign too closely with a film can be a risky business – after all, plenty of films have 'bombed'. But when they are hits, the potential benefits and associations for destinations can be huge. For instance, in the wake of the box office success, *Gandhi*, India experienced a 50 per cent increase in tourism; *Deliverance*, an early 1970s action movie set in Raeburn County, Georgia, was the catalyst for the establishment of its raft and adventure tourism industry; whilst visitor figures to Fort Hayes in Kansas, featured in Kevin Costner's *Dances with Wolves*, increased by 25 per cent during 1990–1 following the film's release. In fact, the three Scottish blockbusters of the 1990s, *Braveheart*, *Rob Roy* and *Loch Ness*, generated an estimated £7–15 million in additional tourism spend in Scotland. Japanese interest in Haworth has increased dramatically on the back of the box office success of *Wuthering Heights* in Japan – so much so that Japanese signs have been erected at the stately home. Similarly, more than 250 000 people a year still visit the Green Gables House on Prince Edward Island, the inspiration for the setting of the books (and subsequent television series) *Anne of Green Gables*.

Attractions, stately homes, regions and countries can all benefit tremendously from the magic worked by film. A guestroom in the Crown Hotel in

Amersham (UK), featured in the hit film *Four Weddings and a Funeral*, has been transformed by Andie McDowell and Hugh Grant's bedroom scene, from a quaint and comfortable room into a destination in demand for romantic couples. Since the film's release the room has been solidly booked until 2000. Likewise the short-break business to Morocco received a considerable boost in 1999 thanks to the publicity generated by the Kate Winslet film *Hideous Kinky* – set in the streets and markets of Marrakesh. As a result Marrakesh became the latest trendy destination – gaining significant newspaper coverage and promotion as a direct result of the film. In such instances, when destination managers find that they do have a 'hit' film that they can exploit, advertising is likely to feature the links either directly by running an ad before the screening of the film (as the Scottish Tourist Board did in the USA with *Braveheart*) or indirectly through a tourism brochure, as mid-Wales tourism marketers did with Hugh Grant's film *An Englishman Who Went Up a Hill and Came Down a Mountain*.

It is critical that success on the big screen is translated into effective marketing if places and attractions are to benefit. To this end, the British Tourist Authority produced its highly successful Movie Map (with a print run of 250 000) highlighting film and television locations across Britain, whilst the Scottish Tourist Board used endorsements from *Rob Roy* stars Jessica Lange and Liam Neeson, seen in full costume in the 1996 Scottish brochure. Recognizing the power that film, television and travel programmes can have in raising the profile of places, tourism destination agencies are now working with film-makers to promote their destinations as possible locations. Locations are important choices for film-makers and tourism agencies have an increasingly significant presence at festivals such as the annual Cannes Film Festival and the Los Angeles Locations Fair. In this ever closer relationship between the media and tourism marketers, this is the ultimate in tourism product placement – to place your destination in a film or television series. It is important to recognize in tourism marketing terms, however, that the value of film link-ups can also be a somewhat transitory affair. Devil's Tower, Wyoming, thanks to the 1977 film *Close Encounters of the Third Kind*, became a household name in the USA in the 1970s. The Devil's Tower plays a key role in the film and during its cinema run and television reruns the area enjoyed a tremendous increase in visitors. The year after its release visitor numbers increased by 75 per cent but today it is no longer such a tourist attraction due to its isolated location and lack of local support.

In terms of creative inspiration, film and television shows do not merely form opportunities for advertising and marketing link-ups – they can also be parodied to create amusing advertising concepts. For instance, Peugeot car ads

193

have parodied the film *Thelma and Louise*, whilst Nissan imitated a famous scene from *Betty Blue*. A young woman throws her lover's belongings out of their shared beach house on to the sand because he borrowed her Nissan without asking her permission. In a similar vein, in 1999 Ben & Jerry's ice cream launched a series of ads using cartoon parodies of cult movies. The £800 000 'Legendairy' campaign (pun intended!) featured four executions based on the movies *Jaws*, *King Kong*, *Close Encounters of the Third Kind* and *Psycho*. The campaign used posters, bus rears, cinema, postcards and underground advertising. Parody or imitation offers a wealth of creative opportunities, but companies and agencies need to ensure that they have secured permissions (where appropriate) or perhaps consider working with the idea's originator in order to produce more effective ad concepts.

Ad highlight 7.3   Opportunities of travel shows

Travel programmes such as *Wish You Were Here* in the UK or the *CNN Travel Show* are becomingly increasingly influential as marketing vehicles. The essence of these programmes is to blend travel and entertainment and the regular presenters are often joined by guest celebrities who present a short personal view of three or four destinations. These travel programmes could be considered in much the same way as music videos, which are at one and the same time entertainment but also advertisements for songs, albums and pop groups. The MTV CEO Tom Freston has described such channels as 'environments that are uniquely conducive to the marketing of music'. Yet viewers of music video channels such as MTV and VH-1 would most likely dismiss the notion that the music video is nothing more than a new type of advertising. Consumers tend not to view either the videos or the channel itself as advertising or as a means by which to increase sales of a specific product.

In many ways, MTV and the music video parallel the development of the travel programme. These programmes are seen as popular entertainment but once again they can also be construed as a form of advertising. In the UK some 8 million people each week watch programmes such as *Holiday*, programmes which could at one level be said to be a series of advertisements for destinations, resorts, even hotels, airline carriers and tour operators. These programmes are clearly vehicles for disseminating knowledge to their loyal viewers – who may well be aspiring tourists. It also seems reasonable to argue that just as consumers of MTV see the product more as about entertainment than advertising, so too do consumers of these travel programmes. Often developed in close co-operation with the area tourism authorities, there is very little research measuring the impact of such programmes, although there is some anecdotal evidence. For instance, for days after featuring on *Wish You Were Here*, the Hythe Imperial Hotel (on the south coast of England) was inundated with more than 1000 calls for information – many of which were converted into bookings.

Striking the right chord: music in advertising

Almost thirty years ago Coca-Cola wanted to teach the world to sing in perfect harmony – the premise matched Coke's global brand values and the pattern was set for an important ingredient in successful advertising – the use of music. Audio plays an important part in creating the right advertising atmosphere, often as soundtracks to accompany visual images and, in fact, it would be a mistake to separate the two as there is a close relationship between the audio and visual elements of advertising. Music, of course, is an important asset in demarcating time and space, and in transporting viewers and listeners to different places, and an emotive song can conjure up accompanying visual images, whilst some places evoke certain sounds and songs. Songs are highly significant components of tourism advertising since music has the ability to stimulate extraordinary emotional feelings. Songs such as 'I Left My Heart in San Francisco', 'I Love Paris' and 'Viva Las Vegas' carry tremendous images. 'If You're Going to San Francisco' became an anthem and a cultural icon in the 1960s for the 'flower power' generation and, for those baby boomers, still evokes strong images. Despite the fickle nature of popular music the song retains those associations for successive generations and has helped to position the city as an easy-going, relaxed destination, just as the music group the Beach Boys symbolized the California surf-beat culture and the Beatles the Mersey beat of Liverpool.

The associations various destinations have with music is often used to great effect by their marketers. For instance, haunting strains of Irish music are the background sounds when the ad is for Ireland, and rock and roll and Elvis Presley are used to sell the USA in general, and blues music markets the southern US states and country music the US corn belt states in particular (Case study 7.1). More recently, the Wales Tourist Board television ad campaign launched in 1998 features the music of the Manic Street Preachers' 'A Design For Life', which sums up the whole brand proposition, whilst Cardiff Marketing Limited has used the CD sleeve for Catatonia's hit single 'Mulder and Scully', which portrays a futuristic scene of a flying saucer over Cardiff's impressive Civic Centre. In such ways, popular music, beyond delivering emotional gratification to a listener, also serves as a ticket to membership in a group with similar tastes. In this sense, music is also orchestrated to appeal to particular social groups and to make connections with these groups, another case being Spain's use of flamenco music in its 'Passion for life' campaign aimed at the cultural, upscale tourist. To see the full use that advertisers can make of music in a campaign, you need only look at the example of the Hard Rock Hotel in Bali (Case study 3.2).

In many of today's ad campaigns the relationship between popular music, and even artists, and the brand in question are central. Levi's ads have spawned twelve top ten hits since 'I Heard it through the Grapevine' launched 'Laundrette' in 1985, an ad which marked a turning point for advertising as, for perhaps the first time, agencies recognized the full power of pop songs as weapons in the battle to win over increasingly jaded audiences. Previously, pop songs had been used because they were cheaper than commissioning jingles, but after this ad they were used to make an immediate impact on the consumer and Flat Eric's success as a result of Levi's 1999 campaign was the latest beneficiary in this symbiotic relationship between the song and the brand. The production of a CD featuring Levi's ad theme tunes in 1993 marked a further development in the relationship between the brand, the song and the advertising. *Originals* featured a pair of Levi's 501s on the CD cover, thus reinforcing the links between the brand, the audience and the cool, trendy persona of the jeans and, by extension, the jeans' wearers. Promotional CDs have since developed into a valuable vehicle in advertising, featuring a range of tracks that complement the brand and brand values. The next step was brands sponsoring pop artists' tours and albums, and we may well see more bands making cameo appearances in movies or in computer games to maintain successful relationships and associations. It would be a mistake to assume that merely using a pop track guarantees advertising success, however. Tracks have to be used intelligently to build brand identity, credibility and emotional relationships with their audience, as in the case of the UK holiday company First Choice which used Katrina and the Waves' song 'Walking on Sunshine' for an ad which is still featured during its charter flights.

Ad highlight 7.4 Getting the music right. Levi's 501s and the 'Refrigerator' ad

Music can be incredibly important in generating and communicating advertising associations, but it is important to select the right piece of music for an ad and it is essential to change it if it does not quite work. 'Refrigerator' was one of a series of highly successful ads produced by Bartle, Bogle, Hegarty for Levi's in the later 1980s and 1990s. In the ad, a boxer-shorted man comes down the stairs of an American motel in the 1950s. The atmosphere is hot and humid and there is an exchange of 'steamy' looks between the man and a young woman working at the counter. She backs away, he follows her to the fridge, where he takes out his chilled 501s.

The music initially chosen to accompany this ad was James Brown's 'This is a Man's World'. However, when the ad team first saw the execution the soundtrack clearly did not work. It did nothing for the ad – in fact it made the acting look bad, the supposedly sexy star appeared downbeat and plodding and there was no on-screen chemistry between the man and woman. The search for a new soundtrack began and the music that completely transformed the ad was Muddy Waters' 'Mannish Boy'. The new soundtrack was added and it completely transformed the ad into a sexy, atmospheric scene – without having to change a single cut in the ad itself. In this instance, Levi's was prepared to allow the agency to delay the ad launch until the right piece of music had been found. Given that music is such a vitally important brand signature for Levi's, it was essential that this happened since a mismatch could have damaged the brand – but how many clients would have been prepared to take such a decision in an era where advertising schedules are contracting and little time is left to get the best out of what you have?

Source: adapted from *Branded*, BBC2 programme screened in 1997.

Sonic brand triggers

Just as the pop song replaced the ad jingle, the jingle itself is now making a comeback after having been shunned as unfashionable for many years – a trend ironically fuelled by the release of CD collections featuring classic tracks from television and radio ads. The jingle or, in modern advertising parlance, the sonic brand trigger can be a powerful brand device. In much the same way as visuals, sounds can also become hugely effective branding devices once they have become associated with a particular brand and such sonic brand triggers are so powerful precisely because (like all music) they have the ability to penetrate the consumer's consciousness almost without notice. Whilst the take-up of sonic brand triggers is slow at the moment (Table 7.1), some brands have consistently used them. British Airways, for instance, has used the 'Flower Duet' theme from Delibes' opera *Lakme* for so long (in its television commercials, for the airline's in-flight music and on its telephone holding system) that it has become inextricably linked with the BA brand.

Table 7.1   Use of sonic brand triggers in radio advertising, 1999

Use of audio techniques in ads	Percentage of ads
No music or jingle	85
Some use of music	9
Background music	2
Use of a sonic brand trigger	2
Music at the end of the ad	1

Source: *Marketing Week*, 1999.

197

The rise and rise of product placement

Whilst advertising and entertainment overlap in music promotions, the greatest synergy between the two can be seen in the development of product placement as an advertising technique. The product placement sub-industry has grown vigorously over the past two decades as Hollywood producers have sought additional sources of income to offset rising production costs, and as advertisers have searched the media horizons for underused and more favourable locations for their promotions. Companies such as the Creative Partnership film marketing agency, established in 1979, are now able to precisely match up brands with the ideal cinematic vehicle. As a result, product placement has grown massively since it began with James Bond endorsing British Airways and Bollinger and ET leaving a trail of Reece's Pieces for Elliott to find in the 1970s. Fuelled by the late 1970s influx of product-shrewd directors such as the Scott brothers and Alan Parker (who all began their careers making commercials), it grew with movies such as *Home Alone II: Lost in New York*, in which the Plaza Hotel is heavily featured and the family spend considerable time considering Avis car rental. Then we had the reverse product placement of *Toy Story* and, most audaciously, *Jurassic Park*, where in one scene the dinosaurs actually enter a toyshop selling *Jurassic Park* merchandising. Now George Lucas is set to make a billion dollars from the merchandising of *The Phantom Menace* alone.

So well known has the phenomenon of product placement become that films can even send up the practice themselves. As well as attracting 100 licensees for products ranging from action-figures to cocktail shakers, half a dozen companies – including Heineken and Virgin Atlantic – paid millions for promotional tie-ins with the 1999 film *Austin Powers: The Spy Who Shagged Me*. Its star and writer, Mike Myers, not only wrote a Heineken joke into the movie but he also promoted the beer in print ads and television spots. There is also a huge plug for 'Virgin Shaglantic' – which Myers also advertised in the USA, appearing on posters for Virgin Atlantic with the headline 'There's only one virgin on this poster, baby'. Whilst Coca-Cola must win the prize for achieving the most product placements, the Swedish mobile phone company Ericsson achieved one of the largest and most lucrative deals ever when it linked up with the 1998 James Bond film *Tomorrow Never Dies*. In the film, Pierce Brosnan uses an Ericsson phone to drive his car on remote, crack open a safe, take photographs and scan fingerprints – not to mention making phone calls!

Tied in with Ericsson's $30 million ad campaign launched simultaneously in sixty countries (which had the dual purpose of advertising Ericsson's phones and promoting *Tomorrow Never Dies*), this is an excellent example that demonstrates how advertising agencies (in this case Young and Rubicam) can get involved in a film project preproduction. The link-up gave both parties what they wanted: for the film distributors the phone company's involvement provided money for promotion, whilst for Ericsson, it was the opportunity to be associated with James Bond – a brand which is strong, likeable, durable (he has survived eighteen movies) and has global awareness. The synergy between the two brands – Ericsson and James Bond – works perfectly: the one is seen as a specialist in high-tech communication and the other is the ultimate product tester. As the ad proclaimed: 'At Ericsson we've cracked the secret of making advanced mobile phones but we leave the testing to our expert'.

Using celebrity endorsement: does the face fit the brand?

In much the same way as products, places and services can be placed in films, celebrities and film stars can also be strategically placed in advertisements. Celebrities such as film or sports stars and fashion models tend to be used because of the feeling that they are able to penetrate the commercial clutter of advertising and arrest viewer attention for a few milliseconds longer. Nike, one of the major exponents of celebrity endorsements in advertising, realized very early on that consumers wanted to wear the clothes and footwear of their sporting heroes. Its celebrity portfolio has grown to be literally a sports pantheon – featuring Michael Jordan (basketball), Tiger Woods (golf), Pete Sampras (tennis), Ian Wright (soccer) and numerous sports teams (in soccer these include Brazil, America, Italy and Holland and, in rugby, France, England and Ireland). In fact, celebrity endorsement is now one of the most popular forms of advertising in the USA: approximately a fifth of all television commercials feature a famous person and approximately 10 per cent of television ad dollars are spent in celebrity endorsement advertisements – a figure which is rising as the costs of endorsement contracts become astronomical. In tourism and leisure, celebrities can also emerge as presenters of tourism and sports programmes and as endorsers of tourism products and, since most stars are available at a price, it is only a matter of time before an individual celebrity takes on a commercial role as a product endorser.

Michael Jordan is one athlete who has reaped huge rewards from endorsements – his total endorsement contracts with companies such as Nike, McDonald's and Gatorade exceed $240 million and in 1999 *The Economist* claimed that the back of his head was more recognized than the faces of Bill Clinton, Newt Gingrich and Jesus Christ.[11] As an articulate, intelligent, highly likeable (and winning) athlete with a reputation for sportsmanship and charity work, Jordan is the perfect endorser with a high degree of consumer credibility – and a multiracial appeal. In the years that Jordan has been a professional basketball player he has had an impact on the world economy estimated at over $10 billion – including an estimated $5.2 billion in sales of Nike products.[12]

| Ad highlight 7.5 | Wales's star-studded campaign |

In the mid-1990s the Wales Tourist Board ad campaigns made effective use of Welsh celebrities, including US Masters-winning golfer Ian Woosnam, Oscar-winning actor Sir Anthony Hopkins and world-renowned singer Tom Jones. The involvement of these celebrities attracted tremendous media attention in an eye-catching poster campaign. The campaign, launched in 1994, was the first time that the Wales Tourist Board used endorsements from the world of showbusiness, fashion and sport. The first phase of the campaign featured giant posters of Sir Anthony Hopkins, Ian Woosnam and Tom Jones against beautiful Welsh landscapes. A surreal approach was used on the poster featuring Tom Jones, whose face was superimposed on a photograph of a rocky outcrop on Tenby beach in south-west Wales. The posters featured on 746 strategic billboard sites in London, the East and West Midlands, North-West England, Wales and the West and in 4000 advertisements on London Underground trains. Subsequent phases of the campaign added Alice of Lewis Carroll's *Alice in Wonderland*, who regularly holidayed in Wales, designs of the (then) Welsh-based fashion house, Laura Ashley, and Dylan Thomas, the Swansea-born poet.

Celebrity endorsements are not restricted to film, music and sports stars – even cartoon characters can find their way into advertising. In the UK, Typhoo Tea licensed Wallace and Gromit from the BBC and, when consumers were encouraged to collect figurines and send away for themed items (more than 2 million products were redeemed), sales of the tea trebled. Brand managers who utilize such characters are buying into consumer goodwill, character credibility and, importantly, a past history, and choosing the right face to represent a brand is an art that is becoming more and more critical as brands increasingly turn to licensed characters to promote themselves in the marketplace. Their use and cost has risen dramatically – in 1997 the global market was estimated to be $112 billion and George Lucas is set for massive rewards through the merchandising rights of the 1999 blockbuster *Star Wars: The Phantom Menace* prequel. Lucasfilm Ltd. (George Lucas's company) commands huge licensing fees from toy-makers who are willing to pay in advance for the chance to cash in on success later. Even before the release of the new trilogy, *Star Wars* toy sales topped $500 million a year. The benefits – primarily linking brands with well-known characters which consumers relate to – far outweigh the costs of licence purchases, although such is the cost (perhaps 10 per cent of a company's marketing spend) that brands must fully exploit any characters which they license.

Securing the right face (whether real or animated) for a brand is also about obtaining a sympathetic fit between the product and the personality. Rights owners now actively promote and sell their characters to the brands they want to be associated with – those which are quality, leader brands. In turn, brand managers are unlikely to want to link up with stars who are likely to bring their name into disrepute. The celebrity halo effect is one of the key effects marketers seek when celebrities are used to advertise brands – the hope is that the repeated association of a brand with a celebrity will ultimately lead consumers to think the brand possesses the same attractive qualities as that figure. If the celebrity can also represent what the brand stands for then that strategy is even more successful. In the UK the Walkers Crisps' strategy was that the snack food is 'so nice that even the nicest people in the world would steal them'. This fitted perfectly with the image of 'nice guy' Gary Lineker (the England soccer star who was never booked in his career) – a link-up which has been startlingly effective. Before the campaign, awareness rates for Walkers Crisps' ads hovered around the 40 per cent mark. Since the Lineker campaign, awareness rates have never fallen below 60 per cent and when the ads are airing, awareness rises to 96 per cent. In terms of sales, Walkers Crisps have soared – prompting Walkers managing director, Martin Glenn, to comment: 'I've never been involved in any advertising that has worked so well'.

Interestingly, it is not just Walkers, but the brand managers of all kinds of products are turning to soccer because of the sport's current popularity and fashionability. Whilst we said in Chapter 3 that soccer is currently the world's most watched sport, some commentators are asking whether the game's bubble is about to burst. In the UK, in particular, soccer has become a major advertising theme following the sport's increasing popularity – regardless of whether the product has any soccer associations or not. Loyalty to a brand's established strategy and commitment to the difficult task of long-term brand-building has been put on hold in the search for soccer themes, which are felt to be safe and saleable to virtually any audience. Horlicks (a bedtime milk drink) have featured Les Ferdinand of Tottenham Hotspur and formerly of England taking his clothes off; Ruud Gullit, Gareth Southgate, Stuart Pearce and Chris Waddle have all featured in Pizza Hut ads, whilst Gary Lineker has been joined by Michael Owen in Walkers Crisps ads. Other soccer-link ups in the later 1990s included: Peter Schmeichel (Danish Bacon), Eric Cantona (Eurostar), Jason MacAteer (Wash & Go shampoo), David Beckham

(Brylcream), David Ginola (L'Oreal) and Ian Wright (Nike, Chicken Tonight and Nescafé). The soccer stars are used to communicate quickly with an audience in much the same way as other celebrity endorsers. Unfortunately, their proliferation may have more to do with the interests of creative executives than the brand consumers themselves. Many creatives are young men interested in sport and soccer in particular, and not surprisingly their creative ideas frequently reflect their own interests. The question is, can this fad continue indefinitely? Industry opinion suggests not, although the jury's out as to when the creatives will score one own goal too many.[13] Certainly, if so many advertisers are using soccer stars as endorsers, it is unlikely to make one brand stand out above another and consumers may well be confused over which product each star endorses.

Ad highlight 7.6　　　**Pizza Hut's success with *Beverly Hills 90210* star**

The brief for this campaign was to assist in repositioning Pizza Hut's position as a fast-food chain into one of a casual, relaxed eatery. The concept centred on a teenage girl on a dream date at a Pizza Hut. The dream date is eventually dispensed with when he eats too much of her pizza. The personality selected as the dream date most likely to appeal to the target audience of young female adults was Luke Perry of the American television show *Beverly Hills 90210*. National television provided the medium for the £9 million campaign, which achieved awareness rates of 66 per cent in the fifteen to twenty-four age group and 62 per cent in the twenty-five to thirty-four age group.

Brand managers are increasingly becoming involved in a guessing game of celebrity success potential since brands that sign up stars before they become hugely successful will reap greater rewards. The trouble is predicting the next band, sports hero or cartoon character set for stardom, whilst avoiding the fallout from negative publicity or box office flops. Other problems include the fact that some celebrities endorse several products, sometimes even switching their endorsements to rival brands. Celebrity endorsements may also backfire when the celebrities themselves fall from grace (witness the examples of Eric Cantona, Mike Tyson and O. J. Simpson) or even die just after the campaign launch, as happened to the actor Gordon Jackson, featured in a Scottish Tourist Board commercial. Pepsi, a company that uses music celebrity endorsers to resonate with its target audience (Case study 7.2), quickly dropped the pop star Madonna when she was seen making love to a black Christ in her video for the 1989 song 'Like a Prayer'. The cola company

Table 7.2 Brand–celebrity link-ups: pluses and minuses

Brand celebrity pluses	Brand celebrity minuses
Quality	Costly
Consumer appeal	Consumer confusion over endorsers
Celebrity halo effect	Celebrity choice backfires
Brand–celebrity synergy	Vampire effect (brand promotes celebrity not vice versa)

replaced her at huge expense with Michael Jackson – who it subsequently dropped following allegations of child abuse. Indeed, such is the risk of scandal and negative publicity associated with celebrities that there has been a recent mini-trend towards using dead celebrities who are well known and respected by consumers in the target audiences to whom they appeal and, best of all, who cannot compromise their reputations and adversely impact on the brands they posthumously endorse! Einstein, Steve McQueen and Marilyn Monroe are just some of those who have featured in ads long after their deaths. See Table 7.2 for a summary of the pluses and minuses of linking up with celebrities.

Ad highlight 7.7   **The British Broadcasting Corporation's 'Perfect Day'**

'Perfect Day' by Lou Reed became the theme tune for Britain's biggest celebrity commercial – selling an institution designed to hold the British together – the British Broadcasting Corporation (BBC). In building its licence fee ad around this cult song, the BBC succeeded in promoting a collective 'feel', even though each line of the song is performed by an individual artist. The ad itself is beautifully executed with big stars (Lou Reed, Elton John, Bono, David Bowie, Tom Jones and many others) chosen for their currency and broad appeal. The setting for the ad is a computer-generated garden that moves from dawn to dusk and slide-projector special effects signal changes in the acts. The ad concept – the range of names and the idea that nobody else except the BBC could attract such a star-studded cast – provides both proof and metaphor for the BBC's very rationale and existence – its mass appeal.

Even the most successful companies can and do get it wrong over celebrity endorsers. Nike, in the build up to Euro '96 (the European soccer championships held in England), ran an ad campaign featuring Newcastle United team-mates Les Ferdinand (of England) and David Ginola (of France). The players faced each other in a showdown with their national flags in the background, whilst the billboard strapline read 'Friendship expires 6/96'. As an ad concept and execution it worked extremely well – the only problem was neither player managed to make it into their respective national squads and thus were not featured in the tournament. Nike bravely tried to rescue the situation by running ads ridiculing the original execution and highlighting the Nike curse, thus when England faced Germany in the competition's semi-final Nike's ads in the UK declared 'Good luck Germany' with 'that should do it' in brackets – unfortunately for Nike in the UK market, Germany won!

Once again, two years later Nike spent $5.6 billion in marketing during the soccer World Cup finals in France, including $4 billion on sponsorship for individual teams and players. Unfortunately the Nike curse struck again and Ibrahim Ba, the French soccer player who featured prominently in Nike's ad campaign, failed to make the French team. Further bad news was to come when the final was contested between France and Brazil. Nike's sponsorship deal with Brazil alone cost £250 million over ten years, yet Brazil lost the final and their star player Ronaldo (also sponsored by Nike) had a very lacklustre performance. Even worse for Nike, it was Adidas-sponsored France who beat Brazil and Adidas star Zinedine Zidane who became a national hero by scoring two goals. Such was the media interest in the event that Nike had to issue press statements denying rumours that they had insisted Ronaldo play in the final despite being unfit. It would be wrong to suggest, however, that Nike is the only company subject to the curse of unpredictability in sport. An Adidas billboard ad campaign in England in the same tournament read: 'Historians, it's spelled B-E-C-K-H-A-M', only to see David Beckham vilified in the English press for being sent off in England's match against Argentina.

The use of celebrities as spokespeople in advertisements constitutes a significant investment in intangible assets by the sponsoring firm – an investment that management hopes to offset with greater future sales revenues and profits. In order for celebrities to be effective in advertising, their selection must be based on their familiarity to the market, the nature of their appeal and the credibility of the celebrity in the consumers' eyes. Even where – as in the case of Walkers Crisps – there is an ideal 'fit' between brand and celebrity, it is almost impossible to accurately measure the direct impact of endorsement on a brand. It does seem to be the case, however, that with products high in psychological or social risk – such as holidays or clothes – celebrity endorsers create greater believability and a more favourable evaluation of the product and the ad than either 'experts' or a 'typical consumer' endorser, probably because these types of style products are highly aspirational.

Chapter summary

This chapter has focused on one of the most challenging aspects of producing advertising: the creative process where ideas are generated and then rationally examined to assess their value. Creativity is about being different and its task is to make the advertising message believable and persuasive, whilst remaining relevant to the consumer and the brand personality. The most effective way to ensure a message is noticed is to:

- reduce the advertising problem to its bare essentials
- aim for simplicity
- isolate the proposition to identify the desired evoked emotions
- determine how to approach the message psychologically
- dramatize the relevant stimulus.

Creative inspirations for advertising campaigns come from a range of sources, but often in tourism and leisure ideas spring from who uses or does not use the product, its inherent value or its past associations. Popular entertainment can also be 'quarried' for ideas and appeals based on literature, art, films and television programmes, music and celebrities are all extensively seen in advertising campaigns, to the extent that there is an increasingly closer link-up between films and advertising through product placement.

Celebrity endorsement has become a significant element of advertising and film or sports stars and fashion models tend to be used because they are able to penetrate the commercial clutter of advertising and arrest viewer attention. Celebrity endorsers can also create greater believability and a more favourable evaluation of tourism and leisure products that are high in psychological or social risk, since these style products are highly aspirational. It is critical, however, to obtain a sympathetic fit between the product and the personality so that the celebrity can represent the brand's values, attributes and qualities. Using celebrities to advertise a brand also risks the product becoming associated with any negative publicity attracted by a celebrity. Other problems include the fact that some celebrities endorse several products, sometimes even switching their endorsements to rival brands.

Case study 7.1

Using music to sell America

Music lovers and history buffs can walk in the footsteps of musical legends like Chuck Berry, Elvis Presley and Louis Armstrong following the launch of the America's Music Corridor joint marketing initiative. America's Music Corridor is a co-operative marketing effort which focuses on the river cities' contributions to America's indigenous musical art forms from St Louis to New Orleans and all points in between. Visitors can sample the flavours of a number of musical styles in one trip to a music corridor which has produced more music and legendary artists than anywhere else in the world, and the initiative is designed to be particularly appealing to baby boomer music lovers and older travellers.

The concept, developed by Nancy Milton and Dawne Massey (co-founders of America's Music Corridor), emerged during the 1993 annual St Louis Blues Heritage Festival. It originally built on the similarities of St Louis's and Memphis's musical heritage, and then New Orleans's blues, jazz, ragtime and rock 'n' roll traditions. As Massey has commented, 'It just seemed like a natural way to promote the . . . cities'. In 1996 the programme won the Odyssey Award for Cultural Tourism and it has received tremendous media coverage in both the US and international press – achieving incredible results from a tiny budget through its unique partnership between cities. The branding initiative relied on co-operation, a joint PR campaign and print material to meet its objectives of increasing international visitor numbers and improving the region's appeal to the New York and California markets. It quickly became a part of international tour itineraries and grew the percentage of New York and California visitor inquiries from only 4 per cent to 34 per cent.

In a similar initiative, Memphis and Mississippi joined forces to promote the region as America's Blues Alley in 1995. Music has been the link between the Southern Tennessee city and the Magnolia State since the turn of the twentieth century and the aim of the branding initiative has been to develop the region as a fly-drive destination using Memphis as the gateway. Between them, Memphis and Mississippi can lay claim to the USA's richest mix of American musical heritage. Mississippi produced not only the king of rock 'n' roll, Elvis Presley, but also B. B. King (the founder of the blues) and Jimmie Rogers (the father of country music). Memphis became the home of Elvis, it is also the home of Beale Street (a showcase location for the blues since the 1940s), as well as the legendary Sun Studio where Elvis, Johnny Cash, Roy Orbison and Jerry Lee Lewis all cut their first records.

Source: St Louis Convention and Visitors Commission and Memphis Convention and Visitors Bureau.

Case study 7.2

Using a band to sell a brand

In the later 1990s the link up between Pepsi and the Spice Girls proved to be exceptionally effective in boosting sales of the cola. Pepsi's sales rose by 5 per cent from 15 to 20 per cent of the cola market – largely at the expense of rivals Coca-Cola. Pepsi signed up the Spice Girls just before the band became a true pop phenomenon. The deal was designed to reinforce Pepsi's appeal to its core teenage market – and in this it can be seen as part of a long-standing musical link-up between Pepsi and stars such as Michael Jackson, Gloria Estefan, Tina Turner and M. C. Hammer.

Pepsi launched a £1 million 'generation next' campaign in the UK – running alongside sales promotion activities, notably one whereby consumers collected twenty pink ring-pull tabs from promotional Pepsi cans, sent them off and received a free Spice Girls CD single *Step to Me* – not available in high street retailers. Collectors were also entered into a free prize draw to see the band play in Turkey. The advertising and the promotion were integral to Pepsi's marketing strategy, and television and press ads and the Pepsi Chart Show (screened on the terrestrial station Channel 5) all spelt out that the only way to listen to the single was to buy Pepsi. Producing 92 million promotional packs of the cola, Pepsi clearly stuck to the premise of saying one thing very clearly and very loudly. Six hundred thousand CDs were redeemed with the promotion. Multiply this by the twenty cans' ring-pulls required and sales from the campaign were obviously hugely impressive (12 million cans). The redemption rate of 10 per cent marked a significant rise on previous Pepsi promotions such as *Star Wars*. Since this campaign the Spice Girls may have been discarded by Pepsi but it continues to use music to push its youth cola signature – the Irish boy band, Boyzone, followed as the next addition to the Pepsi fold.

Notes

1 Simon Anholt (1998). Paper presented at the Second International Travel and Tourism Advertising Festival, Valencia.
2 Jeremy Bullmore (1999). The advertising creative process. In *The Advertising Business: Operations, Creativity, Media Planning, Integrated Communications* (J. P. Jones, ed.) pp. 51–60, Sage.
3 John Hegarty, in *D&AD Newsletter*, March 1998, quoted in Len Weinreich (1999). *11 Steps to Brand Heaven: The Ultimate Guide to Buying an Advertising Campaign*. Kogan Page, p. 152.
4 David Abbott, quoted in Len Weinreich (1999). *11 Steps to Brand Heaven: The Ultimate Guide to Buying an Advertising Campaign*. Kogan Page, p. 121.
5 Len Weinreich (1999). *11 Steps to Brand Heaven: The Ultimate Guide to Buying an Advertising Campaign*. Kogan Page, p. 121.
6 John Hegarty, in *D&AD Newsletter*, p. 143.
7 Courtesy of Tom Rodwell of Court Burkitt.
8 David Dingle and Graham Harding (1994). From Canberra to Oriana: a £200 million investment in the identification and management of brand values. *Journal of Vacation Marketing*, **1** (2), 195–201.
9 Jim Aitchison (1999). *Cutting Edge Advertising. How to Create the World's Best Print for Brands in the 21st Century*. Prentice Hall, pp. 244–5.
10 Ibid.
11 'His airness retires', *The Economist*, 16 January 1999, **350** (8102), 32.
12 R. Johnson (1998). The Jordan effect. *Fortune*, **137** (12), 124.
13 Harriet Green (1998). Why football will not guarantee an ad's success. *Campaign*, 6 February.

Further reading

Agawal, J. and Kamakura, W. A. (1995). The economic worth of celebrity endorsers: an event study analysis. *Journal of Marketing*, **59** (3).
Aitchison, J. (1999). *Cutting Edge Advertising. How to Create the World's Best Print for Brands in the 21st Century*. Prentice Hall.
Bond, J. and Kirshenbaum, R. (1998). *Under the Radar: Talking to Today's Cynical Consumer*. John Wiley.
Bullmore, J. (1999). The advertising creative process. In *The Advertising Business: Operations, Creativity, Media Planning, Integrated Communications* (J. P. Jones, ed.) pp. 51–60, Sage.

Bullmore, J. (1999). Humour in advertising: a practitioner's view. In *The Advertising Business: Operations, Creativity, Media Planning, Integrated Communications* (J. P. Jones, ed.) pp. 175–80, Sage.

Cialdini, R. B. (1993). *The Psychology of Influence*. William Morrow.

Dru, J.-M. (1996). *Disruption: Overturning Conventions and Shaking Up the Marketplace*. John Wiley.

Fletcher, W. (1994). *How to Capture the Advertising High Ground*. Century Business.

Jones, J. P. (ed.) (1999). *The Advertising Business: Operations, Creativity, Media Planning, Integrated Communications*. Sage.

Kotler, P. et al. (1993). *Marketing Places. Attracting Investment, Industry and Tourism to Cities, States and Nations*. Free Press.

Mathur, L. K., Mathur, I. and Rangan, N. (1997). The wealth effects associated with a celebrity endorser: the Michael Jordan phenomenon. *Journal of Advertising Research*, **37** (3).

Morgan, N. and Pritchard, A. (1998). *Tourism Promotion and Power: Creating Images, Creating Identities*. John Wiley, ch. 4.

Weinreich, L. (1999). *11 Steps to Brand Heaven: The Ultimate Guide to Buying an Advertising Campaign*. Kogan Page.

IF YOU'RE EXPECTING JUST ANOTHER
BEACH HOLIDAY, YOU'LL

HAV'A

CULTURE SHOCK IN

TEL AVIV·JAFFA.

Where else in the Mediterranean can you walk straight from the beach into the theatre and see a world famous prima ballerina dance?

Nowhere but Tel Aviv, a thriving metropolis that just happens to be situated on miles of white, sandy beaches. There are art galleries full of Renoirs, Picassos and Lichtensteins. And theatres and concert halls where internationally renowned

orchestras and opera companies perform regularly.

After your evening's cultural entertainment, you can dine out in one of the many restaurants that serve dishes from all over the world.

Tel Aviv is a lively, buzzing city that's no more than a five hour flight away. If you fill in the coupon, we'll send you a book of discount vouchers on theatres, museums, restaurants,

excursions and car rental. Or simply pick up the telephone and call us on 0171-434 3651.

NAME _____

ADDRESS _____

_____

_____

_____ POSTCODE _____

TELEPHONE _____

Plate 8 Israel's HAV'A campaign (Courtesy of Court Burkitt)

Plate 9 Wales's 'Two hours and a million miles away' campaign (Courtesy of Wales Tourist Board)

Plate 10 Elle Macpherson: a celebrity felt to embody the spirit of Western Australia
(Courtesy of Western Australia Tourist Commission)

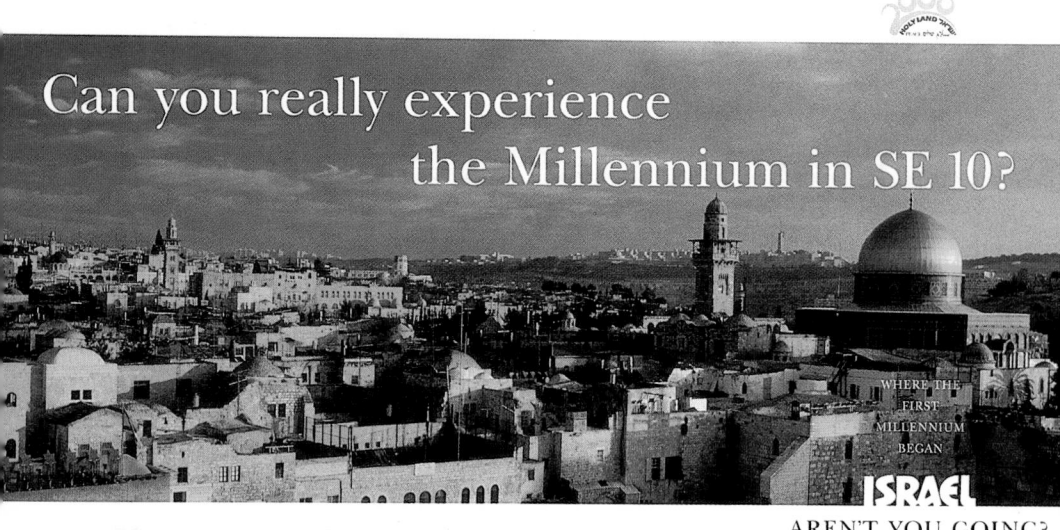

Plate 11 Israel's millennium campaign (Courtesy of Court Burkitt)

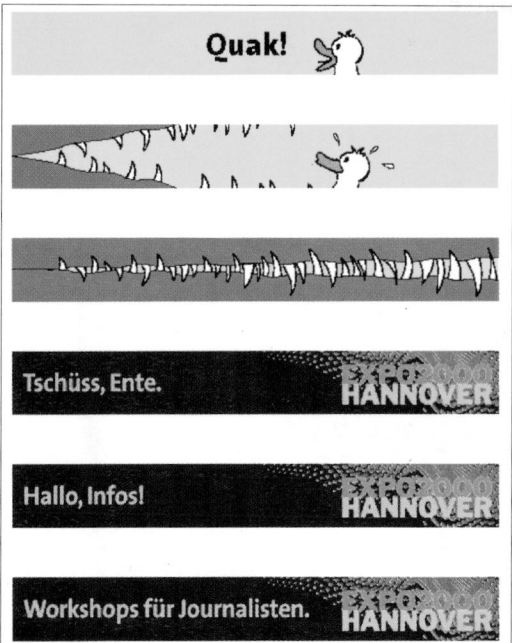

Plate 12 Hanover Expo banner ads (Courtesy of DDBO, Hamburg)

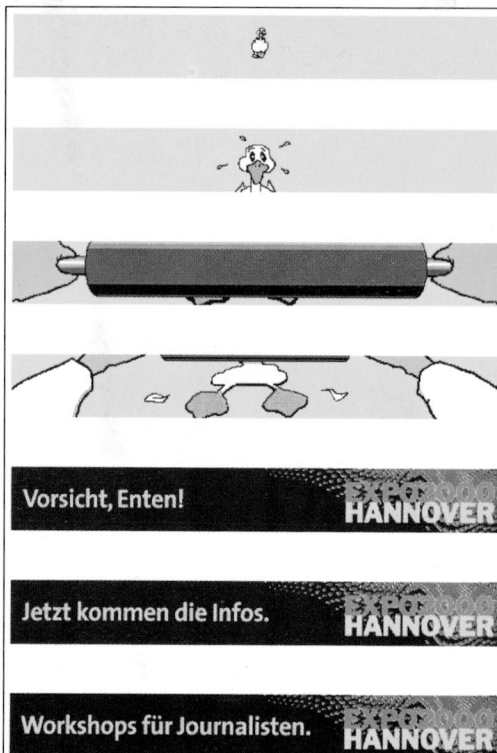

Part Three

Advertising Brands

8

Building powerful tourism and leisure brands

Chapter overview

As the first of three chapters that examine the important relationship between advertising and branding, this chapter discusses brand-building. Whatever values a brand represents, in today's marketplace it is becoming more and more critical for it to be able to shout above the crowd and, whilst a decade ago brand managers knew that if they spent enough money on a campaign some of it would work, in the 2000s they have to communicate with an increasingly sophisticated audience. In this context, the chapter begins by defining brands, and then focuses on brand-building before discussing consumer–brand relationships. The chapter concludes by considering the problems facing the tourism and leisure industries' 'rebel' brands. Key themes reviewed are:

- understanding branding
- building brands
- the brand benefit ladder
- establishing brand architecture

- brands as today's trust brokers
- brand aerobics
- creating brands with consumer resonance
- the challenges to tourism and leisure rebel brands.

Introduction

At the start of the twenty-first century, brands permeate virtually all facets of everyday life – indeed, arguably branding has become today's most important marketing strategy. It has developed into both a valuable equity and a sophisticated science and, whilst it costs millions to develop new brands, around half of which fail, if successful the branding of organizations, goods and services can reportedly increase gross profits by up to 50 per cent. Although the various aspects of branding continue to be the subject of much study, little has been written about tourism and leisure branding and its relationship with advertising. This part of the book seeks to go some way towards redressing this by focusing on the relationship between the brand and the consumer (Chapter 8) brand positioning and repositioning (Chapter 9) and destination branding strategies (Chapter 10).

As tariff barriers break down worldwide and television and the Internet shrink the global marketplace, brands are the real free-market winners, transcending geography, history and management teams. Great brands have proved to be more enduring than companies, products or people, and in the daily battle of American marketing the main consumer brands wage an almost relentless war on their rivals. Clearly for today's tourism and leisure industries, increasingly characterized by mergers and the emergence of large players, branding is perhaps *the* most powerful marketing weapon available. In the fitness sector, for instance, services are basically the same, every club and venue claims to have the friendliest and most customer-focused culture, equipment is no longer a differentiator and location is either good or bad. Equally, when advances are made, competitors quickly incorporate new product features or service innovations. Yet, if two companies offer equal products and services from equal locations at similar prices, what would persuade one potential member to choose one fitness club over another? It will come down to empathy with the club and its values – ultimately which one potential members feel is a truer reflection of themselves. The battle for customers in tomorrow's leisure and tourism industries will be fought not over price but over hearts and minds – in essence, branding (in conjunction with creative communications) will be key to success.

Understanding brands today

Simon Anholt of the WorldWriters agency has defined a brand as 'the goodwill tied up in a name'.[1] He also describes branding as the creation of a distortion field in the mind of the consumer which interferes with his or her sense of value so that he or she is prepared to pay more for a product than its intrinsic worth would suggest. In this way, consumers are prepared to pay a premium price for a product. For example, when buying a can of Coca-Cola consumers are paying for the name on the can and what this name represents rather than for what it actually contains. Indeed, such is the value of this name that the Coca-Cola brand alone (simply the equity of its symbol, not its factories, distribution networks or any of its tangible assets) is worth as much as the gross domestic product of the UK! Yet Coke and brands like it could not sustain their premium prices if they had not originally established a unique position in the consumer's mental picture of the market. The *value* of a brand lies in its ability to polarize consumers and, in creating this sense of difference, the *name* of the brand becomes critical. Unfortunately, in the travel, tourism and leisure industries (particularly in the public sector) little thought has traditionally been given to names: they are often bureaucratic inventions that fail to satisfy the three criteria of a slick and effective name: they are neither distinctive, memorable nor short. Destinations marketed on the basis of political boundaries are particularly forgettable but, at the same time, of course, they have to compete for global consumer mindshare with brands such as Nike, Coke, Sony, BMW, etc.

Such megabrands of course, did not always carry this cachet – Nike only conjures up particular associations because of years of effective, consistent and coherent marketing and advertising. The name of the Greek goddess of victory has become a symbol of sporting success, rebelliousness and attitude because of advertising. As well as tending to be distinctive, memorable and short, the best brand names must also be trademarkable (so that they can be legally protected) and what Anholt calls 'leakproof'. Since a brand name initially means nothing, it is only 'an empty vessel into which you pour brand equity by means of marketing',[2] if possible it should also be a name that will not be confused with any other. If it sounds or looks like another well-known brand, then for every dollar spent on marketing, that competitor will also gain 50 cents of free awareness.

Although commentators are in agreement that branding has much to offer, there remains considerable debate over how its principles are translated into practical marketing activity, and there are few studies which discuss how tourism and leisure managers can use branding strategies to market what are frequently intangible bundles of services. Certainly, managers in the tourism and leisure industries cannot afford to ignore branding as it offers an innovative and effective tool by which organizations and destinations can establish emotional links with the consumer. Just as in the marketing of consumer goods, branding has the potential to engender consumer loyalty and position products, services and destinations to appeal to consumers' self-images and lifestyles. Interestingly, powerful brands such as Coca-Cola, Nike and Levi's share a number of characteristics. They all have a vision which is founded on intensive consumer and competitor research and which is expressed with care and discipline in everything that communicates the brand's personality.

> Modern branding is not just about developing appealing communication strategies, it is also about defining and delivering leading-edge product or service quality to match or exceed customer expectations.

That vision (which must be shared and 'bought into' by the consumer) can be seen to be clearly expressed in the brand's core values which are credible, plausible, durable and deliverable. These values are consistently reinforced through the product, the service and in all marketing communications – both above and below the line – every execution in all media contributes to maintaining brand presence. The challenge for many tourism and leisure brand managers to emulate the success of powerful brands in other sectors remains of paramount importance as we move into the twenty-first century. Tomorrow's marketing environment will be one defined by ever-increasing competition, greater product parity and consumer choice in which intangibles such as brand values, service and celebrity will be the key differentiating factors.

Building rich and complex brands

In marketing, a brand is understood to represent a unique combination of product characteristics and added values, both functional and non-functional, which have taken on a relevant meaning which is inextricably linked to that brand, awareness of which might be conscious or intuitive.[3] Brand advantage can be secured through communication that highlights the specific benefits of a product, culminating in an overall impression of a superior brand. The image the product creates in the consumer's mind, how it is *positioned*, however, is of more importance to its ultimate success than its actual characteristics. Brand managers try to position their brands so that they are perceived by the consumer to occupy a niche in the marketplace occupied by no other brand – thus for marketers, the value of a successful brand lies in its potential to reduce substitutability. Brand managers try to differentiate their product by stressing attributes they claim will match their target markets' needs more closely than other brands and then they try to create a product image consistent with the perceived self-image of the targeted consumer segment. When consumers make brand choices about products – including leisure services and tourism destinations – they are making lifestyle statements since they are trying to buy into not only an image but also an emotional relationship.

> Contemporary brands offer consumers meaning and value – they are modern trust brokers and indicate quality and reliability.

Given the nature of this relationship, there is increased focus amongst marketers on differentiation through loyalty and the emotional appeal of brands, rather than through discernible tangible benefits.[4] As Lury says, 'it is our perceptions – our beliefs and our feelings about a brand that are most important'.[5] However, mere emotion is not enough, the key is to develop a strong brand which holds some *unique* associations for the consumer – 'while emotion has always been an important component of branding, emotion in the absence of a point of difference that can be articulated and firmly seated in the memory is arguably a recipe for consumer confusion'.[6] Such is the importance of this product positioning that it has been described as the essence of marketing and, as we see in the next chapter, since it conveys how the product will satisfy a consumer need, different consumer meanings can be assigned to the same product via different positioning strategies, depending on the audience and stage in the brand life cycle.

The added value which a brand stands for – its equity – is difficult to define or measure yet brands clearly enhance the value of products beyond their fundamental attributes – brand names, brand symbols, brand design, brand logos are all physical reflections of what are intangible assets. Whilst there are various definitions and measures of brand equity, in most cases brand managers are interested in how salient their brand is to consumers (their level of brand awareness and the associations it conveys) and how these are manifested in consumer brand loyalty (see Table 8.1 for a variety of saliency measures). There is no doubt that the significance of branding in leisure and tourism is increasingly recognized – for instance, hoteliers who

> Brand saliency refers to how positive and emotionally close consumers feel towards a brand. Advertising significantly influences saliency levels.

previously looked to product features such as satellite television or upmarket restaurants to make themselves stand out from the crowd are turning to branding to provide that point of differentiation. Naturally, advertising is hugely significant in the creation of brand equity because of its ability to communicate the rational or emotional benefits delivered by a brand: advertising is instrumental in creating awareness, it can affect perceptions of

Table 8.1   Brand saliency measures

Awareness
Purchase
Consideration
Familiarity
Association
Intention
Recall
Affection
Loyalty
Belief/attitude
Emotion
Personality

brand quality and it can transform a brand from an 'also ran' into a major player. If brand managers cease investing in brand advertising, as in Ad highlight 8.1, they must be prepared to lose equity over time, a situation which will be aggravated if key competitors maintain their ad spend.

Ad highlight 8.1	Higher ad spend boosts the Holiday Inn brand

An American study examined the impacts of brand equity on two hotel chains – both of which invested in very different ad spends over a ten-year period, but which offered similar product attributes and reported almost identical consumer service ratings. The study found that the brand with the higher advertising budget (Holiday Inn) generated substantially higher levels of brand equity, which in turn generated significantly greater preference and purchase intentions.

	Ad spend ($ millions) Howard Johnson	Ad spend ($ millions) Holiday Inn
1980	0.6	10.5
1990	4.1	26.2

After making allowances for the size of the hotel chains, Holiday Inn spent between two and five times more than Howard Johnson on advertising during the 1980s. In the early 1990s investigations were conducted into brand awareness, brand associations and perceived quality and the research revealed that Holiday Inn:

- had a brand equity over five times greater than Howard Johnson's
- occupied the coveted 'top of mind' location in the customer's hotel set
- had 55 per cent more advertising awareness

- was felt to be of greater quality than Howard Johnson
- had many more positive associations (reputation, consistency, service, value and room quality), whilst Howard Johnson had far more negative associations (reputation, rooms, cleanliness and restaurant).

The impact of all these measures resulted in Holiday Inn achieving greater brand equity which translated into greater brand preference – the preference for Holiday Inn was nearly ten times that for Howard Johnson – and generated higher purchase intention scores.

Source: adapted from Cobbwalgren, R. et al. (1995). Brand equity, brand preference and purchase intent. *Journal of Advertising Research*, **24**, Fall, 3.

Building a brand is a long, slow process that needs patience and commitment. Brands attempting to take share away from a dominant brand leader face a very long and difficult journey – indeed, some commentators argue that in modern marketing it is far too difficult to attempt. Jones confirms this view by suggesting that advertising dollars spent on larger brands result in more sales than a similar amount spent on smaller ones.[7] Therefore, those who have strong brands hold significant advantage – which is why brands are considered to be so valuable – strong brands equal premium prices. Despite this, even strong brands must be nurtured and require continuous investment. Pat Mann, a director of international brand management at J. Walter Thompson, has argued that this does not always happen, saying that too many 'companies have been living off the legacy of their brands without putting anything back'.[8] As we shall see in the next chapter, brands can often show signs of age, needing refreshment in the face of modern competition and even the most classic of brands need to remain contemporary. Certainly, such is the speed of change in today's market that brands which fail to evolve are brands which will fail, although that evolution has to be controlled to avoid damaging the brand's long-term positioning (see the problems faced by BA in Case study 8.1).

Just like people, brands grow and evolve – they are complex and rich. In fact, the most powerful brands are those with the richest personalities – we all know how Nike behaves, although (just as if it were a person) we all engage with it in a slightly different way. If a brand manager can describe his or her brand in less than a page of A4 then the brand personality is nowhere near rich enough to have resonance with the consumer. Just think of Virgin. Originally a music business, the Virgin brand embraces an airline, a railway, soft drinks, leisure and financial services and now mobile phones. Above all, Virgin has a complex personality enabling it to have become a way of life for many consumers (see Ad highlight 8.3). Yet such complex personalities are quite rare in a world where brand attributes are often arbitrarily and superficially constructed. Traits such as 'friendly', 'caring' and 'contemporary' are popular hoped-for descriptors but they hardly help to build an engaging or aspirational brand. Brand-building is all about developing a rich, relevant brand personality. 'Developing' is the keyword here – brands should never atrophy – instead they should reflect and respond to changes in consumers' lives and, whilst a brand's core values will remain the same, its personality should be able to evolve. Thus, P&O has evolved considerably over the decades yet has retained a powerful and consistent identity which is promoted today using both humour and subtlety in its press and television advertising.

Ad highlight 8.2   **Stakis builds a brand based on a warm welcome**

Stakis is a company operating over fifty hotels, over twenty casinos and almost seventy LivingWell health clubs in the UK, Ireland and Gibraltar. Before it launched its new brand identity in 1998, Stakis conducted one of the most comprehensive research projects in the hospitality industry to establish if the hotel chain had a point of difference and if this was relevant to people's choice of hotel. Three pieces of independent research all came to the same conclusion – that people thought of Stakis as being warm and natural, with intuitive staff who made customers feel special. This research was then used to underpin the new brand identity which promises that Stakis will make its customers feel special, communicated via two 60-second commercials.

The ads, based on people sharing 'Stakis moments', were aimed at all types of people. One ad shows children having a pillow fight being caught by a seemingly stern member of staff who then laughs and leaves them to it. Then a young couple are seen enjoying a Stakis moment, relaxing in bed, followed by a tired businessman cheered up after his warm welcome at the hotel. Finally the ad's last 20 seconds focus on the time to leave and the endline 'Stakis. You won't want to say goodbye' appears. In addition to refocusing its advertising, Stakis also redesigned its corporate identity to reflect warmth and has emphasized staff attitude as a cornerstone of the brand. The new logo is a lamp and a flame and the word Stakis is now written 'in contemporary script, representing informality and individuality'.

Source: Stakis moments. *Leisuremarketing*, 26 October–8 November 1998.

Wolff Olins suggests that there are four phases in identity- or brand-building:

- investigation, analysis and strategic recommendations
- identity development
- launch and introduction – communicating the vision
- implementation – making it happen.[9]

The first of these phases in brand construction or development is to establish just how contemporary or relevant the brand is to today's consumer, which largely explains the recent explosion of investment in consumer research (Ad highlight 8.2). In Chapter 4 we considered the various advertising research techniques available to brand managers and ad agencies but here we need to consider the specific ways in which brand managers can come to understand and build brand value and saliency with existing or potential consumers. Of primary importance in this process are the concepts of the *brand benefit ladder* and *brand architecture*.

The brand benefit ladder

A brand's personality has both a head and a heart – its head refers to the logical brand features, whilst its heart refers to its emotional benefits and associations. Advertising propositions can be based around either a brand's head or its heart: head advertising communicates a brand's rational values, whilst heart advertising reveals its emotional values and associations. Brand benefit ladders sum up consumers' relationships with a brand and are frequently established during the consumer research process where consumers are usually asked to describe what features a brand offers and what the brand means to them. Using the research, it should then be relatively straightforward to ascertain what particular benefit ladders consumers associate with the brand

Level 5	What is the essential nature and character of the brand?
Level 4	What does value mean for the typical loyal customer?
Level 3	What psychological rewards or emotional benefits do customers receive by using this brand's products? How does the consumer feel?
Level 2	What benefits to the customer or solutions result from the brand's features?
Level 1	What are the tangible, verifiable, objective, measurable characteristics of products, services or ingredients of this brand name?

Figure 8.1   The brand benefit ladder
Source: adapted from Word, S., Light, L. and Goldstine, J., What High Tech Managers Need to Know About Brands, *Harvard Business Review*, July–August 1999, 91.

in question (see Figure 8.1). The benefit ladder can be instrumental in helping to distil the essence of a brand's advertising proposition. This refers to the point at which consumers' wants and the brand benefits and features intersect – the advertising should encapsulate the *spirit* of the brand. Whilst many ideas may be initially suggested, the challenge is to develop a proposition which makes the brand relevant, contemporary and appealing – establishing the brand's architecture can be critical to this process.

The need to establish brand architecture

Essentially the brand architecture should reflect all the key components of a brand including its positioning, its rational (head) and emotional (heart) benefits and associations, together with its brand personality. A brand's architecture is in essence the blueprint that should guide brand-building, development and marketing, and is a device which can be used by all tourism and leisure brand managers. As we shall see in more detail in Chapter 10, more and more tourism destinations are looking to establish their brand architecture in order to put themselves ahead of competitors. Of course, when they are whole countries, destinations are often composite brands (being composed of many different places). Yet consumer research which reveals and establishes a destination's brand architecture should enable marketers to clearly see the elements and contributions of these various composite brands. It is a device that is critical to the development of *destination supra-* and *sub-brands*. Our case study of Britain (Case study 8.2 at the end of this chapter) examines the brand architecture of one destination supra-brand and the sub-brands which are both part of and, at the same time, distinct from it. It provides an informative analysis of how different brands can work together, for instance, in the overseas market. It also reveals how the sub-brands (London, England, Scotland and Wales) can differentiate themselves from each other both in the domestic (within the UK) and overseas context, for instance, the marketers of Wales characterize its brand personality in the following terms: 'Wales holds a passion which is drawn from a heritage of poetry and song, legend and mystery. There is a spirituality about the natural and dramatic beauty of the countryside.'[10]

The brand architecture (or the building blocks) which underpin this personality is detailed in Table 8.4. This demonstrates how the British Tourist Authority and Wales Tourist Board are creating an emotional or spiritual bond between the mood of the destination and the consumer. Thus the *positioning* of Wales as a country of nature and legend is translated into the *rational benefit* of encountering rugged landscapes, heritage and friendly people. At a deeper, emotional or salient level these benefits offer the overseas visitor the *emotional benefits* of feeling inspired, uplifted and spiritual. Finally, the culmination of these brand attributes is a destination *personified* by independence, mystery and warmth. This becomes the essence of Wales the brand, with values rooted in the experience of past visitors, credible and relevant to potential visitors and, most crucially, which the product can deliver.[11]

Brands as today's trust brokers

Brands are critically important to today's consumers who tend to place more trust in megabrands than in institutions such as the police or the church. One UK study recently reported that brands such as Kellogg's, Cadbury, Heinz, Nescafé, Rowntree, Coca-Cola, Boots and Marks & Spencer, together with several leading supermarket chains, all achieved higher trust ratings than such institutions. In addition, brand logos have an extremely high recognition value: the Shell and McDonald's logos are in the world's top three most recognized symbols, recognized by almost 90 per cent of the globe and exceeded only by the Olympic rings symbol. This places commercial brands well above religious symbols such as the Christian cross, recognized by about half of the globe. Moreover, a recent report into the UK stock market showed that sixty-eight strongly branded companies such as British Airways, Cadbury-Schweppes and Unilever have consistently outperformed the FTSE 350 index during the last fifteen years. Megabrands like McDonalds, Nike and Coca-Cola are huge global players, recognizable in any language or culture. Can't speak the local language in a bar? You can always order a Coke. Such is the power of the Coke logo that it has moved beyond being a visual trigger or even serving to encapsulate the brand values – it now has the ability to provoke complex consumer emotion.

Brand aerobics

Since brands are increasingly pivotal in consumer choice, today's brand management is also about trust management. Brands that are able to become trust brokers in the eyes of the consumers can position themselves as people-partners in a confusing, troublesome and risky world. Moreover, such brands can also move into all sorts of new ventures, reassuring the consumer that because they express qualities of trust and partnership, they can be relied upon in problem areas of life management – witness Virgin's and Marks & Spencer's successful moves into the UK financial services market. As a result, many companies are in fact engaging in a new brand culture – where they stretch their proven expertise in one field into another. Boundaries are breaking down not merely between sectors but also between manufacturers and retailers. Service-based companies such as Tesco and Virgin are as much a brand to the consumer as traditional product-based brands such as Cadbury or Kit-Kat. This exercise in brand aerobics has been stimulated by a range of factors, including advances in new technology, increasingly detailed customer research and relationship information, together with the costs and difficulties surrounding the development of new brands.

> The vast majority of today's leading brands have been around for a very long time – many of them are over 100 years old.

Despite this, many brands can stretch too far in brand aerobics. In the latter years of the twentieth century the Cadbury brand appeared on savoury snacks, tea bags and mashed potato before returning to its core brand of chocolate and confectionery, whilst Levi's reached into men's suits in the late 1970s before refocusing on denim in the mid-1980s. Herein lies the problem – if a brand overextends itself and loses credibility in one sector, it runs the risk of damaging the whole brand range. Trust and credibility are key and a recent review of a dozen of the world's best known brands suggests that very few brands are truly capable of elastic brand stretching. Marks & Spencer's and Virgin are brands with extensive credibility – although interestingly, at the outset of the twenty-first century even these super-credible brands are suffering. In 1999, the UK retailer Marks & Spencer's reported significantly

Table 8.2 Assessment of brand stretchability

Brand	Brand personality	Stretchability factor
Barclays	1970s-style high street banking	*
Cadburys	Small purple pleasures/world of chocolate	**
Coca-Cola	America for everyone	**
Levi's	Classic style, authenticity	**1/2
Marks & Spencer	Editorial ability, innovative luxury	***
Nescafé	Suburban niceness, familiar product brand	*
Nike	Just do it; youth and attitude	**1/2
Persil	Caring, household cleaning	*
Sainsbury	Middle-class quartermaster	**
Sony	Innovative design gizmos	**1/2
Virgin	David vs Goliath	***

Note: *** outstanding, super-stretchy; ** good, very stretchy; * average, only slightly stretchy.
Source: adapted from Peter Wallis (1996). Brand Assessments. *Sunday Times*, 3 November.

smaller profits and were felt by many commentators to have somewhat lost their way, whilst Virgin has possibly overextended itself with Virgin Vodka and then with VirginRail.

Threats to brand value when trust breaks down

The emphasis on trust brings with it new challenges to brand health management. In addition to the traditional brand warfare tactics of brand attribute and imagery, ethical issues have emerged as significant concerns for competing brands. First, some brands have been challenged for the prices they charge, as in the late 1990s UK 'designer wars' provoked by supermarkets which persuaded consumers that they were being 'ripped off' by premium, designer brands including Ralph Lauren, Nike and Levi's. Second, brands face challenges from 'trust watchdogs' – pressure groups which attempt to mobilize consumer opinion through highlighting unethical company employment practices. For example, when Gilbert (the manufacturers of the official Rugby World Cup 1999 match balls) was alerted by concerned groups to the possibility that children were involved in making its rugby balls, it immediately responded, promising action if the allegations were accurate. Other brands that pride themselves on their community-based values can be damaged by employee disputes – witness the long-lasting protests by Levi's redundant factory workers in Texas. Thus, although it can give a brand a competitive edge, the emphasis on trust makes brand value and equity vitally important. In fact, some commentators have argued that brand value is one of the few things that really matters in today's global economy. Brand value has indeed become a balance sheet entry – Coke is reputed to be worth $35 billion for its brand value alone whilst IBM's brand worth has been put at $18.5 billion.

Successful brands need consumer resonance

Brands offer consumers a short cut to product choice and satisfaction in a world in which they face a bewildering array of products. In a sense this choice has become something of an enemy to consumers, and a strong brand reassures consumers, providing them with safe, reliable, likeable and easy choices, making the buying process much easier and speedier. Their mental map of markets and brand hierarchies usually clusters around factors such as price and quality, and consumers tend to inhabit a brand comfort zone which reflects their own socioeconomic status and psychographics (Figure 8.2). In this marketing saturated world where time is increasingly the prime currency, brands with both trust and authority will triumph, and advertising is critical in this process. In

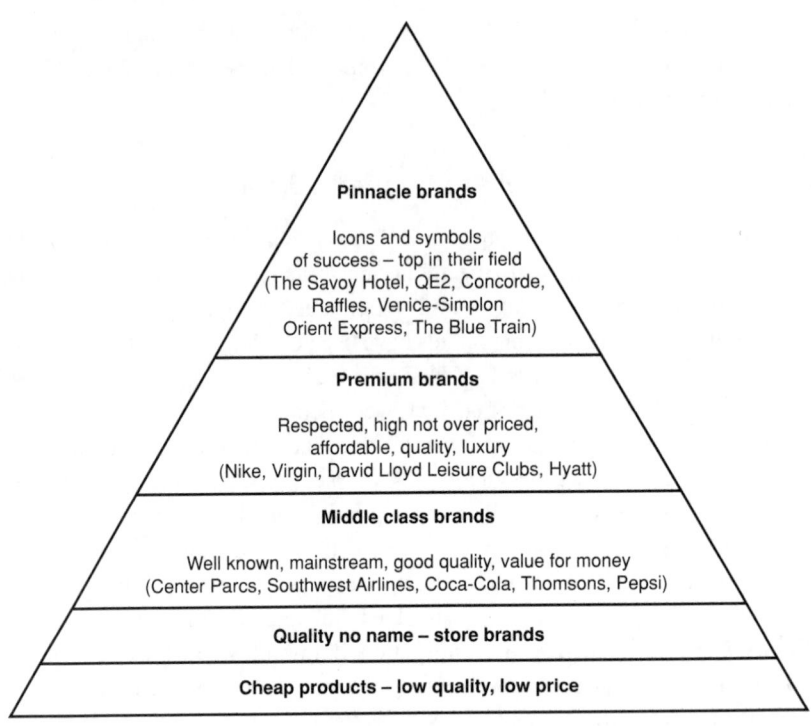

Figure 8.2 The brand value pyramid

attempting to create consumer mindshare, effective tourism and leisure advertising will get people talking about or engaging with a brand – reactions which are essential precisely because people tend not to buy brands they do not talk about. Whilst doubts have been cast on the effectiveness or reach of branding, fortunately for managers, encouraging research suggests that consumers:

> Brands hold practical (habit, convenience, quality, guarantee), emotional (identification, self-expression, links to the past, genuine affection) and social (short hand communication, acceptance and approval) roles for consumers.

- are not as cynical towards brands as commentators frequently suggest
- like or even love brands (as old favourites or new stars)
- attach practical, emotional and social roles to brands.

Recognizing that branding is a two-way process done *with* and not *to* the consumer, Len Weinreich suggests that instead of thinking in terms of the traditional product or brand life cycle, brand managers should be thinking of the S-curve (Figure 8.3) which charts a brand's life and development through birth, growth, maturity, decay and death (although, of course, the time frames are elastic and could encompass anything from weeks to centuries). Instead of seeing the S-curve as tracking sales volume over time, managers should consider it as a series of stages in the brand's relationship with its consumers, revealing useful insights into a brand's communications requirements.[12] In the x section the market is small and many brands succeed in spite of their advertising activities because the product is innovative and excellent. Here the brand is in its fashionable phase and its purchasers are cosmopolitan, trend-setting consumers who, although few in numbers, are influential opinion-formers. Yet, as the brand becomes famous and loses its cutting-edge appeal, these consumers move on to the next new product since they do not want to be seen with something that has become popular and rather passé. In the famous phase, a brand's consumers are loyal and affluent but at any time, the brand may become irrelevant to them – hence the ongoing need for it to remain fresh and appealing. If it fails, it will drift into the z zone where everyone knows about the brand, but no one bothers to buy it any more – its advertising has become 'overwarm, cuddly and sentimental, the antithesis of cool'.[13] The challenge of being friendly leads a brand to extinction or to a renaissance and, if it is badly damaged, a brand's core values may need to be reassessed and its relevance to target markets redefined and revitalized.

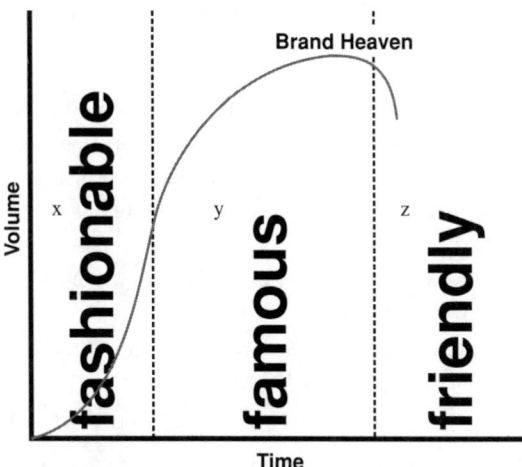

Figure 8.3 The brand S-curve
Source: Len Weinreich (1999). *11 Steps to Brand Heaven: The Ultimate Guide to Buying an Advertising Campaign*. Kogan Page, p. 25.

Brand loyalty: the key to brand heaven?

Consumers' loyalty to a brand is inherently bound up with Weinreich's life cycle of fashionability but as we enter the first years of the twenty-first century, brand loyalty is becoming an ever more intriguing but important concept (Case study 8.3). Some consumers are proud to be loyal, others delight in the fact that they routinely switch, and still more are undecided – sometimes loyal, at other times not. For marketers it is vital to establish the factors which can strengthen or weaken people's connections with brands – good customer service is one example, but a stronger one may be affection for nostalgia as consumers often buy those brands which they knew first as children (Table 8.3). Yet nostalgia is not enough on its own as successful brands also need to be current and contemporary – as relevant today as they were in the past. Remember that consumers can also desert brands precisely because they are so important to them, so those that cut back on quality and disappoint will lose previously loyal customers.

What determines a brand's success?

Is brand loyalty the major factor in determining a brand's success or is it more the case that big brands have more loyal users than smaller brands simply by virtue of size which ensures more store allocation, promotion and bigger advertising budgets? Alternatively, is there a third way – one where loyalty is frequently related to brand size but where change can be achieved through building the perception that a brand is more appealing or better than

Table 8.3 Building consumer relationships into the brand personality

People have relationships with brands – work to nurture their loyalty. Drops in quality and appeal will be punished as consumers turn to more relevant, interesting and self-enhancing brands.

Patience is vital – brand-building is a long-term process. Attempt to achieve a timeless and contemporary appeal.

Appeal to youth – brands often stay with consumers throughout adulthood or are developed through family loyalties and habits.

Don't forget the importance of brand clubs, word of mouth and customer service.

Above all, make people feel good about themselves when they buy your brand.

Source: adapted from Judith Langer (1997). What consumers wish brand managers knew. *Journal of Advertising Research*, November–December, 60–6.

its competitors? Brands can certainly achieve success on small budgets – if a brand's communications are synergized then its impact may well be greater than its resources would suggest. Case study 8.4 illustrates this with the contention that the next stage in brand development is the advent of aesthetics – a development that could provide enhanced opportunities for smaller brands. Certainly a lack of communication synergy or conflicting strategies are likely to dilute a brand's chances of success. Industry research suggests that a brand's strengths and weaknesses can be assessed according to how well it performs in terms of both its size and its competition. Such assessment is vital as, when taken over a long period of time, research also reveals that many brands show evidence of dramatic increases or decreases in brand strength.

Brands can achieve significant success within a category by breaking through the status quo either through increased awareness (stimulated by advertising, sponsorship, distribution, etc.) or loyalty (stimulated by incentives, or some perceived rational and/or emotional advantage). Without this breakthrough, conditions are unlikely to change. Smart marketing is vitally important, as is understanding brand attributes: how loyal is a 'loyal' customer? One who looks to a given brand for 75, 50 or 30 per cent of their purchases of that product or service? Brand managers need to establish appropriate definitions of loyalty. Research shows that consumers who are loyal to a brand and have strong attitudes towards it are more likely to buy it in the future. The question therefore is to identify ways in which a brand can disturb the status quo to achieve both growth and strength.

Whilst the potential for change does exist, it would be naïve to overlook the fact that weaker brands will have to work much harder to keep their place in the market and as a result, will be correspondingly much more vulnerable to competitor brands' actions. Not surprisingly, stronger brands are much better placed to capitalize more on their own marketing, resist competitor onslaughts and hence maintain market share. British Airways, with the launch of its World Images rebranding programme, signalled a sea change in the role and significance of corporate identity in its relationship with consumers. For the first time its corporate identity was made up not just of the logo but extended to include a whole body of imagery encapsulated in the World Images campaign. This move possibly signals a shift in the relative significance of branding and advertising. The brand is becoming far more significant (communicating the true value of your product and service) than 30-second ad slots in which people do not even recognize the advertiser. In this BA has been hailed as a flagship for the design business. BA have set themselves a huge challenge and only time will tell whether their customers appreciate the change but in the world of branding design its impact has already been felt. Case study 8.1 looks at the impact, success and limitations of the World Images rebranding.

The challenge to tourism and leisure rebel brands

The 1970s witnessed the launch and development of what could be described as *rebel brands*, such as Nike, Virgin and the Body Shop (amongst others), which took on the establishment and won, capturing the hearts and minds of many consumers. Yet, once the very epitome of rebellion, these brands (by virtue of their success) have themselves become part of the very establishment that they originally set out to challenge. How has this impacted on consumer perceptions of such brands and what lessons can be learnt by the emerging rebel brands of the new millennium? At the heart of the matter lies an essential conundrum – when a brand's success emanates from the fact that it is new, anti-establishment and (by implication) cutting edge, how can its success be protected when it is no longer new or rebellious? In this, all anti-establishment brands have a built in time bomb and are vulnerable to attack since their marketing ethos centres around their rebelliousness and determination to take on the major players in the interests of their customers.

Anti-establishment brands need to constantly evolve to remain in tune with their consumers or face declining market share. The Body Shop is one such brand that could be accused of failing to evolve. Its original point of differentiation – of ethical consumption – was a great concept, however, when other organizations copied this philosophy the Body Shop failed to come up with other ideas to further develop the brand. Such brands also have to be seen to be maintaining their original rebel philosophies if they are to continue to flourish but, when they are seen to desert such principles, their rivals are keen to maximize their discomfort. Nike is perhaps the essence of the rebel brand turned corporate giant and in the late 1990s it experienced negative press, consumer protest and anti-Nike activism. Nike's employment practices have attracted significant criticism in the tabloid and broadsheet press and on the Internet (with boycott Nike websites) whilst it has also been subject to consumer groups' 'days of action' over its alleged exploitation of cheap Third World labour – a charge Nike vehemently denies. The Nike brand represented the soul of the athlete, but this was seriously devalued by its perceived Asian employment practices – a $6 billion company, selling trainers for $140, produced by people allegedly earning $1.50 a day presents an ethical and an image dilemma. Nike has also been accused of being increasingly arrogant and out of touch with its consumers, and it is running the risk of becoming a victim of its own success and losing credibility with its youth market. Currently Nike contends that it has no problems keeping its brand fresh, passionate and successful but the question remains: how long can Nike maintain its rebellious image when it features sporting stars who are incredibly rich and successful? How can stars like Michael Jordan really be construed as rebels, and is the positioning of Nike now a contradiction?

Another rebel brand of the 1970s, Virgin, is a rather different proposition to Nike in the sense that it does not dominate any one market sector and, as a result, it is still able to position itself as the underdog, fighting the corporate establishment. Conversely, because of the extent of its diversification, Virgin may be in danger of overstretching itself and failure in one sector could have a damaging impact on the wider brand image. However, Virgin has developed strategies to ensure that the Virgin brand remains fresh despite such massive corporate expansion and development (Ad highlight 8.3). A decentralized structure ensures that each 'company' within the group can develop their own strategies and take responsibility for their brand's health. Critically, however, Virgin maintains its anti-authoritarian, youthful and fun image through its consistently effective, quality advertising (Plate 6). Virgin Atlantic's award-winning 1999 poster campaign – with the three executions, 'BA doesn't give a shiatsu'; 'Outrageous legroom' and 'Bald man' – exemplifies this brand attitude. Each ad speaks to the consumer in terms of attitude (poking fun at BA whilst advertising Virgin's business-class massage service), fun (the various legs which draw attention to the amount of legroom in the cabin) and humour (the bald man in front of you constituting the in-flight entertainment). Currently Virgin and similar anti-establishment brands remain hugely successful, although some more than others. The underlying ethos of rebellion and consumer championship are powerful brand concepts but the dangers to these brands lie in a failure to evolve, a tendency to believe in their own press and to appear arrogant and removed from their consumers, whilst they also face the threat of new rebels awaiting their chance to undermine those that have become the new corporate giants.

Ad highlight 8.3	Living the Virgin life

A recent article in *The Times* demonstrated how UK consumers can now 'Live life the Virgin way from birth to old age'. A newborn baby may be covered by her parents' life assurance from Virgin Direct and when a little older, she may soon develop a taste for Virgin cola. At school she could join the 2.2 million listeners of Virgin Radio and follow one of the pop stars signed to the V2 record label – buying her CDs at one of the eighty Virgin megastores. During her teenage romance, Virgin clothing could provide the fashion and Virgin Vie the cosmetics. When it comes to the wedding, the dress would be from Virgin Bride, whilst Virgin Atlantic or Virgin Sun could book the honeymoon – with the happy couple getting to the airport on a Virgin train. Once home, they could keep in touch via Virgin mobile phones and find entertainment on Virgin Net or by reading a book from Virgin Publishers. More energetic activities could be enjoyed in Virgin active fitness centres or at weekend breaks in Virgin hotels. Retirement need not be a worry either – as a prosperous old age could be financed by Virgin pensions.

Source: adapted from *The Times*, 24 April 1999.

Chapter summary

Today's tourism and leisure marketers must understand brand psychology, brand differentiation and brand management if their brands are to thrive in a highly competitive market. In an environment of product and service parity, brand managers must strive to forge brands with values which people can share or to which they can aspire since customers will differentiate in favour of those brands whose personalities reflect their own. Brand extension is often a means to increase market presence but it is also important to nurture brands in the face of increasing competition. Increasing brand loyalty is also critical to sustain brand growth and can be increased through developing strong consumer brand attitudes via advertising.

It is often easier for new brands to challenge the status quo – though their ability to do so will wane after the launch period and half of all new brands fail. Established brands are more likely to be:

- tied into particular ways of doing things
- less keen to attempt anything radical which may put off existing customers
- challenged by the need to respond to new competitors.

Whether new or old, a brand must be relevant to people's needs, and its emotional appeal, saliency and perceived performance need to be stronger than its competitors'. Consumers need to be bonded to the brand attitudinally, and a brand's rational and emotional benefits need to be communicated via *strong* and *consistent* brand communications. Long-term brand-building is essential for future success and managers need to establish their brand's presence, relevance and performance *vis-à-vis* its competitors. They also need to establish its advantages and weaknesses and the extent of consumer loyalty by considering:

- what the brand stands for
- what attributes the brand owns
- how they can use these attributes to make the brand grow
- how loyal the customers are
- how they can be made to be more brand-loyal
- whether a sustained shift in attitude is necessary.

Case study 8.1

British Airways: a brand in transition?

BA underwent a number of changes at the end of the 1990s, both in advertising and product branding, beginning with 'Dreams' in 1996, followed by 'World images' in 1997 and a further repositioning in June 1999. Its 'Dreams' campaign was designed to show how BA carried the hopes and dreams of the 30 million passengers who fly with the airline every year. 'Dreams' resulted from a fifteen-month long consumer research project which involved over 40 000 customers. The research revealed that whilst BA was perceived to be particularly strong on tangible customer benefits, it was also felt to be weak on style and customer service.

The resultant new advertising, launched in 1996 to a worldwide audience of 500 million as part of a two-year £100 million campaign, was warmer, friendlier and more personal than previous BA advertising. In the past, BA had concentrated on linking its appeal to its global airline status. 'Dreams' marked a departure, including ads featuring a woman watching Chinese theatre, a man being chased through the snow by a horseman, a middle aged couple splashing in a lake and a businessman struggling with a huge dollar sign. Later in each ad, these same passengers were then seen to be enjoying the comforts of BA business class. The advertising, which retained 'The world's favourite airline' strapline, cost £1 million to produce and was part of various improvements to the BA product including a revamped First Class service offering individual cabins, a new Club World 'cradle' seat, refurbished arrivals lounges and new in-flight catering, including a business 'raid the larder' service.

In 1997 BA followed 'Dreams' by introducing 'Utopia' – a new corporate identity at a cost of £60 million. The programme, which was to take three years to complete, was launched simultaneously in sixty-three countries linked by satellite. Extensive consumer research had revealed that, despite the improvements, BA was in need of a much more fundamental makeover. The company knew it had to change in order to meet consumer needs and expectations which demanded a much more human and caring persona to replace BA's rather cold and stuffy identity. This identity was one which was valued by white, British middle-aged men but which women and customers from other countries and racial and ethnic groups regarded as outmoded and relatively unappealing. The latest rebranding was therefore designed to embrace the world and shrug off the overtones of empire and imperialism which still dogged the BA brand – replacing the sober blue and red livery with a world art gallery. In rejecting a monolithic corporate identity in favour of a celebration of diversity and humanity, BA was attempting to demonstrate how it differed from its competitors – it wanted to be seen as a global brand striving to maintain identity and consistency through diversity.

The world art gallery programme – 'World images' – was to include fifty different 'ethnic' designs drawn from around the globe. The concept was based on the premise that the language of imagery is one which we can all understand and the world art gallery metaphor was designed to be a powerful tool for bringing people together – portraying BA as British but modern and at home wherever it travelled. This new identity was merely the most outwardly visible sign of a massive organizational change necessary, so BA argued, to meet the challenges of the next millennium. A key aspect of this review was BA's 'Kaleidoscope' training programme for its 20 000 cabin and ground staff. Recognizing that its service style was seen as very formal, this initiative was prompted by a desire to provide a service that reflects the airline's global passenger mix.

Key in this was BA's decision to offer monolingual cabin staff voluntary redundancy and replace these crew with bilingual or multilingual flight attendants able to deal more effectively with BA's varied customer base. The airline's relationships with airlines in France, Germany, Australia and the USA mean that it is handling ever greater numbers of foreign passengers and staff, and 60 per cent of its passengers are now generated from outside the UK. The company's change of identity was thus designed to show its customers that it was both 'global and caring' and able to deliver service to passengers of any background. The airline wanted to appear to be warm and cosmopolitan, not as cold, aloof and chauvinistic – as a company with roots in a modern, rather than an imperial Britain.

BA's revamped identity provoked much debate within the corporate identity industry and beyond. Within the former, opinion was somewhat mixed and whilst there was a recognition that the new identity has both elegance and gracefulness, there was also some concern expressed – particularly surrounding the linkage between the brand identity and the aeroplane tailfin imagery. Some commentators argued that because the tailfin imagery is so strong, BA could in fact be mistaken for another airline – as the BA signature almost gets lost in comparison. Others have argued that a carrier's national identity expressed through the flag it carries gives consumers reassurance. Thus, Lufthansa is well regarded because of notions surrounding German reliability, whilst Swiss Air is valued for the traditional notions of punctuality and precision associated with the Swiss (and this is reflected in its advertising – such as one execution which depicts a farmer setting his watch as a Swiss Air jet flies overhead). As a result, many experts argued that the perceptions of British service and safety standards previously communicated by the flag were now communicated by a mixture of world images and were, therefore, seriously diluted.

In Britain itself reaction to the 'World images' campaign was mixed. Whilst this new identity was deliberately and very carefully chosen by BA, not surprisingly such a radical change of style generated some controversy and criticism. One very 'traditional' UK newspaper accused the airline of dropping its Britishness, of burning the flag and 'desecrating' what it used to proudly 'fly'. The same newspaper also asked 'If the new, self-hating BA really finds Britishness so outmoded and nationalistic, then why not drop the word "British" altogether?' Former Prime Minister, Baroness Thatcher, also entered the debate, describing BA's decision to drop the Union flag as 'terrible, terrible, absolutely terrible', saying, 'we fly the British flag, not these awful things', as she covered the offending tailfin of a model aeroplane at a Conservative Party conference.

Interestingly, the furore over BA's 1997 campaign disguised the processes that lay behind its previous revamp in 1984. Then, BA went to San Francisco-based identity consultants, Lander Associates, to develop an identity which appeared British in a way that American customers would appreciate rather than authentically British to domestic flyers. The result of this mid-1980s reimaging was the adoption of a heritage-themed identity focused on part of the Union flag and a fake crest. Interestingly, this scripted identity was less that of Britain than 'Brit-ish', an identity crafted to appeal to a hugely powerful and profitable US market. In this sense, therefore, the 1997 move to replace the crest with new global 'ethnic' designs, was less the removal of something which was authentic, and more the swapping of one artificially crafted identity for another.

In embracing cultural expressions from around the globe, BA tried to present itself in a different and, it hoped, more attractive way, especially in the Asian market, which its market research showed regarded BA's 'Britishness' as a hindrance. As such, Wolff Olins, a corporate identity consultant, commented at the time of the launch that 'It may not be in BA's interest to appear to be too British any more'. BA itself commented that 'In the 1990s, "global and caring" does not mean post-imperialist flag-waving. It has to mean intelligently sensitive relations with customers and communities.' The company also commented that 'Instead of being a British airline with global operations, British Airways has become a world airline whose headquarters happen to be in Britain'. At the same time, Adrian Day, Director of Lander Associates, predicted that the airline would, in years rather than decades, drop the word 'British' from its name altogether. He said: 'The company's quest is to become the first global airline' – identities are becoming more flexible and the message is one of diversity – 'It makes sense for where the company is at the moment.'

Exactly two years into the 'World images' programme, BA had something of a change of heart. In June 1999 it announced plans to bring back the Union flag on at least 160 of its 340 planes, although BA intends to retain the 180 aircraft which have already been decorated in 'World images' livery because of their success and appeal in the overseas markets. Ironically BA's new tailfin on the 160 aircraft will now be based on a flag used by Nelson in the battle of Trafalgar in 1805. This 'combined' look was designed to reflect the aspirations of BA's customer base, which is split between the UK (40 per cent) and the rest of the world (60 per cent). Whilst the overseas customers regard the 'World images' brand very highly, UK customers have responded much less enthusiastically – believing their community to be underrepresented in the tailfin imagery. BA's about-turn is somewhat embarrassing and comes on the back of a 61 per cent decrease in profits and follows research which reveals that UK passengers want to see the Union flag given greater prominence in BA's global identity – it also came at a time when Virgin unveiled a new Union flag livery for its fleet.

As Virgin rolled out its new livery with a heavy emphasis on the Union flag, it accused BA of panicking and although BA responded that its change of heart was due to customer reaction rather than competitor strategies, Virgin's claim seems to have some truth about it – given that BA's announcement came on the eve of Virgin's launch. Certainly the BA brand went through turbulent times in the 1990s. Profits nose-dived from £580 million to £225 million during 1997–8 and there can be little doubt that the Virgin brand has made significant headway amongst the more profitable business travellers – due in part to its excellent service culture. The BA about-turn over its 'World images' programme does seem to be a case of reacting to, rather than pre-empting, competitor challenges. Moreover, this strategy of combining the 'World images' and the new Union flag logos must surely raise serious questions over what is in effect a schizophrenic brand identity. Whilst BA probably hopes it is large enough to sustain such a dual brand personality, its move seems to undermine the role and significance of brand and identity in a world where the psychology of branding is increasingly important. BA's decision appears to be something of a fudge – only time will tell whether it is a fudge which can be maintained and which will restore its depleted profitability also under threat from losses in the business market.

Source: based on Morgan, N. J. and Pritchard, A. (1998). *Tourism Promotion and Power: creating images, creating identities.* John Wiley, pp. 142–3.

Case study 8.2

Britain's brand architecture

The development of a brand architecture for Britain in the later 1990s was the end product of a large-scale research and development programme conducted by the British Tourist Authority (BTA), together with the Scottish, Wales, English and London Tourist Boards (Table 8.4). There is recognition by the various brand managers within the British setup that different customers, existing or potential, have different ideas and levels of knowledge regarding Britain. These vary depending on factors such as age, lifestyle and the country in which they live. Whilst ideas and messages will obviously vary depending on the markets in question, the intention is to use each brand's core values to inform the advertising overseas and brand-building process.

'Britain' as the destination supra-brand or umbrella brand can be promoted on its own or in conjunction with one of the other main brands. London shares many of the same values of the brand Britain whilst, in contrast to the brand values of Britain and London, those of Scotland and

Table 8.4 Britain's brand architecture

	Positioning	Rational benefit	Emotional benefit	Personality
Britain	Island of traditional heritage and the unconventional	Tradition, heritage and pageantry, landscape, arts and culture, people	I feel stimulated by the enriching, often paradoxical experience of Britain. I feel at ease in the friendly, open culture of the British people.	Great/solid yet accessible, cold in appearance yet deeply friendly, ordered yet quirky, traditional yet innovative
London	City of pageantry and pop	Diverse culture, arts, pageantry, heritage, nightlife, music, glamour, shopping, safe, cosmopolitan, fashion leader	I feel liberated by the vibrancy of London. I feel stimulated by the wealth of heritage and culture of a great city.	Open-minded, casual, unorthodox, vibrant, creative
Scotland	Land of fire and stone	Rugged, unspoilt, wilderness, dramatic scenery, romantic history, heritage and folklore, warm and feisty people	I feel in awe of the elements in Scotland. I feel embraced by the warmth of the people. I feel rejuvenated by the experience of Scotland.	Independent, warm, mysterious, rugged, feisty
Wales	Land of nature and legend	Natural, dramatic beauty, poetry and song, legend and mystery	I feel inspired by the lyrical beauty of Wales. I feel uplifted by the spirituality of the natural environment.	Honest, welcoming, romantic, down to earth, with passion
England	Lush, green land of discovery	Afternoon teas, quaint village pubs, cathedrals, country houses, rolling countryside, meandering roads, hedgerows, rivers, canals, coastline, piers, fetes, morris dancing, cricket, rugged country, moorland, lakes, industrial heritage, B&Bs, rugby	I feel fulfilled by experiencing the quaint culture and history of England. I feel relaxed by the harmonious countryside and bracing walks along the coast. I feel warmed by the hearty, down-to-earth character of England. I feel soothed by the open, unspoilt outdoors.	Conservative, pleasant, refined civilized, eccentric, down to earth, approachable, hearty, humorous

Source: British Tourist Authority (1997). *Living Britain: A Guide to Understanding the Characteristics of the Geographic Brands of Britain, London, Scotland, England and Wales*. BTA.

Wales are much more elemental, natural and spiritual. Research has also shown that 'England' as an entity is rather less well known as it is indistinguishable from Britain and London in the minds of many people. Whilst Britain is an undoubted destination supra-brand, its success in translating its brand benefits and personality into successful and distinctive brand advertising has been rather mixed. Indeed, arguably some of Britain's sub-brands (such as Wales and Scotland) have been developing much stronger consistent, coherent and effective brand propositions over recent years. Recent advertising by the BTA (for instance) has focused largely on the rational benefits associated with Britain. Ads (particularly television and in-flight ads) appear to have tried to pack in virtually every aspect of Britain's product – from its tradition, heritage and pageantry to its landscape, attractions (such as Legoland) and culture. The end execution appears more as a composite picture or amalgam of what Britain has to offer – almost overwhelming the potential tourist with images – rather than a total brand positioning which personifies the rational and emotional benefits of this destination supra-brand.

Case study 8.3

Branding a leisure complex

Branding is a strategic exercise at the Guildford Spectrum in Surrey – it is not simply about the corporate logo, colour or uniforms. One of the biggest challenges to its managers is overcoming potential visitors' perceptions that Spectrum is just a swimming pool, sports hall or ice rink and adopting the name Guildford Spectrum immediately makes it more memorable than, say, Guildford Leisure Centre. Underpinned by the positioning statement, 'The most exciting leisure complex in the UK', with Spectrum a brand has been constructed with a strong identity which is reinforced in every aspect of the operation. Like many such centres, Spectrum is almost totally reliant on pay-and-play customers, which means that maintaining a loyal and profitable client base is essential. Consistent branding throughout the whole marketing mix ensures this occurs and products at Spectrum are not devalued by discounting for promotional purposes, instead added value is used to achieve the same outcome.

To define and segment target markets underneath the umbrella Spectrum brand, a further seven sub-brands have been developed – including Spectrum Ice, Spectrum Aerobics and Spectrum Sports – based on market research into customer loyalty. Each sub-brand has a clearly defined identity with specific logos and colour-coding used in signage, promotional literature and stationery. In addition, there are other branded products with even more distinct target markets in the Spectrum portfolio. These include Ice Xtreme discos, offering a safe weekend venue for the over-fourteens – a particularly brand conscious segment who were targeted by promotions, including features in *The Ministry of Sound* magazine. Other products also include The Prime Time Club, aimed at the over-fifties market, and Fitness Direct, primarily aimed at regular health and fitness users who wanted an easy payment scheme. Although pay-and-play is possible, monthly payments and other benefits attract regular users who were initially targeted with a direct mail campaign. Spectrum are now able to build on the Fitness Direct brand to tactically promote other appropriate products and, since the consumers are a distinct group in which other companies are also interested (sportswear manufacturers and life insurance companies), there are opportunities for joint mailings.

Source: Catherine McGrath (1998). Spectrum. *The Leisure Manager*, December, 18–19.

Case study 8.4

Aesthetics: beyond branding – the case of Absolut Vodka

Aesthetics offer tourism and leisure organizations the opportunity to differentiate themselves from their competitors via consistent, stylish, unusual, leading edge identifiers. Nike's swoosh, Cathay Pacific's brushwing and Absolut Vodka's artistic credentials are all extremely successful examples of the adaptation of aesthetics as a brand positioner. Aesthetics encompasses not only the 'look' of a brand but also how it reflects cultural and quality issues in the 'sensory experience' it provides. Such sensory elements are critical to a brand's identity – customer perceptions of this can be established using the brand fingerprinting techniques discussed in Chapter 4.

Aesthetics is claimed to be the next phase in marketing strategy – supplanting branding – a claim which is of significant interest to all tourism and leisure providers, many of whom it would be fair to say, have yet to seriously grasp the challenges offered by branding. Brands provide the customer with values through their names and benefit associations, via emotional rather than functional attributes. Brand managers focus on concepts such as brand-building, equity, image awareness and recognition – concepts which are visually expressed through brand symbols. Branding itself is about identity management but, unlike aesthetics, branding cannot take full advantage of the opportunities provided via new interactive technology to target customers through a whole range of sensory delights. As such, a reliance on branding may not be sufficient to attract and maintain consumer interest and loyalty. Aesthetics offers the possibility of consumer interest and loyalty from not only brand qualities but also the meanings the brand in question communicates. Aesthetics offers functionally similar products the ability to differentiate via emotional and experiential strategies. As a result, it also allows some products or services to charge premium prices – Nike can charge $150 for its trainers because of its performance aesthetic.

In the same way, Absolut Vodka's adoption of an aesthetics strategy enabled the company to establish a hugely successful brand identity in the USA via distinctively sensory means. Absolut Vodka at the start of the 1980s was a small vodka brand in the USA – selling a mere 5000 cases a year. However, the brand sales increased exponentially so that by the mid-1990s Absolut Vodka sales hit 3 million cases – it had become the number one imported vodka brand. How did it manage to achieve this remarkable transformation in fortune in just over ten years? At the start, Absolut faced incredibly difficult odds – it lacked awareness and distinction. Originating from Sweden – a country not associated with the production of quality vodkas – it faced tough competition from Russian vodkas, a country renowned for the product. The market leader in imported vodkas at the time was Stolichnaya, which accounted for over 80 per cent of the market.

In the USA the brand's success was due to a highly targeted advertising strategy which enabled medium, audience and brand to come together in harmony. Vodka, regardless of brand, is functionally the same product but Absolut launched a brand differentiation strategy based on emotional appeal and aesthetics. This strategy prompted development of a campaign that was visually stunning and witty, sophisticated and stylish. The campaign was ideally suited to the chosen medium – colour magazines, including unconventional and trend-setting titles – and produced print advertising at its very best. Not only was it well targeted, it also carefully reflected the psychographic make-up of its intended audience. The ads were aimed at magazine readers who felt themselves to be subtle, smart and sophisticated – as Absolut wanted its drinkers to be seen.

Central to the campaign were the Absolut name and the distinctively shaped bottle. Absolut was positioned as a cool, cutting-edge brand which was also fun-loving and rather irreverent. Central to the long-running, visually stunning and highly stylized campaigns were its high production values. Each Absolut ad features the bottle above a two-word headline which begins 'Absolut . . .'. The bottle is placed in surprising and ever changing scenarios, featuring special types of lifestyle activities – such as an aerial view of an Absolut bottle-shaped private swimming pool in the case of 'Absolut LA'; ski slopes depicting the bottle in 'Absolut peak'; a martini glass leaning towards the vodka in 'Absolut attraction' and a halo-topped bottle representing 'Absolut perfection'. The campaign still runs today and seems as contemporary as ever. In testimony to its success, the campaign's style and tone have been copied by Absolut's competitors; individual ad executions have become collectable items and in 1996 Richard Lewis (account director at TBWA/Chait Day) produced the *Absolut Book: The Absolut Vodka Advertising Story* which featured the best of the 500-plus campaign executions. Interestingly, the ads themselves were not subject to advertising pretesting – this was deemed to be far too insensitive to reveal how the campaign was designed to stimulate consumer reactions and there was concern that pretesting could kill the creativity so central to the success of the Absolut campaign.

Source: based on Schmitt, B. and Simonsen, A. (1997). *Marketing Aesthetics: The Strategic Management of Brands, Identity and Image*. Free Press.

Notes

1 Simon Anholt (1999). Paper presented at the Third International Leisure and Tourism Advertising Festival, September, Valencia.
2 Ibid.
3 C. Macrae, S. Parkinson and J. Sheerman (1995). Managing marketing's DNA: the role of branding. *Irish Marketing Review*, **18**, 13–20.
4 Sheena Westwood, Nigel Morgan, Annette Pritchard and Elizabeth Ineson (1999). Branding the package holiday – the role and significance of brands for UK air tour operators. *Journal of Vacation Marketing*, **5** (3), July, 238–52.
5 G. Lury (1998). *Brandwatching*. Blackhall, p. 4.
6 G. Hallberg (1995). *All Consumers Are Not Created Equal: The Differential Marketing Strategy for Brand Loyalty and Profits*. John Wiley.

7 John Phillip Jones (1999). Budgeting for advertising. In *The Advertising Business: Operations, Creativity, Media Planning, Integrated Communications* (J. P. Jones, ed.) pp. 77–88, Sage, p. 79.

8 Pat Mann, quoted in Glen Peters (1996). *Imagining the Next Wave of Consumers*. Pitman, p. 54.

9 Wolff Olins (1995). *The new guide to identity. How to create and sustain change through managing identity*. The Design Council and Gower Books, 46.

10 British Tourist Authority (1997). *Living Britain: A Guide to Understanding the Characteristics of the Geographic Brands of Britain, London, Scotland, England and Wales*. BTA.

11 Ibid.

12 Len Weinreich (1999). *11 Steps to Brand Heaven: The Ultimate Guide to Buying an Advertising Campaign*. Kogan Page, pp. 25–6.

13 Ibid., p. 28.

Further reading

de Chernatony, L. (1999). The challenge of services branding: knowledge management to the rescue? *Journal of Brand Management*, **6** (4), 271–7.

de Chernatony, L. and McDonald, M. (1998). *Creating Powerful Brands*. 2nd edn. Butterworth-Heinemann.

Gilmore, F. (ed.) (1997). *Brand Warriors*. HarperCollins.

Hallberg, G. (1999). The future of differential marketing. *Journal of Targeting, Measurement and Analysis for Marketing*, **17** (4), 325–34.

Hallberg, G. (1995). *All Consumers Are Not Created Equal: The Differential Marketing Strategy for Brand Loyalty and Profits*. John Wiley.

Hart, S. and Murphy, J. (eds) (1997). *Brands: The New Wealth Creators*. Macmillan.

James, G. (1997). Britain: creating a family of brands. *Tourism Intelligence Papers*. BTA/ETB, A-21.

Keller, K. L. (1999). Designing and implementing branding strategies. *Journal of Brand Management*, **6** (5), 315–32.

Knox, S. (1996). The death of brand deference: can management stop the rot? *Marketing Intelligence and Planning*, **14** (7), 35–40.

Langer, J. (1997). What consumers wish brand managers knew. *Journal of Advertising Research*, November/December, 60–6.

Lewis, R. W. (1996). *Absolut Book: The Absolut Vodka Advertising Story*. Journey Editions.

Lury, G. (1998). *Brandwatching*. Blackhall.

Morgan, N. J. and Pritchard, A. (eds) (1999). *Journal of Vacation Marketing*, **5** (3). A special issue on branding opportunities in tourism and travel.

Mundell, J. (1999). Advertising, brands and loyalty: making and monitoring the link. *Journal of Targeting, Measurement and Analysis for Marketing*, **17** (4), 349–58.

Olins, W. (1995). *The New Guide to Identity: How to Create and Sustain Change through Managing Identity*. The Design Council and Gower.

Schmitt, B. and Simonsen, A. (1997). *Marketing Aesthetics: The Strategic Management of Brands, Identity and Image*. Free Press.

9

Advertising and brand positioning

Chapter overview

How can advertising create highly
differentiated brands and refresh and
reinvigorate them, changing often long-held
consumer brand beliefs? In this chapter we try
to answer such questions by focusing on brand
positioning and repositioning – the latter
frequently being mentioned but rarely seriously
discussed by the tourism and leisure industries.
In our examples here (which include such
diverse products as Odeon cinemas, Mallorca,
Las Vegas, Torquay, Disneyland Paris, bingo,
Levi's and Alton Towers) we contextualize the
processes which underpin positioning and
repositioning in order to better understand the
role which advertising can play in these
strategies. Occasionally, repositioning involves
refreshing a brand's saliency through
advertising without altering the product – our
first chapter end case study, Levi's, is an
example of an incredibly successful, sustained
campaign which enhanced the image and
boosted the sales of 501 jeans. Much more
often, however, successful repositioning is

achieved by revitalizing or enhancing the product **and** reinvigorating its advertising. Here, the second of our case studies, Alton Towers, is an excellent example of how a theme park repositioned itself through product development and the subsequent advertising campaign. The key themes of this chapter are:

- what is positioning?
- positioning leaders in tourism and leisure
- positioning followers in tourism and leisure
- repositioning tourism and leisure brands.

Introduction

As recently as 1993 when, on 'Marlboro Friday', the financial markets cut Philip Morris's value by $13 billion in one day, marketing gurus declared 'Brands are dead'. If it could happen to Marlboro, it could happen to any brand and the media quickly proclaimed the 1990s a 'value decade', arguing that consumers would always shop for the lowest price and would buy only on sale. Within two years, however, Marlboro's US market share reached an all-time high of 31 per cent as Philip Morris created a 'Marlboro steamroller' based on a strategy of doubling advertising spend and cutting back on coupons and price-off programmes which 'cheapened the Marlboro image'.[1] It does seem that predictions of the death of brands were premature and today branding is as powerful a global marketing device as ever. Furthermore, when many Western marketers were moving away from brand-building, their Asian counterparts were energetically building theirs up and the Asian success has been to build brands not around products, but around reputations. The great Asian names imply quality, price and innovation rather than a specific item; they are 'attribute brands' which relate to a set of values. Thus, Mitsubishi is everything from a bank, to a car manufacturer, to a textiles and an electrical goods manufacturer. In fact, Mitsubishi is not a single company at all but a brand name that belongs to several companies.

What is positioning?

The managers of these 'attribute brands' recognize that the image their product has in the consumer's mind, how it is *positioned*, is more important to its ultimate success than are its actual characteristics. Brand managers try to position their brands so that they are perceived by the consumer to occupy a distinctive niche in the marketplace, a niche occupied by no other brand. They try to differentiate their product by stressing attributes they claim will match the target markets' needs more closely than other brands and then they try to create a product image consistent with the perceived self-image of the targeted consumer segment. As such, they appeal to consumers' values and self-images and in doing so they are thereby appealing to the powerful associations which have shaped those self-same values and images.

Positioning has been described as the essence of the marketing mix. It conveys the concept or the meaning of the product – how the product meets a consumer need – and different consumer meanings, or product images can be assigned to the same product. In this way it can be positioned differently to appeal to different audiences and it can be repositioned for the same audience. Brand choices clearly make lifestyle statements about the consumer and with drinks, as with other products: 'consumers are trying to buy into an image. There is an element of taste, but in blind tests consumers find it difficult to tell the difference between brands.'[2]

> Positioning – The process in which a company communicates with consumers to establish a distinctive place for its brand in their mind. A brand's position is the perception that targeted consumers have of a company's offering relative to the competition.

In today's communication saturated society, it is imperative to create a distinctive product image in the consumer's mind and it is vital to remember that positioning is not what you do with the product, but what you do with *the mind of the prospect*. Similarly, it's no use using a product attribute to position your brand if it has no meaning or relevance to the consumer. The Westin Stamford Hotel in Singapore may be the world's tallest hotel, but if that's not important to many tourists, 'The Stamford Crest at the world's tallest hotel . . . This must be what they mean by the high life', may not make an effective advertising positioning statement.[3] So in a sense, it's not about 'product positioning' at all – you are not doing anything to the product itself but attempting to secure a worthwhile, and if possible unique, position in the consumer's mind. Whilst the first priority of brand managers should be to increase the average net value of a brand (how much consumers like it on average), their second priority should be to increase its distinctiveness. In other words, 'to develop the ability of the brand to "polarise" consumers by differentially developing its appeal to those consumers to whom it is particularly suited'. This also has the effect of reducing the relative competitiveness with the major products in the market.[4] The result of a successful positioning strategy is a distinctive brand image on which customers rely in making product choices.

It is worth pointing out at this stage, however, that as companies and organizations increase the number and range of distinctive claims for their brands, they risk losing consumer credibility and clear positioning. Kotler et al., in their discussion of positioning, note that companies need to avoid three major positioning errors: *underpositioning, overpositioning* and *confused positioning*.[5] The first occurs when a company fails to position at all or lacks a clear vision of its product's unique qualities – this is particularly the case in the tourism and leisure industries. As we pointed out in the previous chapter, many organizations in these sectors (with some notable exceptions that are usually international players) have yet to fully engage with the marketing opportunities presented by branding. Underpositioning, for example, could happen where independent hotels – such as the Hotel du Palais in Biarritz – are trying to capture an international market, yet are unknown outside their own country – in this case France. To combat this, hotels such as the Hotel du Palais have affiliated with the marketing group The Leading Hotels of the World, a luxury group that creates a definite position and image for any hotel. The second positioning mistake is overpositioning – where marketers become so focused on one aspect of a product or destination that they project far too narrow an image of it to the consumer. Finally, the last problem is confused positioning which does the opposite and leaves consumers with an unclear image of the product – again this is very common in the tourism and leisure industries. Good examples of this are many of the UK package tour operators whose advertising switches between price-led appeals and more emotionally based branding positions. Such lack of cohesion has left consumers with ill-defined images of tour operator brands and does little to encourage brand loyalty.[6] Similarly, Burger King's US advertising is also a good example of confused positioning. Since 1986 the company has run five separate campaigns – each with its own positioning statement – which presented consumers with contradictory messages and left the company with declining profits. Now, however, the company has developed a memorable position statement which forms the centre of its ads – 'Have it your way' – which lets customers know that they can have their own choice of burger.[7]

To be successful in positioning a tourism or leisure product today, you must touch base with reality and the only reality that matters is the one which exists inside the potential consumer's mind. To be wholly creative, in other words to create something that does not already exist in the mind, is almost impossible. Instead of creating something new and different, the idea of positioning is to manipulate what is already in the mind and to re-engineer the connections that already exist. In today's overcommunicated society, consumers are increasingly 'screening out' advertising and they will only recognize something which matches their current

> The three mistakes of positioning strategies: underpositioning, overpositioning and confused positioning.

state of mind or which connects with their prior experience. In this communication fog, the only hope for a product to make any impression through its advertising is to be selective, to focus on an appropriate segment (see Chapter 6) and to adopt a 'positioning' strategy. Look at the strategy of Carnival Cruise Lines. In the 1980s it went after less affluent, less sophisticated, first-time cruise passengers (a new cruise market segment which included families), began offering three- and four-day trips and made the ship itself the destination, positioning and advertising itself as the 'fun' cruise company.[8]

Whatever the product, a company must create a position in the prospect's mind that takes into account not only the company's own strengths and weaknesses but those of its competitors as well. In this, strategy is critical. This is clearly the case today in the UK cinema industry, which in the past has tended to be weakly branded. In urban areas that traditionally offer much more choice of cinema venues, people have tended to opt for the cinema closest to them or for one that offers a more personal choice. Cinema operators have been attempting to change this over the last decade in the face of pressure from alternative entertainment such as video rental and the expansion of cable and satellite television. However, as a result of improved facilities and some hugely popular films, flagging UK attendances rose from 110 million in 1993 to 160 million in 1998. Now, however, after a huge, expensive expansion, the UK cinema market has become extremely competitive, with UCI the market leader, closely followed by Odeon and UGC (having bought out Virgin in October 1999), with Warner some way off in fourth place.

Once the leading UK cinema chain, Odeon, with its long-established presence in the marketplace (in excess of seventy years), could be thought to offer heritage but also to be old-fashioned – certainly by comparison with newer, more heavily branded operators such as UCI and the former operator, Virgin. UCI was designed with older, more affluent segments in mind, whilst Virgin cinemas had a meteoric rise – its Premier Screens had armchairs, private bars with waiter service, children's party rooms and stores in the lobbies selling Virgin merchandise. To fight back, Odeon has launched a marketing and advertising initiative which the company hopes will make audiences feel more passionate about the Odeon brand name. Adopting the strapline 'fanatical about film', Odeon feels the key to achieving this is to build anticipation and excitement among audiences, and in each Odeon cinema, prior to the film screening, an ad made by Ridley Scott & Associates is shown. Together with changes to the product support, this branding exercise encompasses new packaging and staff uniforms; the appointment of 'film fanatics' (staff who can advise customers about film) and an updated website (www.odeon.co.uk).

Positioning leaders

How do you position a product? The best way is to be the first into the consumer's mind – the first company to occupy that position is going to be very difficult (if not impossible) to dislodge – such as Coke in cola, McDonald's in fast-food or Hertz in car rental. History shows that the first brand on average gets twice the long-term market share of the number two brand and twice as much again as the third placed brand – and the rankings are not easy to reverse. Coke's 'The real thing' campaign is a strategy which could work for any leader since Coke got into the consumer's mind first and this strapline cleverly reinforces the 'original' concept. Coke is now the standard by which the market followers – the imitators of 'The real thing' – are judged. This works extraordinarily well. Yet it is not a good idea to run ads which actually spell out that a leader is number one because either the consumer already knows that and wonders why the company is so insecure that it has to say so, or he or she does not know it and, if so, why not? A leadership position cannot be built on the company's terms – it has to be on the consumer's terms and, once that position has been built, leaders are in the best position to exploit opportunities as they arise. Market leaders should use the power of their leadership to keep as far ahead of the rest as possible and endorse their position through consistent advertising programmes. In this way a number of companies use advertising to promote identities that are far more controversial than the products or services they market – for example, Benetton or Nike.

Positioning followers

Can new brands take the creative ad high ground or is this position restricted to the market leaders? If you cannot be first then you must follow a strategy of positioning your product against the one that did get there first. However, far too many companies create their marketing and advertising programmes as if the competition did not exist. Yet, is it sensible to create advertising in a vacuum when consumers do not make product choices in a vacuum but use product and brand 'ladders' (see Chapter 8)? In today's marketplace the competition's position is just as – if not more – important than your own. A classic illustration of this is the famous Avis campaign, an early success in positioning. On each rung of the rent-a-car brand ladder is a company – Hertz is first, Avis second, followed by National and Budget, etc. The Avis campaign positioned it against the leader: 'Avis is only No. 2 in rent-a-cars, so why go with us? We try harder.' After losing money for thirteen years in a row, Avis began to make money – enough to attract a buy-out. Avis's campaign was so hugely successful (consumers still remember the ads today) because it did not compete with Hertz head on but *related* itself to Hertz. Yet since running the campaign Avis has consistently ignored the only concept it can really call its own in the consumer's mind and has run much less memorable ads. To be successful, you have to take account of the competition, but you should not walk away from your own position of strength.

The Avis ads are a famous example of the 'against' positioning. There are others and to find them you must look inside the consumer's mind. Al Ries and Jack Trout, in addition to discussing this Avis example, also talk about the 'Seven-Up, uncola' idea.[9] In other words, you can position your brand by saying what it is *not* as well as by saying what it *is*. One of their examples is WLKW, a beautiful-music radio station in the Providence, Rhode Island, market that was going nowhere until McCormick Communications made it the number one station. The theme? 'WLKW, the unrock station.' Ries and Trout describe the follower strategy in terms of the French marketing expression: 'Cherchez le creneau. "Look for the hole."'[10] In other words, rather than introducing a raft of 'me too' products which attempt to improve on those of the brand leaders, try to find a gap in the market and fill it with something different. That gap could be based on a high price – premium perfumes, clothes, cars and beers base their entire product message on the high-price concept – as, in tourism, do the Venice-Simplon Orient Express, the *QE2*, Concorde and the Savoy Hotel. It could also be based on low price and a budget approach – such as the Motel Six brand in the USA. Some companies reject the idea of looking for a specific niche because they want to go for high market share and to produce products that appeal to everyone. But in today's marketing environment it is very difficult to appeal to everyone unless your brand already owns a significant share of the market. Indeed, it is impossible to attempt this approach if you are trying to build a market position from scratch.

Positioning is difficult enough even if you are a number two company in a market – as Pepsi is in the cola market. Over their 100-year rivalry with Coca-Cola, Pepsi has lagged behind – today, although PepsiCo has total sales of $22 billion, in the USA, Coke sells three sodas for every one sold by Pepsi. Recently, however, Roger Enrico, who took over as chief executive of Pepsi-Cola in 1996, has looked to reinvigorate the brand.[11] Pepsi advertising has since adopted a broader, less edgy approach than the 'Generation next' theme which excluded much of the audience and the company launched a new beverage – Pepsi One – to take on Diet Coke. A major part of the plan,

> Three positioning strategies: be the first, relate to the company that is the first, or advertise what your brand is not and fill a marketplace gap.

however, is a sweeping reorganization of the corporation, pulling Pepsi out of the restaurant business (jettisoning Pizza Hut, Taco Bell and Kentucky Fried Chicken, which netted combined sales of $11 billion but which were capital-intensive) and divesting itself of its bottling operation. At the same time, Frito-Lay, a PepsiCo subsidiary which accounts for two-thirds of PepsiCo's sales and profits, is being harnessed for the cola by being teamed with it in supermarket and store displays – everyone who buys one of the company's snacks will have to walk past a bottle of Pepsi in the same section. Such strategies, together with the marketing blitz tied to the *Star Wars* summer 1999 prequel, *The Phantom Menace* (Pepsi spent $2 billion to secure the exclusive rights to the film), places PepsiCo in a position to take on Coke. Certainly the time may be right as Coke itself has problems – the Brazilian devaluation at the end of the 1990s (Coke's third largest market) hit business severely, its sales are weak across Asia and the company is suffering from heavy investment in the volatile Russian market.

Repositioning strategies

As Wolff Olins has commented, identity is a major resource for instituting and managing change, yet despite this, few organizations in any industry have really got to grips with it[12] – certainly not in tourism. Identities surround us, not only in terms of private and public sector companies and organizations, but also – importantly for destinations – in terms of culture and geography. Yet very few tourism or leisure organizations have an identity which is anything like as well known as Coca-Cola, Sony or BMW and, despite the discussion above of the strategy of finding a niche or 'creneau' in the market, there will be situations where there are none left to fill. With an overwhelming volume of goods and services of every size, price and variety in each product category, how can a company, organization or destination use advertising to capture consumer mindshare? In a recent survey two-thirds of consumers in Europe, Asia and America could not find any difference between a wide range of products. If the brand is an established one that has reached market maturity and is facing stagnant sales and decreasing profit margins, one answer may be to reposition the brand. This is a strategy that defines a new role for an ageing product in the marketplace – it could involve changing the product's target market and it would require altering the original positioning strategy.

> Repositioning strategies could involve changing the product or the target market, refreshing the advertising, or all three.

An excellent example of this strategy is the UK bingo industry, which in the late 1990s completely repositioned itself through product development and advertising to try and capture a share of a previously off-limits market. Bingo traditionally has been seen in the UK as a pastime for older women with little appeal for the potentially lucrative but completely 'switched off' youth market. The fact that bingo was, until recently (following a review of the 1960 Gaming Act which had also prevented its listing in *Yellow Pages*), unable to advertise was one of the factors which compounded its image problem. In essence, bingo has been one of the UK leisure industry's best kept secrets since the industry had been unable to advertise the substantial investment which has taken place in the bingo product since the introduction of a major competitor – the National Lottery – in 1994. The lottery threatened to make huge inroads into the core bingo audience and in part it prompted a review and revamp of the bingo product. The Rank Organization, which, with its two chains, Top Rank and Mecca, currently has the largest market share, expanded its Mecca chain in a £100 million investment campaign which ran until 2000. Ancient, dusty halls have been replaced by a new generation of entertainment complexes seating up to 2000 people, serving a wide range of food and drink and offering an all round experience in an attempt to lure younger players. Random number generators that select and display numbers on screens have replaced faded comperes who drew ping-pong balls from a drum. As a result, the new clubs have proved very popular with both traditional bingo players and a new, younger audience – including more young men.

Yet, whilst new product development can initially generate extra business, it will soon level off without advertising and, as a result of the legal changes, bingo is now able to play on a level playing field with the UK's National Lottery. Television advertising has formed the centre point of a number of campaigns intended to reposition the image of bingo and promote the newer clubs. Offering the most cost-effective method of communicating the industry's transformation and positive image, television has been used by both Gala (Bass's bingo division) and Rank's Mecca. Gala, one of the major bingo operators, featured a thirty-six-year-old woman in its advertising that focused on the anticipation and excitement of bingo. The woman goes to bingo, has a great time, wins but then the buzz and magic disappear when she gets home to her husband. The ad's strapline 'Bingo gets you buzzing' is also featured on all promotions. Mecca's campaign also uses humorous advertising to get its message across – although its ads (set to the funky sound of 'Gonna Make This a Night to Remember') are more stylish, young and trendy. The ads are designed to show how much of the thrill of bingo is in the anticipation. Although someone always wins (the strapline is 'You win more at Mecca'), much of the appeal centres on those who come close to winning, the group camaraderie and the laughter. Bingo is presented as a leisure activity that encourages female bonding in much the same way that football promotes male bonding. So far Mecca has been delighted by the results of the campaign which has prompted very positive customer responses and resulted in a younger customer profile.

Repositioning the competition

So far, our examples have all been quite well-established brands, companies and products seeking to reposition, but what if you are launching a new brand? Again, Al Ries and Jack Trout offer one solution – 'reposition the competition'.[13] In other words, to move a new idea, product or brand into the mind, you first have to move an old one out. Thus Stolichnaya, a vodka made in Russia, saw sales soar in the 1980s in the USA as a result of a campaign which pointed out that rivals such as Smirnoff were actually made in America. This kind of advertising is much more common in the USA, where commercials which name rival brands have been legal since 1974, but it is also becoming more popular in the UK (where, incidentally, comparative advertising has been legal since 1975).

The same challenge faced a newer brand that was proving less than successful. When Virgin Atlantic was first established in 1984 it was perceived as a 'backpack' airline, an image compounded by the fact that Richard Branson was associated with his ownership of an entertainment group. This brand image, along with Virgin's original mistake of operating short-haul flights, which were not cost-effective for a small airline, prompted Branson into repositioning Virgin's image. The airline set out to target business travellers and concentrated on long-haul flights offering high quality and service. As a result, Virgin is now second only to British Airways in the UK long-haul market, with prime routes, high load factors and a reputation for high quality and excellent service – two-thirds of its income now comes from the business sector.

Repositioning your name

There are other ways to reposition in addition to changing the target market or product. Of course, the most obvious is to change the name of a brand or organization – as when Trusthouse Forte became simply Forte in 1991. Even the oldest name in travel – Thomas Cook – has used the technique of using a brand new name to create a fresh image and gain competitive advantage for the company. In September 1999 Thomas Cook's familiar brochures (including Sunworld and Sunset) were scrapped, along with two airlines – Flying Colours and Caledonian. In an exercise costing £200 million over five years, they were replaced by a single new brand, JMC, the initials of John Mason Cook – the company founder, Thomas Cook's son. JMC was launched with a £6 million advertising campaign to project the brand as a tour operator with as many as nineteen brochures as well as an airline. Whilst the new brand does offer a more flexible and less impersonal product than previously, the main reasoning behind such an expensive branding exercise was largely to enable the company to sell holidays through as wide a range of agencies as possible. Whereas the Thomas Cook brochure can only be promoted through the group's own 750 retail outlets, the JMC brochure will be sold through up to 6000 other high street travel agents' stores.[14]

Changing names does not have to be restricted to organizations and companies – you can even change the name of a place. Hog Island in the Caribbean was in a much stronger position as a destination once it became Paradise Island.[15] And would Sir William Clough-Ellis's Italianate fantasy village-hotel in North Wales have become world-famous if he had not changed its original Welsh name which meant 'cold river mouth' to Portmeirion – a purely fictitious name? In fact, in a positioning (or repositioning) strategy, the single most important decision to make is what to call the product. Take the Spanish Balearic Island of Majorca. Here, declining visitor numbers in 1989–90 prompted the island's regional government to introduce a number of initiatives. A £115 million refurbishment programme funded by regional government and local district councils improved the resort's environment and infrastructure. Development controls were tightened, limiting new hotel developments to those that were four-star or higher, development was completely banned in conservation areas, which covered 30 per cent of the island, and legislation encouraged older hotels to upgrade.[16] These improvements formed the basis of a promotional campaign orchestrated by the Fomento del Turismo de Mallorca (the Majorcan Tourist Board) and the Balearic Islands Tourism Council. The key objectives were to highlight the improvements, to counter the 'lager lout' resort image by raising tourists' awareness of the island's other attractions and to attract back the family, the older and the more upscale markets.

The aim was to shake off an image of a Majorca linked with a certain kind of tourism – charter flights, crowded beaches, all-night disco-bars and drunken sex. In addition to the infrastructural improvements, however, a key vehicle in achieving these objectives was a public relations campaign, linked to the launching of a new corporate logo. Most significantly, however, the island also renamed itself Mallorca – using the spelling of the local language, Mallorquin – to emphasize its cultural identity and new image. Individual resorts also repositioned and rebranded themselves – Magaluf and Palma Nova became Costas de Calvia. To negate its 'lager-lout' image, Mallorca launched a public relations offensive that drew particular attention to its scenery and to Palma and its associations with Chopin, Miro and Robert Graves. The campaign has been extremely successful, and the 'new' destination of Mallorca has successfully moved upmarket, attracting film stars, celebrities and royalty.

Ad highlight 9.1   **Changing a name to reposition a beer**

Scottish Courage changed the name and look of Molson Dry in a £2 million rebranding campaign. The company simplified the name to simply 'Molson' and redesigned the product packaging to a 330 ml. clear bottle which now highlights the brand's Canadian heritage via a red maple leaf livery, whilst the old bottle merely emphasized the word 'dry'. Research suggested that consumers were put off by the word 'dry' because it implied an unwanted 'dry' lager taste, so on the bottle this is replaced with the line 'Smooth in the extreme'. The rebranding was supported by a national press and poster advertising campaign.

Repositioning by refreshing the advertising

Whilst destinations have their own particular marketing challenges which can make positioning and repositioning difficult (see Chapter 10), even the world's biggest and most marketing-shrewd brands get it wrong sometimes and have to rethink their positioning. When EuroDisney was first launched, even the most cynical observers who predicted some difficulties for the giant corporation failed to anticipate the severe problems that the theme park experienced in its first years of operation. The problem for EuroDisney was reaching an equitable balance between retaining its American 'feel' (which was, after all, its main draw) whilst also reflecting European expectations. Initially Disney merely transferred its concept wholeheartedly to Paris and the project was controlled exclusively by US managers who failed to assess European tastes or, indeed, European vacation habits (including issues of seasonality). After absorbing substantial initial losses, EuroDisney has changed not only its name (to Disneyland Paris), but also its marketing approach and its product policies, to suit European tastes. Reductions have been made in its pricing strategies, alcohol (for so long taboo in Disney) has been introduced, whilst its advertising has adopted a much less glitzy all-American approach. Specifically in order to woo the French market – who were making up only a quarter of visitors in the early months (as opposed to the hoped for half) – American-inspired ads were dropped in favour of more descriptive campaigns.

A similar example of repositioning accomplished largely by advertising rather than any large-scale changes to the product itself is the way in which Skytours, part of the Thomson Travel group, has reinvented itself as the leading provider of holidays to families. Part of a much broader campaign that sees Thomson trying to shift the emphasis away from pricing to brand values, this campaign seeks to persuade people to think about what they want from their break, shifting the focus from the cost concerns that have tended to dominate the package holiday market in the past. Previously launched as a budget brand in the mid-1980s, it lost its distinctiveness as the Thomson brand developed and as price competitiveness became the standard measure for package holiday providers in the UK. By 1996, Skytours was losing business to Airtours, which was seen as a competitively priced, yet not downmarket, holiday brand. To overcome these problems Thomson initially repositioned Skytours as a 'fun' brand targeted at the under thirty-fives. However, the repositioning proved to be problematic because of its attempt to appeal to various subgroups within this umbrella category (young people, couples and families) who do not share similar needs and desires from the holiday package. Thomson elected to redefine Skytours (and other brands in the Thomson Group) to appeal to much narrower target markets, and product and brand differentiation were regarded as key to its marketing strategy.

The Skytours brand repositioning has centred on a £1 million television advertising campaign that focuses on the problems of parents. A 30-second ad shows a young couple in bed, having fun. Before the fun becomes 'serious', a 1950s-style announcer breaks in and asks them to reconsider what they are about to do. The warning is: 'Before you have children you should think about the future . . . you'll have to look after them constantly and think about the effect on your social life, not to mention the expense'. Such dire warnings are countermanded by jolly, happy holiday visuals which show mum and dad at the pool whilst the kids have supervised fun on the beach. A close-up of the Skytours brochure shows a free child place with every holiday – so that means it will not cost a fortune either. The advertising avoids the clichés of sun and beaches through its exclusive focus on the family and their concerns – a theme carried into the brochures, which feature children's drawings of holidays rather than the usual holiday visuals.

Repositioning by product development and fresher advertising

Whilst occasionally repositioning can be successfully achieved without major product development, products which have reached a certain maturity usually require more than just a fresher ad campaign. One such example is the repositioning of Torbay in south-west England at the beginning of the 1980s. At that time British tourism was performing poorly and the number of tourist nights spent in the resort of Torbay dropped by over a fifth between 1977 and 1982 – even in high season a third of its beds were empty. With the assistance of the English Tourist Board, Torbay Tourist Board (TTB) commissioned market research which demonstrated that the resort attracted two main types of holidaymaker: those upscale tourists who saw Torbay as the best resort in Britain for a main or supplementary holiday; and those who could not afford to take an overseas holiday and saw Torbay as the best alternative. In addition to these findings, it emerged that repeat visitors were a high proportion of Torbay's visitors, whilst holiday-makers in the AB socioeconomic groups were underrepresented and awareness of Torbay's attractions and mild winter climate was limited.

The resort's marketers embarked on a repositioning campaign to appeal to the more affluent holiday-makers, those looking for second holidays and short breaks and those desiring a 'continental' feel on holiday. The branding saw the resort produce a series of highly creative and design-led posters, brochures and marketing literature using the phrase 'The English Riviera' with a newly designed palm tree logo. Printed on high-quality paper, the brochures were of a new, larger format and incorporated a controversial new palm tree logo and the TTB's corporate colours of blue, jade, yellow and white. All the brochure designs marketed Torbay as a highly stylized image, not as a location – very different from those of other British seaside resorts at that time which tended to feature photographs of the resort (often the same photograph year after year!). Torbay – by producing a different cover each year – ensured that its brochure stood out from other such publications. Moreover, by embracing a highly branded identity, Torbay was attempting to sell a concept rather than a product – an emotional rather than a resort attribute.[17]

Produced within the resort, these brochures of the 1980s and 1990s achieved a considerable impact and their designs won national acclaim – that of 1988 scooping the Creative Circle Honours Award for the best travel advertisement. Costing £100 000, this particular design was launched at the World Travel Market in winter 1987 and appeared on 200 000 English Riviera brochures. Although its depiction of seaside huts was criticized in Torbay itself as too old-fashioned – local hoteliers commented that it conjured up images of a quaint and antiquated seaside which the resort sought to escape – the poster was highly successful according to TTB research and certainly capitalized on burgeoning trends in the holiday market such as the nostalgia trend.[18]

The 1985 Torbay brochure design (Plate 7) is a good example of the resort's repositioned image. The brochure cover depicts a waiter serving drinks to a young woman in a swimming pool. White-jacketed and bearing aloft his tray of cold drinks at the pool-side, the waiter indicates a high standard of service. His dress means style – evocative of popular conceptions of interwar elegance – an image reinforced by the Art Deco style of the title's lettering of 'The English Riviera'. Yet at the same time the design also incorporates images associated with a very contemporary holiday since the swimming pool and the deeply sun-tanned, bikini-clad woman convey images of sunshine more reminiscent of Mediterranean holiday-making. Thus this design – still typical of contemporary Torbay publicity material – cleverly mixes traditional and modern images, creating an impression of a very modern resort capable of providing old-fashioned service and elegance – a sophisticated and successful blend. Moreover, the campaign was hugely successful – Torbay is now one of the UK's leading year-round seaside resorts with around 10 million staying visitor bed nights a year.

Repositioning a destination is not easy, however. No matter how slick the advertising, it usually requires significant investment in the actual product. Las Vegas, for example, has reinvented itself in the last decade as a family-oriented tourist mecca for sports, entertainment, recreation and the performing arts, in spite of the fact that it is still seen as a vice capital – 5 per cent of the city are employed in the sex industry and gambling is worth well over $20 billion, or 60 per cent of the local economy. It has the world's biggest and most up-to-date casino-hotel-theme-parks and, however fast new ones are built (the $1 billion Mandalay Bay, the $1.6 billion Bellagio, the $1.2 billion Venetian and the $760 million Paris all opened in 1999), room occupancy remains impressively high. At a time of stagnation in many US cities, Las Vegas is enjoying unprecedented prosperity: Greater Las Vegas has become the fastest growing region in the USA, with the valley's population doubling in the same decade. It is also a university town with one of the fastest growing, most prestigious universities in the west of the USA. It has a high-tech regional service centre that attracted almost 100 new companies during the 1980s and at the start of the 2000s is a hugely popular retirement destination.

This year-round, 24-hour resort (the theme of its advertising) has cleverly repositioned itself in the face of the competition. Where ten years ago there were 24-hour gambling joints, topless bars, tacky wedding chapels and tired showbusiness stars at the end of their careers, now there are family hotels, theme parks, musicals and venues designed to appeal to smart, young professionals. The latest 'family' incarnation of Las Vegas began in 1993 with the launch of a group of megaresorts offering an alternative to gambling. The

Luxor (since further extended) has a 360-foot black glass pyramid with a faux-Egyptian theme; and Treasure Island (a mock eighteenth-century pirate village on the edge of an artificial Buccaneer Bay where every evening two galleons fight it out) is another themed hotel that appeals to families. The MGM, the world's largest hotel, has its own sports stadium and a 33-acre theme park, the Excalibur has a turreted Arthurian appearance and the Mirage is a Polynesian paradise with white tigers behind glass in the walk-through lobby and a 40-foot flaming volcano that erupts every quarter of an hour after dark. By the end of the year 2000, Las Vegas will have more rooms than New York, Paris or Los Angeles.

However, in successfully repositioning itself to appeal to families, Las Vegas found that cheap rooms and food meant that those who turned up with their families spent more time with them in the theme parks than in the casinos gambling – since 1990 gambling has fallen from almost 60 per cent of Vegas's Strip's revenue to just about 50 per cent. In response to this and demographics – the target audience is now aged fifty, high-spending and without children (one person in the USA will turn forty-nine every 13 seconds between 2000 and 2015) – the resort's hotels are now moving upmarket and establishing Vegas as a destination for style-sensitive thirty to fifty-year-olds. The $100 million Hard Rock Hotel and Casino with its guitar-neck handled slot machines was one of the first hotels to make Vegas 'cool' – attracting well-heeled generation Xers and rock 'n' roll baby boomers. This hotel has roulette tables shaped like pianos, Harley Davidsons on top of slot machines, underwater rock music in the swimming pool and its gambling chips are so trendy that guests often keep them as souvenirs.

Not only are the hotels themselves now 'cool', but some of Vegas's traditionally poor fare is also being given a major makeover. Whereas the resort was once a food desert with low quality all-you-can-eat buffets as standard, now fine dining has become a feature of the newer hotels (the Bellagio, the all-suite Venetian and Hilton's Paris, Las Vegas), with restaurants franchised from some of America's most celebrated ones in New York, Boston and San Francisco. $3.99 buffets have now been traded for $20 entrées at Wolfgang Puck's and European glamour. Style is also definitely the theme at the designer shops at the recently extended Forum shops at Caesar's Palace, and nowhere more than at those of Steve Wynn's $1.6 billion Bellagio which include outlets of Tiffany's and Chanel. Opened at Easter 1999, this thirty-six storey, 3000-bedroom hotel, fronted by a 3-hectare lake with dancing fountains, has a $300 million art collection (including works by Van Gogh, Picasso, Miro, Gauguin, Cezanne) as its main attraction, together with a stunning flower-filled conservatory.

Chapter summary

One of the most important tasks facing marketers of tourism and leisure products is the challenge of effectively positioning their brand – whether as a leader or a follower. The positioning process involves three stages:

■ identifying potential competitive advantages upon which to construct a position
■ selecting the appropriate competitive advantages which are relevant and meaningful for the chosen target audience
■ effectively communicating and delivering the selected position to the market.

In today's highly competitive leisure and tourism marketplace, brand positions also need to remain fresh and relevant. If the brand is an established one that has reached market maturity and is facing stagnant sales and decreasing profit margins, the answer is often to reposition the brand. This is a strategy that can involve a number of alternatives:

■ identifying a new role for an ageing product in the marketplace – this may involve changing the product's target market and it would require altering the original positioning strategy
■ repositioning the product by changing its image, name or advertising – refreshing a brand's saliency through advertising without altering the product
■ repositioning by revitalizing or enhancing the product *and* reinvigorating its advertising.

Case study 9.1

Repositioning a leisure wear product

Levi's 501s are a low-tech jeans product. Whilst the quality control is good, there is nothing inherently different between a pair of Levi's, Pepe, Wrangler or other branded or own-label jeans product. Despite this, Levi's can make substantially more than its competitors per sale. Levi's make about twice the profit of their rivals in the mass branded jeans market and the success of the brand means that, as consumers, we are prepared to pay for the privilege – we have somehow been persuaded that the Levi's product is worth more than the many other alternatives on offer. Despite the recent downturn in the fashionability of denim, Levi's still makes about $6 billion a year from the global jeans market. Levi's is undoubtedly the market leader but it was not always as successful. In this case study we ask whether Levi's make better jeans or just more alluring dreams?

In the early 1980s Levi's were going through a difficult period. Its sales were declining, its market was maturing and fashion trends (with the emphasis on power dressing) were incompatible with the Levi's product range. Levi's brand image was diverse and confusing and it lacked sex appeal, as evidenced by its move into washable polyester suits. The appointment of Bob Haas as CEO in 1983 marked the turning point in the company's fortunes. Levi's 501s became the flagship product of the company in the drive to capture international markets and was at the heart of one of the most successful brand makeovers ever. The advertising brief for 501s focused on its association as the original, authentic American blue jeans. Thus, instead of positioning Levi's in terms of the strength and durability of the jeans (the product), the ads focused on its associations. The ad makeover transformed 501s into the original, authentic, American, freedom, rebel, individual and, above all, sexy jeans. A series of ads were produced which captured these qualities. Their ingredients were a sexy star and an emphasis on the 1950s – the high point of American youth culture. Music was central to the Levi's makeover, reflecting its significance and role in youth culture, today as in the 1950s.

It was the second ad in the series that was the spark that sent 501s into high orbit and marked a watershed in ad history. 'Laundrette' starred Nick Kamen, accompanied by Marvin Gaye's 'Heard it through the Grapevine'. In the ad, Nick Kamen walks into a laundrette, coolly takes off his clothes, places his 501s with some stones in a washing machine and walks over to the seats in just a pair of boxer shorts – watched with anticipation by the women and with envy by the men in the room. The ad's impact was immediate – sales of 501s rocketed by 800 per cent. Sales of all jeans also benefited – Lee jeans sales went up by 40 per cent without the company spending a penny on advertising. Levi's became the number one market leader – a position it still holds. The ad's impact extended beyond jeans and sparked a revolution in men's underwear almost overnight. When the UK Advertising Standards Authority ruled that the character could not wear Y-fronts, boxer shorts were used instead and became the trendy, sexy, cult underwear for men.

'Laundrette' ran in the mid-1980s. Since then, the Levi's campaign has produced many other executions, all of which communicate the jeans' emotional values. Levi's have stayed cool and at the forefront of youth culture by consistently surprising the consumer with ads that switch between colour and black and white, heroes to heroines and past to future. All the executions incorporate great soundtracks. Yet, from today's viewpoint it is easy to underestimate the scale of the brand's success and the task with which its owners and their ad agency were originally confronted. Unlike trendy niche players (it is, after all, the biggest mass-market brand), it is only able to retain its 'cool' anti-establishment status through cutting-edge advertising and the successful communication of brand associations. Whether Levi's can weather the problems facing the jeans industry at the beginning of the 2000s remains to be seen.

Source: based on *Branded*, BBC2 programme screened in 1997.

Case study 9.2

Repositioning a theme park

The UK theme park market has become increasingly competitive, and the parks are having to refine their product and maximize revenue from every visitor by increasing secondary spend – particularly in the areas of catering and merchandising. During 1993–97 admission charges increased by 12 per cent to recoup money invested in new rides and new technology. Much of the new competition has come from the 'European-ization' of the industry. Currently the European theme park industry consists of nineteen major attractions with annual attendances in excess of one million and forty-five moderate scale parks that attract between half a million and a million. Together they all generate 70 million attendances and £51.5 billion in revenue.

Of course, it is Disney which has redefined the nature of the theme park and such is the dominance of the Florida and Paris parks that they are able to spend over £5 million on main media advertising in the UK alone. As Europe's most visited tourist attraction, attracting 11.7 million visitors in 1998, Disneyland Paris invests heavily in promotion and in the late 1990s became one of the most consistent advertisers in the UK market. Disney has educated the consumer to expect and demand high product quality, but it also provides price leadership in the theme park sector, and its creative marketing programmes generate market awareness and enlighten competitors to the use of effective marketing techniques. This means that advertising is more important than ever in the theme park marketing mix and in 1997 – the year before Oblivion – the new ride at Alton Towers (and our case study here) opened – both Alton Towers and Chessington World of Adventures, the second most visited UK theme park, both spent £1.8 million on advertising.

Two industry experts, Jones and Robinett[19] suggest that the European theme park sector must be aware of four watchwords in the 2000s: anticipation, repositioning, expansion and consolidation. They suggest that in the future a theme park must:

- be unique, a must-see destination
- have large-scale and a critical mass of attractions
- combine high-tech with a human scale and quality service
- encourage overnight stay
- have complementary destination activities
- support media coverage and exposure.

One result of the growing demand among consumers for new, bigger and better attractions is that parks will have to invest more and more money to maintain their market positions. This was the challenge facing Alton Towers in 1996.

The theme park

Alton Towers is the UK's most famous and largest theme park, attracting some 3 million visitors and a £50 million turnover. In the late 1990s, however, there was some concern that it was losing its appeal to the thrill-seeking, teenage market. The problem for Alton Towers was how to win back this market without alienating its other core market of young families. Located in 7 acres of parkland in Staffordshire, Alton Towers is a byword for big rides and even bigger thrills in the UK. Originally opened as a theme park in 1980, it has about 130 rides (open mid-March to early November) and a year-round theme hotel on site (which was the first in a UK theme park) with a 200-room conference facility.

In the 1990s Alton Towers' product portfolio and market orientation had been diversified since its owners were anxious that the park should target the family market in addition to its then core fifteen to twenty-four age-group market. This was in response to population forecasts that suggested that the latter was a declining market which would drop by 1.7 million in the 1990s. When the park was purchased by the Madame Tussauds Group, this strategy continued and, to compensate for the projected decline in the teen market, Alton Towers invested heavily in family-oriented attractions. The Land of Make Believe was specifically aimed at the very young; regular shows featured popular children's characters such as Beatrix Potter's rabbits; and gentle water rides and farm animal attractions were designed for families with young children.

The challenge

Alton Towers' corporate philosophy is based around 'magic' – everything within the park has to be done according to the magic and customers, employees and shareholders alike share in the magical, unreal, fun, fantastical and escapist world offered at the park. Alton Towers' marketing proposition is that it is 'Britain's most magical experience'. However, between 1996 and 1997, the magic was waning and the company realized that the balance had swung too far in favour of family entertainment. There was real concern that Alton Towers was failing to attract its thrill-seeking market. Its last thrill ride, Nemesis, had been launched in 1994 and whilst this had been incredibly successful, it was now considered insufficient to attract fifteen to twenty-four-year-olds. Young thrill-seekers want new challenges, dangers and excitement from a theme park, yet Alton Towers had developed a youth credibility problem – suffering from an 'I've done it all before' image. The Tussauds Group realized that the park needed to bridge the credibility gap with something special – which had edge, which was cool, visually impactful and appealing.

The answer was the development of a new £12 million ride – Oblivion, the world's first vertical drop roller coaster. So important was the new development that the ride was to be central to Alton Towers' new £5 million marketing strategy. The focus of this strategy would be an ad for Oblivion which, at the end of the initial advertising burst, was intended to have been seen by 80 to 85 per cent of the target market three to four times. The J. Walker Thompson agency was appointed to develop the ad campaign and it was agreed that Oblivion would initially be launched with a month-long teaser campaign (February 1998) which would not be directly associated with Alton Towers but which would establish Oblivion's brand, colourways and icon.

265

This teaser campaign for the ride actually began much earlier as Oblivion's construction site itself was turned into a taster. In 1997 great interest was generated amongst roller-coaster enthusiasts and park-goers – visitors knew that something special was going on behind the construction hoarding. The Oblivion construction site was patrolled by orange-clad, dark-glasses wearing, uncommunicative security guards who refused to interact with the visitors – something which went completely against the Alton Towers' usual service ethos. Computer-style announcements authoritatively advised park visitors that 'The time is not yet right . . . please clear the area'.

Oblivion's USP

The ride's USP is that Oblivion is the coolest ride in the land. Riders teeter on the edge of Oblivion, eyes closed, stomach churning, sweat beads and then falls. Riders free-fall forward into a dark hole . . . into oblivion, into 'a state of being forgotten'.

The initial ad concept

The creative team decided not to use traditional images of roller coasters, trying instead to look for images that were much more funky and zany – it wanted to come up with something completely new for what was a completely new development in roller-coaster rides. It opted for a metaphorical approach to the advertising, focusing on the fear of the fall rather than the actual fall itself. Their first ad storyboard opened in the inky blackness of the interior of a Hercules plane. We see a man strapped to the inside of the open loading ramp. He begins to slide towards the edge. As he slides, his feet hook on to the metal railing of the ramp. The ad cuts to: 'What's it like to fall into oblivion?'

As if in answer to this question the ad cuts to a ride car from various angles. Suddenly it hurtles towards the camera at great speed until the logo at the front of the car fills the frame. The camera focuses on the word 'Oblivion' at the centre of the logo. As this sequence runs, a voice-over intones: 'the world's first, face first, sheer drop'.

The focus group

The ad agency's idea was tested using a focus group, which did not appreciate the metaphorical approach taken by the agency. The plane sequence did not appeal largely because it was felt to be an unrealistic and inappropriate comparison. Whilst the guy in the plane was going to die, roller-coaster riders clearly do not. The focus group participants were very uncomfortable with the ad concept which they felt was too extreme, preferring instead a more realistic representation of the roller-coaster experience.

The client/agency response

Both the client and the agency recognized the shortcomings of the focus group research. Respondents tend not to like metaphorical associations and imagery which is 'removed' from the product in question. Despite the fact that people like the creative and highly stylized imagery of, say, Nike or Levi's, when faced with an ad in a focus group, people tend to opt for a 'tell me more about the product' approach. In this case, the group favoured editing out the first part of the ad and focusing on the ride shots at the end. The danger in a too literal interpretation of the focus group's reactions would be an ad that merely consisted of a series of ride shots and had no depth of imagery. Despite these reservations, in the end, the focus group responses proved impossible to resist and the agency had to drop its metaphorical approach. The man in the aeroplane was replaced with ride shots filmed in a studio and a more mainstream approach than originally planned was adopted – although this still left ample opportunities for creativity.

The finished ad

The storyboard opens in semi-darkness. A hand clings to a bar. The ad cuts to a face that is clearly terrified, a bead of sweat forms and then drops down off the man's forehead – at a right angle! Suspended above a sheer drop, the sweat bead plunges down into oblivion. The ad then cuts to someone next to the man – someone strange, manic and weird, someone who is obviously not frightened but who looks back, saying: 'Don't look down!'

Difficult choices

The client still had some reservations about this approach. Of concern was how 'dark' the ad should be. The only colour in the scenes was the safety harness and the ride's logo, both of which were orange. More importantly, how weird should the stranger be? Perhaps he should be more human . . . but was not the essence of the ad the contrast between the ordinary rider and his strange companion? Underpinning this concern was the dilemma facing Alton Towers. The marketing strategy centred around this one ad which was going to be seen by the attraction's two distinct markets – the thrill-seekers and families. If the ad was too scary

Table 9.1 The Oblivion launch media mix

Magazine advertising	Public relations	Trade relations
Targeted audience with tailor-made messages	Highly significant element of the marketing strategy	Organizations and individuals deliver large numbers of people to Alton Towers
Scary, risqué ads in magazines read by young thrill-seekers	Generates more media coverage than purchased media	Coach operators targeted via direct sales calls to capitalize on their interest in new ride's launch
Family-oriented ads in women's magazines	Newspaper/television pieces appear as endorsements and independent of Alton Towers despite the fact that the media releases were generated by the theme park	Schools targeted via direct mail and educational resource packs
Ads designed to trigger pester-power – to get kids to ask parents to take them to Alton Towers now	Secrecy is the key to Oblivion PR. Details to seep out slowly to maintain interest and excitement Competitions and special offers with newspapers/cereal manufacturers, etc. help fill off-peak capacity and generate more coverage	Corporate consumers are a growing market, attracted by Alton Towers' unique environment and off-peak discounts

there was always the possibility that it would alienate the family market – particularly those with very young children. Not scary enough, however, and the ad would fail to attract the fifteen to twenty-four-year-olds. In the end, the ad went ahead and Alton Towers resolved the problem of matching message and market by using a tightly defined media mix (Table 9.1).

The impact

In March 1998 Oblivion was launched on the back of tremendous media hype generated by an extremely successful PR strategy. As well as being tied into promotions with cereal manufacturers, Oblivion was covered by the news media (both television and press) and featured on popular children's programmes. Dedicated roller-coaster riders were driven almost to a frenzy of anticipation by the secrecy surrounding the nature of the ride and the drip-feed PR strategy. When it was launched, the park used interactive telephone lines and a website as well as exclusive ride time offers. In its first season, Oblivion broke all records for a UK roller coaster. On busy days 1800 people an hour rode the attraction, and following this success Alton Towers remains the UK's top paid-for attraction, drawing almost 3 million annual visitors.

Source: based on television programmes BBC1 *Modern Times*, 1998, and TV Choice, *The Alton Towers Story*.

Notes

1 Patricia Sellers (1995). A brand new day in Marlboro County. *Fortune*, 12 June, 16.
2 Frances Brassington and Stephen Pettitt (1997). *Principles of Marketing*. Pitman, p. 123.
3 Ad for Westin Stamford Hotel in *Conde Nast Traveller*, October 1997; Philip Kotler, John Bowen and James Makens (1996). *Marketing for Hospitality and Tourism*. Prentice Hall, ch. 9, p. 264.
4 L. J. Marchant, P. J. Hutchinson and P. Prescott (1990). A practical model of consumer choice. *Journal of Market Research Society*, **32** (1).
5 Kotler, Bowen and Makens, *Marketing for Hospitality and Tourism*, pp. 264–5.
6 Sheena Westwood, Nigel J. Morgan, Annette Pritchard and Elizabeth Ineson (1999). Branding the package holiday: the role and significance of brands for UK air tour operators. *Journal of Vacation Marketing*, **5** (3), 238–52.
7 Kotler, Bowen and Makens, *Marketing for Hospitality and Tourism*, pp. 264–5.
8 Ibid., pp. 241–2.
9 Al Ries and Jack Trout (1986). *Positioning: The Battle for your Mind*. Warner Books, ch. 4.
10 Ibid., ch. 7.
11 Frank Gibney Jr (1999). Pepsi gets back in the game. *Time*, 17 May, 54–6.
12 Wolff Olins (1995). *The New Guide to Identity: How to Create and Sustain Change through Managing Identity*. The Design Council and Gower Publishing.

13 Ries and Trout, *Positioning*, ch. 8.
14 Desmond Balmer (1999). If you can't Thomas Cook it, then dream up a brand new name. *Observer*, 5 September, p. 4.
15 Ries and Trout, *Positioning*, p. 71.
16 M. Morgan (1991). Majorca: dressing up to survive. *Tourism Management*, **12** (1), March; M. Morgan (1996). *Marketing for Leisure and Tourism*. Prentice Hall, pp. 255–6.
17 Annette Pritchard and Nigel Morgan (1998). Mood marketing, the new destination branding strategy. The case of 'Wales the brand'. *Journal of Vacation Marketing*, **4** (3), 215–29.
18 Nigel Morgan and Annette Pritchard (1999). *Power and Politics at the Seaside: The Development of Devon's Resorts in the Twentieth Century*. University of Exeter Press, ch. 5. Also material from a personal interview with Neil Whitehead, Director of the TTB.
19 Jones, L. and Robinett, M. (1997). *The Future Role of Theme Parks in International Tourism*. Economics Research Associates.

Further reading

Camp, L. (1999). Positioning and communication issues in building financial services brands. *Journal of Brand Management*, **6** (4), 243–9.
Dingle, D. and Harding, G. (1994). From Canberra to Oriana: a £200 million investment in the identification and management of brand values. *Journal of Vacation Marketing*, **1** (2), 195–201.
Farnfield, I. (1999). Driving for effective positioning and competitive differentiation. *Journal of Brand Management*, **6** (4), 250–7.
Free, C. (1999). The internal brand. *Journal of Brand Management*, **6** (4), 231–6.
Kotler, P., Bowen, J. and Makens, J. (1999). *Marketing for Hospitality and Tourism*. 2nd edn. Prentice Hall, ch. 9.
Morgan, M. (1991). Majorca: dressing up to survive. *Tourism Management*, **12** (1), March.
Morgan, M. (1996). Marketing for Leisure and Tourism. Prentice Hall.
Morgan, N. and Pritchard, A. (1999). *Power and Politics at the Seaside: The Development of Devon's Resorts in the Twentieth Century*. University of Exeter Press, ch. 5.
Olins, W. (1995). *The New Guide to Identity: How to Create and Sustain Change through Managing Identity*. The Design Council and Gower Publishing.

Ries, A. and Trout, J. (1986). *Positioning: The Battle for your Mind.* Warner Books.

Taylor, H. (1997). Competitive advantage in the hotel industry: success through differentiation. *Journal of Vacation Marketing*, **3** (1), 170–3.

Westwood, S., Morgan, N. J., Pritchard, A. and Ineson, E. (1999). Branding the package holiday: the role and significance of brands for UK air tour operators. *Journal of Vacation Marketing*, **5** (3), 238–52.

10

Advertising destination brands

Chapter overview

This chapter completes Part Three of the book which examines the relationship between advertising and the creation of powerful tourism and leisure brands. Whilst Chapters 8 and 9 discussed brand-building and repositioning strategies, this chapter focuses specifically on advertising, destination marketing and branding. In the tourism and leisure industries, destination marketing (largely co-ordinated and funded by the public sector) is one of the most highly politicized areas and such is the difficulty of producing good, effective advertising that we have devoted a whole chapter to its evaluation. Our discussion here encompasses the advertising strategies of Morocco, Israel, New Zealand, Canada, Wales, Spain and Australia, whilst our end of chapter case studies examine the marketing challenges facing Langkawi and

Jamaica and the opportunities which were presented by the millennium celebrations. The key themes reviewed are:

- the challenges of destination promotion
- destination advertising strategies and the development of branding
- destination branding techniques
- case studies of successful destination branding
- the emergence of destination supra-brands.

Introduction

As tourism expands around the globe, it brings new opportunities in destination marketing, yet one of the outcomes of the increasing number of available and accessible tourist destinations is a dilution of established destination identities and increased competition amongst emergent tourism sites. The relative substitutability in tourism products is well established and destinations offering a similar product at a similar price are highly interchangeable. For example, UK tourists in search of a moderately priced sun and sand experience will accept a range of alternatives – from Cyprus, to Turkey, Spain or Greece. As a result, the need for destinations to project a unique identity – to differentiate themselves from their competitors – is more critical than ever. But most destinations continue to project very similar images. How many ads do you see which portray blue seas, cloudless skies and endless golden beaches with a less than memorable strapline? Yet what does one Caribbean or Mediterranean island really have which is significantly different from its nearest neighbour? Certainly not sun and sand.

This highlights the peculiar problems of tourism destination advertising. Sometimes agencies do not give these contracts to the appropriate creative team – one that is perhaps not fully aware of the complexities of destination marketing. But far more common (and worrying) is the persistent failure of the advertising to create a sufficiently differentiated identity for the tourist destination, so that the place stands out from the competition. Combine this with the highly damaging internal and external politics involved in creating destination advertising with evidence that tourism promotion does not persuade uncommitted potential vacationers (but rather acts to confirm the intentions of those already predisposed to visit), and destination managers and advertising agencies have genuine problems. To counteract such challenges (more of which below), many destinations, be they cities, regions or nations, are developing comprehensive identity programmes in an effort to differ-entiate themselves and to emphasize the uniqueness of their product in today's highly competitive market – most obviously to attract tourism and inward investment – but also to foster self-confidence and self-esteem.

The challenges of destination promotion

Most national tourism organizations have limited budgets and yet they have to market globally, competing not just with other destinations, but also with other global brands. Procter & Gamble, the world's biggest advertiser, may spend millions each year promoting its various products but countries such as Spain, France and Thailand still have to vie with them for consumer mindshare in a crowded ad environment (see Table 1.2 in Chapter 1). Whilst Sony alone spends over $300 million a year on global advertising, the total global government tourism ad spend topped just $350 million in the mid-1990s, accounting for around half of the promotional budgets of national tourism organizations. Table 10.1 illustrates 1997's biggest ad spenders (other significant spenders included Greece, Turkey, Egypt and Canada) – not, of course, including private sector spending. It is worth pointing out here that this table only illustrates national ad spend – where available. It does not, for instance, include countries that have no national tourism organization. In the USA, for example, state promotion is undertaken by a variety of convention bureaux and state travel offices – whose budgets often exceed those of some countries. The Illinois state travel office budget in 1997 topped $35 million, that of Texas was $25 million and Pennsylvania almost $20 million. Compare these figures with the national tourism budgets of Germany ($27 million), Hungary ($21 million) and Morocco ($18 million).[1]

Table 10.1   Top national tourism organizations' ad spend, 1997

Country	Ad spend (US$ millions)
Australia	30
Thailand	26
Cyprus	17
Spain	17
France	16
Puerto Rico	16
Brazil	15
Portugal	13

Source: World Tourism Organization (figures to nearest million).

Thus, the first challenge facing destination marketers is their extremely limited budgets by comparison with the marketers of many consumer goods and services. For instance, the total domestic and overseas marketing budget for Wales (one of our case studies in this chapter) stands at £5 million – clearly a small budget to support a worldwide branding campaign. So how do destination marketers compete with the megaconsumer brands and penetrate the fog of advertising overload? Clearly they have to outsmart rather than outspend the competition – and that means creating innovative, attention-grabbing advertising on a budget and maximizing the media spend. This is a simple, self-evident truth but in destination advertising it seems incredibly difficult to achieve. This is not to say that destination marketers are not good at their jobs, but too often they are not allowed to achieve the best they can because of the politics of destination advertising.

The challenge of politics

The reality of local and national state promotion is that it is about achieving a balance between applying cutting-edge advertising and public relations approaches to a marketing problem and the realpolitik of managing local, regional and national politics. This is the second challenge for destination marketers. Nowhere is the paradox of public policy and market forces more sharply defined than in the creation of destination advertising. One area in which there is a great deal of debate in political terms amongst destination marketers and destination stakeholders is over the use of clichés and stereotypes in marketing and advertising. Often consumers have very clichéd images about countries, yet those clichés are frequently despised in the countries themselves. One view is that if the consumer connects with a cliché about a country, then its marketers should use it since it has recognition and therefore advertising value. That, however, is an agency view – not one tempered by the experience of seeing the media fallout of an ad campaign perceived by residents as perpetuating stereotypes which are (by definition) outdated caricatures of places and peoples. The answer, which is both politically acceptable and which makes marketing sense, is to craft images that use the cliché as a hook on which to hang more detail – the clichéd identity can then be reshaped and given greater complexity through effective and consistent marketing.

> The challenges of destination advertising are: limited budgets, political pressures, a lack of product control and product parity.

Beyond such issues, public sector destination marketers are also hugely hampered by a variety of political pressures – they have to reconcile a range of local and regional interests and promote an identity acceptable to a range of constituencies. As Bob Garfield, editor of *Advertising Age* and long-time advertising critic, has said of destination advertising: 'When you look at the ads . . . you can see transcripts of the arguments at the tourist boards . . . the membership of which all wanted their own interests served . . . you can see the destruction of the advertising message as a result of the politics.'[2]

In addition to compromising the creative process of marketing and advertising destinations, the political masters of public sector tourism organizations frequently demand short-term results – pressure that is inconsistent with the long-term investment required by brand-building. Whilst ultimately it is the politicians who are the destination marketers' paymasters, a destination brand's life span is more of a long-term proposition than the careers of most politicians. Bureaucratic red tape can also often confound effective advertising – the marketers of Valencia, Spain's third city, for instance, are obliged to issue new advertising contracts every year – a practice which can do little to ensure consistency of message. Frequently, political considerations within a local state can even dictate the range of photographs that are included in a campaign. Many a creative execution has had to be amended so that brochures, commercials or posters can include photographs to illustrate all the key areas, towns, or resorts within a region or country. Whilst this has its political advantages in that it appeases local pressure groups and local residents – politicians are vulnerable to bad press and unrest in the trade – it will seriously compromise the effectiveness of the advertising.

Even when all the internal stakeholders are satisfied with a campaign, destination advertising can run into political problems as a result of external pressures. Perhaps one of the most depressing examples of this was the 'Feast for the senses' campaign created by Publicis for the Morocco Tourist Board in the mid-1990s. The campaign was an attempt to craft a homogeneous image for the country in all its generating markets, each of which had previously commissioned quite separate advertising on the reasonable premise that consumers in the UK, Germany, France, Italy, etc. all sought different experiences from a holiday to Morocco. Yet this disparate approach had created a blurred and confused image of the country. Working with the Morocco Tourist Board – total annual tourism budget approximately $18 million[3] – the agency therefore decided to create a new logo and produced a number of stunning visuals in a series of ten posters and in the main brochure, followed through in television commercials – all based around the strapline 'Morocco – a feast for the senses'. The advertising was produced in seven or eight languages, so whilst consistency of brand image was achieved the local Morocco marketing office in each of the markets was to some extent free to choose the visual it thought would sell best in that particular country.

Each of Morocco's main tourism regions was featured in the campaign and such was the positive reaction in the country when the visuals were seen that in the next phase the agency even created posters for those areas where there was little or no tourism infrastructure. Yet, whilst the image-building exercise was warmly welcomed in Morocco – and actually began to change regional policy-makers' attitudes to the potential of tourism – it proved extremely difficult to sell the campaign to external stakeholders. Travel agents and tour operators had to be persuaded to embrace it and a considerable effort was put into trade promotional packs, including displays, maps and a new trade magazine. Ultimately the campaign hit problems because German tour operators lobbied the Morocco Tourist Board, concerned that the campaign was promoting the country as a cultural destination and not as the sun and sea product which their customers were seeking. Whilst the visuals and the logo were retained in the following year, Publicis lost the contract and the dilution of the strong brand values of the original concept began.[4] Whilst this is a quite recent example of the power of such pressure from international tour operators, there are many others – notably in Tunisia in the 1970s when it was German tour operators who again dictated the nature of tourism development and today on the Albanian Mediterranean coast where there is external pressure to opt for high-density development rather than more sustainable alternatives.

The challenge of the destination product

The above examples of countries bowing to external pressures to adopt a particular type of tourism development or to change an ad campaign highlight the fact that destinations are not a single product but composite products consisting of a bundle of different components, including accommodation and catering establishments, tourist attractions, arts, entertainment and cultural venues, and even the natural environment. Destination marketers have relatively little control over these different aspects of their product and a diverse range of agencies and companies are partners in the task of portraying favourable brand images. These could include local and national government agencies, environmental groups and agencies, chambers of commerce, trade associations and civic groups. Whilst packaged goods normally have an obvious core, so that their ads can anchor themselves to product performance and attributes, with destinations the situation is much less clear.

The essence of creating a successful brand is to build an emotional link between product and consumer, but what encapsulates the emotional brand values of a destination – is it the atmosphere of a resort, the hotel the tourist stays in, or the friendliness of the local people? All of these factors can and do affect how the tourist views the vacation experience. In view of the fact that it is a composite product, can a destination ever evoke high levels of emotional commitment? Arguably it can, as the potential to evoke an emotional attachment is even greater for tourism destinations than for fast-moving consumer goods or for services – destinations have very strong and pervasive associations for tourists which, if skilfully manipulated, can provide the basis for brand-building. Today's tourists are not asking 'what can we do on holiday?' but 'who can we be on holiday?' They are increasingly looking less for escape and more for discovery, and that creates the basis of an emotional connection which the marketers can exploit in advertising.[5]

The challenge of creating differentiation

Whilst there are these added political pressures in destination marketing, good advertising can still be produced. To again quote Bob Garfield:

> Smart managers find out what is the meaning of their destination as a product to their potential consumer. They exploit that meaning in finding the value they can add to the sun and sand experience. Their advertising, when it's done well, should reflect that added value . . . that point of differentiation.[6]

Most destinations probably do have something – a unique selling opportunity – that can be translated into a unique selling proposition. The US Virgin Islands, for example, is ultimately a sun, surf and sand destination that is physically absolutely identical to the British Virgin Islands which are 40 nautical miles away. Yet, because the US Virgin Islands' biggest market is the USA, it does have something on which to build a unique proposition. Its marketers can advertise the concept that you can have the exotic experience of a natural paradise – yet with the comfort and security of visiting somewhere that has the familiarity of speaking the same language and using the same currency. For those Americans who want a beach holiday and are predisposed to try something partly exotic but mostly safe and familiar, the US Virgin Islands has a unique opportunity and hence its marketers use the straplines 'They're your islands' and 'The American paradise in the Caribbean'. These differentiate the destination from the British Virgin Islands, which uses the phrases 'Out of this world . . . not out of reach' and 'Nature's little secrets'. As the US Virgin Islands brochure points out:

> As an American territory, the US Virgin Islands offers United States citizens significant advantages over other Caribbean vacation getaways.

Even if you are an international traveler, you will find the American system of laws and customs under which the US Virgin Islands operates to be convenient and trouble-free ... Come experience the majestic beauty and friendly warmth of these American treasures ... The US Virgin Islands. They're your islands. Come see them for yourself and you'll find yourself returning.

Countries often talk about their history, their culture and their beautiful scenery in their advertising but all destinations have these attributes and it is critical to build a brand on something which uniquely connects a destination to the consumer now or has the potential to do so. It must also be a proposition that the competition wants and may be able to copy but which they cannot surpass or usurp. For example, other world cities can claim to be romantic or spiritual, but only Rome is 'The eternal city' – it has that epithet, it had it first and no other place can now claim it. Whatever proposition is used it must also have the potential to last, to grow old and to evolve in a long-term branding campaign, so it is essential to get it right. However, the point of differentiation must reflect a promise which can be delivered and which matches expectations. Good destination advertising is therefore original and different but its originality and difference needs to be sustainable, believable and relevant – not, for instance, as in the case of Philadelphia, USA, whose promise about your vacation memories of the place living with you forever promises far too much.

> Virginia in the USA has had phenomenal success with its 'Virginia is for lovers' campaign but no destination can surpass Paris's associations with romance.

One destination advertising campaign which transcends the commodity nature of the product and which promises a unique (yet credible) experience is the 'India changes you' campaign – a finalist at the 1998 International Travel and Tourism Advertising Awards. There are a lot of exotic countries that a consumer could visit and many of them have breathtaking scenery and fascinating heritage, yet such is the emotional power of the subcontinent with its poignant history and diverse cultures that its advertising promise to the consumer that 'India changes you' is sustainable. Garfield describes this campaign premise as:

> among the most powerful advertising statements I have ever encountered in any category anywhere – it's not 'get away from it all', it's not 'escape the rat race', it's not 'discover yourself' – which are all fairly familiar themes – it's better than discover yourself, it's 'change yourself'. It's breathtaking.

This appeal (which was executed with flawless production) was only a part of the reason for this campaign's success. The other is that in this instance, the marketers of India also managed to transcend the politics of tourism advertising. Despite the fact that India is made up of a number of enormously populous regions, all competing for tourism business, the campaign promoted the whole of India as the destination and, in doing so, succeeded in preventing any dilution of the advertising message that the promotion of the individual regions would have created.

Ad highlight 10.1   **Georgia: 'people, places, things'**

In 1996 Georgia's Department of Industry, Trade and Tourism produced an ad for Georgia's attractions, portraying the state's main associations – ex-President Jimmy Carter, its golf courses and Coca-Cola – set to an Elton John soundtrack. The ad features the ex-President and his wife Rosalyn, who appear in long shot, wearing suits and symbolizing Georgia's 'people'. The ad then moves to Georgia's 'places' (with a voice-over 'take me to your southlands') where a golfer in a sand-bunker illustrates Georgia's '329 challenging golf courses'. Moving on, the ad cuts to a young boy running towards an old pick-up truck (in front of a Waltons'-style shack store) – here we have the birthplace of Coca-Cola, and the 'home of "The real thing"'. After these 'people, places, things', many other images and messages clutter the screen, such as 'It's all in Georgia', 'USA – Georgia on my mind', followed by 'Georgia, Department of Industry, Trade and Tourism'. This ad is typical of those that have too much clutter and include questionable attraction choices – are they really the essence of Georgia as a differentiated destination? 'People, places, things' does not communicate anything distinctive about Georgia and there is no sense of an attempt to craft a unique identity for the destination in this rather pedestrian ad.

The branding of destinations

As we have seen, the lack of overall product control, limited budgets and political pressures pose unique challenges for managers of destinations. In such circumstances, some destinations are adopting strategies whose main goal is differentiation through the creation of brand saliency – the development of an emotional relationship with the consumer through highly choreographed and focused communications campaigns. Whether such strategies can truly be described as 'branding' largely depends on how branding is defined. De Chernatony and McDonald's definition is typical, describing a successful brand as: 'an identifiable product, service, person or place, augmented in such a way that the buyer or user perceives relevant unique added values which match their needs most closely. Furthermore its success results from being able to sustain these added values in the face of competition.'[7]

As such definitions suggest, there is a general agreement amongst academics – as well as practitioners – that places can be branded in the same way as fast-moving consumer goods and services. Indeed, the concept of branding is increasingly being applied to destinations and some, such as San Francisco, Paris, Venice and the French Riviera, have already developed strong reputations, consumer perceptions, associations and expectations. However, although there is this general agreement that branding can be applied to tourism destinations, there is less certainty about how the concept translates into practical marketing activity. Certainly, provenance – where a brand comes from and where it is based – is important and influences consumer brand perceptions. Those such as Coca-Cola, Microsoft and Nike are strongly seen as being American and they derive strength from the brand equity of the USA itself, which is associated with independence, attitude and technological ability.[8] In terms of tourism destination branding, provenance is even more critical because countries pre-exist any identities crafted for them by marketers and neither their advertisers nor consumers can have objective views of them.

How can destination brands be built?

The first stage in the process of building a destination brand is the establishment of the core values of the destination and its brand – these should be durable, relevant, communicable and hold saliency for potential tourists. Once these core values have been established, they should underpin and imbue all subsequent marketing activity – especially in literature text and illustrations – so that the brand values are cohesively communicated. The brand values should also be reinforced by a logotype or brand signature and a design style guide which ensures consistency of message and approach. To successfully create an emotional attachment a destination brand has to be:

- credible
- deliverable
- differentiating
- conveying powerful ideas
- enthusing for trade partners
- resonating with the consumer.

Such destination brand-building strategies have been adopted recently by a range of countries – from Greece to Thailand. Particularly successful examples include the 1980s relaunch of the English seaside resort of Torbay as the English Riviera, the mid-1990s repositioning of the Balearic Island of

Majorca as Mallorca, and the ongoing construction of Spain as the España supra-brand – first begun in the early 1980s. As we saw in Chapter 9, in the case of Torbay (in addition to major investment in the resort infrastructure) its rebirth was facilitated by its marketing managers who successfully blended traditional and modern brand values in a campaign which projected images of a very modern resort capable of providing old-fashioned service and elegance. Key associations for the campaign, first launched in the early 1980s, include a stylized palm tree logo and the strapline – 'The English Riviera' – which is intended to evoke associations of Torbay's long-established rivalry and identification with the French Riviera (see Plate 7).

Whilst there are particular challenges facing those who would brand places, it is clear that more and more destinations are using brand saliency techniques in an effort to create a unique and differentiated identity. In the 1980s there were several highly successful marketing campaigns which centred on a consistent communications proposition. New York's 'I love NY' and the 'Glasgow's miles better' campaigns are two of the best known. In these, and in many other instances, the campaigns focused on logos and slogans but they were not truly branding initiatives. In building a brand for a destination the image should not be confined to the visual, and this is the essence of the latest tool adapted by today's destination marketers – 'mood brand marketing'. It is designed to create an emotional relationship between the destination and potential visitors – as in the current 'Amazing Thailand' campaign. In this, the branding activities concentrate on conveying the essence or the spirit of a destination, often communicated via a few key attributes and associations. Not to be confused with any religious connotations, this is marketing based very much on an emotional appeal – what we have elsewhere termed 'spiritual marketing'.[9]

The value of such branding activities is gaining increasingly more recognition – in the UK, for example, both the Scottish Tourist Board and the British Tourist Authority have appointed brand managers. In the mid-1990s Scotland launched a multiorganizational, joint public-private sector initiative around 'Scotland the brand'. Based on an earlier New Zealand initiative, this attempts to commonly brand products as diverse as whisky, woollen products, shortcake biscuits, the Scottish rugby team and Scotland the country into a coherent umbrella brand identified by the thistle logo. The aim is to raise awareness of Scottish products and to synergize the marketing activities of many disparate organizations and companies under the core brand values of 'Scottishness', 'quality' and 'tradition'.

Such success stories in destination advertising inevitably reflect destination brands that have been able to resist the political dynamic (which is exerted at all levels of the political scene). These brands have strong advertising heritages, are consistent but at the same time are able to change, move with the times and continually refresh themselves in the mind of the consumer. This is easy to write but difficult to achieve and that is why the same destinations are constantly cited as classic examples of cohesive, long-term branding – because they are a rare breed and they succeed against the odds. Thus, Ireland has been running the same basic proposition in its various campaigns for two decades and while marketing directors and executives change the message remains constant – currently encapsulated in the 'Live a different life' strapline. Yet for every success story there are several examples of destinations which have failed to maintain long-term marketing and advertising effort. One place that once had an enviable reputation for luxury and glamour was the Côte d'Azur – Europe's dream destination that was the very essence of chic. Yet since the 1950s it has lost its cachet as the glitterati have moved to other destinations further afield and although such places as Monte Carlo, Cannes and Nice retain their allure, the South of France as a whole has lost its strong associations with wealth and fashion.

Ad highlight 10.2   **Las Vegas, Phoenix and San Diego form Southwestern brand**

In 1997 Las Vegas, Phoenix and San Diego combined to position the three cities as a new 'golden triangle' in the USA amongst international visitors. This tri-city strategic alliance (the first of its kind involving three of the USA's most popular resort destinations) plans to use each city's inherent strengths under the umbrella of a Southwestern theme – the 'Old West, New West' – used to brand each destination's individual attractions. The goal is to emphasize to international travellers convenient fly or drive access to each destination, a broad spectrum of activities and attractions in the Southwest and the widely diverse landscapes – from desert to mountains and ocean. The partnership is based on a three-year agreement, to be reviewed in July 2000 for renewal by each of the partners. Advertising, promotional materials, travel trade programmes, familiarization trips and public relations opportunities are conducted jointly, initially targeting Europe, with gradual roll-out into Asia and Latin America.

Source: Phoenix and Valley of the Sun Convention and Visitors Bureau

---

Four destinations which all show signs of becoming success stories – if they continue to produce consistent advertising – are Israel, New Zealand, Canada and Wales. To look at the experience of Israel first, in the UK, Israeli marketing has fallen into two distinct phases since 1993. Phase One (1993–7) was designed to enable Israel to stand out from the crowd whilst Phase Two (1998 onwards) sought to make maximum capital out of Israel's links with the millennium (see Case study 10.3). In 1993 Israel was a poor performer in what is acknowledged as perhaps the world's most competitive travel market. Research in the UK amongst Israel's primary target market (ABC1s aged twenty-five to sixty) revealed that Israel scored very poorly in terms of people's future (next twelve months) holiday consideration set – considerably below competitors such as Italy and Greece, and well below Spain. Perhaps of even greater concern were the perceptions held amongst consumers in its target market. Israel was variously seen as a Third World country, a desert, a place only for religious fanatics and, lastly (but by no means least), a war zone. The one piece of good news, however, was that these perceptions did not cause people to totally reject the possibility of holidaying in Israel – a potential further boosted by the 1993 Peace Accord.

Israeli advertising in the UK needed to present the country in a very positive and memorable light and, significantly, the Israeli national tourist office was prepared to make additional funds available to stimulate visitor growth – working with a total promotional budget of around $24 million, just under half of which was allocated to advertising.[10] Targets were set to achieve a 30 per cent increase in tourism arrivals in two years, aiming to move from attracting 230 000 to 300 000 UK visitors. At that time, visitors to Israel fell into three categories – the Jewish community (30 per cent), Christian pilgrims (20 per cent) and the ABC1 market (50 per cent). The last group was felt to offer the greatest opportunities for the growth demanded by the national tourist office. Within this target market, the advertising would specifically target twenty-five to thirty-five-year-old couples without children, followed by aged fifty-plus empty-nesters. The advertising needed to communicate that Israel was neither a cheap nor a young sun and sand destination, it also needed to overcome the target markets' misconceptions. Israel was therefore positioned as a 'quality beach holiday offering the texture and atmosphere of the Mediterranean but with a rich heritage and exotic overtones'. The keys to the detail of this positioning were the quality of its four- and five-star hotels and service, its varied beaches and seas (the Red, Dead, Mediterranean and Galilee Seas), its year-round sunshine and activities, and its Mediterranean quality in tone and sophistication (rather than geography). However, the positioning needed to be communicated via a strong, simple, memorable and unique brand hook.

The final execution combined 'Hava Nagila' (an Israeli folk song well known in the UK) with the concept that people want a great holiday. Hence, the strapline: 'HAV'A great holiday in Israel' was used in all ads. The campaign used television (running two 40-second ads portraying Israel's winter and summer sun) together with press and poster ads, all focusing in on the London and south-east region. The Hava Nagila folk song was central to the executions in every medium, being used as the musical accompaniment and also the hook for each scene change in the television commercials, as well as providing the inspiration for the copy in the posters (Plate 8) and the main brochure – for example, HAV'A good cuisine, HAV'A trip to Jerusalem and HAV'A great holiday. In the poster ads HAV'A (displayed in bold central type) linked two separate – although linked – images, for instance, gold beaches and golden Jerusalem; each execution invited tourists to submerge themselves in the country's culture and history as well as its scenery.

The campaign performed remarkably well, and in just one year the growth target of 30 per cent was achieved and then maintained in subsequent years. Whilst the total winter sun market in the UK grew by 7 per cent in 1993/4, Israel's grew by 18 per cent and Eilat (one of Israel's key resorts) by 34 per cent. Israel's spontaneous awareness levels increased dramatically on pre- and post-measures and exceeded the post-awareness levels of all its competitors. The advertising itself became famous and distinctive in a market notorious for its uniformity and lack of brand differentiation and prompted advertising recall grew from 38 per cent in 1993 to 50 per cent in 1994, and reached 57 per cent in 1996 despite a decreasing advertising budget.[11] Whilst the HAV'A ads were suspended in 1999/2000 whilst Israel capitalized on the opportunities created by the millennium, the campaign provides the ideal platform for further branding opportunities based on its positioning of Israel as a Mediterranean destination with culturally exotic overtones.

In contrast to Israel's culturally based position, New Zealand's '100% pure New Zealand' campaign is one based on the destination's natural environment. Designed to double New Zealand's tourism foreign exchange receipts to more than £3 billion by 2005, it is the country's first global marketing campaign. It is intended to recover some of the ground lost to Australia in the tourism marketplace and, whilst it targets Asians in particular, it is a worldwide strategy. The destination is seeking to use events such as the new millennium (New Zealand is beside the international dateline) and the Americas Cup (hosted from Auckland and lasting from October 1999 to March 2000) to build sustainable tourism development. The '100%' logo incorporates an image of the country's two islands – North and South – whilst the strapline '100% pure New Zealand' seeks to position the destination as the ultimate backpacker and thrill-seeker paradise – one of 'awesome sights, breathtaking vistas, indelible experiences – that's New Zealand'.[12] The theme of '100%' and purity is echoed in all the imagery and the copy of the material, with the scenery, its wines and foods, its people and its experiences being seen as being untainted, unadulterated, unaffected and undiluted. Currently, straplines such as '100% pure romance' and '100% pure spirit' are being used. In the long term, Saatchi – the ad agency responsible for the campaign – is aiming to achieve such consumer awareness of the logo so as to be able to drop the '100% pure New Zealand' strapline and let the '100%' logo stand for the brand New Zealand.

This branding campaign is quite similar in concept to how the Canadian Tourism Commission (CTC), in partnership with Canadian Airlines International, has been promoting Canada since 1998. Positioning itself globally as the premier, authentic, four-season travel destination – as the destination to connect with real outdoor adventure and to experience diverse cultures and communities – the CTC is appealing to tourists' desires for exciting nature adventures. In Australia, for instance, the campaign included print ads run in the major daily newspapers of Sydney, Melbourne and Brisbane during October and November 1998. These featured high-flying snowboarders and polar bears close up, packaged in bold themes like Extremeworld and Winterworld. In addition to identifying the campaign's key target segments (couples and families), images of tickets reading 'Admit Two' and 'Admit Family' appearing on these ads helped to heighten the 'authentic theme parks' concept for Canada. Readers of the papers were encouraged to obtain a free vacation planner through e-mail response and a 24-hour toll-free numbers – and the ads themselves could even be clipped as coupons and mailed in for more information. These ads were followed up by CTC's agency (Vickers & Benson Advertising of Toronto) with executions featuring Adventureworld, Waterworld and Natureworld – aimed at spring and summer travel. These were crafted around spectacular visuals highlighting Canada's natural and unspoiled environment: feeling the power of Niagara Falls, hiking in the Yukon and horse-riding in the Laurentians.[13]

This theme of nature forming the basis of a destination's unique proposition is also echoed in the branding of Wales in its domestic market of the UK. Wales has a distinctive natural environment – particularly its coastline and mountains – that is the main motivating factor in attracting domestic visitors. This £5 million three-year campaign, launched in December 1997, is a multiagency strategy based on credible brand values grounded in extensive consumer research in Wales's major domestic market – England (Table 10.2). Research confirmed that potential consumers believe that Wales offers visitors an antidote to modern life because of the revitalizing holiday experiences on offer. Thus, Wales's 'Design for life' campaign is specifically targeted at potential visitors in the Granada and Central television regions, London and the M4 corridor, and focuses on how Wales's landscape and environment can revive an alienated urban population – putting 'back into your life what life takes out'.[14]

**Table 10.2   Key associations of Wales amongst
UK travel consumers**

Going back to childhood
Freedom from claustrophobia
Breezes through your hair
Paddling in cool water
Being yourself as a family
Snow mists on lakes and waterfalls
Screaming at the sea on a beach at Christmas
Dolphins
Seals swimming next to boats

Source: Roger Pride, Marketing Director, Wales Tourist
Board (1997), Creating a tourism brand for Wales.
Unpublished paper presented at the UK Chartered
Institute of Marketing Seminar, November, Cardiff.

The branding concept centres around 'natural revival', conveying that Wales's unspoilt and beautiful landscape – which for many remains 'hidden on England's doorstep' – offers tourists the physical and spiritual renewal so needed in today's hectic society (Plate 9). This is encapsulated in the strapline 'Wales: two hours and a million miles away' – and even the background music in the television ad – the Welsh band Manic Street Preachers' 'A design for life' – echoes this revival theme (see Chapter 7).[15] The 'Design for life' campaign aims to position Wales as the natural antidote to the stressful, non-stop life of the modern world. Grainy black and white images of everyday life are juxtaposed alongside colourful, peaceful, romantic and happier scenes of visitors enjoying breaks in Wales. As part of its wider promotional activity, the Wales Tourist Board also runs a highly effective PR campaign based on the brand's core proposition. Examples of its award-winning initiative included its tree-shaped air fresheners bearing the slogan 'Real fresh air is just two hours away – Wales/Cymru', given away free to London taxi drivers; its hiring of dirty vans with 'Clean air is just two hours away – Wales/Cymru' written in the dirt and parked around the capital; and its sponsoring of maintenance workmen on London's orbital motorway, all of whom wear jackets bearing the slogan 'Clean air is just two hours away – Wales/Cymru'.

This branding of Wales as a 'natural' destination largely builds on previous marketing campaigns, aimed at the domestic market, which have been dominated by images of Wales's scenery and environment. These images which are used by the Wales Tourist Board to market Wales in the UK are those which its advertisers feel to be:

meaningful and relevant to the market segment. For instance, you'll see an emphasis on the notion of being able to get to Wales easily. That is particularly important for second and third holidays. So there has to be this element of getting there quickly and also the element of when you are there you are in a place which must be different to where you were before – the notion of activities and so on.[16]

This branding strategy, like those of New Zealand and Scotland, is developing as a multiorganizational, joint public-private sector initiative. It embraces not only the Wales Tourist Board and the British Tourist Authority, but also economic regeneration agencies such as the Welsh Development Agency and media organizations such as Sianel Pedwar Cymru (Wales's Welsh language television station) and Sgrin (Wales's media and film agency). The core values on which the brand Wales is being built are 'honest, welcoming and romantic. It is a country to inspire and revive'.[17]

It is still far too early to evaluate the success of Wales's brand-building activities. There are, however, significant indications that the strategy is beginning to bear fruit. In 1998 the return on investment from the direct mail campaign was £60 for every £1 spent on promotion, whilst in 1999 direct mail responses were up 100 per cent to 480 000, and for the first time Wales moved above Scotland in domestic market share and its awareness increased dramatically. The ad campaigns themselves captured fifteen national and international awards and the Wales Tourist Board's direct mail agency was voted direct mail agency of the year on the strength of its work for Wales. 'Two hours and a million miles away' is an excellent campaign, superbly executed, with high production values and slick copy. The promise of taking all of the things about your everyday life that you most despise and on the spur of the moment having them disappear because you are only 2 hours away from another experience – is a very powerful idea indeed. There is all kinds of tourism advertising which promises 'getting way from it all", but the 'two hours away' image is very strong – plus the fact that the scenery, culture and language are just exotic enough and remote enough, yet highly accessible.

Destination supra-brands

As the above examples clearly illustrate, destinations can be branded, and the next step in the evolution of destination branding is the creation of the supra-brand. Here, marketers of tourism destinations – primarily countries – attempt to create supra-brands which offer consumers an emotional commitment, moving beyond the mere characteristics of the product to provoke a much deeper response and identification. Crucially, however, in a supra-brand this involves a two-tier but highly integrated approach whereby the country's brand personality is consistently projected at the macro level in all the key target markets, and its sub-brands (whether states, regions or even cities) echo, but embroider in more detail, the same consistent themes in their advertising messages.

The experience of established supra-brands

Once a destination with an image for poor quality service and facilities, perhaps the first destination to have become a supra-brand is Spain. In the early 1980s the Spanish government began what was to become one of the most consistent and successful brand-building exercises in destination marketing supported by a significant financial commitment – which continues today (Table 10.3).

Table 10.3   Distribution of Spain's promotional budget, 1997

Promotional activities	52%
Advertising	43%
Research activities	5%
Total promotional budget	$71 631 000

Source: World Tourism Organization.

Here España is the main brand and its cities (mainly Barcelona and Madrid) and regions (such as Andalusia and Galicia) have become the second-level brands. At the country level Spain has remained remarkably constant in its advertising, with each campaign promoting the diversity and variety of the country, focusing on its heritage and culture, as well as the staple sun and sand product. At the heart of the brand for the last sixteen years has been Miro's logo, designed in 1983 (the year he died) by mixing elements from his own pictures and his own alphabet. As a piece of modern art, this logo both symbolizes Spain's past and looks to the future and incorporates representations of the sun (yellow and red), the stars, and the bullring (black) to portray Spain. The shifts in the campaigns from 'Everything under the sun' (first used in 1984) to 'Passion for life' (1992–5) to 'Bravo Spain' (introduced in 1997) have been gradual and well thought out, and have never compromised the brand values. The one departure from this message of passion and diversity came in 1996 when famous photographers were asked to provide their own interpretations of the essence of Spain. A series of posters were created depicting a photograph taken by each photographer with the strapline – for instance, in David Bailey's case – 'Spain by Bailey'. Whilst the campaign won several awards for its superb photography, it was disliked by the Spanish tourism industry and proved short-lived.

The 'Bravo Spain' campaign, which replaced that of 1996, was tested in the key markets of the UK, Germany and France where it was seen positively – the word 'Bravo' conjured up images of approval – allaying fears in Spain of any negative connotations of its association with bullfighting. Intended to communicate a different, modern Spain, this campaign uses strong, visually impressive images in its television, press and poster executions. In the print ads (which are the backbone of the campaign) the consistent image is of a blurred photograph with a larger, perfectly focused close-up window showing some detail of the photograph. Every region of Spain features in the ads, which mix well-known attractions (such as the new Bilbao museum) with less well-known sites (such as Valencia's new concert hall) and include interesting copy and a small map indicating the location of the scene in the poster.

Constructing emerging destination supra-brands

The supra-brand of Spain is an example of an established destination that attracts 51 million visitors a year and has the world's third largest promotional budget for tourism. But the strategy can be equally effectively applied to newer tourism destinations – such as Australia. Here again, the country itself is being positioned as the supra-brand, whilst its states (such as Western Australia) form the sub-brands. For Australia as a whole, the marketing challenge was similar to that in Wales: the destination was seen as having much to offer but its image was diverse and unclear – in fact, it has so much to offer that its diversity clouds its image in the consumer's mind. In order to create a unified, cohesive global 'Brand Australia', a number of industry experts, academics and researchers were brought together to examine the vacation needs of consumers and their perceptions of Australia. In constructing the brand, the following seven-step model was adopted:

1 Identify the markets.
2 Research the brand values within the key markets and amongst the deliverers.
3 Evaluate the product requirements – identify any need for reinvestment.
4 Construct the brand architecture.

5 Translate the brand personality and proposition into deliverable messages.
6 Implement an integrated campaign.
7 Monitor, evaluate, review.

The first step was to concentrate on the target audience and to isolate those who were potential consumers and those who were not. The marketers of Australia identified that a key target audience for the destination was a younger age group between eighteen and forty-four years old and especially those aged eighteen to thirty-five. These consumers were more likely to consider travelling to Australia now rather than seeing it as a 'once in a lifetime' destination. They are looking for adventure, exhilaration, freedom and personal discovery and thus Australia's core brand values needed to reflect these attributes (Table 10.4). In the next stage, the global brand messages in each of Australia's key generating countries were reshaped to reflect the recrafted brand personality (Tables 10.4 and 10.6). Launched in 1997, the campaign was to cost $100 million in total and was intended to generate 14 million tourists and $44 billion export earnings in markets that were estimated to have 500 million potential consumers. It was an approach based on partnership and synergy and which embraced a range of media, including television, magazines, newspapers, direct mail, cinema and the World Wide Web.

A key element of the new Brand Australia was the creation of a new trademark logo. This was intended to encapsulate the personality and the brand architecture of the destination and had to be bold, exciting, energetic,

Table 10.4   The values and personality of Brand Australia

Brand values	Brand personality
Youthful	Youthful
Energetic	Stylish
Optimistic	Vibrant
Stylish	Diverse
Unpretentious	Adventurous
Genuine	
Open	
Fun	

Source: *Brand Australia*, video produced by the Australian Tourism Commission, 1997.

Logo = Symbol of Australia + Colours + Personality

Figure 10.1   The 'Meaning of Australia' logo

Table 10.5   The heart of the Australia logo

Colours	Symbolize
Red	Earth, desert, centre, outback
Blue	Sky, sea, cool, endless
Green	Bush, rainforest, environment, clean
Yellow	Warm, nights, life, energy, sun, youth, friendly

Source: *Brand Australia*, video produced by the Australian Tourism Commission, 1997.

vital, adventurous and sophisticated, yet friendly and fun. The end result was the creation of a logo depicting a yellow kangaroo against a red sun over a background of green and a blue sea (Figure 10.1 and Table 10.5).

Whilst the core brand values of Australia remain cohesive and consistent, four different facets of its personality are portrayed in four slightly different campaigns aimed at its main tourist-generating regions – the consumers of which are diverse and seeking differing vacation experiences. To be consistent in the brand values does not mean that it is appropriate to run identical campaigns around the globe – a brand will find it difficult if not impossible to be all things to all people. Indeed, that is to erase cultural differences and ignore the fact that consumers in Asia, America and Europe respond to differing advertising appeals and are seeking a diverse range of benefits from a visit to Australia. However, what the marketers must do is to ensure that the individual country-specific campaigns reflect Australia's brand values and communicate its unique attributes. Thus, for instance, the commercial aimed at a European consumer is constructed around the centrality of emotion and the power of holiday memories, whilst the execution screened in cinemas and on television in the USA emphasizes fun, adventure and discovery, and features Australians 'inviting' the viewer into the destination (Table 10.6).

Destination sub-brands

Lying below the overarching brand of Australia, each individual tourism region within the country is also pursuing an integrated sub-branding strategy

Table 10.6 Translating the personality of Brand Australia globally

Region/ country	Asia	USA	Japan	Europe
Australia's attributes	Big nature, outdoors, city life	Fun, diversity, active, adventure, live it	Surprise, undiscovered, culture, lifestyle	Activity, relaxation, intriguing, enriching, diverse, powerful memories
Campaign	Let the magic begin	Holiday	Country of surprises	The sooner you go, the longer the memories
Message	Excitement, shopping, nightlife	Take a break from work and discover people and islands	Fast-paced, sophisticated, cosmopolitan, modern	Emotional, appealing, unique, travel now

Source: *Brand Australia*, video produced by the Australian Tourism Commission, 1997.

which synergizes with Australia the brand. One example of a complete approach to this sub-branding exercise is that of Western Australia where tourism is a AUS$2.1 billion industry. The Western Australian Tourism Commission (WATC) has implemented Brand Western Australia (BWA), a strategy based on intensive consumer research. Its aim is to reposition Western Australia as a premier nature-based tourism destination in the global market. Central to this repositioning has been the development of an inclusive partnership between government and industry to promote the marketing and development of the tourism product and infrastructure. Significantly, it has also prompted an organizational restructuring to better reflect its new corporate mission, increased accountability and customer focus.

BWA sought to develop a clear brand identity based on its core strengths and personality following consumer research in 1994 which revealed that Western Australia and its capital Perth lacked a meaningful identity in the international marketplace. The WATC had AUS$8.8 million over five years to develop, implement and market Western Australia to an international and Australian audience. Interestingly, BWA was not only intended to be a tourism brand – it was also to provide the state brand – hence the need for wide-ranging consultation to ensure that the actions of the Brand Strategy Group – the steering group behind the initiative – were thoroughly endorsed. Also significant was the maximization of BWA's links with the Australian Tourism Commission's (ATC's) 'Big nature–big city' brand strategy. The key steps in constructing the brand personality of BWA were:

293

- consult with possible BWA end users
- conduct comprehensive market research in key national and international markets
- research the key brand values amongst Western Australians and overseas visitors
- select the appropriate target markets.

The research conducted to underpin the branding showed that Western Australia offered most of the things tourists want from their vacation, including relaxation, an opportunity for recharging and an unspoilt natural scenery. Less positively, however, Perth was seen to be quiet and lacking in activity. The research concluded that Western Australia was strong on nature-based imagery and attractions but that it lacked a meaningful identity. To take this research forward, international target markets were then objectively selected using the Market Potential Assessment Formula – a model developed by WATC and the International Advisory Council. These markets (the UK, Germany, Japan, Singapore, Malaysia and Indonesia) were assessed (and continue to be reviewed) in terms of their access, growth, value and synergy with the ATC's broader Australia-wide strategies.

The personality of BWA centres on its pristine environment which then underpins the marketing of the state as a fresh, new, nature-based tourism destination with friendly, spirited people and the freedom and space to travel. BWA's core personality elements were thus defined as fresh, natural, free and spirited, and the positioning statement 'Western Australia. Holidays of an entirely different nature' guides the communication strategy. The visual language of the campaign was not just a logo but a set of design briefs which ensured that the visual elements of Western Australia's marketing always reflected the core personality and added to the brand's overall strengths. In constructing the advertising strategy, the overriding objective was to develop a long-term campaign designed to build awareness of Western Australia as a holiday destination in what is a highly competitive and dynamic global marketplace. Celebrity endorsement was seen as an effective means of providing a point of differentiation between Western Australia and other competing destinations, and television and press ads as the key media. The WATC secured the services of Australian supermodel and actress Elle Macpherson who was felt to embody the personality of Western Australia. As a supermodel she also had the ability to take the message to the world in a way no paid advertising could. Her endorsement has provided Western Australia's tourism industry with high levels of recall and enquiry, as well as millions of dollars in free publicity – well beyond the state's advertising budget (Plate 10).

Post-advertising research has revealed positive changes in attitude and belief measures in all markets and increased awareness across the board. The key evaluation indicators for BWA were:

■ levels of top-of-the-mind awareness
■ post-campaign research to establish 'perceived knowledge' and 'propensity to consider'
■ industry targets for visitor nights and expenditure.

Significantly, although primarily intended to increase awareness, the initial six-week UK campaign in September 1997 directly resulted in almost 6000 visitors generating AUS$7.3 million tourism expenditure in Western Australia – a 500 per cent return on the advertising outlay. Following the success of the initial television ads, Elle Macpherson was contracted for four additional commercials that were broadcast in the core markets from February 1999. Interestingly, in a series of initiatives similar to the 'Amazing Thailand' campaign, BWA has also been integrated into projects with a broad community focus, including BWA vehicle number plates, vehicle registration stickers, welcome signage at state entry points and BWA 'welcome statements' on the rear windscreens of taxis. A merchandise range incorporating clothing and souvenirs has also been created and distributed throughout Western Australia. A brand ownership campaign has been initiated where approved licensees use BWA's visual elements in their own advertising – over 300 organizations had been approved by mid-1999.

Chapter summary

It takes time to establish destination brands and it is unrealistic to expect to achieve immediate results. Building a destination brand is a long-term effort, which yields incremental and not exponential results and any brand manager seeking to create an identity must have long-term commitment to the brand. Moreover, destination brand managers in the public sector face three key constraints that often undermine attempts at brand-building:

■ political pressures and limited budgets
■ a lack of overall product control
■ the challenge of creating differentiation.

By branding a destination, however, the impact of these three constraints may well be reduced. To be successful, a destination brand has to be:

- credible
- deliverable
- differentiating
- conveying powerful ideas
- enthusing for trade partners
- resonating with the consumer.

The first problem of inadequate resources is tackled through harnessing innovation, creating powerful ideas and by employing a multiorganizational approach to constructing the brand. In this way, relatively small individual agency budgets are pooled to underpin a targeted campaign in a very cost-effective way, yielding greater results. The second problem – political pressure – can be tackled by using an 'inclusive' approach whereby the key brand attributes and values are researched amongst the destination stakeholders and residents to ensure that they are not only relevant and credible but also acceptable, representative and not stereotypical. The final problem that often faces destination brand managers is that the actual product must correspond with the brand image and with consumer expectations, yet they are not in overall control of the product. Here again, however, an 'inclusive' approach provides an imaginative way forward. By researching the core brand values amongst its overseas visitors and indigenous population, a tourism organization not only ensures that the brand's associations are acceptable, but also that they reflect the product. In constructing the brand, the following steps should be adopted:

1 Identify the markets.
2 Research the brand values within the key markets and amongst the deliverers.
3 Evaluate the product requirements – identify any need for reinvestment.
4 Construct the brand architecture.
5 Translate the brand personality and proposition into deliverable messages.
6 Implement an integrated campaign.
7 Monitor, evaluate and review the strategy.

There are significant and unique problems facing destination marketers, but these should not prevent them from persevering in their aims – successful branding brings enormous rewards. Certainly, destinations cannot afford to ignore branding as it offers an innovative and effective tool by which managers can establish emotional links with the consumer, particularly if a multiagency-driven supra-brand is constructed.

Case study 10.1

Langkawi: is beauty and peace enough to differentiate?

Can beauty alone differentiate a tourism destination? Langkawi in Malaysia competes with destinations such as Phuket and Bali and is a good example of the difficulties facing those marketing a destination seen by some consumers as simply another Asian beach. Langkawi, unlike Bali, has little by way of cultural attractions and, if anything, is losing its culture. Most visitors come to the destination for its natural attractions and unspoilt beauty – with the emphasis on the unspoilt, a plus point in an age when that is becoming increasingly rare. Yet Langkawi is fast developing as a tourist resort. At the beginning of the 1990s it had only 2000 hotel rooms – now it has three times that number. Amongst its advantages as a destination are its duty-free status and its friends in high places. In recent years the Prime Minister Dr Mahateer has been using every opportunity to promote the island: its museum is dedicated to him and he has staged maritime events and air shows there in a bid to raise its profile.

Despite this development, Langkawi is something of a blank sheet of paper and it is seeking a differentiating identity. However, a headlong rush to craft one would be a mistake as it has to be something that is developed slowly. With tourism promotional budgets shrinking (as a result of the Asian economic downturn), Langkawi believes it can learn much from the way in which one of its rivals – Bali – is being marketed. When you think of Bali, you do not talk of how an individual hotel is marketed – you think of Bali as an island. In Langkawi, by contrast, the promotional strategy has focused much more on individual hotels – with the luxury Datai Hotel being one of the most prominent. At the Datai, naturally, its marketers believe that the hotel comes first. They are promoting the hotel as a destination in itself rather than as a resort in Langkawi because of the hotel's unique position on the island, in the jungle. So, whilst some in Langkawi believe that it should try to compete head on with the likes of Bali and Phuket, others believe that it is not necessary. Typical of the latter are those who argue that Langkawi's difference is its point of differentiation – with many people not looking for a Bali or Phuket, Langkawi offers an unspoilt experience. Yet, with so much riding on tourism on the island, most hoteliers believe that it needs to be marketed much more aggressively to secure its share of the region's tourism dollars.

Case study 10.2

Jamaica: moving downmarket or moving up?

Jamaica – the inspiration of Noel Coward, Ian Fleming and Bob Marley – was the Caribbean's first ultimate exotic holiday destination. It paved the way for the rest of the Caribbean to market itself worldwide. Yet in the 2000s Jamaica seems to have lost its way as other islands overtake its market position and it is attracting some negative publicity. Television screens have recently featured a series on Pleasure Island – a soft-porn holiday camp hotel where naked tourists were encouraged to live out their fantasies on camera. Whilst this represents only a tiny proportion of tourism in Jamaica, the long-lasting image it leaves could prove to be highly damaging to the island's tourism industry. Jamaica has also received bad press for its internal problems (including riots) which caused cancellations and perhaps long-term damage in the mind of the consumer. Faced with these twin assaults on its image, Jamaica has had to stage an upmarket recovery and the Jamaica Tourist Board recently launched an advertising campaign aimed at redressing this situation. However, when a product or destination has slipped so far downmarket, it is incredibly difficult to bring it upmarket again and tour operators are lobbying for much more investment in Jamaica's promotion – highlighting not only its natural and artificial attractions but also the friendliness of hotel staff and the local people.

Case study 10.3

The tactical use of the millennium event within a brand

One of the biggest marketing opportunities in the last decade was the advent of the year 2000. Many countries sought to capitalize on this event – from the UK (home of the first meridian in Greenwich) to a range of South Pacific destinations where the easterly rising sun allowed tourists to see the first day of the new millennium. Using the term 'First to the future', New Zealand capitalized on its proximity to the international dateline in its marketing material: 'New Zealand will be the first nation on earth to glimpse the dawn of the new century. Why not join us and be first to the future?' invited its 1999/2000 brochure. All the country's major cities and resorts scheduled special events to mark the celebration with the biggest event being in Gisborne, New Zealand's most easterly city and the first to see the sun on 1 January 2000.

Other destinations that heavily promoted their millennium connections were those of the Middle East, including Egypt, Jordan and Israel. Egypt launched a television ad campaign in April 1999 in an attempt to improve its reputation in the UK market following the Luxor massacre in November 1997. The ads – based on the slogan 'Welcome to our Se7enth Millennium' – featured images of Aswan, Nile cruising, diving, the sphinx and the number seven. Consumer press advertising also ran alongside the television campaign in an aim to remind consumers that Egypt is entering its seventh millennium. Similarly, Jordan used its biblical links to position itself as an obvious destination for the millennium in its own literature and in link-ups with the Royal Jordanian Airline. Promoting itself under the banner of 'The holy land', Jordan is estimated to have fifty to sixty biblical sites. Bethany – where Jesus was thought to have been baptized by John the Baptist – looks set to become the focal point of a biblical trail and provide an anchor for its millennium campaign, although Petra will continue to be promoted as Jordan's main attraction.

'Israel – where the first millennium began. Aren't you going?'

However, in the Judeo-Christian world, no country has a stronger link with or claim to the millennium than Israel. Israeli advertising has been focusing on this millennium opportunity since 1998. Central to this positioning was the need to communicate with Israel's ethnic and religious market, as well as its mainstream holiday market. The advertising needed to speak to all people who, for whatever reason, were thinking about the millennium in an emotional way. It needed to show why Israel should be considered as a destination, its inherent magic and, of course, its relevance to the millennium.

Central to the proposition created by Israel's agency (Court Burkitt and Company) was 'the best Millennium experience is surely where it all began'. A series of poster ads were produced for the UK market which invited the tourist to Israel whilst juxtaposing Israel's claims with those of other less 'worthy' destinations in which to celebrate the new millennium. One execution headlines 'In the year 2000 do you really want to say you went to Florida?' against a shot of three camels silhouetted against a glorious sunset. In a similar vein, another poster features a beautifully shot scene of divers in the Red Sea with the copy: 'The Millennium and it's not just 2000 years of history you'll want to dive into'. A further poster (Plate 11) asks 'Can you really experience the Millennium in SE10?' above a photograph of Jerusalem's skyline and Jerusalem's dome commemorating the place where the prophet Elijah is said to have ascended into heaven. This poster has particular meaning in the UK market as it contrasts the Jerusalem temple dome with the Millennium Dome – which is located in London SE10. This campaign, a finalist at the 1999 International Travel Advertising Awards, aimed at a UK audience, is a good example of a destination harnessing an event opportunity on a tactical level, whilst ensuring that its tone, image and message remains integrated in its wider strategic position.

Notes

1 Figures from Deborah Lurman of the World Tourism Organization – presentation at the 1998 International Travel and Tourism Awards, Valencia.

2 Bob Garfield, Editor, *Advertising Age*, in a personal interview, Valencia, September 1998.

3 Figures from Deborah Lurman of the World Tourism Organization – presentation at the 1998 International Travel and Tourism Awards, Valencia.

4 Christian Vial of Publicis, in a paper presented at the first International Travel and Tourism Advertising Awards, Dubrovnik, 1997.

5 We owe this discussion to a conversation with Roger Pride, Marketing Director of the Wales Tourist Board.

6 Bob Garfield, Editor, *Advertising Age*, in a personal interview, Valencia, September 1998.

7 Leslie de Chernatony and Malcolm H. B. McDonald (1992). *Creating Powerful Brands: The Strategic Route to Success in Consumer, Industrial and Service Markets*. Butterworth-Heinemann, p. 18.

8 Simon Anholt (1998). Nation-brands of the twenty-first century. *Journal of Brand Management*, **5** (6), 395–404.

9 Annette Pritchard and Nigel Morgan (1998). Creating 'Wales' the brand: opportunities in destination branding strategy. In *Leisure, Culture and Tourism in Europe* (W. Nahrstedt and T. P. Kombol, eds) pp. 165–176, Bielefeld.

10 Figures from Deborah Lurman of the World Tourism Organization – presentation at the 1998 International Travel and Tourism Awards, Valencia.

11 Information courtesy of Tom Rodwell of Court, Burkitt and Company, London.

12 '100% pure New Zealand', 1999/2000 promotional brochure.

13 Information courtesy of Vickers & Benson Advertising of Toronto.

14 Roger Pride, Marketing Director, Wales Tourist Board (1997). Creating a tourism brand for Wales. Unpublished paper presented at the UK Chartered Institute of Marketing Seminar, November, Cardiff.

15 Ibid.

16 Elwyn Owen, former WTB Director of Research, in a personal interview, April 1999.

17 British Tourist Authority (1997). *Living Britain. A Guide to Understanding the Characteristics of the Geographic Brands of Britain, London, Scotland, England and Wales*. BTA.

Further reading

Anholt, S. (1998). Nation-brands of the twenty-first century. *Journal of Brand Management*, **5** (6), 395–404.

British Tourist Authority (1997). *Living Britain: A Guide to Understanding the Characteristics of the Geographic Brands of Britain, London, Scotland, England and Wales*. BTA.

Crockett, S. R. and Wood, L. J. (1999). Brand Western Australia: a totally integrated approach to destination branding. *Journal of Vacation Marketing*, **5** (3), 276–89.

Hall, D. (1999). Destination branding, niche marketing and national image projection in central and Eastern Europe. *Journal of Vacation Marketing*, **5** (3), 227–37.

James, G. (1997). *Britain: Creating a Family of Brands*. Tourism Intelligence Papers, BTA/ETB, A-21.

Morgan, N. and Pritchard, A. (1998). *Tourism Promotion and Power: Creating Images, Creating Identities*. John Wiley, ch. 7.

Morgan, N. and Pritchard, A. (1999). *Power and Politics at the Seaside: The Development of Devon's Resorts in the Twentieth Century.* University of Exeter Press, ch. 5.

Morgan, N. and Pritchard, A. (1999). Building destination brands: the cases of Wales and Australia. *Journal of Brand Management,* **7** (2), 102–19.

Nickerson, N. P. and Moisey, N. R. (1999). Branding a state from features to positioning: making it simple? *Journal of Vacation Marketing,* **5** (3), 217–26.

Palmer, A. and Bejou, D. (1995). Tourism destination marketing alliances. *Annals of Tourism Research,* **22** (3), 616–29.

Singh, A. and Chon, K.-S. (1996). Marketing Singapore as an international destination. *Journal of Vacation Marketing,* **2** (3), 239–57.

Williams, P. and Palmer, A. J. (1999). Tourism destination brands and electronic commerce: towards synergy? *Journal of Vacation Marketing,* **5** (3), 263–75.

Part Four

Advertising Futures

New advertising vistas

Chapter overview

This chapter concludes the book by reviewing the impact of new technologies on advertising, focusing particularly on the implications of two new advertising horizons – the Internet and digital television. Organizations in every sector of the travel, tourism and leisure industries must develop strategies to reach out to customers via these new channels – those who do not will be overtaken in today's highly competitive marketplace. In order to understand the task facing organizations, we look at some case studies of those who have begun to tackle these challenges – including the television Travel Shop in the UK and the Australian Tourism Commission. The chapter ends by discussing the changing nature of the leisure product and concludes with some final thoughts on the future of advertising in tourism and leisure. The chapter reviews:

- Internet advertising
- the profile of today's e-consumer
- what makes a good website
- making search engines work for you
- creating effective banner ads

- the potential of digital television
- the changing leisure product
- threats to the future of advertising
- tomorrow's advertising agenda.

Introduction

The future of advertising will be shaped by fragmented audiences, narrow casting, digital compression technology, more 15-second commercials and the further proliferation of place-based ads. At the beginning of the 2000s, over two-thirds of European customers are reported to be irritated by ads and some commentators are predicting that the future will be an age of advertising diseffectiveness, with the rise of one-to-one media (through smart websites and CD-ROM technology) facilitating interactive and individually tailored ads. Others see in the new technology an opportunity to converge many traditional techniques into web media to produce a more stimulating interactive environment using on-line television, channel websites and enhanced animation and video links. Whatever your perspective, it is certain that the new Digital Age will revolutionize advertising, and ultimately the Internet and digital television will combine into webtelevision – creating an interactive promotional platform particularly suited to the travel, tourism and leisure industries.

Some of the newer media vehicles already being used by leisure, travel and tourism advertisers include audio tapes, video tapes, faxes and interactive kiosks, and further technological change is opening up other new advertising vistas. For instance, virtual reality already allows tourists to see and 'experience' certain destinations, resorts and hotels before ever visiting them. Visitors planning a Hawaiian vacation can, for $8.95, buy the *Visit Hawaii* CD, the Hawaii Visitors Bureau's official travel planner on CD-ROM. The disk contains 'valuable visitor information, hundreds of images of the most beautiful islands in the world, traditional and modern Hawaiian music, a wealth of Hawaii's history and cultures, maps, a photo guide to beaches, parks, and sights of interest, a calendar of events, a talking Hawaiian dictionary, and much more!'

Ad challenge 11.1   The impact of virtual reality

Virtual reality is still in a relatively early development stage, however, it will be a product of the near and not the distant future. It offers marketers huge potential but, at the same time, it could 'destroy' the travel industry as we know it by creating a synthetic tourism experience. Virtual reality offers consumers risk-free opportunities, limited only by their own imagination. A recent survey in the UK suggested that 80 per cent of people believe that 'video visiting' would eventually become a social norm, replacing the need to physically visit friends and relatives. Whether it eventually replaces the travel industry is a matter for future forecasters, but it seems unlikely – at the beginning of the twentieth century the advent of the cinema was predicted to herald the end of travel, yet today both are huge industries. Whatever the future holds, virtual reality's potential as a highly visual, experiential and interactive advertising tool cannot be underestimated.

Such comprehensive, interactive media may threaten traditional promotional methods in the very near future – although at present there is a fee involved whilst many conventional print brochures are free of charge. New multimedia self-booking kiosks could soon become commonplace, as could video links to travel agents allowing customers to see live footage of resorts. Already, brochures are increasingly being accompanied – or as, in the case of Disney World, even being replaced – by video cassettes which allow the organization to show actual images of the holiday resort, hotel or destination. In the UK, the English Tourist Board and the regional boards are developing integrated management systems for tourist information centres – installing touch-screens linked to a bookable Internet site. Eventually interactive kiosks will be installed in hotels and leisure centres, giving information about a range of services – including accommodation, events, attractions and transport – acting as one-stop travel agents.

Ad highlight 11.1　　CD-ROM brochures and business cards arrive

More and more organizations, from fitness suppliers to destination marketing agencies, are using CD-ROMs as tools in their promotional activities. CD-ROMs are now available which can be used instead of business cards. The disk can hold an audiovisual presentation that can be regularly updated. Similarly, Forza Fitness has produced a CD-ROM to act as a corporate brochure, including details of all its ranges and services. Reebok Fitness Equipment's interactive CD-ROM, launched in January 2000, is designed to help people achieve their fitness goals. Users can key in information, such as their diet, and will then receive fitness advice.

Source: adapted from Fitness suppliers set to use CD Roms. Leisure Opportunities, September 1999.

But the biggest shift in recent years has been the growing maturity of the Internet as an advertising medium, and thousands of travel companies – from hotels to airlines and destinations – already have a presence on the Internet. More than 200 million people are now connected worldwide – a number that is growing globally at a rate of up to 10 per cent every month. In 1997 $900 million was spent on Internet advertising and, whilst current revenues are small by comparison with more traditional media (such as television and radio), its growth is outpacing them all. A recent Coopers & Lybrand study showed that Internet ad sales soared in 1998 – 240 per cent up on the previous year – leaving cable television a distant second (up by 16 per cent) with magazines ranked the third fastest growth medium at 11 per cent. That makes encouraging reading for a medium that is still in its infancy, and in the not too distant future it is entirely possible that the Internet will be *the* main tourism advertising tool. Travel agents will be able to download moving images from the operators' sites, and with e-mail and intranet the paperless office is close to reality. There are highly specialized travel agents that have already done away with paper, using a combination of Internet sites for initial information and e-mail for personalized follow-up. Such companies range from the Zambezi Safari and Travel Company (at www.zambezi.com) to the more basic but informative site of ArcJourneys (www.travelarc.com).

For the immediate future, however, such examples are likely to be the exception rather than the rule and the brochure still has many years to run – although CD-ROM and Internet usage will increase. The Internet is, of course, changing every facet of advertising – not simply as a new medium, but also as a shaper of the creative and production processes. For example, Internet-based resources now allow agencies and production companies to conduct tailor-made, on-line searches for ad directors – thus dramatically reducing production time and administrative costs as they are able to instantly view showreels and review regularly updated on-line curricula vitae. More-over, with traffic along America's electronic superhighways tripling each year, the significance of this medium is mushrooming, especially amongst younger people – future consumers who, brought up with such technology, are likely increasingly to use it to make independent travel bookings.

> The summer 1999 blockbuster *The Phantom Menace* signals the way – more people saw the film trailer on the Internet than have so far watched the movie.

On-line advertising

The Internet has tremendous marketing potential, whether it is used to sell directly or as a vehicle to attract and stimulate consumer interest, and it allows small companies to compete on a 'virtual' level playing field with their larger rivals. A quarter of European businesses in the UK, France, Germany, Italy, Spain and the Netherlands with access to the Internet already use it for electronic advertising and more than half expect the revenue generated by e-commerce business to increase in the next few years. An *ActivMedia* survey of 2000 commerce-related websites in 1999 found that almost a half were already profitable and a further 30 per cent expected to become profitable by 2001.[1] For such companies, the real attraction of the Internet is that for the first time ever, they can combine interactivity with advertising – allowing them to both get their message across and process the end transaction. Moreover, whilst the USA has led the way, today the Internet economy in Europe and Asia has a faster rate of growth and in 1999 there were 9 million households on-line in Japan.[2]

As a new medium the Internet is experiencing growing pains – it is an unwieldy tangle of information; it is very slow to look through and as more people get connected they increasingly encounter 'virtual traffic jams'. Moreover, on-line searches can yield some rather strange results. A recent study has shown how one search for 'hotels and Western Australia' resulted in 6340 'hits' using one search engine –despite the fact that there are only 1200 registered hotels in the state, few of which have an Internet site! The hits included professional travel guides, regional tourist offices, travel agents, tour operators, media reports, travel book companies and specialist information providers representing hotel properties on the Internet.[3] At the same time, whilst Internet distribution may be one of the most effective marketing channels for leisure, travel and tourism companies, its costs are rising sharply. Although a basic website could be provided for about £500, to have an effective Internet site requires a strong financial commitment and an advertising and marketing budget to bring customers to the site. According to *New Media Finance* (a specialist newsletter reporting on the web sector), some design agencies command client budgets in excess of £300 000 for each website created. Other research indicates that a hotel seeking to develop a site would need at least £2.5 million a year to support it effectively – a budget which would cover content, promotions, marketing and on-line bookings. Furthermore, these costs would rise with growth in use and greater demands from customers for more products.

Ad challenge 11.2   Today's threats to e-commerce

- Companies' failure to consistently brand on-line.
- Inadequate design expertise resulting in inferior sites and poor quality information.
- Umbrella brand sites (e.g., destinations) are threatened by disagreement amongst members over the content, cost and format of a shared Internet facility. Such sites also face stiff competition from other Internet service providers.
- Supplier bias towards business travellers and higher-priced products.

- Supplier reticence and consumer scepticism.
- Information overload and web complexity for consumers.
- Copyright and legal issues.
- Access costs, particularly high telephone charges in Europe.
- Security and privacy concerns.
- Fear of commitment to the electronic unknown.

Source: adapted from Paul Williams and Adrian Palmer (1999). Tourism destination brands and electronic commerce: towards synergy? *Journal of Vacation Marketing*, **5** (3), 263–75.

Despite such problems, the Internet has created a virtual marketplace in which creative and innovative companies can thrive. Prior to the advent of the Internet, most products and services needed, at the very least, two media for marketing – advertising to get the message across and a sales medium (face to face or telephone) to process the transaction. Today, websites are channels of distribution as well as communication, making the conversion of interest into action and sales more immediate. Websites are particularly useful for last minute and out-of-hours bookings since users are becoming more comfortable about buying on-line. The World Wide Web (the Web) also offers this potential at a reasonable cost – compared to alternatives – in terms of providing, updating and customizing information and of interactively communicating with a potential user. However, whilst the costs might be manageable from a marketing perspective, for the e-consumer they are potentially high; in Europe high Internet telephone charges (by comparison to the USA) remain a major barrier to access. Perhaps even more importantly, there are also high costs in terms of time since anyone using the Web has to search for information – and as a result he or she is often in real danger of experiencing information overload. To get around this problem, web users rely on search engines, 'best of lists' and catalogues to bring some sense and order to a sea of information – more of which below.

Although it is much more flexible, in broad terms the Web has much in common with television – text, pictures, animated graphics and sound can all be used to deliver the advertising message – especially with the advent of cameras relaying 'real-time' film on-line (visitors to Disney's website can see the activity on Mainstreet). This information can be updated quickly and easily and, unlike some promotional tools, you can monitor the usage (the number of hits) and the effectiveness of websites, as well as building up detailed information about your users and tracking bookings. One of the barriers to consumer take-up of e-commerce at the moment, however, is that it has to compete with television and with the consumer's everyday living and working environment. As a result, Internet advertising's primary objective must be to grab attention. Downloadable screensavers have arguably been the most successful attention-getters in Internet advertising so far. The Guinness screensaver – featuring an on-line version of a television ad where a man dances around a full pint of Guinness (with its unmistakable white head) – was perhaps the first major screensaver success in the UK. In contrast to screensavers such as these, however, the majority of Internet advertising tends to be very information and text heavy – unlike the best traditional advertising, which often focuses on emotional appeals. Successful websites will be those which make e-commerce convenient for the web user – providing easy, rewarding access to relevant and related information whilst creating a personal approach. Certainly the Web offers marketers the possibility of establishing effective consumer relationships and dialogues – which, if done well, will culminate in a sale, although web advertisers should be extremely wary of irritating browsers who may take the ultimate sanction and ban them from their personal web portfolios.

Internet marketing clearly has a number of advantages over more traditional forms of promotion. A website has the potential to reach a mass audience directly, which means that although it is a mass medium, each individual who 'hits' a site feels as though they are being personally addressed (unlike a television ad, for instance), since they have made a conscious effort to view the site. This one-to-one aspect of the Web will become further enhanced when organizations begin to produce customized home pages for users, which hold enormous advertising potential. Imagine a scene in the near future – it's a blustery day in March, a family logs into their webtelevision and as they open their own home page, a story appears featuring ads for local all-weather attractions and events: customized advertising and sales all wrapped up in a personal home page and accessed in the comfort of their living room.

Ad highlight 11.2   The interactive ad revolution is here

In 1998 CBS's coverage of the Grammy Music Awards featured a digital process which some believe marks the beginning of the end of the television ad as it exists today since it provided the first large-scale test of digital interactivity. A standard 30-second television ad for NZK Music Boulevard, one of the largest electronic music stores in the USA, aired during one of the lead ad breaks. The majority of viewers probably did not notice anything special about this ad – but webtelevision subscribers did. This Microsoft-owned service enabled subscribers to view an icon on their screen which, once activated, created a picture-in-picture display with the Grammy awards broadcast in the smaller window and NZK Music Boulevard's website occupying the larger window. In the words of J. J. Rosen, President of NZK Entertainment, 'for the first time, music fans were able to access the Music

Boulevard and the Grammy Guide directly from the broadcast for immediate purchase of the music they were hearing and seeing on screen'. This enabled viewers to interact with both a television ad and on-line content, providing a new integrated, hybrid medium encompassing direct response, on-line and broadcast advertising. These next generation ads can provide not only emotional appeal, but also product information, promotions, retail locations and on-line purchasing. In the medium term, their appeal to advertisers is likely to be huge.

Source: adapted from How an interactive icon may change the nature of ad breaks. *Campaign*, 12 June 1998.

Customized home pages and interactive ads hold great commercial promise for web-wise companies. In the near future hotel guests may well find themselves surfing through ads for restaurants, retailers, nightclubs and local attractions which the hotel's smart television will be able to ring automatically for reservations and provide directions and maps. Unlike conventional broadcast video advertising in hotel rooms, the new systems – which have already been run by US West Marketing Resources in 5000 San Francisco hotel rooms[4] – will allow guests to use their television remotes to focus on their interests. Instead of the few dozen ads that can fit on a prepackaged 30-minute video, the new interactive guides potentially offer unlimited ads *and* allow usage monitoring for each advertiser.

Ad highlight 11.3   Doubleclick advertising hits the target

You're at work, daydreaming about sandy beaches and turquoise-coloured water and an ad for a tropical vacation pops onto your computer screen. Coincidence? No. Doubleclick (www.doubleclick.net) – a web advertising company that acts as a middleman, hooking up web publishers and ad buyers and determining which ads you see on the Internet. The clear market leader with a 50 per cent market share, the company can dynamically deliver ads when users go on to a web page – and whilst 1000 users may go on to that same page, they will see different ads based on what the company knows about each individual. New York based Doubleclick offers companies a network of seventy popular websites including Altavista, Dilbert and major league baseball. Founded in 1996, its CEO argues that the Internet offers advertisers the cream of the crop – many of the people who are spending nine hours a week on the Web tend to be highly educated, with higher disposable incomes than the average – demographics advertisers cannot afford to ignore.

Travel and tourism providers should never lose sight of the fact that the Internet is a global community and that the Web offers many opportunities to link with and advertise in the sites of organizations that are perhaps on the other side of the world. Such opportunities are helped by the fact that the Internet is a friendly, helpful place. In fact, website 'linking' is a significant development in web advertising. Here, popular sites charge companies which want to 'hyperlink' with them; users who then click on to these hyperlinked partners are able to transfer from one to another. Companies can look to form partnerships with similar businesses in different parts of the globe and web hyper- or reciprocal links enable like-minded companies to promote each other – be they bed and breakfast operations, country house hotels, farmhouses, or other niche operators. Indiscriminate linking should be avoided – at the moment links to sites in the USA would probably be particularly useful as the USA currently accounts for almost 70 per cent of Internet users, although, of course, other high use generating markets should also be considered. Larger brands have already created very synergistic relationships – for example, when Rough Guides redesigned its identity with the woodcut logo of the running man, it collaborated with Mars confectionery; whilst the Great Outdoor Recreation Pages homepage, using the latest browser technology, is sponsored by the sports goods manufacturer New Balance whose print ads feature on the site. The ultimate in brand advertising symbiosis is Nike which does not even have its own official website but finds it more effective (and in keeping with the brand attitude) to sponsor those of top sports celebrities such as Michael Jordan.

The Internet offers particularly effective marketing for small businesses and one – the self-catering cottages operator, Wales Holidays – has seen business increase by 10 per cent since it started taking bookings over the Internet; in fact the website has generated more sales than any other direct sell distribution channel. Selling on-line has made a tremendous difference to the business because now the product is available 24 hours a day at a low cost – also enabling more upmarket overseas customers access to the business. At times, Wales Holidays has taken more than £2000 a day via the Web since going on-line. The company's senior partner, Julian Burrell, has commented that pound for pound, the website outperforms advertising in the Sunday papers, *Radio Times*, direct mail and Teletext, and he anticipates the website (www.wales-holidays.co.uk) will eventually replace the company's brochures.

It is not just the small operators who benefit from going on-line and the leading hotel companies invested $20 million in their websites in 1998. Internet sales for Hyatt were forecast to double in 1999 to $30 million on-line bookings and Radisson Worldwide attracted $2 million sales in January 1999 – set against $1 million for the same period in 1997. Marriott International, the world's fifth largest hotel firm, attracted nearly 30 million visitors to its website in 1998 and took more than $50 million of on-line bookings – an increase of 213 per cent over 1997 when only 2 million users logged on. As a result, the company has made a major commitment to the Web – creating a separate Internet department to market its 1700 hotels across ten brands. Detailed travel guides, maps, directions, destination information and other features have been developed to attract web users to www.marriott.com. This commitment reflects the upward trend in overall Internet usage and the growing strength of the Marriott brand – more than 80 per cent of its Internet bookings come from its own site (www.marriott.com) and Marriott intends to continually enhance its site to attract new visitors and retain the interest of current users. The company's move is significant in an industry which has largely restricted its Internet offerings to on-line bookings and e-mailing, and last minute discounts to site users could now follow.

Ad highlight 11.4   GeoCities attract advertisers

GeoCities are personal, member-created webpages divided into neighbourhoods of interest. They let like-minded surfers share views on their passions and hobbies. Over 2 million people supply the web content, attracting over 15 million visitors. GeoCities are seen by investors as an ideal medium for advertisers to reach narrowly defined target markets. Examples of GeoCities include IVillage (a popular women's community) and Tripod (a popular twentysomething community).

The on-line audience

The on-line audience is a highly attentive one which actively seeks travel information, advertising and ideas – a quarter of travel users say that they sometimes click on banner ads when using the Internet. Future take-up of the Internet is hard to predict but massive growth is assumed over the coming years – linked to the growth of service providers and set-top television boxes. The new medium is set to revolutionize sales, marketing and distribution, and travel is likely to be particularly affected because as an industry it is largely information-driven. The market analyst Datamonitor predicts a massive increase in on-line European travel sales during the period 1999–2002, estimating that Internet sales (worth £4.7 million in 1997) will top £1 billion by 2002. The company believes the growth will be fuelled by increasingly sophisticated websites with links to picture libraries, virtual tours and tourist offices. Worldwide travel sales on the Internet are forecast to jump from $3 billion in 1998 to $26 billion by the year 2002 – one airline, British Airways, predicts that 50 per cent of its business will be conducted on-line by 2003 – whilst in 1999 this figure was less than 1 per cent.

At the moment, three-quarters of the world's population cannot access the Internet – the 25 per cent who potentially can, however, are proving to be of exceptional interest to advertisers. Numerous surveys have been conducted to estimate the impact of the Internet, the profile of Internet users and the levels of e-commerce activity. Unfortunately, many of these surveys often offer contradictory information and statistics – both in terms of current user patterns and profiles and future use projections. This makes the job of quantifying the Internet's impact on the tourism and leisure industries and their advertising more difficult. What is not in doubt, however, is that the Internet is making a significant impact and in 2000 Internet users already numbered around 200 million.

PhoCusWright Inc., a leading strategy and research company for the on-line Internet travel marketplace expect worldwide travel e-commerce to reach US\$20 billion by 2001 – a 700 per cent increase over the 1998 figure of \$2.5 billion. The company predicts that airlines, hotels and intermediaries (on-line travel services and auction sites) will dominate the Internet travel industry. In 1998, on-line travel agencies accounted for more than half of e-commerce bookings – although in 1999 sales for vacations, tours and cruises grew strongly – and of the remaining e-commerce bookings, airlines accounted for 25 per cent, hotels 13 per cent and car rental companies 8 per cent. In 1999 total Internet travel bookings exceeded \$6 billion and, unlike most new on-line markets, Internet travel is growing faster than even market analysts can predict, with projections continually being revised upward. By 2003, total leisure on-line bookings of \$29.5 billion are expected. Despite this, Internet travel remains hard to predict since problems remain in terms of how speedily

> www.travelocity.com, the on-line booking system run by American Airlines, can book you on 370 different airlines, into 28 000 hotels and at fifty car rental agencies. Tap in your details and in three cursor's blinks you are clicked through itineraries and prices. Enter your credit card number, choose your seat and request your special diet meal.

and simply consumers can get what they want. Simplicity appears to be the key if the example of Sabre's Travelocity website is anything to go by. Sabre's 'three clicks to fly' revamp has resulted in a much faster than expected growth rate – 1998 figures showed over 4 million members and \$7 million in travel sales per week, the same as Expedia.com, which between 1996 and 1998 booked about \$500 million in sales and 'influenced' a further \$3 billion.[5]

Although only a small minority of the world population currently uses the Internet – about 10 million adults in the UK – the trend is upwards (this figure was 1 million in 1994). Yet Internet access remains a major problem at the moment – less than a third of UK consumers have a computer (less than half of these have a modem), and about half of the 7.5 million who do go on-line regularly can only do so at work. By 2005, however, it is predicted that 30 million people – half the UK population – will be using the Internet and in the

Table 11.1   Estimated numbers of users who shop on-line (millions)

1995	1996	1997	1998	1999	2000	2001	2002
3	6	10	16	23	33	45	61

Source: Jupiter Communications, quoted in *Time*, August 1998.

USA 42 per cent of the population already own a personal computer – four out of five of them being able to go on-line regularly via a modem. In addition, the number of web-wise, experienced users is also growing around the world, suggesting that future surfers will be less concerned with security issues and more willing to complete purchases on-line although, interestingly, a survey in the UK suggests that two-thirds of consumers will not make e-commerce purchases unless they know and trust the brand in question. Currently, the Internet is used largely for information gathering, but this will change as consumer familiarity and confidence in its security grows – surveys for on-line shopping estimate that the global number of e-shoppers will have grown from 3 million in 1995 to a massive 61 million by 2002 (Table 11.1).

Ad highlight 11.5   Profiling the USA's 'wired travellers'

A recent study of 'wired travellers' (defined as adult Americans who have travelled by air in the past year and visited a website in the past month) revealed that more Internet users are booking travel arrangements on-line but suggested that converting *browsers* into *buyers* is still the number one challenge for Internet travel services. Four-fifths of wired travellers have looked at Internet travel sites and over half of them have checked prices, yet less than a fifth have used the Internet to book travel on-line. Most of these (83 per cent) have bought airline tickets, 40 per cent have reserved a hotel room, 32 per cent rented a car and 3 per cent have purchased a vacation package or tour. Wired travellers are more likely to use the Internet than other travel information sources (such as magazines or guidebooks) and over two-thirds of them use the Internet to research and plan their trips, but only a tenth regularly buy their tickets on-line.

Nearly three-fifths of wired travellers have 'looked, not booked' and 70 per cent of these have bought their tickets later from either a travel agent or airline. Despite this, travel and travel-related services are one of the top three web purchases: among the 44 per cent of wired travellers who purchase on-line, 44 per cent have purchased computers or related products, 42 per cent books and 40 per cent airline tickets or travel products. Not surprisingly, wired travellers who use the Web frequently are more likely to buy on-line than infrequent users – over half of those using the Web daily have bought on-line, compared to just over a fifth of those using the Web less than weekly. Current non-buyers are stubborn and need to be lured to their first on-line purchase because once they have made their first transaction they tend to repeat. Non-buyers are particularly concerned about the security and personal privacy of on-line buying and three-quarters of them are unlikely to make on-line purchases in the near future. Amongst the vast majority of wired travellers who have not bought travel on-line, nearly half continue to rely on the services of a travel agent they know and trust, and this seems to be a significant barrier to on-line buying.

Source: http://phocuswright.com.

Whilst in a recent UK survey only 1 per cent of web users had actually booked a holiday on-line in 1998, about half had looked for travel or hotel and business information, and almost 40 per cent had read electronic publications (Table 11.3). Expedite UK, an Internet travel agency launched in November 1998, which commissioned research to create a more accurate customer profile, found that those British tourists who book holidays on-line look at an average of twenty-six different sources before booking a holiday. Customers looking for information on possible holiday destinations researched material widely – reading glossy travel magazines, checking Teletext, visiting their local travel agent and talking to friends about their recommendations. However, whilst the percentage of *on-line users* who shop on-line is currently small, it is expected to grow significantly in the early 2000s (see Table 11.2).

> Will 'gadget boy' or 'stone-age man' hold sway in the world of the Internet? 'Gadget boy' is likely to promote the use of new technology regardless of its costs and benefits. By contrast, 'stone-age man' is likely to oppose the implementation of information technology because of innate hostility towards it. The answer is likely to be something of a compromise.

The most popular on-line purchases are CDs, books and software, and research suggests that almost 2 million people in the UK bought on-line in the first six months of 1999 – spending £500 million. However, it is also estimated that 50 per cent of global on-line transactions are travel related.

Table 11.2   Percentage of on-line users shopping on-line, 1998–2002

	1998	*2002*
France	12	35
UK	17	40
Germany	14	40
USA	25	52

Source: Jupiter Communications, quoted in *Time*, August 1998.

Table 11.3   Internet usage in the UK

Purposes (during previous month)	% of Internet users
Searching for business information	51
Reading electronic newspapers/magazines	38
Looking for travel/hotel information	32
Finding out what's on/where to go	30
Looking up addresses/phone numbers	24

Source: Carat Insight/BMRB, *TTG UK & Ireland*, 31 May 1999.

> Today's major Internet challenges: high look to book ratio; security and privacy concerns; building trust and overcoming the pull of existing relationships.

Another survey, this time by Barclaycard, revealed that whilst only 8 per cent of respondents had booked flights over the Internet, 95 per cent of these would book such flights again. Moreover, 61 per cent of respondents would consider using the Internet for this purpose and, despite the low rates of adults currently purchasing over the Web (Table 11.4), e-commerce in Europe is forecast to triple in each of the next three to four years, creating a market worth around a quarter of a trillion dollars by 2002.

Table 11.4   The Internet shopping gap, 1998

Country	% of adults buying on-line
USA	10.1
Sweden	3.8
Finland	3.7
Netherlands	2.5
UK	2.0
Germany	2.0
Ireland	1.4
Italy	0.7
Spain	0.7
France	0.7

Source: International Data Corp., in *Time*, June 1999.

Ad highlight 11.6   **Who buys vacations on-line in the USA?**

A survey in the USA has shown that people who purchase vacations on the Web – and are therefore the target for advertisers – are a special group. Web vacations are purchased by 8.2 million adults, a figure which tripled during 1997–98. These people are more likely to have high incomes – nothing new in that perhaps, but this survey found that web buyers are likely to have more income than web users in general:

- 72 per cent of non-web users' income levels are below $50 000
- 44 per cent of web users' income levels are below $50 000
- nearly 25 per cent of those who bought vacations on the Web had income levels in excess of $100 000.

Vacation buyers are much more likely to be either older generation Xers aged twenty-five to thirty-four, or ageing baby boomers aged between fifty-five and sixty-four, and are less likely to be younger – under twenty-five. What do these profiles mean? Tourism and leisure companies targeting lower- and middle-income households do not need to panic just yet because their customers are not using the Web to make purchases. However, tourism and leisure companies that offer high-quality products and services targeted at upper income adults should be advertising and selling on-line. Leading-edge web vacation buyers are developing web-shopping habits and by extension web brand preferences, and where they lead, others will follow. The Web still only accounts for a fraction of total vacation purchases, but this is not the point – web brand preferences and leaders are being developed now and 'if you're not in, you can't win'.

Source: Dave Tremblay, www.infobeads.com.

The changing face of the e-consumer

The current profile of web users has prompted the on-line marketing of specific services and products – not surprisingly, computer and Internet products dominate but, significantly, tourism products (especially airlines and hotels) are also popular. In the 1990s Internet usage certainly tended to exhibit a skewed demographic profile – well-educated, better-off, white, middle-class males dominated user profiles – in 1999 the UK web users' average annual household income after tax was around £36 000. However, recent research seems to indicate a broadening of the user profiles with increasing numbers of women coming on-line. In fact, girls now outnumber boys amongst UK teenage users. This is particularly significant given women's tendency to be the primary purchasers of consumer products for households and their role as the main decision-makers in holiday choices. Research reveals that both women and men use the Internet to search for travel information; they are likely to be from the ABC1 socioeconomic groups and from all age groups, but especially the twenty-five to thirty-four group.

Yet whilst *web users* are more likely to be aged twenty-five to thirty-four, 60 per cent of people who use the Internet to actually *book* holidays are aged thirty-five to fifty-four and the belief that e-commerce should largely be targeted at a younger audience (as they are the only ones comfortable with the Internet) seems misguided. Indeed, 20 per cent of *all* Internet users are aged over fifty-five, indicating a widening web market. A recent consumer survey conducted on behalf of Going Places, one of the major UK travel agencies, revealed that older generations (particularly those aged forty-five to sixty-four) were much more likely to show a preference for using new technology compared with eighteen to twenty-five-year-olds. Whilst it holds true that the Web provides leisure and tourism organizations with an excellent vehicle to attract highly desirable, upmarket and higher spending consumers, the face of the e-user is beginning to become more representative and is certainly no longer restricted to young males.

Ad highlight 11.7   Who buys hotel rooms on the Internet?

TravelWeb is one of the biggest hotel bookings clearing houses via GDS and the Internet. Its user information shows that:

- three-quarters of users live in the USA
- men are more likely to book than women (3:1)
- 14 per cent are executives
- one-third are between thirty-one and forty years of age
- over two-thirds use TravelWeb from home as opposed to under a third at work
- most users book at least one month in advance
- just over a third of users book one guest per room whilst almost 60 per cent book two guests per room
- over three-quarters are likely to ask for no smoking rooms.

Source: Connolly, D., Olsen, M. and Moore, R. (1998). The Internet as a distribution channel. *Cornell Hotel and Restaurant Administration Quarterly*, August.

The predicted increase in consumer interest will be matched by much greater marketing activity on the Internet and tourism and leisure companies need to be ready for this challenge. For instance, vacation packages need to improve branding to succeed on the Internet as only one – Carnival – has a recognized brand. Although this market is currently growing slowly, Internet travel marketers anticipate much greater significance for it in the future – an anticipation which is matched by the package industry itself. Within five years, the industry predicts that half of all bookings could come through call centres and via the Web or television screens. In the UK, Thomson plans a huge electronic revolution to combat the problems of relentlessly tightening distribution channels and its customers will be able to check products and prices and devise their own packages on screen at the prices they are used to in the travel agencies.

Convenience and the use of interactive digital television are other factors likely to boost on-line activity. Whereas flights lead the way as the most successful on-line travel product, package holidays also have the potential to develop as a successful on-line purchase. In this, operators stand to cut distribution costs by selling on-line whilst travel agents will benefit from higher commissions – making a booking on-line is ten times cheaper than making one through a call centre. The on-line travel agent Microsoft's Expedia (www.expedia.msn.co.uk) offers 75 000 package holiday deals from the leading tour operators, 400 airline timetables, 800 000 bucket-shop fares and details of 50 000 hotels – all of which can be booked on-line (plus destination weather forecasts, maps and an on-line magazine).

The success of such companies demonstrates the value of having an effective on-line presence – a good website provides considerable opportunities to add value to a product or destination. Business-to-business marketing and sales managers are also increasingly turning to the Internet to boost traditional marketing avenues and in terms of consumer goods sales, smaller companies appear to be doing rather better than larger ones. Clearly, the Internet promises to be an ideal medium for advertising and selling leisure, travel and tourism products – regardless of organization size – after all, it provides a highly cost-effective vehicle for distributing related information to potential consumers, no matter where they live.

Creating an effective on-line presence

A few years ago the Web was new and exciting and with few organizations on-line, success was easier to achieve since sites were newsworthy, competition was relatively limited and the consumer was not so discerning. Now, with a proliferation of sites and more experienced consumers, websites must be professionally designed and developed to appeal to a tightly defined target audience. Moreover, whilst English is the current language of the Internet, as markets get bigger in each country, then global sites will need to diversify into local sites which are culturally and linguistically specific – a strategy which some companies – such as Lufthansa/Air Italia – already employ. Sites will also have to have a content that offers added value and which are promoted not just through the Web but also through other promotional activities. The links between web and traditional advertising are already increasing (many print and billboard ads now feature a website address) and in the future ads may well

321

place greater emphasis on the Web dimension, encouraging people – perhaps through incentives – to visit websites. As we will return to below, it certainly makes sense to display web and e-mail addresses on not only all advertising material, but also on all stationery and business cards since it is a waste of time, effort and money to develop a quality website that does not feature loudly in an organization's advertising material.

Despite all the new media horizons, on-line advertising will for the foreseeable future remain a part of a much wider marketing and promotional mix – such as PR activities, print material, direct mail, etc. It does offer many potentially significant advantages over traditional tourism and leisure promotional tools: websites can reach many more people than brochures, web costs per access are much lower than the cost of printing a single brochure, and websites can be updated and amended instantaneously – the Expedia site is updated every 30 minutes – whilst brochure details are fixed until the next print run. Finally, websites, unlike brochures, are a highly interactive medium. However, Kim Bayne, who moderates the Internet's HTMARCOM (High Tech Marketing Communications) e-mail discussion group, argues that 'Seduced by the glitzy on-line world, marketers are making disastrous business decisions'. She thinks that, 'Rather than enhance the established arsenal of traditional marketing tools, they are eliminating it entirely. As a result, they are cutting off communications with their off-line customers.' Many on-line marketers are not evaluating the Internet with the same strategic thinking that they are used to applying to more traditional media. As a result, businesses are discovering the hard way that marketing effectively on the Internet costs more money and resources than they first thought – and poor planning is killing just as many big Internet marketing budgets as small ones.

Internet activity *must* be integrated into the traditional marketing communications mix and it requires a detailed strategic and tactical plan to maximize the benefits of being on-line. Without an effective strategy, an organization's website will look unprofessional, its promotional efforts will be ineffectual and its Internet marketing programme will never realize its potential. On-line advertising should be integrated with all other aspects of the marketing mix from the outset, yet until very recently the creation of websites was totally divorced from the activities of ad agencies because the design expertise lay elsewhere and concepts varied because of a lack of integration between ad agencies, new media developers and clients. There has been a move towards building up ad agency expertise in this area but high levels of creative excellence remain particularly hard to find in travel and tourism. Whilst there are thousands of travel sites, the majority are a waste of web space and it is still not that easy to book on-line.

Ad challenge 11.3   Designing websites

The creative potential of web design is much greater than traditional print media due to the availability of multimedia (combining sound, video, graphics, etc.). However, when briefing a designer, an organization should remember that most web users have relatively slow modems and software which may make it difficult, if not impossible, to load complex graphics. The design brief for websites is similar to that for traditional media, although as well as demanding high levels of strategic and creative thinking, it also requires excellent technical standards. The brief should cover the following:

- Who are you trying to speak to?
- What exactly do you want the website to do?
- How will your site measure up in relevance, reliability, performance and engagement?
- How often will you want to update the contents?
- What will your customers want to find in the site?
- Do you know your target audience and why they will want to visit your site?
- How will your site link to others – if you are a small operator, venue or organization should you join with others to maximize the 'hit' potential?
- How will you monitor the effectiveness of its success?

What makes a good website?

One of the driving forces behind the growth of the Web has been the simplicity of the Hypertext Markup Language (HTML) used to build pages. After a minimum of training it is possible to put up substantial amounts of data, however, this does not ensure that the site will be well presented and enjoyable for on-line users. There are already many useful travel sites and competition is growing fast. Most big travel agents now have at least a micro site and one successful site – www.barginholidays.com – whilst not creatively excellent, achieves 3.6 million hits a month. Similarly, the British Tourist Authority's popular VisitBritain site has images of Britain, travel information, holiday ideas, attractions, accommodation and an interactive map, whilst the Scottish Tourist Board recently launched Project Ossian – a £4 million initiative intended to develop an Internet site for all Scottish accommodation and attraction operators.

Airlines account for a large number of travel sites, although their quality is variable. Some, such as British Airways, Continental and Iberia, have strong design values, good structures and display well-thought-out strategic values. Others such as Go and Easyjet deliberately create a bargain image, the former keeping its identity quite separate from that of its parent company, British Airways, by appealing to a younger audience. Easyjet's site is fully integrated with the company's other advertising activities and echoes their print ads – making a clear design statement to appear as budget-oriented as possible. This is a general rule of Internet advertising – always integrate any on-line activity with other campaigns to endorse the organization's overall positioning. Far too often sites and other advertising have no connections, whilst the better sites strive for a strong and integrated creative, technical and strategic Internet product. One of the best travel sites is Virgin Atlantic, which in 1999 launched a revamped, design-led website (www.virgin-atlantic.com) which, with its better information and more efficient booking engine, is fully integrated with the company's other marketing activities. Using the latest 'flash' Internet technology, the Virgin site simulates the lights of a runway. Part of the Virgin Group's £50 million strategy to establish an e-commerce facility for each of its businesses by 2000, the new leisure-focused service provides information for Virgin freeway members and information on hotels, restaurants and bars.

A good website should be entertaining and informative – ideally it should also encourage consumers to be loyal, repeat viewers. It is critical to ensure that a site is interesting and easy to use – if visitors have to click through several pages to reach the relevant information they will become frustrated – so the site must be self-explanatory with good internal links. To encourage users to return to the site, it is essential that it is updated regularly (otherwise it will look unprofessional) and has useful links to other relevant sites. Some sites have received a huge number of hits because they offer useful or interesting downloads or screensavers which can act as supplementary promotional vehicles for a brand – an attractive screensaver will remind users of the product every time they are on-line. Some of the most effective sites offer virtual reality tours – whether of zoos, theme parks or resorts – and one of the best tourism websites is that of the Singapore Tourist Promotion Board (www.newasia-singapore.com) which offers varied information and an interactive tour agent. This not only provides valuable information for the consumer, but also assists the National Tourism Organization (NTO) to collate feedback on visitors' interests.

Good websites are more about creating and managing customer relation-ships than about operating as vehicles for sensory and information overload, and that of the Arsenal Football club is a good example of how a leisure-related organization can use them to develop relationships with customers. CNN (the 24-hour news channel) has a very good travel-oriented website which offers the channel's partner hotels not only an excellent advertising platform, but also the opportunity to build detailed consumer profiles (see Ad highlight 3.2). The site is designed to collect information on users of cnntraveller.com, registering their business and leisure travel patterns, their accommodation preferences, membership in airline and hotel loyalty programmes, and demographic information.

Not surprisingly, web design has been driven by technology, which dictates what is and is not possible to achieve, but this has meant that many traditional design agencies have failed to engage with the medium and have created badly designed, computer programmer-generated sites. Given that so many companies offer a website design service, it can be very difficult for clients to select the best one for them. To help make the choice, organizations should always look at a range of design and

> Just as other media, the criteria for good sites are creativity, emotional pull and appropriate use of the media.

multimedia companies' sites: those which are uninspiring (with blocks of text, little movement or interaction) should not be considered – after all, the Internet is supposed to be an exciting and interactive medium. As a general rule of thumb, do not expect the reader to read more than 150–200 words in one block and do not underestimate the audience – sites that are garish and cluttered with little design sensitivity will not work, even if they have great content. Moreover, remember that most well-used websites are slightly irreverent in tone and content because the on-line audience is still younger and more open to this approach – so even the most conservative clients often opt for a more 'cool' copy content. Whatever the tone, copy content and visual data must be integrated. The best web design can be simple and quick, using uncomplicated graphics and strong text. Also important is the ability of the company to manage the brand within the new medium – whilst technology-driven companies may excel in providing web solutions, they may know little about the significance of brand management. Take the example of the Lonely Planet website. As a product, the Lonely Planet guides have strong brand values and a particular, distinctive style. Unfortunately, its website, with its boring graphics and high text content, might be a very useful travel site which is quick to load, yet it bears little resemblance to the marketing style or the irreverent thrust of its publications.

In essence, a website needs to be clear – users may well be Internet novices – and well-planned, clearly laid out pages are critical. Too many web encounters are frustrating and time-consuming – good navigation around the site should enhance a website's pleasure factor as will the facility to tunnel down to specifics within the site. Good design should at one and the same time provide the user with the information required and the web provider with good brand enhancement and new business opportunities. Content is therefore key and should be underpinned by integrated text and graphics to maximize the site's effectiveness: the still common practice of tourism organizations merely scanning their brochures into a web page is very unsatisfactory. Customers demand tourism and leisure websites that provide value and service – as a result, the Internet requires more informative and responsive tactics. The ultimate aims of the website should be at least threefold – to inform, to attract and finally to induce purchase on-line. Remember that the website must be able to respond quickly to the user's needs – on average, site hits are incredibly short – lasting a mere 8 seconds. Failure to respond promptly merely encourages the browser to move on, yet successful web design enhances both the Internet's value to marketers and the product or service's brand value.

Making the most of search engines

Once a site has been designed, the next stage is to ensure that it is promoted and that it is visited and revisited. No matter how excellent the website, if people do not know about it or how to find it, then all the time and effort expended on developing it will have been wasted. Take the example of on-line casinos in the USA. They made $60 billion in 1998, but they achieved this by being well supported by traditional print advertising. Internet marketing methods need not require significant sums of money, however, and appropriate selections should greatly enhance an organization's potential for success in today's ever expanding virtual world. Perhaps the first thing to ensure is that the website's domain name is relevant, easy to remember and one that customers will associate with your organization, brand and product.

Tourist boards should have sites which are easily located and straightforward to address – the universal record locator (URL), or website address, must be sensibly structured which means that domain names are valuable as corporate property or a marketing tool. Good examples are swiss.com, etc. Securing the most appropriate domain name may not be that easy, as many URL addresses were bought by speculators in the early 1990s. This means that, although domain names can be bought and sold, it can be difficult for organizations to obtain the most appropriate address. One possibility that most companies have so far failed to consider adopting is the use of their straplines as a web address. 'The Flying Dutchman.com' (KLM Airlines), 'The world's favourite airline.com' (British Airways) or 'Just do it.com' (Nike) have yet to be used as identifiers, but leading industry experts such as Richard Mellor suggest that their adoption is only a matter of time.

> Five million domain names are registered worldwide – 70 per cent to US businesses or individuals and over 7000 new domain names are added to the Internet every day.

A further key move in creating an effective on-line presence is making sure that the finished website is registered with search engines – so that people who

Table 11.5 The major search engines

http://www.altavista.com
http://www.excite.com
http://www.go2net.com
http://www.hotbot.com
http://www.infoseek.com
http://www.lycos.com
http://www.mckinley.com
http://www.metacrawler.com
http://index.opentext.com
http://search.yahoo.com

do not know the domain name will still be able to find an organization. There are over 5000 search engines servicing the Internet, although, despite this overwhelming statistic, there are in fact only a handful of engines which are regularly used by Internet users (see Table 11.5). Search engines apply varied criteria in their indexing processes and an understanding of these is essential so that the appropriate standards and keywords can be adopted in the actual website – speeding up the information search process. Also, since Internet searches regularly generate hundreds, if not thousands of matches it may be useful to employ a specialist company which can 'boost' where an organization will come in any given search – such companies can employ a number of techniques to put a given domain name near the top.

Ad challenge 11.4   Setting up a website

1 Far too often websites are isolated from an organization's marketing – treat your website as an integrated element of your overall marketing strategy. Design and brand it (in tone and style) accordingly (colour, text, imagery, positioning statement). Be creative.
2 Establish what you want your site to do – to increase visibility, to support public relations and publicity, develop sales or facilitate internal communication. Calculate what cost–benefit ratio you are prepared to sustain.
3 Buy a short, snappy and relevant URL – e.g. www.visit.hawaii.org.
4 Register your website with all the major search engines. Do not forget to install META tags that hold indexing information to ensure that the site is easily located by search engines.
5 Plan the mechanics of the site – its features and content. Be wary about overloading a home page – big graphics files take precious time to load, time that browsers can ill afford to spare, although beautiful photos are difficult to resist because of their value in stimulating interest. To get around this problem, consider offering the browser text or graphics options.

6 Your web home page should also offer the browser a variety of other options. Language translations are useful if you are targeting international markets. Dedicated web pages could also offer information – for instance on conventions, short breaks, special events and attractions – at a low cost.

7 Entertain the browser with recipes, postcards, gifts, etc. Encourage feedback or comment from browsers to build consumer relationships.

8 Hyperlink with like-minded products and organizations. Contact key related websites and ask for a link to your site – for instance bed and breakfast establishments, golf courses, fishing-trip organizers and good food guides. Think nationally and internationally – could you include interactive virtual tours of linked products?

9 Site maintenance is essential. Do not treat your website like a brochure, and update it regularly to publicize any special offers or events.

10 Do not forget to market your website via related sites and in traditional media advertising.

11 Be prepared to continually adapt to the constantly dynamic and evolving environment which is the Web.

Creating effective banner advertising

Search engines provide an organization with the opportunities to banner advertise on their websites, and advertising on popular search engines such as Alta Vista could result in a banner ad being seen by over 20 million Internet users a day. These types of ads are the most common form of advertising on the Internet (currently accounting for over 70 per cent of advertising at Yahoo) – partly because their costs are quite affordable, averaging around $6000 per month. These costs could be borne solely by one organization or shared through co-operative arrangements with others. Such web links and banner ads make good marketing sense when organizations want to feature in 'umbrella' information sites which often act as a potential consumer's first port of call. Having said this, they do need to be supported by compelling messages on the pages that link from them if they are to be as effective as possible.

Banner ads should be designed to stimulate interest amongst Internet users and good banner ads are highly visual and send clear messages. They should be placed in web positions most likely to attract readers' attention – successful, eye-catching banner ads should be attractive enough to arrest the attention of people surfing the Internet and intriguing enough to make them want to come and visit your site. The winner of the new media category at the 1999 International Travel Advertising Awards was a series of banner ads produced by KNSK BBDO for the organizers of Hanover Expo 2000. The ads were designed to counter bad publicity over the mismanagement of the event and used humour to great effect (see Plate 12). In German a 'duck' is a colloquialism for a journalist accused of misinformation and in this series of banner ads ducks are seen being flattened in a variety of ways – by steamrollers and rolling pins – under the headline, 'workshops for journalists'.

| Ad highlight 11.8 | The Australian Tourist Commission's banner ads |

There are a handful of publications on the Internet that specialize in providing travel and tourism information on Australia and the Australian Tourism Net currently has the largest database of Australian tourism and travel information – 1700 on-site pages on 532 towns – with links to another 364 sites of interest. It receives over 20 000 hits a day. Operators wishing to advertise in this on-line travel and tourism guide can generate a direct link to their website for only AUS$75 per year, whilst banner ads start at AUS$35 per month. The Australian Tourist Commission itself launched a series of banner ads in 1997/8. These appeared on popular search engines and lifestyle websites, including Preview Travel Network (AOL), *New York Times*, Discovery Channel, Investor.com and Hotmail. The campaign aimed to entice long-haul travellers to join ATC's travel club, which offers special deals to Australia and generates consumer leads for Australian specialists.

Source: http://www.atn.com.au.

Measuring the effectiveness of Internet banner advertising remains a tricky and, as yet, unresolved problem, although in fairness this problem is by no means unique to Internet media. Despite the success of websites such as Australia Tourism Net (Ad highlight 11.8), many in the ad industry are concerned at the costs surrounding banner advertising on the Internet – pointing to the fact that it can cost far more per response than conventional media. Also, despite the tremendous increases in advertising on the Internet, in many ways we remain unsure of its impact, although it should be relatively easy to track whether banner ads have actually stimulated direct sales on the Web. The important point to remember here, however, is that only a small number of banner ads are actually designed to achieve this as they are more likely to be used as alternative ways of communicating with potential users.

As yet, advertisers cannot assess the impact of banner ads on brand saliency or its significance on brand attitudes. Brand awareness measures *vis-à-vis* other media are also elusive. Publishers and ad servers can, however, provide data on different click-through response rates on different forms of banner advertising, and two recent studies have attempted to measure the branding effectiveness of banner advertising in the USA and in the UK. Carried out by market research company, Millward Brown, the studies concluded that good banner ads could at least match and even exceed television and print advertising whatever the click-through rate. With the Internet, advertisers also face the more unusual problem of not really knowing who actually comes across their ads. Unlike other advertising media it is impossible to establish click-through demographic data because many web publishers are wary of site registration, fearing that this will prompt Internet surfers to go elsewhere. However, whilst registration techniques and the quality and reliability of information gathered may be suspect, it is still possible to plan media by targeting sites by interest and geography as opposed to demographics.

The promise of digital television

In much the same way as the Internet, digital television heralds a revolution in the marketing of tourism and leisure products and services, enabling advertising to be combined with purchase transactions. Add to this the fact that television viewers see holidays and travel as their top home shopping preference and digital television would seem to offer tremendous opportunities as an advertising and sales tool. Two-thirds of consumers in a recent survey were enthusiastic about booking holidays via a digital television service although, perhaps not surprisingly, prospective consumers favoured dealing with reputable, established travel brands – suggesting that the future looks bright for existing players in the travel industry. The digital advance, however, also offers often squeezed, smaller specialist companies the opportunity to carve out a distinctive niche in the travel market since people more likely to book via the television screen are upscale and likely to spend more on their vacation purchases than the 'average' consumer.

Digital television will also enable more sophisticated holiday advertising on Teletext as the pages will be enhanced to enable companies and organizations to differentiate their pages with branded messages. Teletext is a widely used source of information for travellers that in the UK carries about 300 advertisers on 1500 pages of text. In the peak summer season 7.2 million people view Teletext holiday pages each week and it now accounts for half of telephone bookings or around a tenth of all UK holiday bookings. Lawrence Lawson, Teletext's commercial manager, suggests that there are four factors in the medium's growth: a wide choice of products and retailers, competitive pricing, the convenience of buying from home and consumer confidence in the information.[6] Compared with press advertising, Teletext's main advantage is its ability to track the up-to-the-minute availability of deals and its success prompted the launch of 5Text, a joint Channel 5–Sky venture, in 1997. With 400 pages of travel information on behalf of 50 to 150 advertisers, 5Text reaches 3.2 million viewers a week. Such a channel of distribution empowers the consumer by providing him with direct, easy access to information – access that will become faster and more selective as a result of digital technology. With the increasing proliferation of television set-top boxes, allowing Internet access and opening up digital television, consumer demand for direct selling seems to be accelerating and retailers cannot afford to be left behind.

In addition to enhanced Teletext services, digital television also offers consumers travel and leisure services via digital travel agents or on-line tour operators – allowing them to make an immediate booking for the property featured on screen – an exceptionally effective sales tool. One such digital travel agent is UK's television Travel Shop which went on air in April 1998 for 5 hours a day with targets of 150 000 bookings in its first year and 500 000–600 000 by year four. Now it is a 24-hour, seven days a week operation and all the majors except Thomson are using it (as are many minor tour operators). The channel has shot over fifty location films in destinations, including Mallorca, the Caribbean, Florida and the Maldives, which are featured on air with professional presenters fronting the programmes. Partner operators are featured in a series of video brochures and viewers can ring the 250-strong call centre to make a reservation when they see a holiday they like. The consensus amongst these operators is that it sells far more of their product at much higher value than they thought possible and preferred operators (such as Airtours, First Choice, Unijet, Kuoni and P&O) receive guaranteed air time.

The television Travel Shop receives about 3000 calls on peak days (Sundays and Bank Holidays) and one in ten television Travel Shop viewers tune in for at least half an hour a day. Once they have discovered it, viewers tend to watch the channel at least once a week and almost 80 per cent of those who had not yet booked via television Travel Shop say they are quite likely to do so in the future. As a selling tool it is very effective and one of the most interesting points is that, although the operators' names are displayed, they are not as prominent as the television show's own branding – consumers are buying what almost looks like the channel's product. Smaller, less well-known specialists benefit from this in-your-home branding as the sense of security and familiarity that the television brings into the living room clearly works well for these businesses – if a well-known travel show presenter fronted the channel it would seem like *Wish You Were Here* or the *Holiday Programme* with a booking facility.

With interactive television and the Internet some years off for many in the UK, the Travel Shop's audience potential is huge, and whilst it is currently only being seen by a small part of the buying public, in the medium term selling travel by the television is a real winner. In the future, the Travel Shop intends to expand to six or seven channels, each of which will specialize in different types of holidays and Harry Goodman, joint managing director, is confident that the service can win 5 to 8 per cent of the total UK market. He also expects to attract sponsorship as tourist boards, luggage manufacturers and theme parks come on board. The company is also set to launch its own website as part of a £20 million investment by the parent company – Flextech.[7]

Going Places, the UK travel agent, has predicted that digital television will be a greater threat to its business than the Internet, precisely because it is an incredibly interactive medium facilitated by a very familiar tool – the television remote control. Initial research suggests that over half the population are interested in using the television for 'other' services and, significantly, 'travel' is the product people are most likely to buy. As yet, few multiples have developed websites that enable a customer to book on-line – pointing to the fact that few customers book via the Internet, seeing it to be too time-consuming and insecure. Digital television is felt to be more of a threat because the multiples know that whilst many of their customers do not own a personal computer, they all have a television which sits in the heart of the home and provides a focus for family activity. Also, using the television remote does not require any computing knowledge and therefore lacks any 'barriers' to adoption, in contrast to the Internet. Once the Web comes into everyone's living room it will open up the travel, tourism and leisure industries to new competitors, and it is not just retailers such as Sainsbury or Marks and Spencer (with their access to huge customer databases) that leisure, travel and tourism firms should worry about but also technology companies such as Microsoft. The proposed £220 billion merger between the Internet giant America Online (AOL) and the media empire of Time Warner is clear evidence of the Internet's importance to the entertainment and media industry. By combining Time Warner's vast media content and AOL's technology, the new company will allow consumers to download films, television pro-grammes and music from the Internet, and will probably herald the merger of other large American and European media and Internet companies.

In some countries, the advent of digital television also offers advertisers the prospect (previously prevented by strict broadcasting legislation) of adver-tiser-funded programming. At the moment in the UK, for instance, a complex web of regulations drawn up by the Independent Television Commission prevents sponsors' names appearing in programme titles unless the title is actually that of a sponsored event – such as the MTV Music Awards. Yet, in the future, strapped-for-cash broadcasters are likely to welcome advertiser funding in programme production and perhaps even as sponsors of whole channels. Significantly, increasing numbers of companies and organizations are interested in creating programming for television and this is likely to lead to the diversion of some advertising money into programme-making – although such programming and sponsorship will only appeal to a niche market since a mass audience is not guaranteed.

The changing leisure product

Much has been written about whether the web-driven, virtual reality revolution will fundamentally change the nature of tourism and leisure experiences. Commentators have pointed to how new technology has and will increasingly generate not only new tourism and leisure products, but also new channels of communications and ever more personal advertising relationships. Some have argued that virtual reality will even eventually replace travel and tourism as we know it. Only time will tell. It is undoubtedly true, however, that organizations in every sector of the travel, tourism and leisure industries must develop strategies to reach out to customers via these new channels. Webtelevision – the combination of the Internet and digital television – will create an interactive promotional platform ideally suited to the travel and leisure industries, enabling much greater consumer–advertiser interaction and engagement, and allowing the building of stronger mutual ties and relationships. It seems as though webcasting is also the future for many radio channels and currently about 7000 of the 12 000 US radio stations have a website and about 1000 of those are webcasting. To take just one example, Chancellor Radio which controls 469 stations has made the Web a central part of its business strategy. During 1999–2001 Chancellor will create sites for each of its local stations, enabling it to offer local and national advertisers tremendous opportunities for targeting and interacting with its 66 million listeners. Such activity promises an advertising and revenue bonanza and in turn enables the radio stations to amass a detailed database on its listeners and their behaviours.

Threats to the future of advertising

This expansion of advertising may well face some threats, particularly in a scenario where companies and organizations are unsure of the benefits that accrue from this element of the promotional mix. Despite the difficulties of establishing clear links between advertising campaigns, consumer perceptions and purchasing patterns, there is a general recognition that advertising delivers long-term brand benefits which tourism and leisure brand managers should ignore at their peril. There will always be a temptation to shift resources to support short-term promotional targets and priorities, but these should be resisted and tourism and leisure organizations should take note that, on average, market leaders spend a fifth more of their budgets on advertising than their nearest competitors. Campaigns need not involve huge sums of money, however, expenditure which many tourism and leisure organizations frequently do not have to invest. More money does not necessarily produce a more effective campaign (witness the 1996 Pepsi next generation debacle discussed in Chapter 3) but the creative use of advertising resources by smaller operators can achieve impressive results – *outsmarting* rather than *outspending* their rivals.

Advertising may also be threatened by the growth in other forms of marketing and the sheer weight and diversity of communications. At the beginning of the twenty-first century there is little fundamentally *new* about advertising – technological advance merely allows more creativity and more selective targeting. Unfortunately it has also stimulated enormous advertising clutter, with new forms of communication, new brands, new consumer choices and more complex media decisions, causing confusion for both advertisers and consumers. As we saw in Chapter 3, the media environment is rapidly expanding as advertisers seek out anything which can carry an ad and very few areas of consumers' lives are now ad-free environments. A rather frightening statistic suggests that the average urban US consumer is confronted with 13 000 ad messages, logos and corporate 'plugs' every day.[8]

Perhaps it is not surprising that as traditional media have become too cluttered, fragmented and expensive, some advertisers have turned to new ways of reaching their target audience – as we have seen, cash-strapped non-profit-making organizations such as museums have turned to corporate sponsorship. Other, much richer organizations such as Nike have excelled in 'ambush advertising' to save on costs but, more importantly, to court additional PR exposure. Yet despite all the threats to advertising, media advertising still accounts for three-quarters of all marketing communications. In the future, the traditional advertising media are likely to remain important, with interactive media complementing rather than replacing their role.[9] Yet, the major task facing tomorrow's tourism and leisure advertisers is, more than ever before, how do they make their ads stand out from the crowd?

Tomorrow's advertising agenda

As this book has discussed, the ability to create good advertising often requires something special but it is often hard to come by and far too frequently ads are uninspired, dull, boring and mediocre and, not surprisingly, these are ads which fail to touch consumers' lives. Worryingly for the industry, more and more surveys are sounding warning signs and suggesting that people are increasingly disenchanted with advertising – finding executions less entertaining and more irritating. Against this backdrop those who can produce creative and engaging ads are even more likely to reap substantial rewards. Without rehearsing much of what has gone before, effective advertising in today's environment is the result of:

- clients being clear about what they want from their advertising and their ad agency
- agencies themselves continually adapting to the rapidly changing (and globalizing) marketplace
- campaigns and executions which are much more creative and slickly produced than ever before
- well-planned, clearly timed advertising research at all the planning stages
- collective goodwill, team-work and the overcoming of advertising politics.

Of central importance is the ability of advertisers to match particular appeals to tightly defined, appropriate market segments. Advertisers who truly understand their consumers' interests, lifestyles and media habits (in whichever country they live) will be one step ahead in the race to produce suitably tailored and effective appeals. Yet the world is a rapidly changing place. Economic power centres are shifting both within and between countries, bringing new opportunities and threats to tourism and leisure organizations: opportunities come from the proliferation of viable market niches, threats from the growing number and diversity of competitors. The globalization phenomenon poses huge problems for advertisers and agencies and, as we saw in Chapter 6, the debate between global and local approaches continues unabated. Certainly, whilst clients and agencies allow their global campaigns to be steered towards the lowest common denominator, international ads will never have that cutting-edge quality which makes great advertising. Yet there are commentators who argue that those who seek similarities across cultures and are able to create advertising on a human scale, with insights into human nature, will succeed in developing superior global campaigns.

'How do you create something that has integrity to it, and has drama to it, yet talks to as many people as possible?' asks John Hegarty.[10] He believes that whilst consumers from different cultures are hugely diverse, in other ways they can be remarkably similar. For instance, whilst fifteen to nineteen-year-olds, Levi's core target market, may have very different lifestyles, they share similar anxieties in terms of handling relationships, talking to their parents and relating to authority. If advertisers can craft messages which tap into those concerns, they can engage with this late teen group globally and with these consumers, as with all groups, the best global ads will strike an emotional chord, possibly through using humour or pathos. If a campaign is based on 'a thought, or an attitude, then it doesn't necessarily lose its power and its life. Attitude travels, words don't necessarily travel.'[11] The message then is to advertise up, to be inclusive and to celebrate *diversity*. This was central to the world's biggest simultaneous ad campaign to date. In November 1999 the Ford motor company spent £6 million to block book air time around the world (known as a global roadblock) to reach 2 billion people or a third of the world's population. Six months in the making and filmed across nine countries, the 2-minute commercial was designed to celebrate and welcome in the new millennium as well as the diversity of Ford's worldwide customers and featured people from many different cultures gesturing hello and goodbye.

Undoubtedly creative, targeted appeals will help to build successful, enduring and, above all, salient tourism and leisure brands – vital in our shrinking global marketplace in which the real winners will be the most powerful, people-partnering brands. Brands need advertising investment to promote, protect and build relationships with their customers, particularly in tourism and leisure where there is considerable product parity. Indeed, the futures of advertising and of branding are intertwined – brands have become an integral part of consumers' lives, standing for quality, reliability and providing differentiation in a crowded market. Whilst advertising can play a leading role in this task, it cannot achieve it in isolation. Every tourism and leisure organization needs to ensure that the product or service meets or exceeds consumer expectations. The importance of delivering on product and service quality and superiority cannot be overemphasized and any amount of slick, highly creative advertising will never compensate for failing customer expectations.

Chapter summary

The Internet offers tourism and leisure advertisers the opportunity to expand the breadth of their promotional mix. The Internet advertising industry is less than five years old but it will be a major medium in the next decade. There are a number of advantages in advertising on-line. The Web offers:

- the potential to reach a mass audience directly, yet each individual consumer feels as though they are being personally addressed on a one-to-one basis
- access to a growing audience of upscale consumers who are rapidly developing on-line brand preferences
- opportunities for organizations to link with partners which are complementary and synergize with their brand
- effective dialogue and relationship-building opportunities between consumers and advertisers
- low-cost, easily updated, interactive promotional and distribution opportunities.

Successful websites are those which are used as part of an overall marketing and promotional strategy with clearly defined objectives, designed to a tight brief and informed by thorough analyses of customer profiles, needs and expectations. The best sites take advantage of the benefits of the Web, using the newest techniques and software – best designed by professionals and not by committees – and should be regularly updated. It is also a wasted opportunity if the site does not have the ability to quantify success, whether this is measured in terms of hits, response rates to requests for feedback or, less immediate, the number of bookings or requests for information. The most successful sites are those which seek to build relationships with users, inviting comments and feedback, collating customer profiles and tailoring more personal promotional messages which can then be 'pushed' to consumers.

Whilst the Internet is undoubtedly the key advertising platform of the medium term, in the short term it must be integrated into the broader promotional mix and has yet to eclipse traditional media. The potential wealth inherent in the Internet, though expanding rapidly, will remain unrealized until more consumers and businesses around the world become wired. Its disadvantages include:

- the necessity for a considerable investment of time and money by the consumer
- the unwieldy tangle of information which swamps the browser
- a high 'look-to-book' ratio and a reluctance to purchase on-line
- consumer concerns over security and privacy
- a lack of understanding of the medium by some advertisers, leading to little synergy in the marketing communications mix between web activities and traditional promotional programmes.

Whether technological innovation will transform the entire nature of the tourism and leisure experience and its marketing in the immediate future remains to be seen. Certainly, there is enormous advertising clutter at the beginning of the twenty-first century, with new forms of communication, a diversity of brands and a bewildering fragmentation of consumer lifestyles and choices. In this challenging environment, it is those advertisers that constantly strive to match particularly engaging and relevant appeals to a tightly defined target segment that will be one step ahead of the competition.

Case study 11.1

Horror film audiences pulled in by the Internet

Daniel Myrick and Eduardo Sanchez, the two film-makers behind the 1999 horror film phenomenon, *The Blair Witch Project*, attribute the movie's overwhelming success to the Internet. 'We started it ourselves by just putting up mythology and coming up with a story and background', said Sanchez. 'The popularity of the sites was incredible – it's fair to say that without the website the movie wouldn't have done even half as much business as it has done. It was crucial.' Made for just £14 000, the film has earned £90 million at box offices around the world. It was the first film to be publicized right from the start on the Internet and the website (http://www.blairwitch.com) became one of the world's most visited websites. Whilst most major films have their own website – the recent James Bond films being good examples – these are timed to coincide with the film's release, going on-line in conjunction with heavy promotion. *The Blair Witch Project* is the first film to use the Internet to build a movie audience from scratch and, as a result, film-makers are now seeing the Internet in a totally different light.

At the heart of *The Blair Witch Project* website is a well-developed chronology, describing the sequence of events in the little USA town of Blair in Maryland which provide the background to the film. It begins in 1785 when a local woman is banished after a group of children accuse her of witchcraft. The next 200 years see a host of mysterious events, including the disappearance of three student film-makers whose journal becomes the basis for the documentary-style movie. The chronology is so well thought out that many people believe *The Blair Witch Project* to be based on real events – and the website allows viewers to run some of the missing students' film footage and audio tapes and to read their journal. On the commercial side, the website offers various merchandise (from T-shirts to comics) and a free screensaver, which is a trailer for the film. There is also a chat forum, accessed by downloading free chat-server software that allows users to assume a pictorial persona based on characters in the film.

Source: adapted from John Williams (1999). Horror film audiences were herded in by Internet. *Western Mail*, 23 October.

Notes

1 *Time*, August 1999.
2 David Weir (1998). The Internet leaves infancy. *The Economist's The World in 1999*, p. 120.
3 A. P. Williams and Adrian Palmer (1999). Tourism destination brands and electronic commerce: towards synergy? *Journal of Vacation Marketing*, **5** (3), 263–75.
4 Neil Weinberg (1994). Push 6 for Seaford. *Forbes*, **154** (13), 5 December, 270.
5 phocuswright.com.
6 Andy Fry (1998). Fantastic journeys. *Marketing*, 26 November, 35–7.
7 Ibid.
8 Carla V. Lloyd (1999). Advertising media: a changing marketplace. In *The Advertising Business. Operations, Creativity, Media Planning, Integrated Communications* (J. P. Jones, ed.) pp. 89–100, Sage, p. 92.
9 Winston Fletcher (1994). *How to Capture the Advertising High Ground*. Century Business, p. 10.
10 John Hegarty, quoted in Jim Aitchison (1999). *Cutting Edge Advertising. How to Create the World's Best Print for Brands in the 21st Century*. Prentice Hall, p. 304.

11 Neil French, quoted in Jim Aitchison (1999). *Cutting Edge Advertising. How to Create the World's Best Print for Brands in the 21st Century.* Prentice Hall, p. 307.

Further reading

Bennett, M. M. (1995). The consumer marketing revolution: the impact of IT on tourism. *Journal of Vacation Marketing*, **1** (4), 376–82.

Hobson, P. J. S. and Williams, P. A. (1994). Virtual reality: a new horizon for the tourism industry. *Journal of Vacation Marketing*, **1** (2), 125–35.

Richer, P. (1996). Should travel companies be selling on-line? *Journal of Vacation Marketing*, **2** (3), 277–85.

Stipanuk, D. M. (1993). Tourism and technology: interactions and implications. *Tourism Management*, **14**, August, 267–78.

Stone, M. (1995). Marketing, wrong answers and the learning organization. *Journal of Vacation Marketing*, **1** (2), editorial, 120–1.

Williams, A. P. and Palmer, A. (1999). Tourism destination brands and electronic commerce: towards synergy? *Journal of Vacation Marketing*, **5** (3), 263–75.

The following websites are also useful:

http://innovate.bt.com/viewpoints/travel_weekly/index.htm
www.labs.bt.com/people/walkergr
graham.walker@bt-sys-bt.co.uk
Internet Information Centre – general infosite (glossary of terms)
Cyberatlas – reference desk for webmarketing
Web Marketing Information Center – Wilson Internet services – links and services plus free subscription to an e-mail magazine
Commercenet – industry consortium for companies operating on the World Wide Web (statistics, link, general resources)
Bookmarks for Cybermarketing – range of links to web marketing sites
iTropolis: Internet Resources – advice on website development and management
Thunderlizard – advice on web advertising
Davesite – teach yourself html
Whose marketing online? – Internet marketing magazine
Australian Tourism Net – articles and information on Internet tourism marketing
PhocusWright – on-line travel industry statistics, forecasts, strategies and analysis

Index

Package tour operators, 157–8, 165–6
  and advertising, 19, 34, 58, 61, 65, 68, 83–5,
    165–6, 248, 254–5, 257
  on-line, 320–1
Packaging, 7, 8, 59
Paris, *see* France
Pepsi, 17, 59, 171, 202–3, 207, 225, 251–2, 334
Personal selling, 6–8
Persuasion, 7, 14, 15, 20, 21, 39, 100–1
Peru, 146
Peters, Glen, 91, 134
Philippines, 140
Planning, 28, 40, 45, 50–5, 78, 87, 89, 183, *see
    also* Advertising objectives; Strategy
Playboy, 26
Point-of-purchase activities, 7, 8, 58, 153, 185
Poland, 141
Politics in advertising, 23, 43–5, 97, 335
Portugal, 224
Positioning, 7, 14, 25, 36, 41, 152–3, 214, 216,
    217, 219, 222–3, 231, 238, 239, 242, 249, 284,
    299
  defined, 246–7
  of followers, 250–2
  of leaders, 250
  problems of, 248
  see also Repositioning
Posters, *see* Billboard advertising
Press advertising, 8, 9, 61–3, 186, 207, 220,
    268–9, 284–6, 290–1, 294, *see also* Print
    advertising; Magazine advertising
Pretesting, 88, 98–9, 242
Pricing, 7, 8, 52, 54, 153, 225, 246, 248, 256–7
Print advertising, 37, 50, 56, 58, 60–3, 67, 82, 155,
    276–7, 290, 300
  effectiveness of, 82–5, 98, 185–9, 241–2, 326,
    330
  future of, 69
  see also Press advertising; Magazine advertising
Product placement, 6, 182, 198, 205
Production, 37, 46
  costs, 56–7
  values, 30, 37, 45, 242, 288
Projective techniques, 105–7, 110–12
Promotion management, 7–9, 51
Prosumerism, 126
Public relations, 4, 6–8, 25, 38, 51, 52, 69–70,
    206, 256, 268–9, 287, 294, 334
Publicis, 276–7
Publicis Eureka, 49, 79
Psychographics, 29, 80, 175–6, 225, 241

Qantas, 167
Qualitative research techniques, 87, 91, 95, 98,
    102–7, 109–12, *see also* Advertising research;
    Focus groups; Stimulus material
Quantitative research techniques, 98, 100, 102–3,
    105, 113–14, *see also* Advertising research

Radio advertising, 3, 8, 9, 57, 61, 63, 65, 69, 70,
    84, 308, 333, *see also* Webcasting
Radisson Worldwide, 313
Railway company advertising, 33, 72, 186–7
Rainey Kelly Campbell Roafe, 32
Recall rates, 18, 20, 98, 101, 102, 202, 218, 294
Reebok, 76, 161–2, 307

Repositioning, 101, 104, 153, 183, 214, 233–7,
    252–69
  defined, 252
  of attractions, 263–9
  of companies, 254–6, 257, 261–3
  of destinations, 255–6, 258–60, 293–5
  see also Positioning
Resorts, *see* Destinations
Rome, *see* Italy
Royal Peacock Hotel, Singapore, 188
Rugby, 75, 77, 170, 171, 199, 225
Russian Federation, 139, 140

Saatchi & Saatchi Co., 38, 142, 161, 166, 185–6,
    188
Sales promotion, 4–7, 9, 14, 38, 51, 52
  campaigns, 200, 207, 246, 268–9
  defined, 8
  planning of, 5
Sales response model, the, 15, 20, 21
Saliency, 15–16, 20–1, 97, 101, 108, 109, 183,
    217, 221, 222, 232, 245, 261, 280–2, 336
  defined, 101, 217
  measures, 218
Satellite television, 18, 50, 63–4, 133, 134, *see also*
    Television
Saturation advertising, 59, 336
Scotland:
  branding of, 222, 237–9, 282, 288
Scottish Tourist Board, 282, 323
Search engines, 305, 309, 310, 326–8
Segmentation, 18, 29, 56–8, 95–6, 122, 150–1
  as a strategy, 152–4, 167–74, 239–40, 246, 249,
    288
  defined, 152
  see also Micro-marketing; Targeting
Senior consumers, 124, 131, 154–8, 240, 262–3,
    319, 320
Sex appeal, 105, 151, 165–6, 177
Sexism, 163–5
Singapore, 140, 170, 185, 186, 188, 247
Singapore Tourist Board, 324
Singles market, 129, 165–6
Skywriting, 70
Slogans, 34–7
Slovak Republic, 141
Slovenia, 141
Socio-demographics, 29, 80, 127–32, 139, 153,
    265, 325, 330
  and advertising appeals, 154–64, 166–74, 264–9
  and target marketing, 150, 151, 284, 319
  see also Audience appeals; Advertising audiences;
    Consumers; Geodemographics; Targeting
Sonic brand triggers, 182, 197, *see also* Music in
    advertising
South Africa, 141–2
South America, 141
  as emergent market, 120, 140
  financial crisis in, 142
Space tourism, 13
Spain, 245, 255–6, 273, 276, 308, 318
  advertising of, 272, 274
  branding of, 282, 289, 290
Sponsorship, 4, 7, 51, 52, 64, 113, 133, 146, 167,
    229, 332–4
  defined, 8, 58
  of sports, 73–7, 170, 171, 199–204
  risks of, 203–4